WITHDRAWN

SOCIETY, GOVERNMENT
and the
ENLIGHTENMENT

Note:

This book is concerned with the workings of institutions,
with types of officials and with categories of people which
have long since ceased to exist and whose very names have
disappeared from modern dictionaries. In order to make
the main arguments as clear as possible without doing
violence to the facts or to the concepts of the period, such
detailed information and evidence as may be required by
the specialist or more enquiring reader has been relegated
to the end notes.

SOCIETY, GOVERNMENT AND THE
ENLIGHTENMENT. Copyright © 1985 by C.B.A.
Behrens. All rights reserved. Printed in the German
Democratic Republic. No part of this book may be used
or reproduced in any manner whatsoever without written
permission except in the case of brief quotations embodied
in critical articles and reviews. For information address
Harper & Row, Publishers, Inc., 10 East 53rd Street,
New York, N.Y. 10022. Published simultaneously in Canada
by Fitzhenry & Whiteside Limited, Toronto.

FIRST U.S. EDITION

ISBN: 0-06-430386-1
LIBRARY OF CONGRESS CATALOG CARD NUMBER: 84-48823

85 86 87 88 89 10 9 8 7 6 5 4 3 2 1

SOCIETY, GOVERNMENT
and the
ENLIGHTENMENT

*The experiences of eighteenth-century
France and Prussia*

C.B.A. Behrens

1817

HARPER & ROW, PUBLISHERS, New York
Cambridge, Philadelphia, San Francisco, London
Mexico City, São Paulo, Singapore, Sydney

CONTENTS

Introduction

It must by now be plain to everyone who has reflected on the causes of the French Revolution that for some considerable time our understanding of this problem has been growing increasingly uncertain and confused. To contemporaries, whether they welcomed the Revolution or condemned it, it commonly seemed attributable to the abuses of a corrupt and arbitrary despotism and a degenerate aristocracy. Even at the end of the eighteenth century, however, and at the beginning of the nineteenth, there were writers in France and Germany who ascribed it to more profound causes and saw it as the expression of a conflict between two social classes with different ideologies, one of which they called feudal and the other bourgeois. Under the impact of the Russian Revolution and the interest in Marxism which it stimulated, this explanation in terms of a class struggle was elaborated in France, and for the space of fifty years or so achieved there the status of an orthodoxy. This orthodoxy, however, has increasingly been coming under attack during the last decades from British and American scholars and is now openly repudiated by some of the French themselves.

As various eminent scholars concerned with the Middle Ages have pointed out,[1] it would be pedantic to quarrel with the orthodox because they assert, following the revolutionaries themselves, that the Revolution destroyed "feudalism". There are good reasons for saying this[2] even though conditions at the end of the eighteenth century differed very greatly from those described, for example, in Marc Bloch's famous work on feudal society. Because, however, of the ambiguities in the term feudalism and the arguments they have provoked, the present writer has preferred to substitute for it the term "société d'ordres", the meaning of which will be discussed below. Nor is there any reason to object to the adjective "bourgeois" when it is applied to the political, social and economic relations which the Revolution introduced into France, and which, to a greater or less extent, later spread to most of the other states on the continent of Europe. On the other hand, it is no longer possible to accept the reasons which the orthodoxy gave for why revolution broke out in France in 1789.

These reasons, most of which are to be found in Tocqueville's *Ancien Régime et la Révolution*, first published in 1856, can be summarized in a series of simple propositions, though as more and more facts at variance with them have come to light their proponents have increasingly felt obliged to qualify them, and in so doing have involved themselves in contradictions which have reduced the subject to confusion. Broadly speaking, the orthodoxy in its original form maintained that the Revolution was triggered off by the threat of bankruptcy which finally led to the summoning of the Estates General, but that its fundamental causes lay in the tensions that developed between an unprivileged bourgeoisie, which throughout the eighteenth century had been continually growing in wealth and self-consciousness, and a privileged nobility that was becoming increasingly impoverished and reactionary.

From the start, these assertions must have seemed somewhat implausible to anyone who reflected on them seriously; for a major tenet of the orthodoxy was that one of the principal advantages conferred by privilege on its possessors was the virtual, or, as Tocqueville said, the complete immunity from direct taxation, which fell with all the greater weight on the unprivileged. In these circumstances it would, to say the least, have been curious if the privileged had grown poorer and the unprivileged richer.

In fact, all the main assertions which the orthodoxy has made on the subject of bourgeois and nobles have now been shown to be either demonstrably wrong, or else unproven or inexact. There is no evidence to support the view that the nobles as a body got poorer in the course of the eighteenth century and much evidence that suggests the contrary. Whenever statistical analyses have been made they have shown that at the end of the Ancien Régime in France the richest individuals were still nobles and the nobility much the richest group in the community.[3]

The so-called noble "reaction", which has been the theme of many works, also appears to have little basis in fact in the form in which it is commonly described, even though it is plain that, judged by the enlightened standards of the time, the members of many groups and institutions held views which may reasonably be described as reactionary. According to the orthodoxy the nobles increased the feudal dues they levied from their peasants in order to restore their shattered fortunes; but there is no evidence that in general they did so. Indeed, one eminent and generally accepted authority[4] goes so far as to assert that, again in general, the burden of the feudal dues diminished; and similar views have been expressed by other writers. The nobles, further, are said to have brought about a reversal of the policy of Louis XIV who, it was believed, gave all the important posts in the state to bourgeois. The noble reaction is held to have manifested itself particularly in the laws and regulations which in the second half of the eighteenth century closed the higher ranks of various professions to everyone who could not show four generations of nobility on the father's side. Tocqueville maintained that in the Middle Ages the nobles had constituted an "aristocracy", by which he meant "the principal people in the nation". Under the Ancien Régime, he said, the nobility had become a "caste", or was becoming "more and more of a caste"; that is to say, their "distinguishing characteristic was their birth". Modern research does not support most of these assertions.

The orthodoxy's pronouncements on the bourgeoisie are equally mislead-ing. The principal exponent of orthodox opinion since 1945, Georges Lefebvre, saw the business world as the source of a new form of wealth – wealth in money (*la richesse mobiliaire*) as distinct from wealth in land – and as inspired by a new vision of the future. A new vision of the future certainly emerged, but its apostles were to be found among both nobles and bourgeois – of the famous *Philosophes* of the Enlightenment most were either born or bought themselves into the nobility – and the first people who tried to translate the enlightened ideas into practice were members of the government, all of whom, apart from Necker, were nobles. Though trade and manufactures grew in this century, principally as a result of bourgeois effort, both nobles and bourgeois held the bulk of their wealth in the same forms, that is, they invested it in land and in the purchase of office and annuities. Commercial and industrial wealth formed only a very small proportion of France's total wealth in 1789.[5]

Such studies as have been made of bourgeois attitudes in the upper reaches of the business world before the Revolution show that the bourgeoisie was on the whole conservative and satisfied with the existing order. Its members adapted themselves as a matter of course to a constricting economic system which, on *a priori* grounds, might have been assumed to be contrary to their interests.[6] The outstandingly successful who could afford to buy themselves noble status apparently always did so. Their desire was to enter the nobility and not to pull it down. In Prussia at the end of the eighteenth century and the beginning of the nineteenth there are instances of bourgeois in high official positions who were offered titles but refused them.[7] In France during the Ancien Régime this kind of class consciousness had no occasion to develop because noble status was always sufficiently easy to obtain, and sufficiently admired and materially advan-tageous, as to seem the prerequisite of any position of eminence.

There is in fact no major item in the catalogue of long-term causes generally held responsible for the Revolution that is now left standing, and this must affect our interpretation of the histories of other countries besides France. The absence of revolution in Germany, for example, and particularly in Prussia – the only German state in the second half of the eighteenth century and the first half of the nineteenth that can be compared to France – is always attributed to the fact that the bourgeois there were less wealthy and less numerous than in France. That they were less wealthy seems beyond dispute. Relative to the population, however, the difference in numbers is unlikely to have been significant; and since it was not the wealthier members of the bourgeoisie who made the revolution in France – they were, on the contrary, among its principal victims – this argument also falls to the ground.

An enormous amount of work has recently been devoted to social conditions in France in the eighteenth century, principally by French scholars themselves, who in one doctoral thesis after another have disposed of this, that or the other item in the orthodoxy while nevertheless refraining from committing themselves to any general conclusions. One or two bold French spirits have launched a frontal attack on it. No one, however, has so far attempted an alternative explanation. At one time we accepted the answer which Tocqueville gave to the question he posed himself when he asked why the Revolution, which he saw as the expression of forces European in scope, should have broken out in France and not elsewhere. Now that many of the views he expressed have been proved wrong or inexact by the facts which research has brought to light since his day, we can no longer delude ourselves that, notwithstanding his remarkable insights, he provided a satisfactory explanation.

The present account cannot aspire to the ambitious task of providing one either, but has nevertheless attempted to make some contribution to the problem by comparing the experiences of France and Prussia in certain important matters that have a bearing on it.

This comparison is not undertaken in the belief that France and Prussia in the eighteenth century resembled each other to a greater extent than is commonly supposed. On the contrary, it seems that the differences between these two states have been underestimated. To compare conditions in France and Prussia nevertheless seems more illuminating than to compare them in France and Britain, as is the usual practice; for Prussia in the second half of the eighteenth century, though burdened like both France and Britain with the commitments of a first-class military power, was ruled, like France, by an absolute monarchy while Britain was not, and by a monarchy, moreover, that was superimposed on a société d'ordres. This term has its equivalent in the German term "Ständegesellschaft", but it cannot be translated into intelligible English because the social and legal phenomena it describes had either never existed in England or had disappeared there long before they became an object of attack on the continent of Europe.

The British and the French, it is true, were close neighbours, with standards of living, education and manners that in the eighteenth century were sufficiently comparable, among sections of the upper classes, to permit, notwithstanding the frequent wars between the two nations, a continuous interchange of ideas and fashions. Prussia, by contrast, until the middle of the century, was a poverty-striken principality, so inconspicuous that in an excellent recent survey of international relations in the reign of Louis XIV[8] it proved virtually unnecessary to mention her. Even as late as 1765 a former French Secretary of State, the Marquis d'Argenson, in his *Considérations sur le Gouvernement Ancien et Présent de la France*, when commenting on the various states of Europe, devoted only a few lines to Prussia in which he merely referred to her disproportionately large army.

At the time he wrote, Prussian nobles were forbidden to travel abroad without the royal consent, which except for official purposes was consistently refused, and Prussia had no attractions for western visitors other than those offered to the small number of French *Philosophes* who could be persuaded, for shorter or longer periods, to take up residence in Berlin as members of the Prussian Academy of Sciences.

Up till the end of Louis XIV's reign, and indeed for several decades afterwards, Prussia bore a much greater resemblance to the countries of eastern Europe than she did to those of the west. During the Thirty Years War, from which a century after its conclusion Frederick the Great continually insisted that she had not fully recovered, she had been one of the principal disaster areas, suffering a loss of population, wealth and skilled labour greater than any experienced, then or later, as a result of any calamity in the west. In the relations between landlord and tenant, in the organization of agricultural production, in the poverty of her upper classes and their lack of cultivation, and in the absence, with the single exception of Leibniz, of any thinker of European stature, she can more easily be compared with Russia than with any western state. Frederick William I could say that Peter the Great was his dearest friend at the time when Louis XIV pronounced him a barbarian unfit to be received in the court of a civilized country.

Remarkable changes nevertheless occurred in Prussia in the eighteenth century, and particularly in its second half, as a result of government action undertaken on a scale, and with a degree of rational planning, unequalled anywhere else. It was then that the Prussians began to outdistance their eastern neighbours and to embark on the work of economic reconstruction and development that was to culminate, a century later, in the creation, under Prussian leadership, of the most powerful industrial state in Europe.

The eighteenth-century Prussian monarchs, Frederick William I and his son Frederick the Great, deliberately applied themselves to the tasks which Colbert half a century earlier had urged Louis XIV to undertake; and in so doing they encountered difficulties comparable to those which faced the French but from many of which England was immune because she was a united country without internal tariff barriers and with one language, one currency, one system of laws and institutions. The dominions of the French and Prussian kings, by contrast, even when absolutism reached its prime, were composed of a number of separate provinces, acquired piecemeal over the centuries, often in only the recent past, through marriage, inheritance, conquest or the dispositions of peace-conferences. These provinces were distinguished one from another by their particular laws, customs, institutions and tariffs, and by the consciousness of a separate indentity, which, strong though it was in France, was much stronger in Prussia, and which the absolute monarchs strove to overcome, as far as seemed practicable, by means of their national armies and bureaucracies.

While the French and the Prussian monarchs faced similar problems, though at different dates, they responded to them differently. French absolutism reached its prime in the early years of Louis XIV's reign but Prussian absolutism not till fifty to a hundred years later. Partly because of the different traditions of the Protestant states of northern Germany, but partly also because of its later origins, and its consequent exposure to ideas hostile to those which prevailed in France throughout most of Louis XIV's reign, Prussian absolutism operated differently from the French and might be described as a newer, more efficient model. Indeed, nineteenth-century Germans, who gave the term Enlightenment a somewhat different meaning from that accorded to it in the west, saw the Prussian autocracy in the reign of Frederick the Great as the supreme example of enlightened despotism and the French autocracy in the eighteenth century as not enlightened at all.

This judgment, though in many respects misleading, is not wholly devoid of truth. Such enlightened policies, nevertheless, as the Prussian rulers were able to enforce more successfully than their French counterparts, were able only to a limited extent to insulate Prussia against the social changes and currents of ideas that began to spread across Europe in the latter part of the eighteenth century and that were hostile alike to the société d'ordres and to absolutism in its existing form.

As wealth and education among the Prussian upper classes increased, and as the success of the British in the struggle for wealth and power inspired an admiration, in Prussia as in France, for British ways of life and government, many of the phenomena which had disrupted French society began to appear in Prussia also, though after a time-lag of a quarter of a century or more. The abolition of the société d'ordres came to seem a necessity in Prussia as it had done in France. The transition to bourgeois society, however, proceeded differently in the two countries, to a large extent because of the different relations between the government and the various social orders that must be the subject of the present discussion.

PART ONE

I

Society in France & Prussia in the age of absolutism: the société d'ordres or Ständegesellschaft

Lefebvre once asserted that "the very essence of the Revolution was the ruin of the aristocracy"[1] and by the aristocracy he meant the nobility, although to the revolutionaries these terms were not synonymous.[2] His words expressed a view which was long popularly believed and is doubtless often believed still, but which is nevertheless misleading.

Admittedly the French nobles were among the Revolution's principal victims, and although the numbers who were guillotined, died in prison or were otherwise disposed of by revolutionary action, were very much smaller in absolute terms among the nobility than among other sections of the population, the Revolution permanently diminished the nobles' power, wealth and prestige. The lands of those who emigrated – and a high proportion did so, including the heads of the richest and most powerful families – were confiscated by the state and after the restoration their owners recovered only such parts of them as the government had been unable to sell.

The seigneur's feudal dues, which until 1789 had often formed a considerable part and occasionally the whole of his landed income, were abolished without compensation in 1793 and never restored. For these and other reasons the nobles' wealth was substantially diminished. Nor were they ever able to recover, except partially under Charles X, the monopoly of the highest posts in church and state, and the social pre-eminence, which they had enjoyed under the Ancien Régime.

One can nevertheless hardly maintain that, as a group, they were ruined by the Revolution since they retained much of their wealth, and even under the July Monarchy their social prestige and political power were considerably greater than used to be supposed.[3] Indeed it seems contrary to common sense to speak of their ruin in a country where, more than a century after this supposed event, Proust could write his *A la Recherche du Temps Perdu*. Nor can it be maintained that the losses they experienced were due, as Lefebvre believed, to an incompatibility between the conditions necessary for economic expansion and the dominance of a noble class. In both Britain and Prussia, where the growth of industry and agriculture increasingly outdistanced that of France, the nobles maintained their social and political pre-eminence for three-quarters of a century or more after 1789.

In their heyday the nobles derived their social prestige, their political power and a large part if not all of their incomes from the land. All these attributes, and their style of life itself, were placed in jeopardy once the land ceased to be a principal source of national wealth. In every European country, however, this state of affairs lay in the more or less distant future when the Revolution broke out. Even in France, where commerce and manufactures were more highly developed than in central Europe, some 21 million people, on the eve of the Revolution, or 85 per cent of the population, are believed to have been peasants, and agricultural production to have accounted for 80 per cent of total production.[4] It was not, in fact, the economic developments of the eighteenth century which caused a relative or absolute decline in the profitability of land-ownership, but the industrial revolution, the iron ship and cheap grain from North America. It was not the French Revolution but the two world wars of the present century which gave the prestige of nobility in Europe its *coup de grâce*. The French Revolution's essential achievement, which was never reversed, was not the destruction of nobility as such – though noble status and titles were abolished in 1790 they were restored by Napoleon, who between 1806 and 1815 created 29 dukes, 44 counts, 1,468 barons and 1,289 chevaliers[5] – but the destruction of the société d'ordres, which removed from the nobles, and from the members of a great variety of other groups, the particular social and economic privileges guaranteed them by law.

The *société d'ordres* or *Ständegesellschaft* was a form of social organization which came to an end in France in 1789 when the deputies of the third estate to the Estates General, then in session at Versailles, decided to call themselves the National Assembly, and forced the king and the other estates to accept this decision, and to abandon the claim that each estate should sit and vote separately.

Before this event, though there had been no meetings of the Estates General since 1614, the groups which had constituted it, either in the persons of all their members or through representatives, had continued to exist as legal entities, endowed with particular privileges and duties, and had done so also in Prussia after they had lost their political power. As is well known, the French estates, in this sense of the term, were the first order or estate of the church, the second order or estate of the nobility, and the third estate which included everyone who was neither a noble nor a cleric. In Prussia, a Protestant country in which the church had less power, the arrangements though similar were somewhat different. The *Allgemeines Landrecht*, the Prussian legal code whose compilation was begun under Frederick the Great though it was not published till 1794, besides various "subsidiary" estates, recognized three "principal" estates: the *Adelstand* or estate of the nobility, described as the first estate, the *Bürgerstand* or estate of the bourgeoisie, and the *Bauernstand* or estate of the peasantry.[6]

These estates, and the comparable ones in France, owed their origins to conditions in which the minimal tasks of government – administering justice, keeping the peace, defending the territory against attack – had to be delegated to groups, because in the largely subsistence economies of the Middle Ages in Europe, and the type of feudalism that prevailed there, the rulers were unable to afford standing armies and bureaucracies, but were forced to leave the functions which these institutions later discharged to groups which were granted or arrogated to themselves privileges supposedly appropriate to their respective functions – functions that have commonly been summarized by saying that it was the duty of the nobles to fight, of the church to pray, and of the other estates to provide them with the means of doing so.[7]

This state of affairs was gradually, and in the course of the eighteenth century markedly, changed by the increase in the power of the absolute monarchies – an increase that was both cause and effect of the growth of trade and manufactures, and, in consequence, of money wealth, of which the rulers appropriated a large share by means of taxation and which permitted them to assume functions beyond the reach of their predecessors.

As a result of these developments, and of the growing sophistication of economic techniques and of the arts of government, the correspondence in many cases diminished or ceased to exist between the rights and duties assigned to the members of the various estates and the functions they performed. Moreover, so many different social and professional groups grew up within the nobility and the bourgeoisie that in France by 1789 the very term estate had come to seem "a word devoid of sense".[8]

The sense which it had had before the advent of the revolutionary changes can be understood most readily from those passages in the *Allgemeines Landrecht* which set out in precise detail the rights and duties which the law conferred on the members of the various Prussian estates and their subdivisions. In Prussia, where the church did not count as a "principal" estate, only the estate of the peasantry could be defined in terms of function. "All the inhabitants of the countryside", the *Allgemeines Landrecht* laid down, "are to be reckoned peasants if they are directly engaged in agricultural work, unless by virtue of noble birth, office or special privileges they are exempted from belonging to this estate".[9]

The estate of the nobility, by contrast, could not be defined in terms of function in Prussia any more than in France. In both countries membership of this estate belonged to a person by right of birth, though subject to two important qualifications which the *Allgemeines Landrecht* set out and which also applied in France. Nobility could be acquired by prescriptive right or by gift from the crown.

To say what constituted the *Bürgerstand* or estate of the bourgeoisie presented the authors of the *Allgemeines Landrecht* with much greater difficulties. For in Prussia, as in France, the bourgeois, unlike the noble, did not owe his legal status primarily to his birth, nor, like the peasant, to the pursuit of a particular kind of occupation. On the contrary, in both countries bourgeois pursued a great and continually increasing number of different occupations, some of which were also open to nobles. The Prussian bourgeois appear in the *Allgemeines Landrecht* as merchants, government officials, members of the learned professions, artists, factory owners, artisans, clerics;[10] and their legal privileges and duties fell into so large a number of different categories that it took fifteen "Abschnitte", or sections, to describe them, as compared with the one section devoted to the nobility.[11]

Not surprisingly in these circumstances, the authors of the *Allgemeines Landrecht* found it difficult to explain in general terms what the word *Bürgerstand* meant. "Strictly speaking", they said, a bourgeois was a person who lived in a town and had been granted the freedom of the town. This definition had nevertheless to be qualified because there were bourgeois who pursued their avocations in the countryside. "In general", the authors of the *Allgemeines Landrecht* concluded, the *Bürgerstand* "includes all the inhabitants of the state who by virtue of their birth cannot be deemed to belong either to the nobility or to the peasantry and have not subsequently been incorporated in either of these estates". Even this definition, however, was inexact because, as appeared later, there was a category of people, the so-called *Schutzverwandte*, who were also neither nobles nor peasants but yet – "strictly speaking" as well as in common estimation – were not bourgeois either since they lacked the professional or property qualifications generally required before a person was eligible for the freedom of the town. The fact nevertheless remains that in Prussia – and equally in France and the other countries with a société d'ordres – the bourgeois could only be defined negatively. He was neither a noble, a peasant, an unskilled urban worker, nor, in the Catholic countries, a cleric.

To the question what was meant by the term "estates" in the eighteenth century, the only answer, in the light of the *Allgemeines Landrecht* and of what happened in practice, is that they were mere legal categories; that is, they were groups distinguished from each other simply by virtue of their legal rights and obligations. Admittedly each estate had its subdivisions and hierarchies which, as in a modern army, were subject to special provisions. The estate as a whole, however, constituted a group whose members might not, and commonly did not, have any sense of unity, but all of whom were subject to certain laws different from those which applied to the other estates.

Though sometimes all the members of an estate might, as in the Prussian peasantry, be engaged in the same kind of work, this was far from necessarily so, and particularly was not so in the estates of the nobility and the bourgeoisie in Prussia, and in the estate of the nobility and the third estate in France. The *Allgemeines Landrecht*, for example, stated that the nobles, as members of the first estate, were entitled to the highest positions in the monarchy provided the monarch judged them competent. The requisite degree of competence was, however, hard to find.[12] Even under Frederick the Great, who continually expressed his contempt for the bourgeoisie, though the top posts went to nobles the posts just below the top often went to bourgeois. Many Prussian nobles in his reign occupied subordinate positions with bourgeois as their official superiors.

In France similar adjustments to the needs of the expanding state were made, though by other means and ones more disruptive of the société d'ordres. The wealth of the French bourgeoisie was greater and of much longer standing than that of the Prussian. The French kings were always in financial straits and prepared to sell noble status for money, which the Prussian kings throughout most of the eighteenth century were not. For centuries before the Revolution the French bourgeois had been able to buy his way into the nobility by various means.

In consequence, whereas in Prussia bourgeois discharged administrative functions which according to the ideology of the société d'ordres should properly have belonged to nobles, in France the ease with which a bourgeois could buy noble status and the temptation to do so because of the prestige and privileges which it conferred, ensured that every person of wealth was a noble, even though the trade or profession he followed – that of tax-farmer or receiver of taxes, for example – was by any standards at variance with the idea of *noblesse*.

It is because of circumstances of this sort that one can describe the estates only as legal categories, for they bore no necessary relation to function and yet were not social classes, either in the Marxist sense of a group whose members stand, as do workers and capitalists in industrial societies, in the same relation to the means of production, or in the more common sense of people with comparable incomes and ways of life. Precisely because an estate is a legal category, whereas a social class, however defined, is a group which the law does not recognize and whose composition is determined by socio-economic circumstances, estates and social classes are unlikely to coincide. In the eighteenth century, a period of expanding economic and state activity, they increasingly failed to do so.

In both France and Prussia, for example, all the children born into a noble family were noble and (unless they engaged in occupations which deprived them in law of their noble status) they remained so even if they were reduced to penury, against which their legal privileges did not commonly provide protection.

In both France and Prussia the nobility was thus a very numerous group (the French nobility in 1789 is usually though dubiously reckoned at some 100,000 families or between 1 and 2 per cent of the population,[13] and the Prussian nobility seems to have accounted for about the same proportion); this group was increasingly divided by great differences of wealth as new opportunities for making money became open to nobles through State patronage or employment. In both countries before the Revolution the nobles' financial circumstances varied from destitution at one end of the scale to the possession of large – in France of enormous – fortunes at the other. In France in 1789, Louis XVI's cousin, the Duc d'Orléans, admittedly the richest man in the kingdom, had an annual gross income of approximately 10 million livres (say roughly £440,000 in the English currency of the time).[14] In Brittany, on the other hand, a province unusual though not unique in this respect, there were villages where one-third of the nobility was reduced to beggary.[15] A similar state of affairs existed in Prussia.[16]

Common assumptions are equally misleading when it comes to the ownership of land, overwhelmingly the most important of the means of production in these agricultural communities. In the popular as well as the Marxist estimation the noble before 1789 was not merely a landowner but a seigneur or *Gutsherr* – that is, a lord of the manor entitled to feudal dues. This belief, however, is hardly more justified than the belief that to be a noble was to be rich. In France there were nobles who were not seigneurs as well as many bourgeois who were, and nobles are commonly believed to have "owned" (in the sense of cultivating or drawing some kind of commercial rent from) only about 30 per cent of the land in the kingdom, the bulk of the rest belonging in more or less equal proportions to the peasantry, and to the bourgeoisie in the nieghbourhood of the towns. In Prussia, even though the sale of *Rittergüter* or manors to commoners was until 1807 prohibited by law except with the express consent of the king, the proportion of landless to landowning noble families in 1800 was 3:1.[17]

To say, however, that before 1789 neither the nobility nor the bourgeoisie constituted social classes and that the origins of the French Revolution, and of comparable movements for change elsewhere, cannot be attributed to a class war between them, is not to deny that there developed in France, in the course of the eighteenth century, and in Prussia at the end of it, two antithetical conceptions about how society and government should be organized. Nor is it to deny that in the ensuing struggle between the protagonists of change and the defenders of the existing order, the privileges of the nobility became the chief target for an attack that was launched against them in the name of principles that contemporaries, as well as later ages, described as bourgeois.

That the nobles in France should have been the Revolution's principal victims can hardly seem surprising. Though not legally, as in Prussia, the first estate, they were so in effect. The fortunate minority among them occupied all the posts of importance in church and state and possessed the largest fortunes. They were the principal beneficiaries of a discredited regime for whose failures and injustices they seemed responsible. That many nobles possessed neither wealth nor power and that their legal privileges were of little if any material advantage to them was overlooked, since in times of crisis such as existed in and after 1789 public opinion demands scapegoats. The complicated causes that are responsible for the collapse of a regime are hard, indeed generally impossible, for most contemporaries to understand. It is easier to point to the wickedness of groups. Revolutions, like wars, cannot succeed without an object to hate. In France, and to some though to a much smaller extent in Prussia, the nobles filled this role.

It would not, however, have been possible to remove the privileges of the nobles while leaving the rest of the société d'ordres intact, nor was this ever the intention of the revolutionaries in France or of the Prussian reformers after 1806. As these people realized, though the historians of countries without experience of a société d'ordres have not always done so, what was at stake was not merely the privileges of one particular group, but privilege in general in the original meaning of that term; for in the société d'ordres, before the ideas which undermined it gained currency, privilege did not mean, as it came to mean later, the possession of some unwarranted advantage; it was a term devoid of ideological content which meant merely the kind of rights already described – rights granted sometimes to individuals but essentially to groups and also to geographical areas.

Besides the privileges of estates and their subdivisions, every province and every town had its own particular laws and customs, or in other words its privileges, which conferred advantages on its inhabitants or on some favoured sections of them, and usually included exemptions from what in later ages came to be seen as the common obligations of citizenship. In Prussia, for example, at the end of the eighteenth century, all commoners were exempted from military conscription if they lived in Berlin, Potsdam, Magdeburg, Danzig, Brandenburg and many other towns, or in various provinces, particularly those west of the Elbe, where flight over the borders was easy. Only certain categories of commoners, however,[18] enjoyed this privilege elsewhere. In France a commoner paid the principal direct tax, the *taille*, if he lived in the country but not if he lived in a "ville franche", a category which included all the major towns. Because of the different tariffs in force in different provinces, the price of articles of common consumption could vary fantastically from one place to another. In France, for example, where the government salt monopoly extended over most though not all of the kingdom, a given quantity of salt which cost 60 livres in some areas cost under 2 livres in others.[19] These examples could be multiplied indefinitely.

Privileges, moreover, were granted not only to individuals, to groups, and to the inhabitants of particular localities; they were also attached to material objects – to buildings and to land. In Prussia Felix Eberty, the son of a Berlin merchant, who began his career in the judiciary but ended it as a professor, and who published his reminiscences as a very old man in 1878, recalled how in his childhood the family house had had inscribed on it the word "Freihaus" in token of the privilege granted to his great-grandfather by Frederick William I, and attached to the house thereafter, which exempted its inhabitants from the obligation to billet soldiers.[20]

In both France and Prussia land in the countryside was divided into categories, principally into various kinds of peasant and noble land, which were subject to different obligations and immunities and to different laws regarding sale, purchase and inheritance.[21] In both France and Prussia peasant land was burdened with a great variety of feudal dues, which in the Prussian provinces east of the Elbe often included compulsory labour services. In certain parts of France, the so-called "pays de taille réelle", noble land was exempt from the *taille* and peasant land subjected to it, even if it was owned by a noble. A similar state of affairs existed in most Prussian provinces.

In France in the second half of the eighteenth century and in Prussia at the end of it, a combination of circumstances brought all these arrangements under attack. Speaking in the Constituent Assembly in 1789, Rabaud de Saint-Etienne declared that the privileges of "all these towns and other portions of the kingdom" had come to form "a monstrous and contradictory mass of inequalities" – a legal chaos "created by time, chance, abuses ... favouritism and despotism".[22] To abolish them seemed as necessary as to abolish the privileges of individuals and groups from which, as Montesquieu had pointed out earlier, it was impossible to separate them. Thus the Declaration of the Rights of Man, drawn up by the Constituent Assembly in October 1789, was supplemented by a decree of the Legislative Assembly issued in June 1791, which declared that "the territory of France, in its full extent, is free like the people who inhabit it".

These pronouncements epitomized the essential differences between the ideology of the société d'ordres and that of bourgeois society, to which the facts came gradually to correspond. The transition from one type of society to the other was necessarily slow, whether it was accomplished by revolution or not. But, as Burke once observed, though no one can say when night merges into day, everyone can distinguish night from day. Similarly it is possible to distinguish the société d'ordres from bourgeois society without implying that it was possible to move immediately from the one to the other; and as one German historian has observed: "It is only when one fully understands the ways of life and inherited attitudes of mind which char-acterized absolutism and the société d'ordres, that one can fully under-stand the vastness of the changes" which their abolition brought about.[23]

The société d'ordres was based on a belief in the sanctity of custom and on the diversity of law and administration which it entailed; the apostles of the new order believed in progress – for which a greater degree of centralization and uniformity seemed essential.

The ideology of the société d'ordres was corporative, that of bourgeois society individualist. The first of these ideologies stressed the rights of groups and of provinces and towns; the second stressed the rights of man (that is, of the individual) and of the nation. The société d'ordres was based on inequality, and bourgeois society on equality, before the law. Montes-quieu, who in spite of the enlightened notions he held in many respects was the most famous of the société d'ordres' protagonists, saw the legally privileged groups, among which he particularly singled out "the seigneurs, the clergy, the nobles, the towns", as a bulwark against despotism. To the French revolutionaries of all persuasions, the legal privileges of all these groups, so far from protecting against oppression, were themselves a cause of it since they placed limits on the freedom of the individual.

By the freedom of the individual the apostles of the new order understood, to start with, the absence of serfdom and all comparable institutions including the feudal dues. As the Bavarian lawyer, Anselm von Feuerbach, put it in 1808 in an exposition of the essential principles of the Code Napoléon: "Every subject stands to every other subject in the relation of a free man."[24] Feuerbach pointed to articles 1780 and 1142 of the Code which laid down that no man could be compelled to serve another man for life or for an unspecified period, such a compulsion being, as he said, an affront to human dignity.

And besides what Feuerbach described as freedom of the person, the apostles of the new order demanded various other kinds of freedom incompatible with absolutism and the société d'ordres – freedom of speech, of the press and the other freedoms included under the head of the civil liberties, political freedom in the sense of government by means of an elected assembly to which the executive was responsible; economic freedom in the sense of freedom from all the restrictions on the individual's right to dispose of his property freely – restrictions, that is, that were placed on him by the monopolistic bodies of the société d'ordres with which, admittedly, the monarchs had often interfered but which they had accepted in principle, attempted to use for their own purposes, and supplemented by monopolies of their own creation.

For in the société d'ordres, though admittedly to a diminishing extent as its practices were eroded by the growth of a money economy, almost all kinds of human activity – the pursuit of trade, for example, of commerce, of manufactures, of agriculture, of learning – were conducted by groups to which a man had to belong, and whose rules he had to obey, if he wished to engage in the activity in question. Even to the authors of the *Allgemeines Landrecht* who, while inspired by some liberal sentiments, were essentially conservative, the monopolistic rights of guilds and other corporate bodies seemed "contrary to natural or civil liberty."[24]

Rights of property had seemed as important in the société d'ordres as they were to seem in bourgeois society, but in this case as in many other cases the Revolution changed the meaning of words. When in the Declaration of the Rights of Man property was described as a sacred and inviolable right, what was meant was individual property in material possessions. In the société d'ordres it had also meant this but it had had other, and more important, meanings as well. In this society where the methods of agriculture had not changed significantly since the early Middle Ages and where the open field system still generally prevailed, one of the most important kinds of property for the majority of people was the right to pasture their beasts on the fields of the village after the harvest and on the meadows after the hay had been cut. The French revolutionaries saw these communal property rights, though in the event it proved impossible to abolish them, as incompatible with the right of the individual to dispose of his property as he chose.

Again, in the société d'ordres property could include the right to exact payments and services from other people and to exert power over them. To the Paris *parlement*, for example, the seigneur's feudal dues were his property, and to suggest abolishing them, even with compensation, was to put property rights in general into jeopardy.[25] Svarez expressed a similar view in the lectures he gave in 1792/3 to Frederick William III when he was crown prince. The most prestigious of the rights which belonged to the owners of *Rittergüter*, or manors, he observed on one occasion, were their rights of justice over their peasants. These, he said specifically, were "ihr Eigentum" – their property.[26] Similarly, the offices which had been sold by the crown in France were their owners' property in law.

To the majority in the Constituent and Legislative Assemblies these forms of property appeared, as Mirabeau put it, "gothic oppressions of the centuries of barbarism".[27] The revolutionaries in consequence abolished them while affording a greater degree of freedom and protection to the kinds of property they found legitimate. They did this in various ways but particularly by providing that all forms of property transactions should be freed from the restrictions previously imposed on them in the société d'ordres. Since land was the principal form of property, these provisions were of particular significance where the land was concerned. In France, for example, though seigneuries had always been bought and sold, the feudal dues to which they conferred a right, and which the peasants owed, were not the result of a commercial bargain but were attached to the land in perpetuity. They were obligations which were due to the seigneur by virtue of his status, just as a commoner who owned a seigneurie paid the franc-fief to the crown because he was a member of the third estate and not a noble.

The abolition of all these distinctions between different categories of buyers and sellers, as well as between different kinds of land, made land a commodity whose price was determined by purely economic considerations and which everyone, regardless of birth or status, could buy or sell at the market rate.

By their insistence on the freedom of the individual and freedom of property, the revolutionaries changed the relations of the individual to the state, since these two freedoms were incompatible with the existence of the legally privileged groups which Montesquieu had in mind when he spoke of "pouvoirs intermédiaires". "In a free country", Mirabeau said, "there are only citizens and public officials."[28] All the public functions hitherto discharged by the seigneurs and by hereditary office-holders and other corporate groups were in consequence transferred to officials paid and appointed solely by the state. The revolutionaries thus distinguished between the sphere of activities of the citizen and that of the state – a distinction which it had been impossible to make as long as, for example, hereditary office-holders in France had been responsible for the collection and administration of the direct taxes or had administered justice, as a means, however honestly pursued, to promoting their private profit as well as the needs of the crown.

The revolutionaries believed, albeit with some exaggeration, that the concept of citizenship and of its corollary nationalism, was their invention. "What is a nation?" Sieyès had asked in his famous pamphlet *Qu'est ce que le Tiers Etat?* and had concluded that it was a body of associates living under a common law (*une loi commune*). In the société d'ordres there had been no common law in Sieyès' sense of the term and therefore no citizens. "The title of citizen", Rabaud de Saint-Etienne said in 1789, "is a new word in our language as the ideas for which it stands are new in this country. The title of citizen is now your glory".

To the French revolutionaries, 1789 marked the beginning of a new era in which poverty, injustice and oppression would be abolished together with absolutism and the société d'ordres which, as they supposed, had caused them; and their vision was shared by many people in other countries. The vision did not materialize. Nevertheless Anselm von Feuerbach spoke the truth when he said: "Where the Code Napoléon comes there begins a new age, a new world, a new state."[29] This new age saw the more or less rapid development of an industrial revolution which, whatever its causes, was not compatible with a société d'ordres.

The French, however, who made the revolution which brought the new age to birth on the continent of Europe, were not among its principal beneficiaries. Economic historians in France are now prepared to admit that the Revolution was a "national catastrophe".[30] By this they do not mean that it would have been better if the Ancien Régime had been allowed to continue. This was in any case impossibe, since the regime had disintegrated before the revolutionaries attacked it. They meant that, because of the destruction for which the Revolution and the wars it engendered were responsible, France in the nineteenth century was unable to retain, let alone to surpass, the position of relative power and prosperity which she had enjoyed in the eighteenth century, but was increasingly outdistanced economically, first by Britain and then by Prussia, which in 1870 defeated her in war.

The reforms in Prussia which made this state of affairs possible were imposed from above and not by revolution. To many people this has seemed regrettable because of Germany's subsequent history. The present account cannot be concerned with these might-have-beens. Its concern is with why the Prussians were able, and the French unable, to remove without revolution the obstacles placed by the société d'ordres in the way of economic development and the growth of military power.

II
The ideology of absolutism
in France and Prussia

Absolutism was an institution which, like other institutions, went through a period of development, of maturity and of decline. These experiences occurred at different dates in different countries, the period of maturity being achieved in France in the reign of Louis XIV and in Prussia in that of Frederick the Great who succeeded to the throne a quarter of a century after Louis XIV's death.

The term "absolute monarchy" (*la monarchie absolue*) was commonly used in France in the eighteenth century. "Absolutism", however (*Absolutismus* in German, *absolutisme* in French), was a nineteenth-century invention,[1] used to describe a form of monarchy that differed on the one hand from the constitutional monarchies that succeeded it and, on the other hand, from the medieval monarchies from which it evolved.

In the Middle Ages narrow limits were set to the monarch's power by difficulties of communication and lack of money. From the earliest times the monarch had always claimed more extensive rights than had any of his vassals; but even in theory and to a still greater extent in practice he was hardly more than *primus inter pares*. He was expected to "live of his own" – that is, from the proceeds of the royal estates and certain royal rights such as customs duties – and to demand help from his subjects only on extraordinary occasions. He had his particular privileges (such as those known in England as his prerogative) just as the various groups in his kingdom had theirs. The idea of one law binding on all citizens, and indeed the very notion of citizenship itself, were unknown. In the later Middle Ages, under that form of government known to German historians as the *Ständestaat*,* it was believed that the kingdom was divided into two parts, of which one belonged to the ruler and the other to the estates.[2]

By the *Stände* or estates of the *Ständestaat* were meant assemblies, such as the *états généraux* or estates general in France. These bodies were composed of the members of the principal estates (in the sense defined earlier of groups with special rights) who met together from time to time, though they sat in different chambers in accordance with their rank. The rulers summoned these assemblies at irregular intervals when they needed help or

*From *Stände* meaning Estates and *Staat* meaning State.

advice in emergencies, particularly emergencies of a financial kind. The assemblies were thus in a position to extort concessions, and in many German states, Brandenburg-Prussia included, they permanently discharged executive functions, such as collecting the taxes, by means of their standing committees.[3]

Substantially, though not altogether to the extent that has sometimes been supposed, the absolute monarchs gradually managed to rid themselves of these encumbrances. In contrast to the state of affairs in the *Ständestaat*, and also to that in constitutional monarchies, the absolute monarch in theory shared his power with no one. The doctrine of absolutism was evolved in France by French jurists at the end of the sixteenth century and the beginning of the seventeenth, and, though increasingly undermined by ideas incompatible with it, was reiterated throughout the eighteenth century till the Revolution. Its constitutional implications were epitomized in 1760 in the words of the chancellor Lamoignon when he said that His Majesty "alone possesses the plenitude of power. It is he alone who draws up ordinances and laws which all his subjects are bound to obey; and it is he alone who has the right to lay them aside." "It is in my person alone," Louis XV declared in 1766, "that sovereign power resides . . . It is from me alone that my courts of justice derive their existence and their authority. The plenitude of this authority which they exercise only in my name, remains always with me. I alone possess legislative power without sharing it with, or depending for it on, anyone. . . . The whole system of public order emanates from me."[4]

The claims of the Prussian kings in the eighteenth century were equally sweeping – and more effectively exercised – but were justified on different grounds. Though French absolutism was often defended as a bulwark against the anarchy which had preceded it, its essential sanction was religious. Though unlike the Roman emperors the French kings did not wear the halo of divinity, they nevertheless had a sacred character, bestowed on them at their consecration when they were anointed with holy oil. This oil was stored in a phial in Rheims and was said to have been brought down from heaven by a dove for the consecration of Clovis in the fifth century.[5] Though it did not endow the king with the attributes of a priest, it nevertheless bestowed on him miraculous powers by means of which he could cure people of scrofula – a common glandular disease, with a tendency to attack every tissue in the body and known in England as the "king's evil". Though in the course of the eighteenth century these miracles became increasingly suspect – Voltaire is said to have been the first to deride them – until the Revolution the French kings persisted in their attempts to perform them, and with little diminution in the number of believers, 2,400 of whom presented themselves to Louis XVI after his consecration in 1774.[6]

Though ideas similar to this were held in England – the last British monarch to touch for the king's evil was Queen Anne in 1714 – they were not held in Prussia in the eighteenth century, since they were contrary to the teaching of the early German Enlightenment, to which Frederick William I became converted at the end of his life and of which Frederick the Great was a convinced apostle, notwithstanding the contempt he professed for German thinkers and his admiration for the French.

In so far as it was concerned with social and political questions, the eighteenth-century Enlightenment could be invoked in defence of many different kinds of government and society. Particularly in its French and most famous manifestation, it produced a great variety of mutually incompatible ideas. But even in its German version (throughout the greater part of the eighteenth century generally ignored by the French or ridiculed when brought to their notice), it was similarly capable of different interpretations. One German historian, in a work on the reign of Frederick William II, enumerated eight different definitions of its essential characteristics (and he did not suggest that this list was exhaustive) which were put forward by Prussians in important positions in the 1780s and 1790s.[7] For all this, nevertheless, there were points on which people with any claim to be called enlightened were agreed in every country. Particularly, enlightenment meant repudiation of the irrational and the superstitious. To be irrational was to show a disregard for logic, to be unaware of the need to relate ends to means and to refuse to submit one's beliefs to argument and investigation. To be superstitious was to believe in the supernatural.

In the early eighteenth century irrationality and superstition characterized the thinking of all classes of the population in ways and to an extent incredible to later generations of educated Europeans, though now they are becoming better understood. These attitudes were fostered by the sanctity attached to custom in all underdeveloped countries; by the churches whose doctrines were based on the assumed occurrence of miracles; and by the persistence of pagan beliefs in magic and witchcraft. Though not necessarily atheists, deists, or even anti-Christian, the enlightened set themselves to combat these ways of thinking in the name of "reason", whatever the interpretation they placed on that word.

In the early eighteenth century the principal exponent of the Enlightenment in Germany was Christian Wolff. Born in Breslau in 1679 the son of a tanner, he was appointed in Halle in 1706 to the chair of mathematics. He did not, however, confine himself to this subject, but sought to embrace all knowledge within a single system, writing and lecturing on logic, metaphysics, ethics and politics.[8] Seeing God, the creator of the universe, as the embodiment of reason, he believed that everything in the world was as capable of rational explanation as were the workings of a machine. "Since God," he said, "possesses reason in the highest degree he can never act irrationally or lay his wisdom aside. In consequence it is not possible that he should have recourse to miracles in order to achieve results that can come about naturally."

These views made Wolff suspect to the Pietists,[9] then dominant in Halle, and when in a lecture on "the practical philosophy of the Chinese", he pointed to the similarity between European and Chinese ethics as proof that morality was not based on revelation, the Pietists accused him of atheism. Apparently at their instigation, in November 1723, Frederick William I ordered Wolff to leave Halle within 48 hours under pain of death by hanging.

Wolff betook himself to Marburg, followed by his students, and there established himself as the leading philosopher in Germany and in the German-speaking lands in the Habsburg dominions. This was a situation which Frederick William I came to deplore, not only because of the loss of prestige, but also because of the loss of much needed foreign exchange which it inflicted on Brandenburg-Prussia. In his childhood, Frederick William had seemed educationally subnormal. The despair of his tutors, he was unable at the age of nine to count up to ten or to learn the alphabet.[10] Throughout his life he remained incapable of writing a grammatically correct sentence in any language. In his old age, nevertheless, he professed himself a convert to Wolff's philosophy and set himself to read Wolff's works,[11] of which it may reasonably be assumed that he failed to understand a word.

Wolff resisted Frederick William's various attempts to bribe him back to Prussia but responded in 1740 to the overtures of Frederick the Great, then his devoted admirer, who saw in Wolff's rehabilitation, as he wrote to Voltaire, the triumph of "freedom of thought and reason over barbarism, ignorance and superstition". Frederick expressed to Voltaire his admiration for the strictly logical nature of Wolff's thinking, which was, he said, "applicable to all kinds of subjects and could be of the greatest value in political matters if one knew how to use it".[12]

Voltaire did not share these views. To Wolff truths were established by syllogistic reasoning – that is, by logical deductions from premises which, as he assumed, were naturally self-evident and which he never attempted to put to the test of the facts. This approach was anathema to the *Philosophes* of Voltaire's generation who, inspired by the great progress made in the natural sciences, to which Wolff was indifferent, believed that the road to understanding lay though empirical investigation. Voltaire, not unjustly, described Wolff as merely another German pedant and in the end succeeded in convincing Frederick that this was so. The fact nevertheless remains that Frederick's attitude to the state, and to his own relation to it, was far more influenced by Wolff's teaching than it was by Voltaire's.

Among the premises which, in political matters, had seemed to Wolff self-evident was that absolute monarchy had originated in a contract between the monarch and his future subjects, whereby the latter had given up their freedom in return for settled government. Their compensation was the opportunity of "Volkommenheit" or perfection – that is, of a moral life lived according to the precepts of reason as expounded by Wolff in his other works.

That monarchy was justifiable in terms of a social contract became official gospel in Prussia in the eighteenth century and Frederick the Great himself accepted this belief as axiomatic. It received its most plausible and sophisticated defence in the lectures which Svarez delivered in the winter of 1791-92 to Frederick William III when he was crown prince.

From this theory was deduced, to use the words which Frederick made famous by his continual repetition of them, that the king was the "first servant of the state". Frederick believed that he embodied this principle, though literally interpreted the claim was absurd, since a servant by definition is a person who obeys a master and Frederick owed obedience to no one. On the contrary, he justified his autocracy with more precise arguments if not with greater conviction than did any other ruler of his day.

When he proclaimed himself the first servant of the state what he meant – and he lived up to his professions – was that there was no personal sacrifice he would not make in the state's interests – as he himself understood them. For these interests he was prepared if necessary to ignore the claims of his family and dynasty, and to forego pleasure, comfort and even life itself, for he constantly exposed himself to death in battle. The ruler of dominions whose poverty continually obsessed him, he pushed his contempt for the luxurious courts of other princes to the point of always going about in filthy clothes – at his death, it was said, there was not even one clean shirt to be found in his drawers.[13] The cliché, repeated for generations and even now still sometimes accepted,[14] that the Prussian government in the eighteenth century was enlightened while the French was not, owed its origin principally to the distinction between Frederick's attitude in these respects and the attitude of the French kings. The point at issue, for the present argument, is how this distinction affected the ways in which these founding fathers of absolutism in France and Prussia understood their functions.

To some extent they understood them in the same way, notwithstanding the different premises from which they started. In France at Louis XIV's accession, as in Prussia throughout the eighteenth century, the circumstances of the time made it seem essential that absolute power should be concentrated in the hands of a hereditary monarch. In France revolts had been endemic long before they exploded into the major rebellion of the Fronde during Louis' minority. Professor Mousnier has described in detail[15] three great peasant revolts that occurred in the first half of the seventeenth century, as well as another (and it was not the only one) that took place after 1660.

In these revolts enormous numbers of peasants, amounting sometimes to 12,000 or more in a single province, rose in organized rebellion against the taxes imposed by Richelieu. They were supported by many other groups in the population – on one occasion by a provincial *parlement*, often by minor officials, commonly by the curés, frequently by members of the nobility who provided the leaders – a fact on which Louis XIV commented three centuries before Professor Mousnier substantiated it.[16] Voltaire can hardly be said to have exaggerated when he observed that, before Louis XIV began to govern, French civilization had continually been stifled by "a gothic government distracted by divisions and civil war".[17]

In the various provinces which composed Brandenburg-Prussia when absolutism began to establish itself, a comparable mood of general rebelliousness does not appear to have existed, but there were other, more menacing dangers. As Frederick the Great put it in 1768, the size of his dominions was equal to that of half Europe but they were poor, sparsely populated and without defensible frontiers. Their heartland consisted of the Mark of Brandenburg and of the provinces of Pomerania, Magdeburg and Halberstadt and, after 1745, of Silesia. But in addition to these territories there were the province of East Prussia (separated until 1772 from Pomerania by Polish West Prussia), the province of Cleves on the Rhine (an enclave surrounded by foreign states), and various territories on the Ems and the Weser, so remote from the centres of authority in Berlin and Potsdam that Frederick described them as being "au bout du monde".[18] As was commonly observed, even as late as the beginning of the nineteenth century, "Prussia", in the words of Freiherr vom Stein, one of the leaders of the reform movement after 1806, "is made up of a federation of states."[19]

In France, notwithstanding the tenacity with which, throughout the eighteenth century, the various provinces defended their identity against the crown's attempts at centralization, there were peasants even as early as 1636 who, in protesting their devotion to the king, maintained that they were "bons Français".[20] More than a century after this even the officers of the Prussian army, as Frederick the Great complained, referred to themselves as men of the Mark, of Pomerania etc. and would not accustom themselves to the common name of Prussians. As late as 1794 the *Allgemeines Landrecht* appeared under the title of the code not of Prussia, but of "the Prussian states",[21] and was preceded by a proclamation declaring that its provisions did not apply when they contravened any provincial laws then in force.[22]

Without some kind of autocracy it is inconceivable that the Hohenzollern dominions should have been welded into a state, and still less that they should have been welded into a nation. Yet this is how they came to seem to Frederick and his officials, and to the principal writers of the time, who commonly referred to them as the "Vaterland" in the second half of the eighteenth century.[23] It is equally inconceivable that the relative degree of order that prevailed in France throughout the eighteenth century, imperfect though it was not only by modern but also by contemporary Prussian standards, could have been achieved except by autocratic means.

Comparable circumstances in both France and Prussia thus played a part in the rise of the institution of absolutism and similarly endowed it in both countries with certain common features. The doctrine that the king shared his power with no one was interpreted in both France and Prussia to mean not only that all authority emanated from him, but that he must exercise it personally at least to the extent of taking every important decision himself, of seeing that every institution functioned as it should, and of ensuring, in

Louis XIV's favourite term, that his subjects were "soulagés" – that is, were protected from burdens too heavy for them. Even Frederick the Great, in spite of his belief that he owed his position to a social contract and that he was the first servant of the state, sometimes referred to himself as the "father" of his people, and clearly always saw himself in that light. Finally, the ideology of absolutism in its prime dictated that the king must personally lead his army in battle since the conduct of war was his most important function. "Always bear in mind", Frederick wrote for his successor, "that there is no prince who has not got in his head the idea of extending his dominions . . . the first task of a prince is to maintain himself. The second is aggrandizement."[24]

From these common ideas of the monarchs' functions certain consequences seemed to follow, the first of which was that the king should have no "first minister" – indeed it was Frederick's view, as must be shown presently, that he should have no ministers at all in the modern sense of the term. This belief, which Frederick observed in practice, but the French kings only with very considerable qualifications,[25] was also a natural consequence of existing conditions.

A "first minister" (not to be confused with a prime minister who can exist only in a system of parliamentary government) was understood to be a person to whom the monarch perpetually deferred and who ruled in his name – as Richelieu had done under Louis XIII. Throughout the greater part, if not the whole, of the period of absolutism the great mass of the population of Europe was illiterate and living on or below the margin of subsistence; a bureaucracy trained in traditions of honesty in public affairs was for long wholly or largely absent; a secure standard of life was enjoyed by few if any families, and the best hope of making a fortune lay in service to the crown, particularly in a financial capacity. In these circumstances the monarchs not unnaturally supposed that anyone on whom they bestowed a position of authority would use it, at the expense of the rest of the community and of the royal power, to further the interests of himself and his relations.

Both Louis XIV and Frederick the Great were obsessed by the fear that their servants would cheat them and that a first minister must have the best opportunities for doing so. As Louis XIV put it in one of his memoirs: "Where the people who should help me in my work are concerned, I resolved above all things never to have a first minister, and if you believe me, my son, and your successors do so after you, the term will be for ever abolished in France."[26] While Louis supposed that God would endow a ruler with the necessary intelligence and judgment, and that all that was required was that he should be educated in youth in the nature of his duties and the need for self-discipline, Frederick, who did not believe in the divine origins of monarchy, had no such excuse for assuming that his successors could be trained to discharge their functions properly. This was an assumption which he nevertheless made in defiance of his usual practice of providing rational grounds for his beliefs.

At an international congress held in 1955 two eminent scholars, one French and one German, agreed that absolutism was not "despotism, tyranny or totalitarianism".[27] That it was not totalitarianism is obvious, since however that form of government is defined, all the conditions which gave rise to it in the present century were absent in the seventeenth and eighteenth. Despotism and tyranny were, however, then as now, pejorative terms which different people at different times applied to governments whose behaviour they disliked. The Habsburgs always described Frederick the Great as a despot, as did many French *Philosophes* at the end of his life.[28] The members of the Prussian establishment, however, denied the charge, which they admitted was commonly brought against them, and themselves levelled it against the Habsburg Joseph II and against the French government at the end of the Ancien Régime.[29] Before the Revolution there was in fact no consensus in any group of European states on which absolute monarchies should be called despotisms and which should not.

In France long before the days of Louis XIV it had been customary to distinguish between absolute monarchy and despotism on the grounds that the monarch was morally obliged, and must generally be assumed to observe in practice, the laws of God and nature. Despotism was equated with the governments of the Far and Middle East whose rulers acted merely in accordance with caprice without regard to law, religion or humanity. They were said to rule by force alone; the life and property of everyone was at their mercy; their subjects, whom they treated like slaves, developed a slave mentality incapable of understanding even the idea of honour and self-respect.

This stereotype, which received its most elaborate and sophisticated explanation in the writings of Montesquieu, and of the Physiocrats[30] in the second half of the eighteenth century, was already present to the mind of Louis XIV. "There are nations", he wrote at the beginning of his reign, "where the majesty of the king consists, in large part, in not allowing himself to be seen, and this may be a consequence of attitudes of mind among people who are accustomed to servitude and who are ruled only by fear and terror. The French character is different, and as far back as our history teaches us, if this monarchy has a special characteristic it lies in the ease and freedom of access to the prince which his subjects enjoy. There is, as it were, an equality of justice between him and them which maintains them within a society that is honest and gentle, notwithstanding the almost infinite differences in birth, rank and power."[31]

The arbitrariness, violence and misery which disfigured French life during the greater part of Louis XIV's reign as a result of war, persecution and famine belied all these assumptions with one possible exception. Louis constantly insisted on the need to respect human dignity and in consequence to behave politely. "Treat everyone well", he wrote to the Dauphin, "and never say anything disagreeable to anyone." He specifically condemned those "cruel and bloodthirsty casts of mind which are unworthy of any man, let alone a king."[32]

31

In expressing these sentiments, which obviously left large areas uninflu-enced by them, Louis doubtless had in mind principally those people with whom he came into personal contact. Since, however, the ideas of the ruling class proverbially become in the course of time the dominant ideas of society, what he said cannot have been without significance. By the middle of the eighteenth century Montesquieu could write that in a monarchy "la tête du moindre citoyen est considérable".[33]

No such ideas as these entered the heads of Frederick William I and his officials, and began to develop only during the last twenty years or so of Frederick the Great's life. Frederick William was not only accustomed to hurl insults at his officials, but to take his stick to them, breaking the heads and knocking out the teeth of judges whose sentences he found objectionable.[34] The behaviour of Frederick the Great, though he did not resort to physical violence, was often comparable.[35]

Throughout the eighteenth century, particularly during its second half, though in Prussia the king's obligation to rule for the benefit of his subjects was insisted on at least a strongly as in France, the interests of the individual were always assumed to be identical with those of the state which the monarchs themselves determined. The idea that the individual as such, in any walk of life, had claims which the state should take into account among its objectives, was far more lacking in the ideology of Prussian absolutism than was the case in France.

The laws, for example, which forbade the Prussian landowner to appropriate peasant land, and which Frederick issued in deference to the principle that it was the duty of the crown to hold the balance between lord and peasant in such a way that neither should be able to ruin the other,[36] afforded the individual peasant no protection. It was merely decreed that if a peasant family were expropriated it must be replaced by another one.

Similar principles governed the crown's policy in relation to the industries it fostered or established. The success of the enterprise was always the primary consideration to which, if necessary, the individual workers and entrepreneurs must be sacrificed.[37]

Even the nobles provided no exception to the attitude that the needs of the state were paramount. Frederick assigned the nobles a role of primary importance. He had, he maintained, always treated them well,[38] but this was true of them only in their collective capacity. He subjected their private lives to a degree of regimentation which their French counterparts would have found intolerable. No officer in the Prussian army, for example, might marry without the king's consent, which was very commonly refused (in most regiments only between one-sixth and one-seventh of the officers were married).[39] Nobles might not travel abroad without permission – granted only for official purposes – and when admonitions to this effect proved ineffective a law was passed ordering that the estates of the delinquents should be confiscated.[40]

Though the civil liberties, including immunity from imprisonment without cause shown, were not recognized by any continental absolutism, high officials in France were commonly treated by their royal masters with a degree of respect to which their Prussian counterparts had no claim. The nobles in the Prussian bureaucracy lacked even such rights as the army officers enjoyed who, when accused of offences, were subject to trial by court marshal (though even this right was one which the eighteenth-century Hohenzollerns did not always respect[41]). Under Frederick the Great, as under his father, high civilian officials from the nobility could be thrown into prison, and kept there indefinitely, for offences which were sometimes never disclosed or of which they were later proved innocent.[42]

Though Louis XIV insisted that the king must take every important decision himself, he also insisted that he should always listen to his ministers' advice. (In cases of the first importance three ministers seemed to him the proper number.)[43] In Prussia, by contrast, Frederick the Great's common response to any suggestion of criticism was "nicht räsonieren" – "don't argue". He commonly described senior officials to their faces or their colleagues as liars, cheats or lazy idiots. Though not in a physical sense a cruel man – he found the sight of physical suffering repugnant – he often took an obviously sadistic pleasure in humiliating people, including nobles in high positions, whom he found irritating or thought incompetent.[44] To judge by the fragment of a memoir written by Graf Schulenburg-Kehnert, who held at different times, and sometimes simultaneously, a variety of important posts (he was the only noble in authority in Frederick's reign who is known to have written his autobiography), even officials who enjoyed, as he did, the royal favour over long periods, could not rid themselves of the fear that one serious mistake, even if committed *bona fide*, might land them for years in Spandau prison.[45]

We lack the evidence to form any general judgment on how Frederick's civilian officials reacted to this treatment. Some plainly felt for him, because of his great achievements, a sense of admiration that could border on idolatry; others while recognizing his faults felt them to be outweighed by his virtues; others harboured bitter grievances. It can nevertheless hardly be doubted that the way he treated his servants, whether bourgeois or noble, was calculated to breed in them, and many individual cases could be cited where it did so,[46] that servile attitude to authority which to the French was one of the hallmarks of despotism.

The different attitudes which the monarchs in France and Prussia adopted towards their functions appear most clearly in their Testaments Politiques and analogous documents which they wrote to justify their actions and to provide guidance for their successors. This practice was begun in France by Richelieu, whom Louis XIV in this respect is said to have taken as a model. In Prussia it dated from the time of the Great Elector who ruled from 1640 to 1688.

Louis first conceived the idea of writing what he called his memoirs when he took up the reins of government in 1661. These memoirs were composed in consultation with his ministers who wrote both the earlier and the final drafts. Louis, however, examined the earlier drafts carefully and corrected them where he thought necessary. Altogether five memoirs were produced by this procedure and covered the years 1661 to 1668. Nothing further, however, was written after this, apart from one or two short pieces, including a few pages in 1679 entitled *Reflexions sur le Métier de Roi.*[47] Louis' failure to complete his project was doubtless due to the onset of the great wars, which began in 1672, continued more or less without intermission till his death, and left France in a calamitous condition.

Overwhelmingly the greater part of the memoirs, designed as a testimony to Louis' achievements, consisted of detailed accounts of diplomatic negotiations and military campaigns, interspersed from time to time with general observations on the rights and duties of a monarch.

Though Louis is commonly supposed to have said "l'état c'est moi", there is no evidence that he ever made this statement, which indeed is hardly compatible with his view of his position. Believing that "we exercise on earth a function wholly divine",[48] and occupy "the place of God",[49] he assumed his relations to his subjects to be comparable to those of God towards humanity. He was the father of his people. He owed them love and protection and the duty to devote himself to their welfare, but they, in their turn, owed tribute to his majesty. He continually referred to the need to maintain "my own splendour of life", my own "magnificence", my own "honour". A propos of a dispute over precedence which occurred on one occasion between the French and the Spanish ambassadors in London, he remarked that this might, had it not been amicably settled in France's favour, have been "a legitimate cause for war in which I should have been able to acquire honour by putting myself at the head of my armies."[50]

When the disasters that overtook the French nation at the end of his reign made plain the incompatibility between his conception of his rights on the one hand and his duties on the other, he accepted the need to give up some of the former but saw this as a meritorious sacrifice. With reference to the peace proposals made to him in 1710, to which he had been prepared to listen, he wrote that in considering them "I can say that I departed from my character, and did supreme violence to my nature, in order to procure an immediate peace for my subjects at the expense of my reputation."[51]

To any high Prussian official in the second half of the eighteenth century (not to mention the modern reader), the most remarkable feature of Louis' instructions for his heirs must have seemed not only the semi-divine attributes with which he credited himself, but the total absence from his writings of any description of the social and economic conditions of his country or of its administrative arrangements. His failure to see the need for any rational analysis of the problems of government, combined with the desire, which Necker found characteristic also of his successors and described as "to make war with the sole object of increasing the royal power or diminishing the power of its rivals",[52] proved fatal after the accession of

William III to the English throne and the consequent alliances which led to France's undoing.

Louis' vision of himself as God's representative on earth, and thus as the defender of the Roman Catholic faith, led him to persecute the Huguenots in an age when religious intolerance was coming under attack from the best minds of Europe. He thus drove thousands of his most skilful and industrious subjects into exile, to the profit of his enemies. In his attempts to expound the principles on which absolutism should function he overlooked, notwithstanding the instruction which Colbert tried to give him, the economic and financial basis on which victory in war depended and, except in his remarks about his council, totally failed to consider how the various institutions of his administration either did or ought to work. As Frederick the Great was fond of observing about Louis XIV's successors: their policy and their government were wholly lacking in "system".

In consequence, as French historians are now pointing out after centuries of adulation,[53] his reign was essentially a disaster. It not only saw the rise of Britain to the position of a world power, and the start of French decline in Europe and overseas which accelerated throughout the eighteenth century till the Revolution; before he died it had transformed France, in Fénelon's words, into "a great and desolate hospital without provisions". French trade and agriculture were in ruins; the taxes and other financial expedients had in Vauban's words "totally impoverished such people of moderate means as could once spare something for the poor".[54] According to the most recent estimates, one-tenth of the French population died in the famine of 1693/4[55] and one-fifth (say some 4 million people) in that of 1709/10[56] – disasters for which the crushing taxation which the wars made necessary must have been at least in part, if not to a considerable extent, responsible.[57]

All these misfortunes, combined with the contrasting state of affairs in England and the growth of the rational, secular outlook of the Enlightenment, undermined the belief in the divine origins of absolutism in France and its defence on grounds of utility became increasingly difficult.

Louis XIV himself evidently recognized, before his death, the bankruptcy of his principles, since he tried to burn his memoirs which were only saved for posterity by being plucked from the flames by the Maréchal de Noailles.[58]

Louis' gesture was symbolic. Though absolutism continued to be accepted for three-quarters of a century after his death, the way it functioned became increasingly subject to criticism, in the name of a variety of different principles all essentially though not explicitly hostile to it.

To read the Testaments Politiques of the eighteenth-century Hohenzollerns, and particularly those of Frederick the Great, who for all his much greater intellectual sophistication to a large extent only elaborated and systematized his father's principles, is to move into a different realm of thought. Though statistical data are lacking, all such evidence as is available strongly suggests that in 1740 when Frederick acceded to the throne,

Brandenburg-Prussia – in terms of wealth, education and technical skill – was more backward than France had been in 1660. While, however, Prussian absolutism rested on a more primitive material and cultural base than the French, it was inspired by an ideology in many respects more modern.

Frederick the Great was more given to putting his thoughts on paper than any monarch of his own or perhaps any other age. But he summarized his main political ideas in his Testaments Politiques of 1752 and 1768, each consisting of over a hundred substantial pages, and in various shorter documents, notably his "Exposé of the Prussian Government and the Principles on which it Operates", of 1776, and his "Reflections on the Administration of the Prussian Finances" which he wrote in 1784 two years before his death.[59]

"The principles on which the Prussian government operates" was a typical and significant expression of Frederick's way of thinking which, in a fashion not uncommon among his countrymen then and later, combined an addiction to philosophizing with a strongly practical bent.

Frederick, in this as in many other ways a follower of Christian Wolff, believed that all governments must be based on some "system", by which he meant that "in every country with a good administration all the various branches of government are so closely connected one with another that they compose a perfect whole. This is what one understands by system."[60]

There are, Frederick said, "principles for everything and every country" – a belief which, like the prophets of the early German Enlightenment, he found most perfectly exemplified in a clock, all of whose parts were designed to work in harmony. He commonly referred to the state as a machine, though always with the proviso that the various parts of its mechanism were liable to be disturbed by unforeseeable circumstances and must therefore be designed to allow for the maximum degree of flexibility.

"It is evident", he wrote in 1776, "that politics, military matters and finance are branches of government so intimately connected that they can never be separated."[61] In other words, to use a phrase that became current during the Second World War of the present century, he thought that his resources should be distributed on a system not of priorities but of allocation – i.e., that no particular need, except in moments of the direst emergency, should take precedence over every other but that all should be considered in conjunction.

To say this, however, is not to deny that, because of the vulnerability of his dominions and his determination to weld them into a defensible unity, military needs, particularly after the end of the Seven Years War seemed to him of primary importance. "This state", he said, "cannot maintain itself without a large army" since "we are surrounded by enemies more powerful than ourselves against whom at any moment we may have to defend ourselves."[62] "Modern French writers", he observed in one of his many sardonic reflections on the French *Philosophes*, "in order to excuse France's military failures, endeavour to ridicule the military profession and to vilify it as far as they can. This temerity should be put a stop to by the police since there is no art so beautiful or so useful as war when it is practised by honest men."[63]

When he said that war, politics and finance were so intimately connected that they could not be separated, he meant in the first place that war should never be entered on lightly without regard to its consequences for all other aspects of the national life. The Prussian population suffered more disastrously from the Seven Years War of 1756-63 than did that of any other nation, and Frederick, who personally commanded his armies, and in no fewer than six battles had horses shot under him,[64] was better aware than any other monarch, for he was not a man to whom physical courage came naturally, of the horrors of the battlefield, as well as of the miseries, which he described in detail, that were inflicted on civilians by plundering foreign armies.

A declaration of war, be believed, should only be made after the most careful calculations of the cost and the benefits likely to accrue from it. A typical illustration of this attitude was his conviction that Prussia should not attempt to build a navy because, without intolerable sacrifices in other spheres, she could not afford the men or the money necessary to compete with the great maritime powers. It was wiser, he concluded, to have the best army than the worst navy in Europe.[65]

Success in war, which seemed to him to turn on a proper allocation of resources, was necessarily connected in his mind with material prosperity (though not with the accumulation of wealth in the hands of the few – a feature of all eighteenth-century economies, his own increasingly included, which he never ceased to condemn), for the government drew its revenues from the taxes raised from the population. Money, he continually repeated, was the sinews of war, provided the government managed it prudently. Without, by contemporary standards, an adequate economic base and an intelligent financial policy, success in war and in the conduct of foreign affairs must, he assumed, be impossible.

At the same time, he realized that the achievement of these objectives also demanded a population that, particularly in its leading groups, was not only dedicated to service to the state, but trained to be honest, intelligent, hard-working and efficient. He strove to improve education, particularly secondary education, though his attempts were largely frustrated by lack of money, and increasingly insisted that entrance into the bureaucracy should be conditional on academic qualifications. He attached great importance to maintaining justice – justice (as far as the needs of the state seemed compatible with it) between one individual and another and one group and another, so that law, order and security of property might prevail, and so that within the bounds of the société d'ordres, which he took for granted, the more powerful should not be permitted to deprive the weak of the necessities of life.

Notwithstanding the arbitrary, capricious and vindictive actions of which he was often guilty, and his general incapacity for ordinary human affection, no one who has read his elaborate instructions to his officials (on this matter a more reliable source of evidence than his various memoirs and Testaments Politiques) can doubt the genuineness of his sympathy for the poor, and particularly for the peasants.

Von Schlabrendorff, then minister for Silesia, observed in 1765, that His Majesty had had a great deal of contact with the common man during the campaigns of the Seven Years War and in the course of military marches through the province. From the peasants he had learned how the nobles oppressed them.[66] To the best of his ability, Frederick intended to put a stop to such practices though his power to do so, as it turned out, was very limited. In his instructions to the General Directory of May 1748, he had written that he would punish with the utmost severity any official who knowingly tolerated or permitted the infliction of any injustice on "even the humblest peasant".[67] He told the Frenchman de Launay, whom he put in charge of the indirect taxes in 1766, "Take only from those who can pay. These I hand over to you."[68] "I well know", he once said, "that the rich have many advocates, but the poor have only one, and that is I."[69] He saw the state as a collection of groups each with its specific functions and rights defined by law – groups which nevertheless were, or rather should be, educated and coerced into becoming united on a basis of justice, morality and patriotism.

As militarism is commonly understood in the west – that is, the exaltation of the military virtues above all others and the diffusion of this spirit thoughout the population – Frederick the Great's Prussia, which in relation to the number of its inhabitants maintained an army four or five times larger than the French, was the most militaristic state in Europe.[70] In the famous words of Frederick's minister von Schrötter: "What distinguishes the Prussians from other people is that theirs is not a country with an army. They have an army with a country that serves it as a headquarters and a commissariat." To many German historians, on the other hand, and notably to Gerhard Ritter, to whom militarism meant the pursuit of military objectives regardless of the claims of and the virtues bred by peace, Frederick the Great, in contradistinction to Louis XIV, Napoleon or Hitler, was the very reverse of a militarist.[71]

The fact nevertheless remains that war and the need to prepare for it were his major preoccupations. The military profession came to seem to him the noblest of all professions. He prized physical courage above all human qualities (even when, as Christian Garve once complained, it was unaccompanied by other virtues). He felt for his officer corps a sense of comradeship, and elicited from it a devotion, which had no parallel in his relations with any other group.

His Testaments Politiques are essentially elaborate analyses of the material conditions of his dominions and their interlocking institutions whose proper manipulation seemed to him the basis of his own and of future military success.

He described what he saw as their principal features in considerable and often minute detail – the nature, for example, of the central and local organs of government; the commodities produced, imported and exported by the various provinces; the sums these provinces could raise in revenue with the proportion they kept for their own needs and handed over to the central government; the numbers of troops in the Prussian army, the extent to which they could be increased in war and the cost in thaler involved; the stocks of grain, in such and such quantities, in such and such depots, in this, that and the other locality, that were needed not only to feed the troops but to keep prices stable for the benefit of the civilian population in times of bad harvest. No wonder, he observed, that the French could not regulate grain imports and exports, and so mitigate the effects of scarcity, when they had no figures of production and consumption.

Above all he insisted on the importance of prudent, methodical management of the royal revenues which, he said, are "the pulse by which one judges the strength of its [the state's] constitution."[72] Alone among the absolute monarchs of his day he realized that there could be no proper financial administration without an "exact assessment of receipts and an orderly system of expenditure", though the methods which he adopted (and also described in detail) with these ends in view were later much criticised.

As the most famous and successful of the absolute monarchs of eighteenth-century Europe, in his old age, not surprisingly, he came to see his system as sacrosanct, though he could hardly be labelled conservative without qualification since he was always aware that change, as he said, was "one of the immutable laws of nature".[73] At the end of his life he did indeed foresee some of the changes Europe was to undergo – the overthrow, sooner or later, of colonial rule; the collapse of the French government through bankruptcy; the secularization of church property.[74] The most important changes which the French Revolution was to introduce, however, he did not foresee. The famous German historian, Meinecke, compared his intelligence to "a bright light in a dark space that illuminates sharply and accurately all the objects on its vicinity but casts no beam beyond them."[75]

He clung to his belief that his kind of absolutism was the best and an enduring form of government, although after his death it increasingly became the fashion to attack it for its defects in both theory and practice, and to stigmatize it, in a constantly repeated phrase, as a "mechanischer Staat" or a "Maschinenstaat" – a state in which people were treated as cogs in a machine. He himself seems not to have doubted that autocracy could subdue the human spirit to obedience by some combination of force and persuasion. He could contemplate no kind of society except the société d'ordres in which, long before he died, the legal barriers which separated the various estates from each other, and which he did his best to preserve, had become obstacles to economic growth.

A combination of circumstances undermined and finally destroyed his system. Brandenburg-Prussia, like the other European states during the period of the revolutionary and Napoleonic wars, had its advocates of drastic change who, there as elsewhere, were prepared to fight not only the vested interests which the old regime had created, but the instincts which in the bulk of all populations in all ages make people unwilling to change their habits.

In the present connection the significant point is that the ideology of Prussian absolutism, as Frederick expounded it, was far closer – not in detail but by virtue of its rationality – to the thinking of the bourgeois age than was its French counterpart, which increasingly in the decades after Louis XIV's death ceased to deserve the title of an ideology at all.

PART TWO

I

The bureaucracies'
tasks in France and Prussia,
and the conditioning circumstances

Absolutism was essentially warlike and war on the continent of Europe provided the principal motive force for change between the end of the seventeenth century and the Revolution. It was the demands of the war for conquest or self-defence that drove the monarchs of the principal European countries to create navies and standing armies under royal control and continually to increase their size at a cost, in the second half of the eighteenth century – if one reckons in the interest on the debt incurred in past wars – of some 70 per cent or more of government revenue, even in peace.

The monarchs' principal preoccupation was to find sufficient money by means of taxes and loans to pay for the armaments necessary to maintain or increase their prestige and power; and the extent to which they could achieve these objectives turned essentially on their ability to promote economic growth and to tax the population sufficiently for their purposes without at the same time damaging the economy or engendering dangerous inequalities or discontent.

These tasks, whether or not their implications were fully realized, drove the monarchs, as far as seemed practicable, to centralize their administrations and to extend their scope, which meant increasing the number of their paid servants who are commonly, though in the French case somewhat inexactly, said to have constituted a bureaucracy; and together with the standing armies it was these so-called bureaucracies, whose authority came to extend throughout the kingdom, and whose members were paid a wage or salary in money, which distinguished the rule of the absolute monarchs from that of their predecessors.

These institutions, nevertheless, did not enable the monarchs to achieve the degree of centralization or obedience which the word absolutism suggests. To describe a ruler as absolute is to imply that his power is without limits, and this is how absolutism has generally been understood by the naive, as it was, for example, in his childhood by the Prussian judge and later professor, Felix Eberty. In his autobiography Eberty said that in the early nineteenth century he and the other children with whom he associated accepted without question "that the king could cut off the noses and ears of all his subjects if he wished to do so, and that we owed it to his goodness and his gentle disposition that he had left us in possession of these necessary organs".[1] Even, however, in more sophisticated adult circles, then and later, the extent to which circumstances limited the absolute monarchs' power to do as they would have liked, and to command obedience, was commonly underestimated.

In every major country on the continent of Europe in the eighteenth century the monarchs ruled over populations that, even in France which was the most densely populated, were small by modern standards but scattered over large areas. Communications were poor, and the great majority of people illiterate, hard to discipline and wholly impervious to rational arguments in favour of change. In these circumstances no ruler could so much as form an idea of what policies were practicable without information provided by people on the spot, and between what was practicable and what might seem desirable there was always a large gap.

The power of the absolute monarchs is commonly attributed to their standing armies, and these were certainly potent weapons which made it possible to repress opposition to an extent previously unknown. The standing army was nevertheless a weapon of limited use in the enforcement of domestic policy, and in any case its efficacy depended on the loyalty of its officers and their ability to preserve discipline – conditions which the French had become unable to fulfil by the end of the 1780s. Even more than on their standing armies, such ability to command obedience as the absolute monarchs possessed turned on the organization and competence of their civilian officials or bureaucracies.

The authority of these officials themselves, however, necessarily turned on their relations with the more powerful groups in the population. The disciple of the economist Quesnay and the popularizer of his doctrines, Le Mercier de la Rivière, pointed out that even the despot, that arbitrary tyrant of contemporary imagination who was supposed to rule by force alone, owed his power to an "association of ambitions and interests" among groups who saw an advantage in allying with him.[2] This was equally true of the absolute monarchs who were held to be distinguished from the despot only by their respect for the laws of God and nature.

In Europe in the eighteenth century 80 per cent or more of the population lived on the land; the land was the principal source of wealth and the landed nobility the group that enjoyed the greatest prestige. In every country where these conditions prevailed, the monarchs risked an opposition that would jeopardize the success of their policies, and indeed the possession of their thrones, if they provoked a significant degree of hostility among the noble landowners; for though the nobility as an estate had lost its right to participate in the making of policy, it retained many means of frustrating its execution.

The truth of this proposition can be demonstrated by many examples, of which the Emperor Joseph II provides the most famous. Joseph attempted to free the landholding peasants in the hereditary lands of the house of Habsburg from the compulsory labour services which they owed to the landlords, and to subject all landholders, whether noble or peasant, to an equal rate of tax. These measures provoked widespread unrest or revolt among the peasantry because they benefited some categories of peasants at the expense of others and raised expectations it was impossible to fulfil. At the same time they threatened with ruin the majority of landowners who were granted no compensation for the loss of their free labour. The result was a threat of chaos which could be exorcised only by the repeal of most of Joseph's measures of reform.

All the other eighteenth-century monarchs and their ministers, however strongly they came to desire reforms, were naturally anxious to avoid comparable catastrophes. On the other hand, those in the countries that were major military powers could not achieve their ends either unless, by combining in some way the use of the stick and the carrot, they could induce the more prominent noble landowners to cooperate with them in their efforts to increase the yield of trade, manufactures and agriculture, to maintain law and order, to raise armies and to introduce workable systems of taxation – all tasks which necessarily interfered with the noble way of life as it existed when absolutism began to establish itself.

Given the prestige of the nobility and the impossibility of dispensing with it, the extent to which the absolute monarchs could achieve their objects depended largely on their ability to educate and discipline the nobles to play the part required of them. But it also depended vitally on the ability to prevent peasant unrest on a scale such as occurred in many countries, where it disrupted the administration, if not, as in France, overturning the government; for in communities where the peasantry constituted the bulk of the population, as Namier once observed in discussing the revolutions of 1848,[3] no major revolution, such as occurred in 1789 and 1917, was possible without peasant support.

In the eighteenth century there was a continuous increase in the spheres of activity of the French and the Prussian bureaucracies, and in the sophistication of its leading members, if by bureaucracy in France is understood those officials who had not bought their offices on a hereditary basis.[4] Since representative institutions, in so far as they had continued to exist, had lost the right to participate in policy-making, the bureaucracy provided the only milieu in which projects of reform could be formulated in concrete terms. In Prussia by 1806 it had become a platitude, to quote one of Stein's collaborators, that "wherever new ideas develop, it is in the bureaucracy that they are seized on with the most resolution".[5] The same could be said of France in the second half of the eighteenth century.

In a famous and often quoted remark, Adam Smith observed that "commerce and manufactures can seldom flourish long in any state which does not enjoy a regular administration of justice, in which the people do not feel themselves secure in the possession of their property, in which the faith of contracts is not supported by law and in which the authority of the state is not supposed to be employed in enforcing the debts of all those who are in a position to pay. Commerce and manufactures, in short, can seldom flourish in any state in which there is not a certain degree of confidence in the government."[6] Because it seemed axiomatic in the nineteenth century that these were the attributes of every civilized state, and because it was assumed that they had originated in the business world, it was easy to overlook that, as the eighteenth century progressed, most of them came to seem necessary to the leading officials in the absolute monarchies.

It was, for example, plain to Colbert, and to his successors particularly from the middle of the eighteenth century onwards, but also to the Hohenzollerns, and to the Habsburgs after the loss of Silesia in 1740, that their countries were underdeveloped by comparison with their more powerful neighbours or by the best contemporary standards, set first by the Dutch and later by the British. In consequence, the monarchs or their ministers in these relatively backward states were seized by the desire to catch up, and to do so by the only means available, that is, by government action deliberately directed to promoting economic growth, to diminishing, as far as seemed practicable, the privileges of the groups that impeded it, and to rationalizing law and administration in the interests of efficiency. All these tasks came increasingly to demand creating the conditions which Adam Smith described in the passage quoted above, and were seen to do so particularly in Prussia, where at the end of the eighteenth century Adam Smith's doctrines were taught as gospel in the universities in which aspiring bureaucrats were educated.[7]

It was not in fact the business communities which provided the solvent of the société d'ordres, however much consideration of their needs may have contributed to it, for they were not only small in numbers and exercised little or no power; even in France where they enjoyed more wealth and independence than they did in central and east-central Europe, they were less open to new ideas than were the progressively-minded members of the administration.[8] As Tocqueville emphasized, it was absolutism itself, by means of its bureaucracy, that rendered the société d'ordres obsolete.

The organization of the bureaucracy, however, and its ability to deal with the increasingly complicated tasks that faced it, could only develop slowly. To suppose that eighteenth-century officials could have functioned in accordance with the standards that came to be accepted in the nineteenth century in the west is to suppose the impossible; for in the primitive societies of the pre-revolutionary age not only were officials with the requisite degree of intelligence and education, particularly in Prussia, hard to find in sufficient numbers; to provide them with the salaries and other conditions necessary if large-scale corruption and dereliction of duty were to be avoided was much harder still, and the further one proceeded down the official hierarchy the more obvious these difficulties became and the more urgent the need to solve them, particularly in the countryside. For in the countryside was produced that most vital of all commodities – the grain which was the principal source of food for the bulk of the population and the only form of mass production of which these primitive economies were capable. It was in the countryside, as the Prussians always saw more clearly than the French, that the task of educating the landowners in the need for agricultural improvement – an essential prerequisite of economic growth – must start if it were to start at all; it was in the countryside where the assessment and collection of taxes gave rise to the greatest problems, and where the riots and revolts, which food shortages and any increase in taxation were always likely to provoke, were the most dangerous.

In the eighteenth century the bureaucracies, then in process of being created, could cope with these problems with at best limited success, but the degree of success varied from absolutism to absolutism. In France it was so limited that it failed to avert a revolution whose principal achievement, in Tocqueville's eyes, was that it completed the task which absolutism had begun but left unfinished. The Revolution, Tocqueville said, must remain incomprehensible as long as it is studied out of relation to its antecedents. Though its first acts dismantled the centralization of the Ancien Régime, its later acts resurrected and extended it. Though, as Tocqueville put it, the government of the Bourbons fell, their administration, purged of its defects, continued.[9] "The administrative monarchy", in the words of a recent writer, "killed the monarchy."[10]

In Prussia, by contrast, Frederick William III's minister, von Struensee, could observe to the French chargé d'affaires in 1799, "the salutary revolution you have made from below will come about gradually in Prussia from above"[11] – a prophecy that was fulfilled to a greater extent than is now commonly admitted in the English-speaking world.

That this was so, as has been said, cannot be attributed to the fact that the Prussian commercial and industrial bourgeoisie was less developed than the French, true though this is. It can more plausibly be ascribed to the much greater degree of success achieved by the Prussian than by the French government, judged by contemporary standards, both at home and abroad. The reigns of Frederick William I and Frederick the Great extended over the best part of a century. In this period they created not only the best army in Europe but a bureaucracy endowed, in Tocqueville's words, with a "power and a command of detail" unequalled in France.

Though both the French and the Prussian monarchs were forced, and indeed were to a greater or less extent willing, to accept the continuance of old practices and attitudes of mind, they did so in different ways and degrees. It would be impossible to say of the eighteenth-century Prussian rulers, as Tocqueville said of the French, that "they destroyed practically nothing of the old administrative edifice".[12] On the contrary, Frederick William I, for all the old institutions he left standing, established a new machinery of government when in 1723 he set up the General Directory and its subordinate organs in the provinces – the *Kriegs- und Domänenkammern* or boards of war and domains. By this means he combined in one body control over financial and other aspects of policy, which his son continued to consider in conjunction, even though he progressively weakened the powers of the General Directory by creating new ministries independent of it. It was to this situation that the greatest German historian of the eighteenth century, Otto Hintze, attributed the fact that Prussia was able to afford her enormous army without ruining the country.[13]

Writing in 1765, in the light of the French disasters in the Seven Years War, the former minister, d'Argenson, observed that France had always made the mistake of attaching primary importance to foreign affairs while neglecting domestic ones. The great periods of French history, he said, had always seemed those when new provinces had been conquered, while the havoc which these conquests had created in the existing provinces had been ignored. He found the French military record, which at the time he wrote had culminated in the British conquest of the whole of the French overseas empire, a proof that this policy was self-defeating. Though the other sciences, he concluded, had made great strides, "the science of politics is still in its infancy".[14]

This was certainly not true to the same extent in Prussia for reasons and with consequences that will be considered in the following chapters by comparing the composition of the bureaucracies in the two countries and the extent to which, in internal affairs, they were able or failed to fulfil the tasks generally accepted at the time as binding on every monarch.

These tasks remained the same throughout the period of absolutism, though as the eighteenth century progressed their nature and their relative importance (for to a greater or less extent they were always incompatible) came to be interpreted differently. They were raising the money needed to defend the territory against attack, or to increase it by conquest for the sake of added power or prestige; maintaining justice, always seen as a principal if not the most important of royal functions, however justice was understood; and finally increasing wealth – a task essential both to waging war successfully and to promoting the welfare of the population which all the absolute monarchs believed in principle to be their duty. Like Louis XIV, every French king spoke of the need to "soulager mes peuples". Frederick the Great, though he used the language of the Enlightenment, expressed the same sentiment when he said in 1770 that he considered it one of his principal tasks "to make people as happy as is compatible with human nature and the means at my disposal."[15]

II

The composition of the bureaucracies: nobles and bourgeois in the service of the crown and in the social élite

(a) THE FRENCH EXPERIENCE

The groups from which the absolute monarchs in France drew their principal servants have always been a matter of confusion and dispute. For a long time it was held that Louis XIV ruled the country by means of bourgeois ministers, but this belief was later challenged[1] and is indeed demonstrably false if "bourgeois" and "minister" are understood in any modern sense. Contemporaries, however, gave these terms a meaning they no longer possess and by their standards the belief was not without substance.

In Louis XIV's day a minister was not a secretary of state or other comparable office-holder in charge of a government department, though the term increasingly came to have this meaning in the course of the eighteenth century. He was anyone whom the king summoned to his council for consultation. In France in the seventeenth century, and indeed for long afterwards, it was comparatively rare to live to old age and even monarchs were continually exposed to the hazards of death from disease or assassination. In these circumstances the princes of the blood who had claims to the succession felt they had a right to share in determining policy. They and their supporters among the other noble grandees thus constituted a threat to the monarch's authority and became a focus for discontent in other sections of the population. It was people in these positions whom Louis XIV was determined to exclude from his council and whom he supplanted by men drawn from what was known as the "robe".

The *robe*, as one its most eminent students has pointed out,[2] was in the eighteenth century a vague term which included all the holders of administrative and judicial offices under the crown. For the purposes of the present argument it may be understood to mean people in the upper echelons of what were known as the "sovereign courts", of which the most important were the Paris *parlement*, and the eleven provincial *parlements*. These bodies were the highest courts of justice in their respective areas, but they also discharged important administrative and legislative functions, and no edict or ordinance had the force of law in any area unless the *parlement* in question had agreed, willingly or under royal pressure, to register it.

The *parlements*, of which the most important was the *parlement* of Paris, dated from the Middle Ages. They were a part of the administrative legacy which the absolute monarchs inherited, and which even Louis XIV never contemplated abolishing. In the eighteenth century it proved impossible either to bypass their authority or to induce them to accept the ideology of absolutism which was adopted by the king's council.[3] By means of a procedure to be described presently, all their members had bought their offices, which in the case of the principal officials, the magistrates, conferred hereditary nobility after twenty years' service, though throughout the eighteenth century nearly all magistrates enjoyed noble status before they assumed office, being the scions of families ennobled in the more or less distant past.[4]

Throughout the reign of Louis XIV, and in the case of many offices up till the Revolution, the holders of the principal posts in the government – the chancellor, the four secretaries of state and the *contrôleur-général* who was responsible for financial and economic affairs – began their careers in the *parlements*, and it was from these officials that Louis XIV chose his advisers.

It has been calculated that, on average, they came from families ennobled for three generations[5] but by the standards of court circles as described by Saint-Simon this was far from enough to remove the stigma of bourgeois origins. Writing of the beginning of Louis XIV's reign, when the King's principal advisers were Lionne, Le Tellier and Fouquet, all of them from families ennobled in the previous century, Saint-Simon quoted the grandees at court as having asked how it could have come about that the kingdom was governed by three "bourgeois". He maintained that Louis chose his ministers from "la pleine et parfaite roture"* and that they could divest themselves only with difficulty of the "filth" in which they had been born. He compared the scene in governing circles to a pair of scales in which those who had previously been everything had sunk to the bottom and those who had started from nothing had been raised to the top.[6]

Saint-Simon plainly wrote in total ignorance of the elaborate hierarchies that prevailed in the walks of life below his own. In terms of rank, wealth and cultivation, most of Louis' ministers were parvenus only by standards long since forgotten. As hereditary nobles they would not have been accounted bourgeois in later ages or even for the purposes of elections to the Estates General in 1789. In 1660, nevertheless, and indeed for long afterwards, people in their position were often so described not only because they had acquired their noble status in (by court standards) the relatively recent past but also because of their *robe* origins. From time immemorial, it is true, there had been nobles of ancient families who had served in the *robe*, and there had been other such nobles who had complained that they had been prevented from doing so by lack of the money necessary to buy an office under the crown.[7] But in this and other matters during the Ancien Régime,

---

* *La roture* means the condition of a commoner as *la noblesse* means that of a noble. To say that a person came from *la pleine et parfaite roture* meant that he was a perfect example of someone of common origin.

as in all forms of society, popular beliefs bore little relation to facts or logic, and it was long commonly accepted that the church and the pursuit of arms were the only occupations befitting a gentleman. Not only trade was thought demeaning, but any kind of work for money, including serving the crown in a civilian office for a salary.

Up to the Revolution the idea persisted, though with diminishing strength and relevance, that the true (as distinct from the parvenu) noble was a "gentilhomme" and that he was distinguished by his "blood" or "race" and by the pursuit of arms. As the famous jurist Loyseau put it at the beginning of the seventeenth century, "Our *gentilshommes* are those whose race has always been free from all contamination by common blood, and we do not reckon any nobility as perfect except that which can be shown to have no plebeian origins – in other words whose origin cannot be demonstrated. *The origins of the true noble lie beyond the memory of man* [author's italics] . . .[8]

"The sword", Loyseau said, "is the ornament and distinguishing mark of the nobility." "The *gentilhomme* cannot engage in any occupation to maintain his family. His only means of preserving his distinctive attributes (*sa qualité*) is by advancing himself in the profession of arms by means of the favour of the great." Professor Mousnier, in his *Fureurs Paysannes*, quotes the mother who said: "My son, do not give yourself airs and remember you are only a bourgeois. I am well aware that your father and your grandparents were . . . councillors of state [that is, possessed noble status in law] but believe me that in France the only nobility that is recognized is the *noblesse d'épée*. The nation is wholly warlike and finds its glory only in arms."[9]

It may have been these standards that Tocqueville had in mind (though even if this is so he exaggerated) when he said that the French administration at the end of the Ancien Régime was in the hands of men who were "almost all bourgeois".[10] For he cannot have failed to know what kind of people constituted the leading *robe* families, since he himself, on his mother's side, was directly descended from one of them – the Lamoignons,[11] whose members had provided the *robe* with many distinguished servants and had been counts and marquises, and men of wealth and cultivation,[12] for nearly two hundred years before the Revolution.

Whatever reasons Tocqueville may have had for this misleading assertion, the belief was certainly held, though with continually diminishing social and political significance, that even such old and distinguished noble families as the Lamoignons were inferior to the so-called "noblesse chevaleresque" and "noblesse d'ancienne extraction", whose origins were lost in the mists of antiquity but whose owners could prove that they had been nobles before the beginning of the fifteenth or the sixteenth century respectively.[13] In the second half of the eighteenth century only the members of the families in the first of these two categories were entitled to the so-called "honneurs de la cour" (of which nevertheless they could not avail themselves without a substantial income) – that is, they were entitled to a seat in the royal carriages, to participate in the royal hunts, and in these and other ways to associate personally with the monarch. Whether or not any given individual had a right to these privileges was a matter for investigation by the court genealogist. The ultimate decision, however, rested with the king, who made exceptions as he chose, and in an increasingly arbitrary fashion, but nevertheless had always, since the days of Louis XIV, granted the honours as a matter of principle – so greatly had the needs of the state come to outweigh ancient prejudices – to ministers and their descendants, even though commonly they were not entitled to them by their birth.[14]

In the second half of the eighteenth century the number of nobles who were so entitled formed only a small proportion of the total nobility, for there were many other ways of achieving noble status. It could be acquired by prescriptive right, that is, by posing as a noble and getting away with it for a specified period of time. This practice, described in the *Allgemeines Landrecht* as *Verjährung*, was a recognized way of rising into the nobility in Prussia where the number of years during which it had to proceed unchallenged was laid down as forty-four.[15] Similar provisions existed in France. For several centuries before the Revolution bourgeois had acquired seigneuries – that is, in effect noble property with the right to feudal dues[16] – and had done so in large numbers either by purchase or by foreclosing on impecunious nobles to whom they had lent money by a procedure analogous to a mortgage.[17] A bourgeois in law, however, might only own a seigneurie on condition that he paid a heavy tax known as the franc-fief, from which nobles were exempt. But if he managed to evade this tax, and if his son and his grandson did likewise, then, in the fourth generation, this family, having successfully escaped the attentions of the tax-officials and the commissions appointed from time to time to unmask "false nobles", was entitled to count itself noble.[18]

Nobility could also be acquired by direct grant from the king either in reward for service to the state or, and much more commonly in the reign of Louis XIV, by purchase. Louis, for example, sold 500 titles of nobility by a single edict in March 1696 and many hundreds more during the last fifteen years of his reign.[19]

He also created nobles in large numbers by the sale of offices. This practice dated from the Middle Ages but assumed its final form in 1604 by means of an arrangement known as the *paulette*,[20] which permitted the purchaser of an office, who put down a capital sum in return for interest paid him in the form of "gages" or salary, to hand the office on to his descendants or to sell it at whatever was the current market price. Subject to certain qualifications[21] the office thus became his personal property, like his house or his land. Many such offices conferred noble status, though on terms which varied according to the prestige attached to the functions which the office-holder discharged. In his *De l'Administration des Finances de la France*, first published in 1784, Necker calculated that at the time he wrote the number of offices which conferred hereditary nobility, either on purchase, or after a period of service, or in the second or third generation, amounted to over 4,000.[22] The inferior offices, which did not confer noble status, but were often a stage in the progress to those which did, were very much more numerous. The officials who owned them discharged a great variety of different functions but were chiefly employed in the administration of justice and the collection and distribution of the direct taxes. It has been estimated that at the end of the Ancien Régime the total number of these so-called venal offices was approximately 51,000.[23] The amount of capital sunk in them at any given time is impossible to assess with any approach to accuracy. Colbert believed that it exceeded the value of all the land in the kingdom.[24] At the end of the Ancien Régime, according to a recent estimate, it was certainly far greater than the annual revenue of the French government.[25]

The traffic in offices as practised in France, extraordinary even by contemporary standards in other countries, profoundly affected the French social structure, the workings of the administration and the mentality of all French people above the level of those too poor and ignorant to entertain hopes of bettering themselves. Essentially it was the product of two causes working in combination. On the one hand was the desire for status and its attendant privileges, which every office, however humble, conferred in some degree and which made it seem desirable even when, as happened not uncommonly, it became a financial liability; and of all the forms of status and privilege the most highly prized were those derived from nobility. To become a noble was the dream of every ambitious bourgeois – a goal in pursuit of which he was prepared to take any risk and make any sacrifice and which frequently caused his ruin. On the other hand, a means for satisfying this passion was provided by the perennial poverty of the French monarchy resulting from its addiction to war and display – an addiction that was not restrained by any institutional checks or habits of rational calculation and that drove it to sell offices to augment its revenue. For in the reign of Louis XIV, and to some, though to a smaller, extent under his successors, to sell offices was a cheaper and easier means of raising money than any more orthodox form of loan, though it mortgaged the future to a greater extent.

One of Louis XIV's ministers once told him that among the most valuable of the crown's prerogatives was that of creating offices, since "as soon as the crown creates an office God creates a fool willing to buy it."[26] This was not, however, wholly true. At the end of his reign Louis created so many offices – doubling, tripling and even quadrupling existing ones, and in these and many other ways defrauding the incumbents – that they became unsaleable.

The practice, however, began to flourish again, though in a better regulated, less unscrupulous fashion, with the onset of the great wars towards the middle of the eighteenth century. At this time the successful bourgeois who wished to enter the nobility could do so by the purchase of any one of various offices, but if he could afford it he commonly bought the office of *secrétaire du roi* in the grand chancellery in Paris or in one of the chancelleries attached to the sovereign courts in the provinces.[27] This office was not new, but being a virtual sinecure it could be multiplied without many of the inconveniences which had attended Louis XIV's creations. Available to anyone who could pay the price (in 1789 it cost 120,000 livres,[28] or £5,200 sterling at the current rate of exchange), it conferred not merely hereditary nobility but fourth-generation nobility – the hallmark, in the latter part of the eighteenth century, of a *gentilhomme* as distinct from a *bourgeois gentilhomme*. It was bought by successful writers (Voltaire and Beaumarchais, for example), merchants, manufacturers and financiers – 86 per cent of the general tax farmers were nobles in 1786.[29] Though such people usually continued after their ennoblement to pursue their original avocations, sooner or later they or their descendants, though admittedly to a diminishing extent, commonly sold the office in order to buy one in the government service that carried greater prestige.

The sale of offices was thus, as it has been said, the principal "méchanisme d'ascension sociale" – the means by which people from the humbler walks of life could rise by gradual stages, purchasing successively more prestigious offices until, after several years as a magistrate in the Paris *parlement*, a man acquired the position of *maître des requêtes*. Contemporaries described this office, whose holder discharged a variety of functions at court, as a "passe-partout" which, as the Chancellor d'Aguessau once put it, was "like the desires of the human heart whose object is their extinction",[30] since it was coveted because, for men of the *robe*, it was the gateway to the highest posts in the government – the *intendances des provinces* and the ministries, which were not put up for sale but bestowed, as far as circumstances permitted, according to merit.

The final stages of this ascent to the pinnacles of power were generally, though there were exceptions, more difficult after Louis XIV's death than they had been in his lifetime.[31] Tocqueville, however, appears to have been right when he said that noble status had never been so easy to obtain as at the end of the Ancien Régime. The numbers of bourgeois who acquired this status between the years 1774 and 1789 alone are such as to amaze anyone misguided enough to assume that the institution of nobility in France was comparable to that in Britain. The British peerage consisted of little more than 200 members throughout the eighteenth century. In France, according to the careful calculations of an American scholar, 2,477 heads of bourgeois families can be shown to have bought themselves into the nobility in the fifteen years before the Revolution.[32] The lack of obstacles in the way of such an achievement must surely have been unparalleled in any other continental country. Professor Bluche's meticulous researches into the period 1715-71 have led him to conclude that "the passage from the middle ranks of the bourgeoisie to the nobility in two generations and from the peasantry in three was not uncommon",[33] though the people who managed to achieve these feats constituted only a minute proportion of the population.

According to Loyseau's and Saint-Simon's criteria the successful bourgeois families whose members bought themselves noble status and climbed the official ladder through the purchase of office remained bourgeois indefinitely notwithstanding their power and wealth and the titles and seigneuries they acquired in consequence. In the second half of the eighteenth century views as extreme as this were heard increasingly rarely. In an age, however, still deeply imbued with the belief in hierarchy and the mystique of noble blood, the more or less unabated traffic in offices perpetuated the attempt to distinguish between the true and the bourgeois *gentilshommes*.

In the last decades of the Ancien Régime this attitude found expression in the provisions drawn up by various bodies, notably by the *parlements*, whose consent was necessary to the admission of new officials, but also, in the notorious *Loi Ségur*, by the government in relation to the officers in most regiments of the army, restricting appointment to men with at least four generations of nobility on the father's side. These measures have commonly been described as reactionary and undoubtedly were so by the enlightened standards of the time, though not for the reasons usually given. Contrary to common sense, it used to be supposed that they were directed against the bourgeoisie, though if this had been so the requirement of four generations of nobility would have been superfluous. In fact, their purpose was to keep out the nouveaux-riches nobles who had bought themselves into the nobility.

They were a testimony to the fact that throughout the reigns of Louis XIV and his two successors the old noble families and their protagonists had fought a losing battle against the claims of money and talent. Contrary to Tocqueville's beliefs, the French nobility never succeeded in turning itself into a caste, and for the reason that Tocqueville himself – a perennial source of illuminating ideas as well as of mistakes of fact – gave when he said, "The permanent separation of nobility and wealth is a chimera which after a certain time always results in the destruction of the first or the amalgamation of the two."[34]

The men of more or less recent nobility who governed the country under Louis XIV, and largely continued to do so under his successors, occupied the principal posts of power in an autocracy where success in almost all walks of life – the church, the army, trade, manufactures, the pursuit of letters, not to mention the government service itself, turned on the good will, if not the active support, of people in the official hierarchy whose pinnacle was the monarchy. Ministers became rich through the perquisites of office and the royal favour. Because they were accorded the honours of the court, not only they, but their descendants who inherited the privilege, enjoyed a status at court equal to that of dukes, whom no one ever presumed to call bourgeois because their rank, unlike that of baron, count and marquis, was only sparingly bestowed. In consequence any desire on the part of the old noble families to ostracize the parvenus commonly yielded to the more urgent needs for wealth and favour. Even Colbert, the most obviously bourgeois holder before Necker of an important ministerial post, counted three dukes among his sons-in-law.

In these circumstances the line between the *gentilhomme* and the parvenu could easily be obliterated in a generation or two if one judged by any standards other than those of the genealogist and often, indeed, even if one judged by these; for a wealthy man could always hire a competent person to invent for him an ancestry which might be difficult to disprove and which, if he was sufficiently powerful and behaved himself like a gentleman, no one might even have an interest in disproving. The direct descendant, for example, of that Fouquet whom in 1661 the grandees at court had called a bourgeois, was the Duc de Belle-Isle, a field marshal in the French army, who led the party at court which pushed Louis XV into war in 1741, and did so in pursuit of the ideals of military glory for which the *noblesse de race* had always stood.

The rise of the bourgeoisie in France in the eighteenth century, so often invoked but also mocked as a cause of the Revolution, was thus a reality in the state service in the sense that this service was continuously infiltrated by bourgeois, who nevertheless, before they reached a position of any importance, had always acquired noble status and were commonly anxious to conceal their bourgeois origins. Even as late as the 1780s it could be said that "the man who has been ennobled, astonished by his metamorphosis, is ashamed of having been a commoner. He devotes all his energies to separating himself from the class from which he sprang. The son of a *secrétaire du roi* is more noble than his father. Thus the purchaser of this office looks on his son with a certain respect because, having purified the race, he has become the scion of a family of *gentilshommes*. In his delighted imagination he prostrates himself before his grandson who has nothing in common with the original stock."[35]

The rise of the bourgeoisie in the service of the state was thus distinguished by a process for which there is no word in French or English but which the Germans, who also experienced it, describe as *Feudalisierung* or *Aristokratisierung* – the process by which a commoner adopts the standards and manners of the nobility. This was, however, a process which could be accomplished only gradually, and which in the course of its accomplishment in France in the eighteenth century also altered the attitudes of the old noble families.

Though at the beginning of Louis XIV's reign the members of these families would have felt that they demeaned themselves if they worked in an office, this notion came to be abandoned in the second half of the eighteenth century though not without heart-searchings. In 1757 the Duc de Belle-Isle, no doubt sensitive on this subject because by ducal standards his origins were not irreproachable, was offered the post of secretary of state for war. At first he refused it. He was, according to his predecessor, the Abbé de Bernis, "still a victim of the old error that a *duc et pair* and a field marshal of France could not without derogation become a secretary of state", as if, Bernis added, "it was beneath his dignity to govern a great kingdom."[36] Much argument was needed to disabuse the duke of these ideas. He suggested various ways by which he might direct the affairs of the department through a deputy and avoid assuming the derogatory title of secretary of state. But in the end he gave way, though on the condition that he should not, as was customary, sign papers with his family name – Fouquet – but simply "Maréchal Duc de Belle-Isle". He was the first of many dukes and members of old and distinguished families to assume ministerial office before the Revolution.[37]

In the course of his lifetime Belle-Isle discharged the functions of both the *robe* and the sword and he was by no means the only one to do so. His career was a refutation of the old belief, refuted in many other ways as well, that the church and the army were the only professions befitting a *gentilhomme*. Admittedly this belief continued to be professed and even acted on in certain circles. The military reformers who laid the basis of Napoleon's victories were convinced that the "armée pure et dure" they desired to create could only be officered by men of ancient lineage, uncorrupted by the wealth which had permitted the purchase of ennobling offices, including that of *secrétaire du roi* notwithstanding the right to fourth-generation nobility which it conferred.

This attitude was dramatically illustrated in 1783 when the Marquis de Ségur and his friend the Duc de Castries threatened to resign from the council because of a quarrel with the secretary of state Vergennes, the son of a recently ennobled *robe* family. "This", they said, "is a war to the death between the *robe* and people like us."[38]

Ségur's and Castries' war, however, was an ancient affair which few had any longer a wish to go on fighting, and which the facts of life were increasingly making appear ridiculous. It is true that in the continental monarchies of the eighteenth century the army officers were always apt to look down on the *Federfüchsern* or pen-pushers, as Blücher liked to call them,[39] and to equate their profession with social superiority. In France, in both the *robe* and the army the children tended to follow in their fathers' footsteps. But they did not do so always. Montesquieu may not have been typical of the *robe* but he was not extraordinary when he said to his son, "You can be a man of either the *robe* or the sword . . . it is for you to choose. The *robe* will give you more independence and liberty, though the sword will offer you greater chances."[40]

Thus within the government service in France, notwithstanding the lip-service which continued to be paid to the old myths, the line between the functions formerly held to be appropriate to nobles and bourgeois respectively became increasingly blurred, as did also the differences in manners and attitudes to life which in Louis XIV's day had been held to distinguish the *gentilhomme*, who was essentially a soldier, from the *bourgeois-gentilhomme* ennobled by civilian office.

This transformation was the result of a combination of causes for all of which, as Voltaire rightly said, the triumph of absolutism was, directly or indirectly, responsible. For absolutism brought civil war to an end – thus permitting an increase in trade, manufactures, and the arts of peace generally – and greatly augmented the scope and power of the government. Among the consequences of these developments was not only the growth in wealth which made it possible for rich bourgeois to buy themselves into the nobility in large numbers and thus to undermine the old hierarchies in the ways described; this process was fostered by great increases in the publication and sale of books and periodicals – notably the *Encyclopédie* – which disseminated the ideas of the French Enlightenment – ideas to which it was impossible that the members of the governing circles themselves should remain immune, however much they might at the same time cling to the old practices and values.

Saint-Simon complained, and by his own standards rightly, that Louis XIV debased the nobility, for he set in train changes that increasingly diminished the importance of birth and the superiority of the soldier over the civilian. Louis' own attitude to his nobles was always ambivalent. Like his counterparts elsewhere he was determined to be master in his own house and to assert his authority against the great noble families who had disputed that of his predecessors and of the regency during his own minority. For all this, nevertheless, it has been justly said that he, like his successors, was bound to his nobility by an umbilical cord – a fact which he himself recognized, as the enormous importance he attached to court etiquette demonstrates. The kings of France were the first *gentilshommes* and the first seigneurs of the kingdom. "Point de noblesse point de monarque", as Montesquieu said. Yet, on the other hand, the needs of the state increasingly demanded, and the growth of wealth and education increasingly permitted, an influx of bourgeois into the government service; and it was always one of the cardinal doctrines of absolutism that the monarch could create nobles as and when he chose, and appoint whom he desired as his ministers and advisers.

This power, nevertheless, was exercised by different monarchs in different ways and with different consequences. The French kings divided their nobility and weakened their administration by continually putting office and noble status up for sale. The Prussian kings, though subjected to the same pressures as the French, proceeded otherwise.

(b) THE PRUSSIAN EXPERIENCE

In his simple-minded fashion Frederick William I, who ruled from 1713 to 1740 and established the administrative foundations of Prussian absolutism, described in his Testament Politique of 1722[1] the conditions which seemed to him essential if his dynasty were to retain its possessions and increase its prestige. He did not, he said, believe in wars of aggression, which were contrary to the will of God and usually brought disaster on their perpetrators; but he wished to defend his rights in a predatory world, and in order to do so it seemed to him essential to build up an army which would, as he put it, enable him to seem respectable to his friends and formidable to his enemies. For this purpose he saw that it was necessary to create the economic base on which military power depended and to organize his government accordingly. Except that their object was aggrandizement rather than survival, these were also the ambitions of Louis XIV and Colbert and were indeed the only ones appropriate on the continent of Europe at this time for a ruler who wished to preserve his patrimony from decline, if not from extinction. In pursuit of these aims the Hohenzollerns, from the days of the Great Elector but principally in the reign of Frederick William I, changed the institutions of government in Prussia to a far greater extent than had ever been contemplated, let alone carried out, in France by Louis XIV's predecessors or by Louis himself; and Frederick William I's agents in this undertaking were for the greater part bourgeois.

The problem of who might properly be described as noble and who as bourgeois, which so greatly preoccupied the French upper classes in the eighteenth century and the historians of later generations, never arose in Prussia during the reigns of Frederick William I and his son because the conditions which gave rise to it in France were absent. These Prussian kings never sold the right to noble status as Louis XIV had done wholesale, nor did there ever develop in Prussia the traffic in offices which prevailed in France. Frederick William, it is true, sold offices for money, particularly offices with judicial functions which he held to be fit only for fools incapable of more useful employment.[2] But he did not sell them in perpetuity or permit their holders to trade in them, and Frederick the Great would not tolerate even the degree of venality in this matter which his father had allowed. In his reign the sale of offices in any form was forbidden and few things seem to have been more calculated to send him into a rage than the suggestion that status or titles could be had for money.

When, therefore, high officials in eighteenth-century Prussia were, at the time and later, described as bourgeois, this word meant something different from what it meant when applied in France to men in comparable positions; for these Prussian bourgeois, unlike their French counterparts, did not enjoy the status and privileges of nobles, but were born and remained members of the *Bürgerstand* in law.

It has been said of the government of Frederick William I that "no other Prussian government until the destruction of the monarchy had at the summit of the executive hierarchy a larger porportion of social *nouveaux arrivés*".[3] The origins of these parvenus have unfortunately never been subjected to the kind of detailed analysis that has been applied to the ministers and to the members of important institutions – the *parlements*, the king's council, the tax-farm – in eighteenth-century France. As far as is ascertainable, most of them came from circumstances so humble that they might justly, in Saint-Simon's phrase, be said to have been raised from nothing, and this was no doubt inevitable. For Frederick William I, though he came to the throne half a century later than had Louis XIV, was much more restricted in his search for competent administrators, ruling as he did over a poverty-stricken country, largely lacking in education, where the destruction of the towns and their urban skills during the Thirty Years War had still not been made good. Of the bourgeois to whom Frederick William gave high office some were merchants, or, like the entrepreneur Andreas Kraut, had begun their careers as clerks in merchants' offices; others were non-commissioned officers like the cabinet secretary Eichel; others again were the so-called *Domänenbeamten* or *Domänenpächter*, that is, men who leased the farms on the extensive royal domains and were always bourgeois.[4]

The reasons which prompted Frederick William to give power to people of this sort seem to some extent to have been the same as those which had moved Louis XIV when he excluded the great noble families from his council and took as his advisers men from the *robe*. Neither of these monarchs had any intention of attacking the social privileges of the nobility or of interfering in any other way with the structure of the société d'ordres. At the turn of the seventeenth century projects of this sort were so far removed from what was practicable as to be beyond contemplation in either France or Prussia, both of them overwhelmingly agricultural communities in which social relations were based on a still unchallenged belief in hierarchy and in which the nobles were the landowners par excellence.

Like Louis XIV, Frederick William believed that he must be the "Herr" or master, and that the nobles were his "vassals" who should not aspire to what he called "condominaht" that is, to sharing power with him. The nobles seemed to him, even more clearly than they had to Louis XIV, the people who should provide his army with its officer corps; nor is it likely that he could have found among them a sufficient number of men competent to undertake the tasks of economic reconstruction which he saw as the basis of military power. As the deputy head of the royal administration in Küstrin, Kammerdirektor Hille,[5] deputed to instruct Frederick the Great when he was crown prince, said to his august pupil when the latter complained that nobles were subordinated to bourgeois: "The world is indeed upside down, since otherwise how should princes who are not particularly clever, or occupy themselves with trifles, give orders to sensible people?"

Sentiments of this sort, which it is unimaginable that any Frenchman in the eighteenth century should have expressed to the heir to the throne, were by no means uncommon in the Prussia of Frederick William I and were fostered by the Pietists, of whom the King himself was a devoted disciple and patron.

A religious sect with apocalyptic beliefs,[6] the Pietists had established their headquarters in Halle at the end of the seventeenth century. Believing that God had visited Germany for her sins with a more terrible punishment – the Thirty Years War – than any meted out to other peoples, they compared the Germans to the Jews of the Old Testament and saw them as destined to reform the world once they had been converted to a godly way of life.

The leader of the movement in the reign of Frederick William I, August Hermann Francke, saw himself as an emissary sent by God to bring this conversion about. He professed a puritanical asceticism which, though hostile to all worldly pleasure, did not preach withdrawal from the world but a godly life within it. Salvation, the Pietists taught, though won by the grace of God, did not manifest itself, as the Lutherans believed, by a single experience of conversion, but by a life lived continuously in accordance with the divine will, that is, a life which not only eschewed all worldly vanities but was dedicated to the service of the community and particularly to service of the poor.

Whereas the Catholic Church preached that the poor were the beloved of God and that the rich were redeemed by charity, to the Pietists poverty was an evil to be cured by education and by providing the poor with work – a task which they clearly saw involved increasing trade and manufactures.

Though believers in hierarchy and not hostile to the nobility as such, to whose regeneration, indeed, they devoted much attention, they were profoundly hostile to the noble way of life as it manifested itself in Prussia at the beginning of the eighteenth century where, particularly in its upper reaches, it was a great deal more primitive than in France. The Pietists condemned the nobles' addiction to feasting and display, their pride in their ancestry, their arrogance, indiscipline and general unruliness. In church, they complained, the nobles marched about with swords and daggers as if intent on a crusade against the Turk, and made such a clatter with their boots and spurs that one might assume one were present at a knights' tournament and not in the house of God.

Though the Pietists produced a large number of fanatics, Francke himself was a man of shrewd business sense and considerable political acumen. His original ambition had been to turn the Prussian state into a theocracy which should serve as a centre for the conversion of the world. Since, however, all his projects depended on the crown for support, this aim quickly revealed itself as impracticable. In order to retain the royal favour Francke was forced to abandon a number of his ideas, particularly his international ambitions, his opposition to war and his hostility to the press gang which was active in Halle at the beginning of Frederick William I's reign, seizing not only tradesmen and domestic servants but students from the university and even members of congregations during divine service.

Francke evidently found it prudent to refrain from protests against these outrages, which a number of years later were diminished by the introduction of a more orderly system of conscription; and as the price of his submissiveness he gained many concessions from Frederick William, who provided him with money, and with very extensive privileges, by means of which he set up orphanages, hospitals and a number of educational institutions, together with various quasi-commercial undertakings – breweries, bakeries, chemist shops and a printing press – in order to supply their needs. The alumni of his institutions spread the gospel of Pietism in the administration, the schools and the churches of Prussia, and during the reign of Frederick William I enjoyed a monopoly of the post of army chaplain.

Pietism in Prussia thus entered into alliance with the crown instead of opposing it as did most other forms of Protestantism in the other European monarchies where they took root. It became a bulwark of autocracy, not a movement for political liberty.

The support which Frederick William gave to it, and his attempts to order his state and his personal life in accordance with its precepts (a task in which he believed that he had succeeded, for he began his Testament Politique by saying "Mit Gott dem aller höchsten stehe ich Wohll"),[7] must no doubt account in large degree for the preference he showed for bourgeois when he reorganized the Prussian machinery of government in the 1720s.

In this matter his son held different views. Frederick the Great conceived a great dislike for the Pietists, who had persuaded Frederick William to exile from Prussia the leading luminary of the German Enlightenment, Christian Wolff, and whose religious fanaticism was anathema to his French mentors in his youth. From the beginning of his reign, moreover, unlike his father who fought no wars, Frederick the Great led his armies in battle and from his experience of warfare at first hand appears to have convinced himself that upbringing in a noble household was an essential prerequisite for the training of a good officer. Only the noble, he was fond of repeating, had a sense of honour.

Unlike the French kings whose financial difficulties led them continually to encourage the infiltration of the nobility by bourgeois through the purchase of titles and offices, Frederick attempted as far as possible to ensure that the Prussian nobles remained pre-eminently a class of soldiers and landowners, distinguished by function, as in law, from the other groups in the population, though his ideas on this subject did not extend to marriage. No obstacles in his reign were placed in the way of nobles who wished to marry women from the more prosperous bourgeois families, and such marriages (as well as those between noblewomen and bourgeois) were very common[8] – a state of affairs to which the *Allgemeines Landrecht* bears witness in the passages in which it lays down that nobility is transmitted by a noble father even when the mother is not noble, and that a noble, without prejudice to his privileges and the status of his children, may marry a woman from the upper bourgeoisie though not from the lower bourgeoisie or from the peasantry.[9]

For the rest, as Frederick wrote in 1763, to Ernst von Schlabrendorff, then minister for Silesia, "Let me make it plain once and for all that I will not sell titles and still less noble estates for money to the debasement of the nobility. Noble status can only be gained by the sword, by bravery and by other outstanding behaviour and services. I will tolerate as vassals only those who are at all times capable of rendering me useful service in the army, and those who because of exceptionally good conduct and exceptional service I choose to raise into the estate of the nobility."[10] In the most famous of the utterances he made on this subject he said of the nobility that their race "is so good that it deserves at all costs to be preserved".[11]

Given these views, Frederick could hardly have tolerated the prominent role which his father had assigned to bourgeois in the civil administration and he did indeed do something to reverse it, though not as much as is commonly believed. In general his attitude to the nobility was a good deal less favourable than the remarks quoted above might suggest. For every occasion on which he praised its good qualities there were many others when he inveighed against its defects. The nineteenth-century writer Theodor Fontane, who devoted much research to eighteenth-century Prussia, seems to have been nearer to the truth than many historians when he made the hero of his novel *Der Stechlin* say: "We had the honour to hunger, thirst and die for the fatherland though we were never asked if it suited us to do so. Now and then we were told that we were 'noblemen' and as such had a greater sense of 'honour'. But that was all there was to it. In his innermost soul Frederick required of us what he required of the grenadiers at [the battle of] Torgau. We were cannon-fodder and for the greater part he looked at us with a very critical eye."[12]

Partly from a desire not to deflect the nobles from service in the army, which he saw as their principal function (by the end of his reign, though there were some 6,000 nobles in the officer corps, there were only about 100 in the higher ranks of the bureaucracy), and partly, no doubt, from respect for his father's arrangements, he made many fewer changes in the bureaucracy's social composition than is usually believed.

At his accession, as we have seen, the principal organs of government were the so-called General Directory, and its offshoots in the provinces known as the *Kriegs- und Domänenkammern*, or boards of war and domains. In 1740 the General Directory consisted of four departments, which were later increased to eight. At the head of each of these was a minister of state, with a staff whose executive officials were known as privy councillors (*Geheime Finanzräte*). Decisions, however, were reached on a collegiate basis – that is, all the ministers and their privy councillors met together and on every important matter reached a collective judgment. In the course of time, various independent departments, to which the collective principle did not apply, were created outside the General Directory.

In every province there was one *Kriegs- und Domänenkammer* and occasionally two. Each was subordinated to the department of the General Directory responsible for its affairs. Each had as its head a so-called "president" and one or two deputy presidents, called "directors". As in the General Directory, there was a staff of executive officials with the title of councillor (*Kriegsrat*). At the summit of the official hierarchy was the king in his "cabinet". This however, was not a cabinet in the modern sense but consisted of men generally referred to as "secretaries", later elevated to the rank of cabinet councillors. At the end of his life Frederick the Great is reported to have described them as his "Schreiber" or clerks. They lived with the King in Potsdam and transmitted the royal commands to the ministers in Berlin (or to any other body or individual with whom the King chose to deal personally). The ministers, for their part, commonly communicated their questions and memoranda in writing to the secretaries for transmission to the King.

In the reign of Frederick William I most of the ministers were bourgeois, whereas under Frederick the Great they were with one exception nobles. The importance of this change can, however, easily be exaggerated. Frederick William's cabinet secretaries had all been born bourgeois though he ennobled a number of them. Frederick the Great's secretaries were also born bourgeois but he ennobled none. At Frederick William I's death the number of councillors in the General Directory was nineteen, of whom three were nobles. In 1748 (apparently the last date for which there are any figures) of the eleven councillors only one was a noble.[13] Because the boards of war and domains had to deal directly and continuously with the noble landowners, even Frederick William had judged it prudent to appoint nobles as board presidents. Frederick the Great continued this policy. The councillors, however, remained predominantly bourgeois though the proportion of nobles among them was somewhat increased. The directors, whose position was one of considerable importance, were frequently bourgeois. It was, however, in the courts of justice, where towards the end of Frederick's reign the qualifications required of candidates were subject to the most testing examinations, that the bourgeois' chances of success were always greatest. At the time of Frederick's death, in the principal appeal court in Berlin only one-third of the judges were nobles.[14]

In these circumstances the assumption, that is often made, that the Prussian government was in the hands of nobles is plainly an exaggeration, and particularly so if the power that could be exercised unofficially by the cabinet secretaries is taken into account. No man seems ever to have enjoyed Frederick the Great's confidence to the same extent as did his principal secretary, Eichel, who served him for twenty-eight years and had previously served his father for ten. Eichel died irreplaceable in 1768 in his early seventies while still in office. A mysterious figure of whom little is known with certainty, and who inspired the most diverse judgments among his contemporaries, he served his capricious and exacting master to the latter's complete satisfaction, accompanying him wherever he went, even on his campaigns. Though the foreign ambassadors who tried to enlist Eichel's services never succeeded in so much as gaining a glimpse of him ("He is watched over", Sir Hanbury Williams wrote in 1750, "as if he were a state prisoner . . . one can live seven years at the Prussian court without even seeing him",[15] the documents printed in the *Acta Borussica* show that ministers and others in high positions in Prussia courted his favour, and not without reason, for he was in effect a *chef de cabinet* and an *eminence grise*, who knew everything that went on, including many matters concealed from the ministers concerned.

No other secretary in Frederick's lifetime ever enjoyed an influence comparable to Eichel's, though in the reign of Frederick William III, who came to the throne in 1797, there were members of the kitchen cabinet who acquired an even greater and more openly acknowledged power.[16] They, like Eichel, were born and remained bourgeois.

The affection which Frederick the Great, not much given to this sentiment, felt for his "guter alter Eichel", and which Frederick William III similarly felt for his bourgeois cabinet councillor Beyme, the son of a regimental surgeon, who exercised a great influence over him, and from whom he persistently refused to be parted, is a significant commentary on the Prussian social scene. In the eighteenth century and at the beginning of the nineteenth, Prussians of the highest birth frequently associated on a footing of intimacy with men of humble origins. Freiherr Vom Stein, for example (and his is only one other case among many that could be cited), had as his greatest friend and confidant, with whom he travelled all over Europe after Napoleon had exiled him from Prussia, the poet and professor Ernst Moritz Arndt. Stein was the scion of an old noble family in the Rhineland and proud of his aristocratic heritage. Arndt was the son of a prosperous peasant who had been born a serf.[17]

Though status in Prussia had no less, perhaps more, importance than in France, the differences in manners in different walks of life were less subtle, complicated and hard to acquire by people not brought up to them, than they were in France. No Prussian ever experienced the kind of difficulties in how to behave like a gentlemen which tortured Julien Sorel in Stendhal's *Le Rouge et le Noir*. Even in the second half of the nineteenth century Bismarck maintained that it was impossible to put what he called a "European varnish" on the Prussian Junker.[18] The differences in outlook between the fighting man and the civilian might certainly be very great, but these apart, the psychological obstacles to intimacy between people in different social groups were plainly less formidable than in the older, more sophisticated civilizations of western Europe.

The organization of the Prussian bureaucracy is a testimony to this fact, and in Frederick the Great's reign almost as much as in his father's. The frequent subordination of noble to bourgeois, against which Frederick had protested to Hille in his youth, was an anomaly which he not only tolerated but sometimes even increased as, for example, when, in recognition of their importance, he raised the salaries of the councillors in the General Directory, who were often bourgeois, above those of many board presidents, who were always nobles. When examinations were introduced for candidates for the bureaucracy in 1770 the board of examiners was composed of four bourgeois and only one noble.[19]

The needs of the state, in fact, in Prussia as in France, permitted, though in different ways, the members of bourgeois families who possessed the necessary combination of luck and talent to rise to positions of considerable power and prestige.[20] Their chances of doing so were greatest in the army.[21] Proverbially in Frederick's lifetime, except during the Seven Years War, the Prussian officer corps was composed overwhelmingly, and in the higher ranks almost exclusively, of nobles. We do not, however, know how many of these nobles had begun their military careers as commoners, though evidently a considerable number had done so. According to a recent historian of the Prussian army, "dozens of deserving men were raised to the nobility", or faked noble ancestry which was not called in question, if they convinced the King that they possessed the necessary qualities.[22] Among them were some of the most famous commanders in the wars against Napoleon, notably Gneisenau and Yorck von Wartenburg.

In the bureaucracy in Frederick's lifetime the bourgeois' chances, though they were, as has been shown, considerable, were nevertheless smaller, since Frederick (his successors were more liberal) commonly refused to promote civilian officials into the nobility. The distinction in law between the noble and the bourgeois (although even in the higher ranks the latter might be the former's official superior) continued to exist and appears generally to have been taken for granted.

This would hardly have been possible, however, had it not been that the bourgeois civil servants enjoyed privileges which set them apart from other, inferior, bourgeois and placed them in many important respects on a footing of equality with nobles.

While the *Allgemeines Landrecht* recognized three "principal" estates of nobles, bourgeois and peasants, it also recognized various "subsidiary" estates,[23] which it subsumed under the heading of "servants of the state". These included the *Soldatenstand*, or estate of the army; what came later to be called the *Beamtenstand*, or estate of the bureaucracy; the *Gelehrtenstand* which embraced the academic professions; and the *Geistlicherstand* or estate of the clergy. The civilian members of these so-called Estates constituted a superior or upper bourgeoisie. They were known as the *Eximirten*,[24] or the exempted, because they were not subject to the town law-courts, but only, like the nobility, to the higher courts of the province. This privilege was accompanied by others. The exempted were punished less severely than the unexempted for certain offences, notably libel and slander; they were immune from the more degrading punishments; like the nobles (who were nevertheless expected to serve in the army) they and their sons were not subject to compulsory military services; they might marry into the nobility, and in the upper ranks of the bureaucracy they often did so. Bismarck, who boasted that his ancestors had been settled in the Mark of Brandenburg before the Hohenzollerns, was the offspring of such a marriage.

The state service in Prussia, in fact, as it had done earlier in France, provided a means, and for long the only one, by which the barriers between nobles and bourgeois could be breached. The memoirs which people in important positions began to write at the beginning of the nineteenth century, but of which there are hardly any in earlier periods, provide many instances of this process. Friedrich von Raumer, for example, an official in the Prussian bureaucracy, who as a very young man was *chef de cabinet* to Hardenberg, though he left this post to become a professor, counted among his close relations members of the court of Dessau on the one hand and Prussian schoolmasters on the other.[25] A. L. Mencken, Bismarck's bourgeois grandfather, who was born in 1752 the son of a professor, became while employed in the Prussian Embassy in Stockholm the friend and confidant of the Swedish Queen Ulrike, Frederick the Great's sister. (When Ulrike died in 1782 Frederick and Mencken spent an evening alone together lamenting her departure, Frederick often with tears.)[26] Von Raumer's relations and contemporaries, the brothers Gerlach, of whom one became a judge, one a high administrative official, one a general and the fourth a pastor, counted among their friends members of some of the oldest and most distinguished Prussian families – an Alvensleben, a Bülow, a Stolberg, Alexander von der Marwitz – but also many artists, scholars and men of letters.[27] Varnhagen von Ense, a bourgeois ennobled during Stein's administration, when writing of Berlin society on the outbreak of the French Revolution, maintained that "estate, rank and money retained their importance as they always will but they did not determine the rules to which one conformed in social relations". If Varnhagen's statement may be believed, and there is much evidence to support it,[28] not to mention the career of his famous Jewish wife Rachel, in Prussia by the end of the eighteenth century, as in France some half a century or more earlier, there had emerged a social élite to which entry was possible not only by virtue of high birth (if accompanied by money) but also by virtue of distinguished official position and talent; and as in France this phenomenon was promoted by a great increase in the production of literary works and periodicals and the emergence among the educated of a common culture.

In 1765 that "sovereign", as his contemporaries called him, of the literary world during the late German Enlightenment – the writer, publicist and bookseller Friedrich Nicolai – brought out the first issue of the *Allgemeine Deutsche Bibliothek* – a periodical which, though only one of many, sold more copies than any other. An accessory, as its editor saw it, of the French *Encyclopédie*, it attempted to provide critical reviews by the best authorities of the day, of every important work in every language, and in the course of its existence brought 80,000 works to the public notice.[29]

Learned societies were founded in Berlin, notably the Montagsklub and the Mittwochsgesellschaft, in which men of letters, and high officials, both noble and bourgeois, met to discuss philosophical, legal and social problems. Towards the end of the century there began to appear in Berlin salons on the French model, run by clever, mainly Jewish, women, and principally concerned with literature and the arts. Here, even more than in the learned societies, social barriers were broken down and a "gute Gesellschaft", or society with a capital S, was created in which, legal differences notwithstanding, people from different *Stände* could meet on equal terms.

In his old age Goethe observed that when he was a young man (he was born in 1749) German literature was still "a clean state" (*eine reine Tafel*). But then, starting in the last decades of Frederick the Great's life, came the dawn of the great age of German literature and philosophy to which many of the principal contributors were Prussians – Herder, Hamann, Kant, Fichte, to mention only some of the more famous.

Whereas the prince-bishop of Salzburg had considered it fitting that Mozart should take his meals with the servants, in Prussia by the turn of the eighteenth century it had come to be said that the man of genius, whatever his origins, was the equal of kings. Goethe, pre-eminently, provided evidence for this belief, for he enjoyed a social prestige greater than that achieved by any French *Philosophe*, including Voltaire at the height of his fame. Goethe not only corresponded on intimate terms with many crowned heads in Europe; the most eminent personages – the crown prince of Prussia, for example – sought the honour of visiting him. (The only exception to this practice, which Goethe reported to his friend Eckermann, was the English Lord Bristol, who, when in Weimar, instead of making the customary pilgrimage to Goethe's house, invited Goethe to call on him.)[30]

For most of the present century it has been customary in France to describe the ideas of the French Enlightenment as a bourgeois creation. Whatever the amount of truth in this assertion, the writers of the German Enlightenment, and of the literary movements which followed it, were certainly in point of social origins and outlook much more bourgeois than the French *Philosophes*, and wrote for a more bourgeois public, however the term bourgeois is understood. For whereas in France almost all the famous *Philosophes* were either born into the nobility or bought themselves titles, and found their first audience in high society – even by the end of the Ancien Régime, the latest authority on the subject has concluded that "the main appeal of the *Encyclopédie*" – that embodiment of enlightened ideas – "was to the traditional élite"[31] – in Prussia, as in Germany generally, the writers were virtually all bourgeois, and bourgeois moreover – Goethe, the grandson of a well-to-do tradesman, is the outstanding exception – from very poor families. The Breslau professor Christian Garve, one of the few writers of the German Enlightenment to concern himself with sociological questions, observed in 1802 that it was the bourgeois who had instructed the noble in knowledge and taste,[32] and this became a common point of view.[33] The process of thinking, it was sometimes said, was a bourgeois activity which, to their credit, the nobles had begun to cultivate. The same may once have been true of France but had long ceased to be so by the time Garve wrote. Even before the end of the seventeenth century M. Jourdain's music master had contrasted this "ignorant bourgeois" with the "enlightened grand seigneur".[34]

From whatever angle, in fact, one looks at the people who exercised power and influence in France and Prussia at the end of the eighteenth century, it is plain on the one hand that similar causes were at work to increase the importance of the bourgeois, but, on the other hand, that the reciprocal processes of *embourgeoisement* and *Feudalisierung* – of noble standards influencing bourgeois ones and vice versa – were producing a different mixture in the two countries.

In Prussia in the eighteenth century, and indeed for long afterwards, the military virtues, of which in pre-revolutionary Europe the nobles were everywhere the principal exponents, were rated more highly than in France, notwithstanding the honour there paid them. The complementary attitudes of authoritarianism and subservience, which exaltation of the military profession fostered at this time, were also more deeply and widely embedded among the Prussian than among the French upper classes. On the other hand certain qualities which writers from Sir William Temple in the seventeenth century to Sombart in the twentieth saw as essentially alien to aristocrats but typical of bourgeois – hard work, sober living, thrift, honesty, and careful accounting in financial matters – became official gospel in the Prussian state service in the eighteenth century and among the social elite to an extent that they never did in France. The aspirants to elegance among Prussian aristocrats enamoured of French culture were often ridiculous (like Graf Lehndorff who kept a diary in French of his life in the service of Frederick the Great's wife) and also the subject of ridicule, as they were to Stein. Many attributes of the French upper classes in the eighteenth century – the "douceur", as Tocqueville described it, among people in high positions, the subtlety in the analysis of human relations, the distinction of behaviour, the refinement of taste – often seemed to famous German intellectuals at the beginning of the nineteenth century (to Wilhelm von Humboldt, for example,[35] and to Clausewitz,[36] not to mention distinguished but uneducated members of old noble families such as Field Marshal von Blücher) mere characteristics of French superficiality.

The insistence in the last half-century or so on the class struggle between nobles and bourgeois which is said to have led to revolution in France, but not to have done so in Prussia for lack of prosperous bourgeois entrepreneurs, has made it possible to overlook how many values commonly seen as characteristic of the bourgeois age had come to influence the thinking of the Prussian ruling classes by the end of the eighteenth century. This fact was nevertheless emphasized by eminent German scholars before a vulgarized Marxist interpretation of European history became dominant. In his life of Gneisenau published in the 1860s Delbrück observed that "in the true sense of the word there was never an aristocracy in Prussia."[37] Writing of the influence exercised by the "new culture" produced by Germans born around 1750, and in the two succeeding generations, Treitschke said that "Germany, more than any other country, became a land of the middle class whose moral judgments and artistic tastes were the determinants of public opinion".[38] Thomas Mann expressed a similar view when, in his *Betrachtangen eines Unpolitischen*, which he wrote during the First World War of the present century, he said "das Deutsche und das Bürgerliche das ist eins" – German and bourgeois are the same thing.[39]

III
Taxation and government finance

France was at war for over half the period of 129 years that elapsed between 1660, when Louis XIV began to govern, and the outbreak of the Revolution in 1789. Since in this period it was impossible for western governments to assume control over manpower and production, they had to buy on the market the military equipment they needed as well as to pay their naval and military personnel. Money in consequence, as Colbert said, was the sinews of war. The question at issue here is how the French raised it and with what consequences.

In common with his forebears and his successors, Louis XIV's attitude to government expenditure, whether for purposes of war or peace (though war was by far the most expensive of his indulgences), was to decide on his objectives without attempting to estimate the cost, and afterwards to search for the means of paying for them. At least in his uncalculating love of war – that "manie des conquêtes", as Turgot described it – and in his irrational, if more sophisticated, forms of extravagance, he had inherited the tastes of his medieval predecessors, though with greater means of satisfying them. Louis' indifference to financial questions, and the complete absence from his thinking of even the idea of financial honesty, put him at a great disadvantage vis-à-vis his principal enemies, the English and the Dutch, whose economies were more developed, and whose financial institutions were organized and directed in a more rational fashion and in awareness of the need to relate ends to means. This should nevertheless not be allowed to obscure the fact that the great wars waged in Europe and overseas between 1672 and the Revolution created serious financial difficulties for all the belligerents.

In the west it was never possible to pay the cost of war from current revenue, and an increasing proportion of war expenditure had in consequence to come from loans. The interest on the loans, nevertheless, and a proportion of the war expenditure itself (except in France during the War of American Independence) had to be paid for out of taxes. The amount that was raised in taxes and their incidence were determined by the government's policies and the functioning of its administration, which in France in the eighteenth century they were largely responsible for bringing into disrepute.

From Louis XIV's reign onwards it was common to say – as Vauban said in 1707 in his *Project d'une Dîxme Royale,* one of the first projects designed to reform the tax-system – France was not only the most beautiful country in the world, she was also the richest. Her fertile soil and her, by contemporary standards, enormous population – over twice as large, when the great wars started, as the combined populations of her principal enemies, the English and the Dutch – should have made raising the necessary taxes no problem. "One does not", Vauban wrote, "need to know much about what goes on in the countryside to see clearly that the *tailles* [then virtually the only direct taxes] are the cause of disaster, not because they are always and at all times too heavy but because they are assessed inequitably . . in a word they have become arbitrary, bearing no proportion to the wealth of the taxpayer. In addition they are levied with extreme rigour and at costs so great as to amount to a quarter of the sums raised."[1]

Views similar to this were repeated continually thoughout the eighteenth century. In 1732, for example, the *contrôleur-général* Orry wrote that "Although the *tailles* have been raised to a point which appears excessive having regard to the state of the provinces, to the difficulties of collecting the money, and to the meagre possessions of the peasants in the way of furniture, domestic utensils and animals, one can nevertheless maintain with certainty that the miserable condition of the inhabitants of the countryside can be attributed less to the excessive extent of the taxes than to the vices in the methods of assessing and collecting them".[2] Many other statements by contemporaries to this effect could be cited, and modern research has not refuted them.[3]

The vices of the tax-system increasingly became a major preoccupation in all circles in which government policy was formulated or discussed – in the king's council, in the *parlements*, in all the intellectual milieux where the ideas of the Physiocrats gained currency, as they did among many people who, like Necker for example, professed themselves hostile to Physiocracy. Even among the educated reading public in general, financial questions evidently excited great interest, since otherwise it would be impossible to account for the huge success achieved by Necker's *De l'Administration des Finances de la France*, first published in 1784. This title, one might suppose, was hardly calculated to have a popular appeal. The work has nevertheless been acclaimed by a recent authority as the best-seller of the century.[4] An American scholar maintained in 1971, on the basis of a sample of 741 of the *cahiers de doléances* drawn up in 1789, that the abuses of the tax-system were overwhelmingly the largest single source of complaint.[5]

In France, as opposed to Prussia, though in common with many other countries, the government distinguished between "ordinary" and "extraordinary" sources of revenue. The "ordinary" were those which were supposed to suffice for ordinary occasions, that is, principally periods of peace. The "extraordinary" sources were those to which recourse was had in periods of emergency, principally war, although in France the failures to observe this distinction were so common as to render it virtually meaningless. Apart from the relatively small sums yielded by the royal domains and regalian rights, the "ordinary" sources of revenue were the direct and the indirect taxes, for which the responsibility devolved on two different, though in some essential respects analogous, types of authorities.

The bulk of the direct taxes was provided by the group of associated taxes known as the *taille*, from which, over the greater part of France, the nobles and the clergy were exempt. This exemption was, however, mitigated from Louis XIV's reign onwards, though not significantly till the middle of the eighteenth century, by other taxes, notably the so-called *vingtième*, the equivalent of the English land tax, which fell on nobles as well as commoners.[6] The various people responsible for seeing that these taxes were collected and delivered to the appropriate destination (they might be used to meet local needs or handed over to the crown) were all royal officials. Apart from the *Intendants des provinces*, however, these were officials who had bought their offices, which were their private property and from which, given luck and skill, they could make a large profit.

The indirect taxes were imposed on the purchase and sale of a very large range of commodities, a number of which – notably salt which in 1788 accounted for approximately a quarter of the yield of indirect taxation[7] – were government monopolies. These taxes were levied by the tax-farmers who, subject to a considerable degree of government interference, were private entrepreneurs.

The "extraordinary" sources of revenue – the so-called "affaires extraordinaires"[8] – embraced a great variety of expedients, but principally they consisted of loans of various kinds. Unlike the English, the French before the Revolution had no national debt. The crown raised both its short- and long-term loans though the agency of people always known as "financiers"[9] who placed their personal credit, skill and financial contacts at the service of the crown in return for a rake-off that could be very large, but that also exposed them to ruin.

In the past it had done so more often than not. It has been estimated that between 1315 and 1522, of the twelve people principally responsible for managing the French kings' financial affairs, eight were put to death and three condemned to prison or exile. Only one survived to enjoy his fortune in peace.[10] As time went on, these risks diminished but even in the reign of Louis XIV the practice continued, in times of disaster, of bringing the financiers before so-called "chambres de justice".

The justice which these institutions administered was not justice as that term came to be understood in the second half of the eighteenth century or during the nineteenth. The judges were chosen for the occasion from among lawyers presumed willing to condemn the defendants, who in any case had usually acted with the acquiescence of the crown if not under its explicit orders. The *chambres de justice* meted out a primitive form of what might be described as "social justice". Its victims were the rich, commonly the nouveaux-riches, in a community reduced to destitution largely by their activities. Their punishment satisfied the popular desire for vengeance while permitting the crown to confiscate their fortunes and to replace them by other financiers (as Colbert replaced Fouquet) assumed likely to serve it better.

The last *chambre de justice* was held in 1716. Thereafter – until comparable practices were adopted during the Revolution and on a larger scale – the institution fell into disrepute both because of its failure to achieve its purpose (the richest financiers frequently bribed themselves out) and because its composition and ways of proceeding seemed an outrage by the new standards of the Enlightenment. In the volume of the *Encyclopédie Méthodique* that dealt with finance and was first published in 1784, the author expressed a long current view when he referred to the "horror" which "all right-thinking people felt for this kind of tribunal". In consequence of this attitude the financier, whatever other risks he might run, had no cause to fear that his property would be seized and he himself imprisoned or put to death merely because he had amassed a fortune.

By the second half of the eighteenth century the financiers had become accepted members of the Establishment. They had always bought themselves noble status, titles and seigneuries and married their daughters into distinguished families which coveted their wealth. In the literature of Louis XIV's reign, however, they had been the bourgeois-gentilshommes *par excellence* whose principal preoccupation was money, who were vulgar, uneducated, insolent when they dared and cringing to the powerful. In the second half of the eighteenth century by contrast, at least the General Farmers – the financiers whose wealth was greatest and most secure – had for the most part learned to behave themselves like gentlemen. They became patrons of the arts, even including among their number men of outstanding intellectual distinction, notably the philosopher Helvetius, and the famous chemist Lavoisier, guillotined in 1794 because he was a tax-farmer. They maintained salons frequented by the highest aristocracy though their relatively recent noble origins stopped them being received at court.[11]

The tax-farmers constituted a private company, which collected the indirect taxes and managed the royal monopolies. They entered into contracts with the crown, known as "baux" or leases, over a succession of six-year periods, by virtue of which they paid the crown a fixed sum annually, pocketing the profits and bearing the losses (theoretically, for they saw to it that there were none) which might result from these arrangements, besides lending the crown money in a variety of other ways.[12] Though not responsible for the nature or weight of the indirect taxes, they developed in the course of the eighteenth century an increasing efficiency in collecting them, and in the management generally of their financial transactions with the Crown. They evolved a nation-wide organization which yielded enormous profits and also protected its members against the disasters which not uncommonly overtook those other financiers, responsible for the direct taxes, who worked for the government independently and had bought themselves offices under the crown.

The government raised both its short- and long-term loans through the agency of these financiers on the strength of their personal credit. Its long-term loans came from a number of different sources – from the sums, for example, provided by the General Farmers; from "rentes" or money lent to the crown on a great variety of different terms and commonly managed for it by bodies, notably the Paris Hôtel de Ville, in which the subscribers had more confidence than they had in the government; further, and to a very large extent in the reign of Louis XIV though to a relatively diminishing one under his successors, the crown borrowed by means of the sale of offices whose purchasers paid it a capital sum in return for a salary, as well as for the perquisites of the office itself, and various privileges, including total or partial immunity from the principal forms of direct taxation.

All these and other "extraordinary" ways of raising money were the means by which the crown augmented its revenues when the "ordinary" sources, derived principally from taxation, proved insufficient. This, however, in France they always did to an extent and with consequences for which the operation of the "affaires extraordinaires" bore considerable responsibility.

To raise taxation, whether direct or indirect, in the kind of communities here under discussion, raised problems much less easily soluble than those which face industrial societies with sophisticated financial techniques, large numbers of experienced, honest officials and literate populations prepared to accept that in peace as well as war the government has a right to tax them.

All these conditions were to a greater or less extent absent in the communities of eighteenth-century Europe. No rational system of indirect taxation was possible as long as the various provinces which composed the monarchies insisted on preserving their ancient privileges, so that each province was separated from its neighbours by tariff barriers and different systems of weights and measures. The only source of livelihood which could be subject to direct taxation without total arbitrariness was the land, which is visible to the naked eye; but even the yield of the land could not be assessed with any approach to accuracy except by means of some form of land-survey – what the French call a *cadastre* and the Germans a *Kataster* – revised from time to time.

In these circumstances the heavier the taxes to which the needs of war gave rise the greater the likelihood of arbitrariness, and the greater the temptation to bribery and evasion which in the poverty-stricken eighteenth-century societies were in any case rife; and the greater these evils the greater the inequalities, the uncertainties and the sense of injustice. This sense of injustice could easily spread throughout all the groups of the population, including the noble landowners, who in matters of direct taxation are commonly held to have been the privileged *par excellence*, but in fact were much less privileged than the people who engaged in finance and other business activities and whose incomes, for lack of any means of estimating them, could not be subject to direct taxation at all. The noble landowners, moreover, and the better-to-do generally, even when they were prepared to admit that they ought to pay taxes, were imbued with the traditional belief, in the existing conditions extremely difficult to uproot, that the state had no right to pry into their affairs. Adam Smith spoke for all of them, in England and elsewhere, when he said that any attempt to assess an individual's wealth or income would involve inquisitions which "would be a source of such continual and endless vexation as no people would support".[13]

It was in these conditions that the French government had to raise the taxes required to meet its long and increasingly expensive wars. In France until the Revolution, as noted before, the principal source of direct taxation was a number of associated taxes known as the "taille". Over the greater part of France, in the so-called "pays de taille personelle", the *taille*, from which the nobles and clergy were exempt, was imposed on all the assets of the "taillables", or persons subject to it. Elsewhere, principally in the more recently conquered provinces which had kept their estates and were known as the *pays d'états*, the *taille* was a "taille réelle" – that is, it was imposed not on all forms of income and means of subsistence but only on non-noble land, even if a noble had bought and owned it.

The total amount to be raised from the *taille* was fixed by the government which had no means of estimating at all precisely what sums it might be reasonable, or even possible, to expect that the population could pay. This total was then divided up among the various "généralités" – administrative divisions, more or less coterminous with the provinces, each of which was subject to the authority of an *intendant*. Here again the estimates of the amount to be levied – as Turgot demonstrated when he was *intendant* in the Limousin[14] – bore little relation to reality, and each *intendant* argued with the council (though without hope of justice, according to Turgot, because the council had no means of judging) in order to get his quota reduced at the expense of the quotas of his colleagues. Except in the *pays d'états* where the procedure was different and taxation always lighter, the *intendant* then divided his quota up among the various districts known as "élections". In the *élections* it was subdivided among the parishes.

In the parishes the task of deciding what each individual should pay devolved on the "collector". The collector was theoretically elected by the parish but the office exposed its holder to so many dangers that, as Boisguilbert put it in the reign of Louis XIV, "there is no one, even the most miserable, who would not sell his shirt to escape this servitude."[15] It was, however, precisely the most miserable who failed to escape. The more powerful groups among the villagers so arranged things that it was the miserable, being defenceless, who were chosen.[16] In the nature of the case they were impoverished, ignorant and illiterate peasants. Though supposed to keep a register of the sums that the various parishioners should pay, being unable to read or write they could not do this but employed some literate person who used the opportunity to protect himself, his friends and relations[17] at the expense of the other *taillables* and thus commonly of the collector himself; for if the collector failed to raise his quota, or if, having done so, he was robbed of the money, he was thrown into prison, and the deficit arbitrarily exacted from the richest parishioners until Turgot changed this practice in 1775.[18]

On the other hand, the collectors who managed to escape disaster at the hands of the government became the natural objects of rage to parishioners who believed themselves to have been overtaxed and who exacted vengeance by beating up the collectors and destroying their property. In 1767 it was estimated that in one district, which in this respect was doubtless not unique, at least 10 per cent of the collectors were reduced to beggary after one year in office.

The collectors manoeuvred as best they could between the Scylla of official retribution and the Charybdis of peasant vengeance, seizing such opportunities as presented themselves to exact bribes and pay off old scores. Among the *taillables*, meanwhile, the small minority who were relatively prosperous had their own ingenious means of cheating. Since, for example, the *taille* was imposed on a person in the parish in which he lived, it was common for peasants in a position to do so to move their dwelling to a parish other than that in which their main property was situated and so to evade or diminish their obligations.[19] In Burgundy, and doubtless elsewhere, prosperous peasants left their villages at Easter when the taxes were collected and only came back a month or so later, with the result that "in many places only the miserable remained, all the well-to-do having fled".[20] Those too miserable to pay the sums which were required to meet the quota – and which fell on them all the more heavily because their richer neighbours had evaded their share – then had their property seized, in cases of recalcitrance by soldiers from the nearest garrison. In this way they lost not only their personal possessions but the implements and animals on which they depended for their livelihood.

All these abuses, and they were far from the only ones, were described by the *Contrôleur-Général* Orry in 1732 as responsible for "the ruin of an infinity of parishes". "All the subtlety and malice of which human nature is capable," Orry said, "operate to render the assessment of the *taille* unjust".[21]

The most successful of the eighteenth-century monarchies, the Prussian and the English, raised a much higher proportion of their tax revenue than did the French by means of indirect taxes;[22] but long before the reign of Louis XIV the French had realized that direct taxation could not be imposed in the towns, since to make arbitrary assessments (and no other kind was possible) of the yield of business activities was plainly to kill the goose that laid the golden eggs. All the major French towns were in consequence exempt from the *taille*. It was not, however, until the middle of the eighteenth century that the French ministers came to believe that increases in the yield of agriculture were at least as important as the development of trade and industry, if not more so. Promoting agricultural growth became in consequence a major objective which seemed among other things, and particularly, to demand reforms in the tax system. Though, however, the sophisticated

French *intendants*, and the *contrôleurs-généraux* who were chosen from among them, were fully aware of the existing abuses, and though they did indeed succeed in putting a stop to the worst outrages that had disfigured the reign of Louis XIV, they were unable, except on rare occasions, to remove the major sources of injustice because to have done so would have involved changing the whole administrative system. Comparable reasons prevented a reform of the indirect taxes which were an equal if not greater source of discontent, because of the violent and arbitrary proceedings of the police – the private employees of the tax-farm – in their pursuit of smugglers and other law-breakers.

Among the reasons for this state of affairs was that practice of the "affaires extraordinaires" which consisted in the sale of offices. Louis XIV, as was shown earlier, created offices on an enormous scale, not only in the higher reaches of the administration but, and in much larger numbers, for the discharge of more or less humble functions in the smaller as well as the larger towns. Not only the offices of mayor and of lesser municipal dignitaries were put up for sale; offices were sold conferring the right to sell fish, pork, wine and other commodities, or to supervise their sale, or to discharge one or more of a great variety of other tasks. Between 1689 and 1715, 2,461 offices were created on the quays and in the markets of Paris alone for capital sums amounting to nearly 80 million livres.[23]

Admittedly many purchasers of office were ruined by the various devices which the government found for cheating them[24] but – until these practices were seen to outweigh the advantages which office conferred – the purchasers who were rendered destitute were replaced by others equally tempted by the prestige and the material benefits which office seemed to offer; for every office, however humble, conferred in some degree immunity from the *taille*, or from its arbitrary assessment, which besides involving material risks became a symbol of inferior status. In consequence every peasant prosperous enough to do so bought himself an office in the nearest town.

That these proceedings greatly added to the inequalities inherent in the methods of assessing the direct taxes needs no emphasis. The writer to whose precise and detailed studies we are principally indebted for our knowledge of this subject, but who was as hostile to the nobility as have been most French historians in the present century, expressed his conclusion on one occasion in the following words: "The exemption [from direct taxation] of the church and the nobility was so to speak of little account compared with this enormous mass of privileged commoners"[25] – commoners admittedly who, besides the office-holders, included all the bourgeois of the major towns, all those peasants who, while remaining on the land, practised the tricks described earlier, and the inhabitants of the *pays d'états* where the direct taxes were lighter than in the remaining and much greater part of France. Had the nobles and clergy been deprived of their tax-privileges, as in fact the nobles were in the second half of the eighteenth century to a much greater extent than is usually supposed, the sums, other things remaining equal, that could have been raised in consequence would have contributed only minimally to solving the financial difficulties which were the immediate cause of the fall of the monarchy.[26]

These difficulties were not in fact due primarily to the reasons usually invoked to explain them but were the consequence of the way the whole financial system was organized, or, more accurately, of the absence from it of anything that can properly be described as an organization at all – a state of affairs for which the sale of offices, and the analogous arrangements with the tax-farm, bore an even greater responsibility than has hitherto been suggested.

The tax-farmers were private entrepreneurs, subject to a considerable degree of government intervention. The other financiers who had bought offices under the crown were in a comparable position; and apart from the provincial *intendants* and the *contrôleurs-généraux*, these two categories of people held all the principal posts in the financial administration.

The men, for example, who were responsible for handing over to the government the sums collected in direct taxation, and also the men, the two keepers of the royal treasury included, who paid the money out to the spending departments, had bought and owned their offices.[27] They kept their own "caisses" (or, in German, "Kassen", terms which in the present context can be translated into English only somewhat inaccurately as private treasuries). They engaged and dismissed their own staff, who were responsible only to them though the government contributed a sum to help pay their salaries.[28]

The profit to be derived from these offices may be judged by their price. At the top of the scale they were very expensive, though socially somewhat looked down on. The office, for example, of the *receveurs-généraux*, of whom there were altogether about fifty, and who were responsible for handing over to the government the sums collected in direct taxes, cost on an average during the last decades of the Ancien Régime about three-quarters of a million livres (or some £33,000 in English money at the then current rate of exchange).[29] The holders were apparently always nobles or entitled to noble status at some stage in their career or that of their heirs.[30] Though they commonly borrowed to buy the office, they were men of substance who in fortunate circumstances might, and often did, become very rich. If, however, they managed their affairs badly, or were overtaken by a slump, they were liable to go bankrupt, and many in fact suffered this fate, particularly during the recession that preceded the Revolution.

In such circumstances they became unable to pay the government the sums for which they had contracted, and were dismissed and prosecuted even if their failure were due to misfortune and not to fraud. For the rest, however, they managed their affairs as they saw fit, making no distinction between those they conducted on their own behalf and those they discharged for the government, of which a principal one was the provision of short-term loans. The receivers general, for example, advanced to the government, in return for interest, the sums due from the taxes before these had reached them or in anticipation of taxes to be raised in future years. As a result of these arrangements bankruptcies among the financial officials, if they occurred to large numbers, as they did during the slump at the end of the 1780s, placed the government in serious difficulties.[31] They seem in fact to have been the immediate cause of that situation which in the summer of 1788 caused the *Contrôleur-Général* Lambert to announce that the treasury was empty, and which, combined with the inability to raise further loans from the public, constituted the so-called bankruptcy that led to the summoning of the Estates General.

As these examples demonstrate, the government had no direct control over its financial affairs, but worked through agents. Its servants who had bought their office were known as "officiers". They were not *fonctionnaires* or civil servants as these terms are now understood. The government itself "was never equipped to collect taxes, to borrow, to hold royal funds or to spend them, and this was one of its most persistent and striking deficiencies."[32]

The huge number of separate *caisses* and the ways in which money was allocated to meet different needs made it impossible to keep track of the sums collected and disbursed. The king, for example, was entitled, by means of so-called *acquits de comptant*, to give orders to the treasury to make such payments to such individuals or bodies as he saw fit without explaining to any of his officials either the nature or motives of his expenditure.[33] As Louis XVI himself put it in 1779: "The registers of the Royal Treasury ought to have details of the entire body of receipts and expenditure, but in fact have no record at all of the business done in many *caisses*, . . . because only after a great number of years are all the individual accounts rendered and audited, and also because these are divided among all the chambers of accounts of our Kingdom, so that only by an immense labour could the total results be formed, and this work, always too late and confused, would never be useful".[34]

The government, in fact, was never in a position to see what its financial position was. At the end of the War of American Independence, which Necker had financed entirely out of loans, no one so much as knew the size of the government debt. It was impossible to draw up a budget or anything approximating to one, and the very conception of such a procedure was unknown, until Necker, to justify his own administration and because he believed that publicity was good for credit, published his notorious *Compte Rendu au Roi* in 1781.

This extraordinary document purported to show – though by means of calculations so obviously incomplete and inadequate as to astonish any modern reader – that revenue exceeded expenditure. In fact, as shortly emerged, it was the very reverse that was true. Yet no one ever impugned Necker's financial honesty. Whatever the explanation for his conclusions, it is plain that he lacked the data to reach even approximately correct ones.[35]

Given this state of affairs – of which Necker, to do him justice, had often complained and done his best to remedy – there was no way of relating ends to means. "If money", Necker once said, "is the nerve of war and credit is the source of money, a minister of foreign affairs who is insufficiently informed [of the country's] resources and of their difficulties and limits, cannot speak with assurance or adapt his negotiations to circumstances, with that foresight and enlightened wisdom which alone can preserve him from error."[36]

The French financial system made such foresight and enlightened wisdom unattainable. "By its very nature it defied planning and control",[37] and did so at every level from the king's council, where policy was formulated in ignorance of the financial resources available to meet it, to the villages where the *taille* was collected by methods which made any fair distribution impossible. A recent analysis of how this system worked described it as "a bottomless pit capable of absorbing any amount of revenue",[38] and there is indeed no reason to suppose that as long as it remained unchanged any increase in the yield of the taxes would not have been squandered on inessential projects, wasted by careless management, or lost in transit from the tax-payer to the spending agencies.

The amount of waste of which the French government was guilty, though impossible to estimate, was plainly enormous. Signs of it were visible everywhere and a source of growing criticism in and outside the government. Nations whose international power is growing rapidly commonly tolerate abuses which in other circumstances become a focus of discontent. As French international prestige diminished, so did the self-confidence and reputation of the government, and the profligacy of its financial management increasingly became a target for criticism on moral as well as material grounds. Turgot put the matter in a nutshell when he said: "One cannot prevent oneself from being amazed that we should be so inferior in [military] strength when we are so superior in resources."[39]

(b) THE PRUSSIAN EXPERIENCE

The French government abdicated in 1789 because of its inability to solve its financial problems, and that some such situation as this must occur sooner or later had been foreseen by Frederick the Great nearly forty years earlier. He always attributed his own success, by contrast, to the ways in which he managed financial matters in his own dominions, a subject on which he continually pontificated.

His "Exposé of the Prussian Government and the Principles on which it Operates", which he wrote in 1776, began with the words: "I start with finance which is like the nerves in the human body that set all its limbs in motion." Any misfortune, he maintained, could be overcome by the state more easily than could financial disorder which, in his Testament Politique of 1752, he predicted must bring France to disaster.

How to avoid disaster in this sphere of government posed, he admitted, problems of the greatest difficulty, but he nevertheless believed, in accordance with his usual way of thinking, that they should be approached by means of rational analysis which could yield, as he put it, "solid principles"[1] from which one should never depart.

In describing in his memoirs the changes for which his father was responsible, Frederick wrote on one occasion that the nature of the state "changed completely under Frederick William. The court was dismissed, the big pensions reduced, many people who had kept carriages now had to go on foot ... under Frederick I [Frederick William's father] Berlin had been the Athens of the North, under Frederick William it became the Sparta. The whole government became military ... luxury, magnificence and pleasure disappeared; the spirit of economy penetrated every estate among the rich as among the poor ... our customs no longer resembled those of our ancestors or our neighbours. We became 'des originaux'[2] – eccentrics.

In financial matters, judged by comtemporary continental standards, the Prussian government may indeed be said to have been eccentric in a variety of ways – in the sources from which it drew its revenues; in the importance it attached to thrift and meticulous accounting; in the administrative arrangements designed to facilitate them; and in the criteria of honesty and equity (as he understood it) which Frederick strove to inculcate into his officials.

At Frederick's accession, when Prussia first embarked on her career of conquest by seizing the Austrian province of Silesia, the Prussian government possessed a large source of revenue which the French had long since lost. In France the domains of the crown had been whittled away by gifts and sales, and in the second half of the eighteenth century made only a negligible contribution to the government's revenues. The crown domains in Prussia, by contrast, had been greatly increased by Frederick William I who, with or without justification, had confiscated territories in the hands of the nobility to which he claimed a right. These proceedings had led to so dangerous a discontent that Frederick the Great on his accession immediately put a stop to them.[3] By the end of his reign, nevertheless, his minister, Herzberg, claimed that the royal domains accounted for "nearly one-third of the landed property" in the Hohenzollern dominions.[4] They were let out to tenants, known as *Domänenpächter* or *Beamten*,[5] subject to the supervision of the royal organs of government in the various provinces – the *Kriegs- und Domänenkammern* referred to earlier. They yielded rents which amounted to between two and three million thaler in 1740 and between six and seven million thaler in 1786, that is, to nearly half the government's revenue at Frederick's accession and to an order of 30 per cent at his death.[6]

To the apostles of free enterprise in western Europe in the second half of the eighteenth century, crown lands of this magnitude must (if the fact were known) have seemed an absurdity. Adam Smith complained that such estates as the crown possessed in England would have been much better managed had they been in private hands,[7] and similar views began to be expressed in Prussia from 1806 onwards.[8] What may have been true, however, in England by the 1770s and in Prussia by the early nineteenth century, was certainly not true at Frederick William I's or even at Frederick the Great's accession. In eighteenth-century Prussia, in Otto Hintze's words, the royal estates and their administration "had a much greater significance than in the nineteenth century. They provided so to speak the ballast which the ship of state needed in the storms of the times and because of an underdeveloped money economy."[9] Moreover, improvements in agriculture and in the treatment of the rural population could be introduced more easily in the royal estates than elsewhere at a time when all classes of the population clung to the old ways of doing things and the government was the principal agent of change.

That the Prussian government could draw from 50 per cent to 30 per cent of its revenues from the careful management of its own possessions was not an accident but symbolized the different attitude to financial and economic questions which distinguished it from the French. So too did its immunity from crippling debt charges.

By the end of the 1780s some 50 per cent or more of French government revenue was required to service the debt. The Prussians, by contrast, had no long-term government debt at all. This was not because they had no sources from which to borrow,[10] although admittedly these were much smaller than in the west; it was because financing wars on borrowed money was contrary to Frederick's principles. His views on this matter were not unusual at the time. Neither Necker nor Adam Smith, for example, would have repudiated them. He was exceptional only because he put them into practice. In the west to have tried to do so would have been wholly impracticable, given the inadequate means of raising taxes and the attitudes of mind which Adam Smith described when he said that the growth in wealth had accustomed its principal beneficiaries – the members of the government and the better-to-do classes generally – to indulgence in "frivolous passions" which precluded "parsimony in peace".[11]

Parsimony in peace – saving against a rainy day, that cardinal bourgeois principle – was a doctrine which Frederick continually preached and practised to the best of his ability. Implementing it involved a meticulous system of accounting and, as he himself put it, "a larger number of honest men than a state normally possesses". It required a deliberate attempt to educate the upper reaches of a primitive population in behaviour uncommon if not unique in the societies of central and eastern Europe at the time.

The system of government accounting that prevailed in Frederick's day was admittedly primitive by later standards – so much so, in fact, that one of the leading reformers, Freiherr von Altenstein, observed in 1807 that it was "such as no merchant would tolerate".[12] For the government, though it had various substitutes for a budget, had nothing that could be described as one. Government money, as in France, was paid into and out of a great number of separately managed *Kassen* or treasuries; the financial affairs of Silesia were kept entirely separate from those of the other provinces, and very large sums, of which no one in authority except the king himself had any knowledge, were paid from the various *Kassen* into several different depositories where they were kept in bullion for use in emergencies. In these circumstances, as Altenstein pointed out, it was impossible to obtain a general view of the various sources of government income and expenditure except at the cost of a great amount of work and then often incompletely. Nevertheless, in spite of the inefficiency of these methods they were never, as Altenstein pointed out, disorderly. Altenstein judged the financial administration in Frederick's day to have been more orderly and more honest than that of any other contemporary government. He may well have been right.

During Frederick's lifetime, though not after his death, Prussian financial affairs were managed in a way that made it possible not only to meet current commitments from current revenue but to permit the accumulation in bullion of sums which Frederick judged sufficient to meet the cost of a four-years' war; and this in fact they did except during the war of 1756 to 1763, which lasted for seven years and not for four, and whose expenses he could only defray by means of subsidies from his British allies, by plundering the foreign territories he occupied – notably Saxony, which though culturally and economically more advanced than Prussia, was militarily much inferior – and, finally, by debasing the coinage.[13]

Debasing the coinage caused an inflation, and when at the end of the war Frederick called in the depreciated currency, he contributed to a commercial crisis of a magnitude which he himself described when he said, speaking of the bankruptcies in Berlin and elsewhere, "in the whole of my life I have never heard of anything comparable".[14]

Prussia at the end of the Seven Years War was, as he himself put it, "like a man with many wounds who has lost so much blood that he is on the point of death".[15] The inflation and its consequences were among the "scourges and calamities", as he described them, for which the war was responsible. Their financial and economic legacy was, however, less enduring than that created in France by the attempt to increase direct taxes and loans.

With many Prussian provinces invaded by foreign armies at various times in the war, with East Prussia occupied by the Russians for the greater part of it, and with the administration thrown into confusion for these reasons, and because the King was absent with the army at the front, it would have been impossible to increase taxation, whose yield in fact inevitably diminished.

In any event, however, increasing direct taxation was, like borrowing, contrary to Frederick's principles. It was one of his most tenaciously held convictions that the principal direct tax, the *Kontribution*, which in most provinces fell only on the peasant, should (except in certain contigencies which he enumerated) never be increased, even in war, but on the contrary, should whenever possible be reduced.[16] That the *Kontribution* was in fact never increased is generally accepted, and such evidence as appears available, though insufficient to confirm this judgment, at least supports it.

Notably, Friedrich August Ludwig von der Marwitz, famous for his reactionary opinions and the courage (compared at least with that of his *soi-disant* supporters) with which he defended them in 1811, maintained in 1820 that the taxes paid by his estate had remained unchanged from the reign of Frederick William I until 1806.[17]

Unlike the French, who raised approximately half their tax revenue from direct taxation, the Prussians, and increasingly after 1763, raised the bulk of theirs, as did the British, from a variety of indirect taxes. Frederick justified this proceeding on the ground that of all forms of taxation indirect taxes were the least burdensome to the subject "because when one buys goods or other things", as he put it in his Testament Politique of 1752, "one pays one's debts to the state without feeling it". Indirect taxes, he repeated in his Testament Politique of 1768, "are the most equitable of all taxes, they do not fall on the poor; bread, meat and beer must be cheap . . . They fall only on the luxuries of the rich."

This was not in fact true since indirect taxes imposed only on luxuries could not yield sufficient revenue. According to the most reliable of contemporary estimates, a mere 7 per cent of these taxes fell on goods consumed only by the rich.[18] Nevertheless, it is far from clear that the weight and abuses of Frederick's indirect taxation, in spite of the complaints against them, were as socially disruptive as would have been an increase in direct taxation, given the existing attitudes toward this and the difficulties of apportioning it equitably.

To the Physiocrats, the founders of the science of economics, whose doctrines were creating a great stir in France and elsewhere in the sixties and seventies, Frederick's views on taxation could not have been more misguided, and so they seemed to Mirabeau when in 1788 he wrote his *De la Monarchie Prussienne sous Frédéric le Grand* (or in all probability caused some Prussian official, discontented with official policy, to write it for him, since it is well known that he wrote none of his works himself).[19] In his judgment on Frederick's fiscal and economic policies generally, Mirabeau observed that "were they not odious they would be highly ridiculous."

Many arguments can be adduced in support of this view. They do not, however, invalidate the contention that Frederick's financial policies were designed to prevent, and succeeded in preventing, the practices which powerfully promoted a revolutionary situation in France. He may have been wholly indifferent to, and indeed ignorant of, the new economic ideas which by the end of his life were filtering into German universities and the heads of his officials. He had, however, a compensating advantage in his awareness of certain popular attitudes and circumstances unfamiliar to more economically sophisticated thinkers – an awareness he doubtless acquired as the commander of peasant armies, officered by nobles for the greater part uneducated, with whom he lived in intimate association over many years. As he once said to Voltaire: "Through the duties of my office I have got to know this two-legged species without feathers very well".[20]

He knew, as for that matter did also Necker,[21] who though Swiss by birth and French by adoption was the son of a Prussian father and the nephew of a Prussian official, that the population in general, but the peasants particularly, would submit patiently to heavy burdens to which they were accustomed but would become restive or rebellious if the burdens were increased, or unfairly distributed by traditional standards. These, as we have seen, were the conditions which prevailed in France. They were conditions which Frederick was determined to avoid and, as far as it seems possible to judge, did in fact succeed in avoiding to a greater extent than any other ruler of a major continental country.

In the numerous instructions which he issued to his officials and which are printed in the *Acta Borussica*, he continually insisted (to quote the words in the instructions to the General Directory in 1748) that "each subject as far as possible must be burdened in the same proportion as every other, so that shoulders of an equal strength shall carry an equal burden."

Equality in this context did not have its modern meaning. What Frederick had in mind was equality within the *Ständegesellschaft,* that is, equality among the members of each group or estate as distinct from equality between one individual and another. The *Ständegesellschaft* was the only kind of society which he could imagine and whose permanence he never doubted. But he never doubted either that it was his duty to see that it functioned equitably – even though his standards of equity were repudiated by later generations and had begun to be called in question before his death.

It was notably, for instance, a cardinal principle with him that he should hold the balance between the various estates so that none should be in a position to cause the ruin of another. He was never a protagonist of the immunity from taxation which the nobles enjoyed in many provinces in his dominions, and he diminished – indeed largely abolished – their tax privileges in Silesia, where, after he had conquered it, he had a relatively free hand.

That he tolerated the continued existence of these privileges elsewhere was presumably for the same reason that he tolerated the more oppressive forms of serfdom which prevailed in many places and which he continually described as a disgrace to humanity, but whose abolition he held to be impracticable except at a cost of social and economic disruption, and a loss of military power, which he was not prepared to pay. "Agriculture", he once said, "is run on serf labour. If one wished suddenly to put an end to this abominable system one would throw the whole agricultural economy into chaos."[22]

Within the limits, however, which this view of things imposed on him he strove to distribute the burden of direct taxation as fairly as he could, and he saw the first prerequisite of this undertaking in the *Kataster* or land survey, on whose proper compilation, it was continually repeated, turned "the welfare or the ruin of so many poor people."[23]

Compiling land surveys for tax purposes was no easy task in the conditions which existed in Prussia and elsewhere in the eighteenth century, when the income or means of subsistence of the landholding peasant turned not only on the produce of his land, but on various communal rights, such as the right to pasture his beasts on the common lands and the fields of the village after the harvest, and to free firewood from the forests belonging to the landlord.

In France, from the middle of the eighteenth century when the problem of taxation became a burning issue, the need for land surveys was continually stressed but they were made only in rare cases.[24] They always encountered a furious opposition from the *parlements* and individual nobles, and plainly not without reason, since no organization existed to undertake the task competently. When Turgot set himself to attempt it on his appointment as *intendant* in the Limousin he confessed that had he known what it involved he would not have had the courage to embark on it; "although I was convinced of its necessity," he said, "it was impossible for me to conceive of the confusion in which this part of the administration was plunged" and how "innumerable were the difficulties".[25]

In Prussia, by contrast, a land survey appears to have existed in every administrative district, or *Kreis*, the responsibility for seeing that it was kept up to date resting with the *Landrat*[26] – that official who was elected by the local nobility, subject to considerable intervention by the crown, and subordinated to the control of the local *Kammer*.

To the best of the present writer's knowledge no general account exists of how these surveys were compiled or how regularly they were revised, though the government plainly attached a great importance to them.[27] If one may believe the testimony of various foreign observers, they constituted a remarkable feat of administration. John Quincy Adams, for example, who made a tour of Silesia in 1800 to 1801, wrote that Frederick the Great had "employed a small number of officers to make an accurate valuation of all the lands in the province and of the income proceeding from them. This work . . . is asserted to be one of the most exact and detailed evaluations ever made."[28] The French, not generally much given to praising Prussian institutions, commented similarly on various occasions. One undated and anonymous report, written apparently in the 1760s when the French government was trying to discover how other countries dealt with the tax problems which it found insoluble itself, reached the following judgment: "Everything", the writer said, "is done with the utmost economy . . . everything turns on economy, legality and moderation . . . These methods should serve as a model. They may be looked on *à juste titre pour un chef-d'oeuvre*."[29] The French ambassador to Berlin, La Touche, had made a similar judgment in 1756. Because, he said, there was no arbitrariness, no bribery, no exploitation, though the taxes were heavy no one complained.

These judgments would be misleading if they were interpreted to mean that arbitrariness, bribery and exploitation were wholly expunged from the Prussian financial scene. The belief that Prussian officials were always honest (at one time asserted though later denied) is not supported by the facts. The printed documents relating to Frederick the Great's reign contain many references to financial scandals in which, admittedly, the ministers were rarely involved but which were not uncommon among the *Landräte* particularly in the early years of the reign, in the *Kammern* where the ministers usually started their careers, in the *Regierungen* or provincial courts of justice, and in the government-owned undertakings which increased in number after the end of the Seven Years War. The frauds which were detected, and of which the records have been preserved, often implicated several or all of the senior officials in the organizations concerned, either because of deliberate conspiracy or because the principal offenders had, as it was said, "verführt" the others – i.e., led them into temptation – or frightened them into silence or complicity.

An example is the scandal that shook high society in Breslau between 1750 and 1753 when an examination was conducted into the accounts of the principal court of justice and large sums were found to be missing.[30] The principal delinquent was the President, von Benekendorff, a noble of such high social and official standing that he made light of the whole affair, assuming no one could touch him. But this was not so. After elaborate investigations he was found guilty, deprived of all his possessions which were put up to auction, and imprisoned for life. (When sentence was pronounced against him, as the Fiscal General, his long-standing enemy, reported with *Schadenfreude* to Eichel: "All his assurance suddenly disappeared, he went deathly pale and his whole face became distorted.") The other members of the court were also pronounced guilty, for responsibility was collective, but those who, one might suppose, bore a particularly large share of the guilt – Baron von Kitlitz and Graf Matushka – because it was their job to audit the accounts, were pardoned by the King on the grounds that they had been "verführt", though why Frederick should have believed this, or found it an excuse, is not revealed.

No attempt apparently has ever been made to assess the proportion of senior officials who were convicted of fraud or who were suspected with good reason of being guilty of it though no action was taken against them (and such cases certainly occurred) because their usefulness was held to outweigh their misdemeanours.[31] It seems unlikely, however, that fraudulent actions can have occurred on a large scale because of Frederick's determination to prevent them at almost any cost.

This determination admittedly could have amounted to no more than a pious hope without the administrative machinery for enforcing it, and the creation of such machinery was a slow process. As in every other absolute monarchy, disobeying the law was common. One German historian once observed, as Tocqueville observed of France, that the gap between law and practice was so large that no importance should be attached to any law without evidence that it was carried out. In Silesian villages the traveller who asked whether the regulations written up in the pubs were observed was, it is said, always given the answer: "Sir, only by the nail on which they hang."[32]

Evasion of the law occurs under every government. That it was far more common in the illiterate and ill-policed eighteenth-century societies than it became later is obvious. Then as now, however, in comparing one contemporary state with another, the question is one of degree. It is hardly possible to doubt that the machinery devised in Prussia for ensuring order and honesty in financial affairs achieved, by contemporary standards, an unusual degree of success.

Every year, for example, on the 1st of June, every provincial *Kammer* was required to make an estimate of its likely revenue and expenditure for the coming twelve months, and the various estimates were then examined by the General Directory and submitted to the King in the so-called "Minister Review". Elaborate arrangements were devised to ensure that as far as possible these estimates once acepted were adhered to, and precise explanations were required if they were not.[33]

In every *Kreis* the *Landrat* was issued with elaborate instructions[34] as to how to collect the direct taxes and as to the sanctions to be applied to the recalcitrant. He was provided with a "Contributions-Einnehmer", or tax-collector, who, it was stipulated, must always be able to read and write and might exact no payments without the *Landrat's* written authorization. The money collected in the *Kreis* was then delivered to the *Übersteuerkasse*, or provincial treasury, where the accounts were checked and signed by every individual member of the *Kammer*, which was collectively responsible for their accuracy. All the accounts, apart from those relating to Silesia, and the sums kept for emergencies of which the King alone had knowledge, were then checked by the General Directory every month, every quarter, and every year.

These precautions against fraud, described here only in an oversimplified form, were certainly not foolproof. To evade them with impunity must nevertheless have been difficult, particularly because of the periodic investigations made on the spot by the ministers, and the King himself, into the workings of every organ of government in the provinces, and because of the employment of an army of spies, notably those known as *Fiskale*, or fiscals.

The fiscals, in the words of Otto Hintze, were "the eyes and ears of the King". Advocates by profession, who sometimes maintained a private practice in addition to their work for the government, they had developed by the end of Frederick's life into a "vast organization"[35] under the control of a fiscal general who reported directly to the King. Their numerous and never precisely defined functions were comparable to those nowadays associated with a secret police, though their office was not secret. Their principal duty was to keep a look-out for financial malpractices among officials.

The standards of honesty they were required to enforce were far more rigorous than those applied at the time by western governments. Practices which in France, and even in England, were seen as perfectly legitimate were not held to be so in Prussia. In England until late in the eighteenth century (to cite only one, though perhaps the most glaring, of many examples) the paymaster of the forces could accumulate a huge fortune, as did notably the first Lord Holland, the father of Charles James Fox, by investing for his own benefit, in the intervals between when he received the money and had to pay it out, the sums allocated by Parliament for the upkeep of the fighting services. In France, as has been shown, using government money for one's own private purposes was a regular practice carrying no imputation of corruption, but this was not so in Prussia. Under Frederick every penny of government money had to be accounted for and it was a cardinal principle that no official should ever, under pain of the direst penalties, fail to keep his personal accounts separate from those of the government.[36]

In consequence, what appear in the Prussian documents as scandals would often not have seemed scandalous elsewhere. A typical instance is that of the unfortunate Christoph von Goerne,[37] a well-to-do noble of some social standing, who in 1774 was made head of the *Seehandlung* – a government institution founded two years previously with a monopoly of certain import and export trades. Goerne, who appears to have been more of a fool than a deliberate swindler, used the funds of the *Seehandlung* for various private purposes, including the purchase of estates in Poland. Like other people in such circumstances, he maintained that he had always intended to pay back the sums he had borrowed, but unlike many others he was in a position to do so. When the facts came to light all his personal possessions were seized and his estates put up for sale. They more than sufficed to pay his debts. He himself, nevertheless, having together with his family been reduced to destitution, was imprisoned for life, though Frederick William II authorized his release after Frederick the Great's death.

Frederick was determined that Goerne's fate should serve as an example, and so it and other comparable cases may well have done. Financial honesty, beyond what was generally achieved or expected elsewhere in the eighteenth century, appears to have been instilled into most branches of the state service (the excise seems to have been an exception) by a combination of circumstances – by the principles of the Pietists which deeply influenced some people in authority, notably Frederick's ablest and most trusted minister, Ludwig Philipp, Freiherr von Hagen[38] – and by the risks of detection and its penalties. It would seem that an ideology, which was sometimes willingly accepted but whose observance at other times, and doubtless more frequently, was enforced by fear, produced a degree of order and economy in Prussian financial affairs without which the achievements of Frederick's reign would be inexplicable.

Prussian military achievements were much greater than those of any other eighteenth-century country except England, despite the paucity of her resources, and were particularly so compared with those of France. France by 1789 had a population of about 26 million while that of the Hohenzollern dominions amounted to only 5½ million at Frederick's death three years earlier. Prussia, moreover, as Frederick put it, has "neither a Mexico nor a

Peru nor any of those foreign establishments whose trade enriches their proprietors"[39] – in other words, there was a smaller amount of wealth in the upper strata of society. From this admittedly it does not follow that average income per head, supposing it were possible to measure it, would turn out to have been as much smaller in Prussia than in France as Frederick's lamentations might suggest. Certainly this cannot have been so.[40]

For all this, nevertheless, the French population was five time larger than the Prussian and the French government revenue – as far as the highly unreliable figures make it possible to hazard an opinion – was very much larger still[41] (an assumption from which, if it were correct, it would follow that per capita taxation in France was higher than in Prussia). The French and the Prussian armed forces, however, bore little relation to these figures. The French, it is true, had to maintain a navy with which the Prussians could dispense, but at the end of the Ancien Régime it cost much less than the army and the army was barely larger than the Prussian, which in point of quality had an acknowledged superiority.

Adam Smith maintained that "Among the civilised nations of modern Europe it is commonly computed that not more than one hundredth part of the inhabitants of any country can be employed a soldiers [i.e., presumably in the armed forces] without ruining the country which pays the expense of their services."[42] Throughout the second half of the eighteenth century the Prussians consistently maintained an army equivalent in numbers to 4 per cent of the population, and though a high proportion of the rank and file consisted of mercenaries, these, like the Prussian conscripts, and the officers who were all Prussians by birth or adoption, had to be paid, equipped and fed by the government.

This enormous military establishment, moreover, whatever the social, economic or psychological distortions it may have caused, did not ruin the country, as according to Adam Smith it should have done. Prussia suffered more severely from the Seven Years War than did any of the other belligerents, but the period of recovery which began in the middle '60s saw percentage increases in trade, in manufactures and in the wealth of the land-owning classes that are unlikely to have been less, and may have been greater, than those in France and England, where the rate of growth has been judged comparable.[43]

All these achievements would have been impossible without the provisions which have been described for preventing the waste of government money and in which Frederick the Great saw the key to his success – a point of view echoed by Frederick William III's cabinet councillor, Lombard, when he said in his diary relating to the years 1805-07, "Les finances étaient en Pruss plusque partout ailleurs la première condition de l'existence de l'Etat"[44] (in Prussia more than anywhere else [government] finance was the first condition of the existence of the state).

IV
The administration of justice

(a) THE NATURE OF THE PROBLEM

From the earliest days of absolutism, the administration of justice was seen as a principal if not the most important function of government. To the French jurists of the sixteenth and seventeenth centuries the king's first duties lay, in the following order, in the fields of justice, war and finance;[1] and in all the absolute monarchies the monarch himself, and everyone else, believed that it was the royal duty to see that justice was done. Louis XIV referred to that "precious depository of justice which God has placed in the hands of the king as a part of his wisdom and power".[2] The chancellor d'Aguesseau declared in 1738 that "the king can never renounce the right, which he possesses as universal judge and the source of all justice, to pronounce himself on all those matters which seem to him sufficiently important to merit his personal judgment".[3] The Prussian *Allgemeines Landrecht* of 1794 declared that "the general and supreme right of justice . . . belongs to the head of the state and is an inalienable royal right".[4]

The way these pronouncements were interpreted and applied differed in France and Prussia, and in Prussia it changed markedly in the course of the eighteenth century. In both countries, nevertheless, it became increasingly inevitable that the vast majority of legal cases should never come to the monarch's notice, but were decided in the various courts established within his dominions.

What is meant by justice and seen as the best means of enforcing it, have changed from age to age and from country to country. These matters, however, are still largely understood in the west in terms of the beliefs of the Enlightenment. Whatever modifications these beliefs have since undergone, a good system of justice is still held in the west to imply that the judges should be independent of the government in the sense that the government cannot dismiss them and is itself answerable to them if its actions are in breach of the law; that they should be skilled in their profession, and immune by virtue of their professional standards and the salaries paid them by the government from the temptation to accept bribes or other inducements to modify their judgments; that torture should be prohibited and punishments should be humane and proportionate to the offence committed; that there should be equality before the law in the sense that no one should be subject to special courts, laws or punishment by virtue of birth, creed or race. Most of these principles were incompatible with absolutism and the société d'ordres, in which the monarchs and their ministers, until they began to come under the influence of enlightened ideas, attempted to enforce principles of a different kind.

In Prussia the views of Frederick William I were by enlightened standards brutal and primitive in the extreme. The Calvinist God whom he worshipped (for though the bulk of their subjects were Lutheran the members of the Hohenzollern dynasty were Calvinists) was a God of wrath. Frederick William is said to have been obsessed with the belief that if he, as king, did not punish criminals with the utmost severity the divine vengeance would be visited on his dominions. In consequence he extended the list of offences that should be classified as criminal and increased the severity of the punishments for crime, resurrecting, for example, a law long fallen into abeyance, which condemned the murderer of a child, usually an unmarried mother (a condition which in itself involved a criminal offence), to be tied in a sack and drowned. As one German legal historian, far from hostile to the Hohenzollern tradition, put it, "one cruel form of execution followed another to the joy of the pickpockets who never had it so good as on the days when the sensation-loving public crowded to the scenes of these executions".[5] No idea of the prerequisites of justice as described above ever entered the head of Frederick William I.

In this respect his son was markedly different, particularly in his attitude to crime and punishment. In his abolition of the death penalty for many offences, Frederick the Great was more enlightened than the monarchs or their ministers in any other contemporary state, Great Britain included.[6] In his efforts to abolish torture (except in the army where the practice known as *Spießrutenlaufen*, or running the gauntlet, can hardly be otherwise described) he showed a degree of humanity certainly unequalled in France, where punishments as barbarous as those prescribed by Frederick William I continued to be inflicted until the Revolution, and to draw equally enthusiastic crowds of spectators.

Except, however, in the matter of crime and punishment, the famous reforms which Frederick the Great introduced into the administration of justice and which altered existing practices in ways often, though unsuccessfully, advocated in France, had little direct connection with the enlightened ideas on justice as described above. The chancellors in both France and Prussia who advocated and carried out, or attempted to carry out, these reforms – Cocceji in Prussia, d'Aguesseau, Maupeou and Lamoignon[7] in France – are not reckoned as apostles of the Enlightenment. Otto Hintze did not think that Cocceji could be so described;[8] nor could d'Aguesseau and still less Maupeou. Maupeou, for all his ineptitudes, was a clever man and a man of vision; but he was arbitrary, harsh, tyrannical, authoritarian, and by the standards of the *Philosophes* uncultivated.[9] He was the bugbear of every *Philosophe* with the single exception of Voltaire, who had his own particular reasons for hating those sovereign courts of justice, the *parlements*, which

Maupeou abolished in their existing form though they were restored after he fell from power.

What these reformers did, or tried to do, was to create conditions perfectly compatible with the société d'ordres but necessary to a more efficient functioning of autocracy. Their aim was to establish what Otto Hintze once described as "eine patriarchalische Billigkeitsjustiz"[10] – the sort of justice required of a fair-minded, conscientious head of family, though of a family whose members became increasingly numerous and its affairs increasingly complex. In both countries, fulfilling this task posed many similar problems which on occasion were even described by identical words. Its fulfilment demanded that means should be found for settling civil disputes and bringing criminals to trial without undue delays or, in civil cases, excessive cost; that the judges should be uncorrupt, and that they and the advocates should be deprived of the incentive to drag out cases for the sake of the fees obtainable from the litigants, and should have the training, knowledge and intelligence necessary to discharge their functions properly; that the limits of the jurisdiction of the various courts should be clearly defined and an orderly and rational system of appeals established; that a code of laws applicable to the whole kingdom should be drawn up so as to put an end to the confusion created by the great variety of laws and customs in the various provinces. The reformers did not suppose that it would be practicable to abolish these provincial laws and customs entirely, but they hoped, by bringing as many of them as possible within a general system, to minimize "their obscurity, their contradictions and their enormous volume" which "frighten the jurist, discourage the judge, and offer to the people an unintelligible body of legislation".[11]

The legal reformers of the eighteenth century, in other words, before the age of the *Philosophes*, and during it largely without reference to its thinking, strove to introduce some honesty, order and system into the administration of justice; and to do so because it became increasingly evident – as various of Stein's associates said after 1806 when the idea was already a platitude – that "the maintenance of law and justice is the first prerequisite of internal order"[12] and "unity in administration is the soul of government without which everything is at sixes and sevens and the state disintegrates and is destroyed".[13]

The difficulties in the way of achieving these objectives are so unfamiliar to the experience of western societies that they have commonly been overlooked. They have paled into insignificance by comparison with the violation of human rights which was a daily and accepted occurrence and to which, until the ideas of the French Enlightenment gained widespread currency, no obloquy was attached. For most of the rights for which the Enlightenment stood – notably freedom of speech and publication, freedom of worship, freedom of association, freedom from arbitrary arrest and imprisonment without trial, and an independent judiciary – were beyond most people's imagining.

The introduction of some degree of honesty and order into the administration of justice was nevertheless a stage in the progress towards the enforcement of enlightened ideas – a stage, however, whose attainment in both France and Prussia encountered great, and in France insuperable, difficulties.

(b) THE FRENCH EXPERIENCE

Though added to by modern research in some respects and corrected in others, Marcel Marion's long article on Justice in his *Dictionnaire des Institutions de la France au XVIIᵉ et XVIIIᵉ Siècles* is still the most comprehensive account of the subject available to the general reader. It begins with the words: "In the study of the Ancien Régime there is no question more vast, more important or more complicated than that of justice." Unfortunately this opinion has rarely been shared by the students who during the last half century have, in increasing numbers, examined the nature of the Ancien Régime.

Marion enumerated under four headings, still accepted by modern scholars, the various kinds of justice to which the French population was subjected – ecclesiastical and municipal justice (of such relatively minor importance as to make it unnecessary to describe them here), seigneurial justice and – by far the most important – royal justice, which he divided into two main categories: "ordinary" justice in civil and criminal matters, and "exceptional" justice.

The lowest courts which administered "ordinary" royal justice were those known as the *baillages*, or in the Midi and the west as the *sénéchaussées*, of which there were some 400 to 500 located in towns throughout the country. They were courts both of appeal and of first instance. They heard appeals principally from the seigneurial courts in which some, though by no means all, seigneurs were entitled to exercise one or more, and commonly all three, of the kinds of justice known as "haute, basse et moyenne", the first of which conferred the right to impose the death penalty. This was a right – the "symbole de la glaive", or power of life and death – that was greatly prized, particularly by the newly-created noble or the commoner who owned a seigneurie. In the eighteenth century, however, it was very rarely exercised and when it was so, it appears, only with the consent of the local *parlement*.[1]

It is commonly said, as it was by Marion, that in this century the seigneurial courts had fallen into decay because most seigneurs lacked the means to maintain the necessary prisons and officials. Where major crime was concerned this seems to have been largely true. We have the word of the chancellor Maupeou, supported by recently discovered evidence, that criminal justice "lay uselessly in the hands of the seigneurs" and hence (for there was virtually no public police force) "the impunity and multiplication of criminal offences".[2]

Except in relation to major crime, however, the decay of seigneurial justice appears to have been exaggerated. It was the only means available to most peasants for settling the minor disputes that occurred continually in every village. However haphazardly it was administered, and its haphazard nature would be hard to exaggerate, it was a great deal better than nothing. So far from being obsolete it was, at least in some areas where its operation has been investigated, more active in the eighteenth century than it had been previously.[3] Though the lawyers who wished to reform the judicial system believed that according to the principles of absolutism it ought, ideally speaking, to be abolished, they realized that its abolition was in fact impracticable. (D'Aguessau, Maupeou and Lamoignon all felt it must be left standing.) Nor was this desired by the rural population. According to Professor Taylor's analysis of the *cahiers*, referred to earlier, among the 488 *cahiers* of those drawn up in parishes and small market towns which he examined, only 11 per cent wanted the seigneurial courts to be done away with.[4]

Besides hearing appeals from these courts, the *baillages* were also courts of first instance in a large number of cases, with appeal to the most important of the so-called "sovereign courts",[5] the *parlements*, whose judgments could be overriden only by the crown. Since, however, the *baillages* could not pronounce a final judgment in criminal cases, or in civil cases except when the sums involved were very small,[6] the *parlements* were always flooded with appeals, a state of affairs they strove tenaciously to preserve, notwithstanding their inability to cope with it, because of its financial advantages.

Many other circumstances also restricted the *baillages'* competence. Notably they had no jurisdiction in financial matters which were tried in a variety of different courts with appeal (in most though not all cases[7] and subject to frequent interventions by the king's council) to the sovereign court of the *Cour des Aides*. Further, the "exceptional" justice removed many matters from their competence.

This "exceptional" justice was justice delegated to administrative bodies in matters relating to their functions. There was, in fact, under the Ancien Régime no administrative body without rights of justice, as well as many bodies, most conspicuously the *parlements*, whose primary duties were judicial but which also exercised important administrative ones.

The so-called "exceptional" justice was in practice anything but exceptional. It was possessed, for example, by the administration of the *Eaux et Forêts*, which by the end of Ancien Régime maintained twenty separate organizations thoughout the country; by the seventeen *Cours des Monnaies* in which coins were minted; by the twenty-six *Bureaux des Finances* which in the seventeenth century and earlier had dealt with an enormous range of matters though their jurisdiction was increasingly contested and diminished by other authorities, notably the *intendants*; by the *greniers à sel* – the buildings in which the General Farm kept and sold its stocks of salt and in which royal courts were located to try in the first instance all breaches of the law relating to its sale and purchase.[8] This list could be greatly extended to the confusion of the reader, as the organization of justice itself confused those who had to live under it. As one legal authority put it in the eighteenth century, "the ordinary courts of justice are like a mighty river which suffices for all needs but which one has almost drained of water to fill, at a considerable loss, particular canals, each of which has its use but which by their competition often embarrass the course of justice and create uncertainty as to the road to follow."[9]

This was to put it mildly. The famous jurist Loyseau, whose works were first published in 1660 though he was born nearly a century earlier, complained that the confusion of jurisdictions in France was no less than that of the languages in the tower of Babel,[10] and it increased as the crown created new courts and more officials in order to raise money from the sale of offices. The rights of jurisdiction with which these courts were endowed were a source of continual dispute; the area over which they extended was never precisely defined and frequently conformed to no rational principles. A *baillage*, for example, could cover two miles or thirty; a single house could be subject to the authority of two *baillages*, so that the owner had only to move from one room to another to escape from authorities he had reason to suppose unfavourable to him. The *baillage* officials in one province which has been the subject of research, and doubtless for the same reasons in other provinces, did not know which seigneurial courts came, or did not come, within their purview.[11] The powers of the *intendants* and of the king's council to try cases themselves, or to override the decisions of the lower courts, were subject to no precise rules. The complexities and confusion resulting from this situation were such that, as an eminent lawyer observed in 1763, "one could be forced to plead for two or three years [merely] to discover before which judge one had the misfortune to be heard".[12]

The writer of this sentence – the *Procureur Général*[13] Joly de Fleury, in the reign of Louis XV – doubtless used the word "misfortune" advisedly, for the legal competence and disinterestedness of the judges – and most significantly of those in the *parlements* where the bulk of cases ended up – was continually subject to question. The chancellor d'Aguesseau had observed in 1738 that the cupidity of the magistrates in the *parlements* should make them blush.[14] Their appointment was not conditional on any rigorous form of training or examination; the law faculties in the universities were "plunged", as it was said, "in debauch",[15] and in any event, as d'Aguesseau put it: "At present the multitude and the variety of laws are so great that it often happens that one studies none because of the difficulty of knowing all."[16]

Particularly the magistrates in the *parlements* were accused of dragging out proceedings in order to augment their incomes. The sums they received in salary as interest on the capital they had invested in the purchase of their offices were, after tax which was deducted at the source, always small, often negligible and sometimes even non-existent.[17] They were therefore faced with the temptation if not the necessity to increase their earnings by other means, notably by the *épices*, or fees, they received from the litigants, and from what were known as *"vacations"*, that is, in effect, by overtime working which could be extended and calculated in various disingenuous ways so as to yield large sums. How far the magistrates did in fact pursue these practices and how much they earned from them, appears not to have been seriously investigated. Particularly in the Paris Parlement there were many rich men who had married daughters of successful financiers and had no need to pursue them. On the other hand there were some – possibly many – who did so. In the reign of Louis XVI the first president of the Paris Parlement, d'Aligre, famous for his great fortune and equally great avarice, earned, according to Marion, enormous sums from his *vacations*.[18]

In any event it is beyond question that the impediments to an efficient administration of justice were such that suspected criminals could be kept in prison for years before they were brought to trial and that civil cases could drag out for decades, lives, and even generations until, as d'Aguesseau put it, they became "immortal".[19]

Many eminent officials in the eighteenth century, all of whom had begun their careers in the *parlements*, attributed the maladministration of justice to the sale of offices, which, inspired as it was by the desire to raise money for war, had increased the number of courts and their personnel regardless of the need for them. Admittedly there were people – notably, for example, Voltaire, Montesquieu and Malesherbes – who defended the practice and whose eminence makes it impermissible to overlook their judgment. As Malesherbes once put it: "As to the sale of offices, one might justly think that the right of judging ought not to be sold. But given the existing circumstances it has its advantages. It prevents the sanctuary of justice from being opened to all the men who would like to enter it by means of intrigue, illegitimate influence and bribery. Further, the sale of offices keeps out of the courts people who lack sufficient means to put them beyond the reach of the temptations bred by indigence." Malesherbes admitted that the sale of offices made it impossible to guarantee that the position of judge should go to the most worthy, but he thought there were means by which this situation could be remedied.[20]

It was indeed true that there were among the magistrates individuals of indisputable learning and integrity, and even dynasties in which the father who exercised the office instructed the son who would inherit it in these virtues. Malesherbes' arguments were thus not without substance. In general, however, they were refuted by the facts – particularly by the multiplication of offices with the consequences already described, and by the difficulty of abolishing them. For an office was a piece of private property for which, if dispossessed, the owner had to be reimbursed, and even if he were so (which always proved impracticable except temporarily and on a small scale) he felt the kind of grievance which an owner of a house feels today if the public authorities turn him out of it, even with compensation.

Malesherbes' arguments, at the time, had many opponents among his colleagues in the sovereign courts and among ministers who had started their careers there. D'Argenson, for example, in his *Considérations sur le*

Gouvernement Ancien et Présent de la France, of 1765, described the sale of offices as "that miserable invention which has produced all the evils now in need of reform" – evils which he proceeded to enumerate *seriatim.* His views were shared, among others, by d'Aguesseau and Maupeou. Maupeou held the sale of offices to be "a shameful monument to the errors of the administration which should be abolished for ever",[21] a point of view which he induced Louis XV to endorse publicly. On 13 April 1771 Louis declared: "We have recognized that the sale of offices, introduced because of the misfortunes of the times, was an obstacle to the choice of officials and often prevented those who were most worthy from entering the magistracy."[22]

The confusion in the administration of justice became increasingly apparent as the tasks of government multiplied, and necessitated more frequent interventions by the council, where the king personally or through the agency of the councils' various committees had the ultimate responsibility for seeing that the lower courts performed their functions properly, for settling (as far as was possible) the conflicts over jurisdiction which arose between them, and for hearing appeals from individuals with grievances.

The organization of the royal council and its development in the eighteenth century have been described in detail by Michel Antoine in his illuminating work entitled *Le Conseil du Roi sous le Règne de Louis XV.* He has shown that the justice administered by the council, where there were no *épices* or *vacations,* was better and quicker than that provided by the lower courts. He has much to say of the learning, intelligence and honesty of many of its members and of the work it performed in promoting a unified national administration. The fact nevertheless remains that, speaking generally, in the sphere of justice which was one of its principal concerns, the council did little if anything to remedy existing abuses and in some respects even exacerbated them.

Of the victims of injustice or delays in the lower courts, only a minute proportion were able to bring their grievances before the council. Among those who succeeded, the most famous were the surviving members of the Calas family whose head, without any proper examination of the evidence, had been tortured and put to death by order of the *parlement* of Toulouse for a crime he had not committed. The Calas only succeeded, however, in getting their case before the council, which reversed the judgment of the *parlement* of Toulouse and gave the family a large sum in compensation, because of Voltaire's enormous efforts on their behalf which made their case a *cause célèbre* throughout Europe. There were other cases, comparable to theirs, in which even Voltaire would have encountered greater difficulties.

These were cases in which people were accused of breaking the tax-laws, particularly those relating to the General Farm. Such cases were not heard before the committees of the council which commonly dealt with the grievances of individuals, for in matters of finance the council had virtually ceased to function.[23] Though one of its committees, the so-called *Conseil des Finances,* continued to exist in name, it met increasingly rarely. The *contrôleur-général*, usually with one of his subordinates, issued edicts on his own authority and annulled the judgments of the lower courts, notably those of the sovereign court of the *Cour des Aides*. What this could mean in practice may be illustrated by the case of Monnerat,[24] which arose when Malesherbes was first president of the *Cour des Aides*.

Monnerat, a merchant of Limoges, was arrested in 1767 by order of the officials of the General Farm who claimed he was a certain Comtois, alias La Feuillade, a man accused of smuggling salt. Monnerat protested that he was not Comtois and had never smuggled salt in his life. It was not, however, until he had been in prison for six months that he succeeded in obtaining a hearing which, even then, was only of a most perfunctory kind. He was imprisoned under a *lettre de cachet*, a document signed by a secretary of state which, among its other purposes, was used to order a person to be imprisoned or exiled. In the reign of Louis XV *lettres de cachet* were issued like blank cheques to officials who filled in the names of the people they or their friends wished to put out of the way.

Monnerat was taken to the prison of Bicêtre, where he was incarcerated in a dungeon totally devoid of light, and tied to a wall by a chain weighing 50 lbs which was hung round his neck. After six weeks, when he appeared to be on the point of death, he was removed to a cell where the conditions were less likely to kill him. Altogether he remained in prison seventeen months and was ultimately released only because of the intervention of some person powerful enough to exert pressure. Once free he brought a case against the General Farm in the *Cour des Aides* which under Malesherbes' direction ordered the General Farmers, among other things, to pay him 50,000 livres compensation. The General Farm, however, procured an order from the council – that is, in reality from the *contrôleur-général* – annulling the judgment of the *Cour des Aides* and ordering it to let the matter drop. This in the end it did, though only after one of those disputes between the council and the sovereign courts which brought the country to the verge of anarchy in the 1750s and 1760s.

Though Malesherbes in his pursuit of the Monnerat affair has, rightly or wrongly, been accused of wishing to make himself popular by championing the cause of the oppressed,[25] one can hardly doubt the truth of what he said, a year before this affair started, in a private letter to a friend on the subject of "Les grands, la noblesse et l'inégalité".[26] *Les grands* (the grandees), he maintained, could always escape punishment whatever their misdeeds – an opinion echoed by a member of the Constituent Assembly, who observed in 1789: "Was a man protégé?" – i.e., had he protectors in high places? In that case "his adversary was judged in the council and lost his case".[27] Whether or not such justice, or the lack of it, should be described as a "justice de classe", or class justice, it was certainly not denied or granted to a person by virtue of his estate. The poor noble was likely to be as helpless as Monnerat. Malesherbes reminded his correspondent of three nobles they both knew of, who had been broken on the wheel and executed. He could, he said, name many others, and "M. de Pleumarten would have been executed like them if he had merely been a man of condition and not close enough to *les grands* to be thought one of them himself." Malesherbes added that he wished to correct a mistake he had made in one of his previous letters: "I told you", he said, "of a great family which recently committed three murders. I was wrong. There were four." All apparently went unpunished. For this reason, as well as for the other reasons discussed earlier, Milovan Djilas's phrase "land without justice" might fairly be applied to France.

Two major attempts to reform the judicial system were made in France in the eighteenth century, one by Maupeou in 1770, the other by Lamoignon on the eve of the Revolution in 1788. The impetus in both cases was in the first instance political – the need to reduce the *parlements'* power to frustrate government policy by refusing to register the royal edicts and, in the 1750s and '60s by going on strike, that is, by suspending all their judicial functions, when the King tried to override their remonstrances. The political aspects of these disputes, however, are not at issue now but only the reforms of the judicial system which in the course of its attempts to curb the *parlements* the government tried to introduce.

The abuses which Maupeou and Lamoignon set out to remedy were those which were described in the first section of this chapter and which had been stressed by French jurists from the sixteenth century onwards. Particularly Maupeou and Lamoignon attempted to bring justice within easier reach of the population by reducing the number of courts, notably those which exercised "exceptional" justice, and restricting the right of the *parlements* to hear appeals. The huge area, variously estimated at half or a third of France, which was subject to the jurisdiction of the Paris *parlement*, and the fact that it tried nearly all the cases which arose in the *baillages* subordinate to it, was "infinitely prejudicial"[28] to those accused of crimes, who commonly spent years in the *parlements'* atrocious dungeons, as well as to the litigants in civil matters. Because of the enormous backlog of cases awaiting trial, the only hope of getting to the head of the queue was to establish oneself in Paris, which might mean travelling from as far off as Lyon; to interview all the officials concerned with one's affairs; to bribe the judges' secretaries and solicit the help of those who could get the judges' ear. The unfortunates without money or powerful friends, who were forced or misguided enough to make the attempt, were more likely than not to be ruined. Both Maupeou and Lamoignon tried to remedy this state of affairs by establishing, within the area of jurisdiction of the *parlements*, courts with the right to decide finally cases which the *parlements* had previously judged. This, it has been estimated, was the greatest benefit which the reforms, had they been implemented, would have conferred on the French nation.[29]

Maupeou, further, set out to abolish the sale of judicial offices, but he was able to do so only to a limited extent and with dubious success; for the salaries of the magistrates he appointed who were paid by the crown were so low that it was commonly said, whether rightly or wrongly, that they found illicit means of earning more than had their predecessors.[30] Apart, in fact, from all the other difficulties with which Maupeou had to contend was that which d'Aguesseau had lamented when, in 1738, he spoke of his misfortune in having to live in a country long accustomed to find superfluous any government expenditure on the administration of justice.[31]

Lamoignon, notwithstanding his dislike of Maupeou, followed in his footsteps and proceeded further. His projected reforms have been described as "the boldest, the most profound and in many respects the best, attempted under the Ancien Régime".[32] In addition to changes of the kind that Maupeou had tried to introduce, he proposed to provide greater safeguards for the accused in criminal cases (though not to mitigate the barbarity of punishments) and to set up a body to codify the law. These projects, however, like Maupeou's, and the many others concerned with different spheres of government, collapsed beneath the weight of the opposition they encountered, and France remained a land without justice till 1789.

That this was so was widely believed. Marion, in his work on Lamoignon's reforms, claimed to have found, as a result of examining a large number of *cahiers*, including parish *cahiers*, that denunciations of the system of justice were common to all of them from whichever group or estate they emanated. This was also the judgment of Arthur Young. "The administration of justice," he said, "was partial, venal, infamous. I have, in conversation with many very sensible men, in different parts of the kingdom, met with something of content with their government, in all other respects than this; but upon the question of expecting justice to be really and fairly administered, everybody confessed there was no such thing to be looked for."[33] "In England", Mirabeau said, "at least in my view on this matter, only emendations are needed, whereas with us one needs to begin again from scratch."[34]

(c) THE PRUSSIAN EXPERIENCE

The problems that arose in Prussia in connection with the administration of justice, the complaints to which they gave rise and the remedies seen as necessary, though in detail very different from those in France, were nevertheless in broad outline similar.

There were many different kinds of justice in France. Yet in Prussia there were even more, because a higher proportion of the Hohenzollern dominions had been acquired at more recent dates than had those of the Bourbons, and had retained many institutions dating from the time when they had been separate states. These various forms of Prussian justice may nevertheless be subsumed under categories similar to those used by Marion. The most important were on the one hand seigneurial justice – the justice exercised by the lords of the manor or *Gutsherrn* as well as by the *Domänenpächter* or tenants of royal domains – and on the other hand, and to an increasingly important extent, royal justice. In Prussia as in France royal justice was divided, to use Marion's terms, into "ordinary" justice and "exceptional" or administrative justice.

Ordinary royal justice in Prussia was the justice exercised by bodies dating from the Middle Ages, of which the most important were those known as the *Regierungen*. These were the principal courts of justice in every province, though there was a right of appeal from them to a higher court in the province concerned, or in Berlin. Originally the *Regierungen* had borne a considerable resemblance to the French *parlements*, exercising a variety of legislative and administrative functions. By the eighteenth century, however, unlike the *parlements*, they had been shorn of all but their judicial powers. [1] They differed from the *parlements*, too, because their members were not hereditary office-holders who had bought their posts by payment of capital sums in return for interest in the form of salary. The principal judges in the *Regierungen* before the reforms of the middle of the eighteenth century were local nobles who saw their office as a source of prestige and as a means of safeguarding their rights and augmenting their incomes.

The "exceptional" justice as Marion described it in France had its counterpart in Prussia principally in the rights of jurisdiction granted to the army and to the *Kriegs- und Domänenkammern* which had originally been set up to provide for the army's needs and to administer the royal estates. In France military justice evidently affected civilians to so small an extent that it did not figure in Marion's categories. In Prussia by contrast it impinged, directly or indirectly, on a great number of people.[2] In relation to the population, the Prussian army was not only vastly larger than the French; its powers of justice embraced not only soldiers but civilians, since most Prussian soldiers, whether they were conscripts or mercenaries, were employed in peace in civilian occupations, where not only they but all the members of their families were subject to military discipline. Moreover, the power and prestige of the army were such that, even in the second half of the eighteenth century when arrangements were more orderly than they had been under Frederick William I, the military commanders, with the tacit if not explicit consent of the king, were able to bend or defy the law to their own or their service's advantage. As one of Stein's future collaborators put it in 1802, "we shall wait wholly in vain for the community spirit of the English and the French to awaken in us until we put such limits as are consistent with it on the power of the army".[3]

Equally, the rights of justice granted to the *Kriegs- und Domänenkammern* extended over a much wider field than did those of the bodies which exercised "exceptional" justice in the French monarchy. The *Kammern* had indeed no French equivalent, for unlike the bodies with "exceptional" justice in France they were departments of state whose members were appointed and paid by the government, and unlike the French *intendants*, who in this respect were comparable[4] to them, they had a large staff at their disposal and a power to resist the opposition of competing authorities which the *intendants* increasingly lacked.

Subject to the control of the General Directory, the *Kammern* were responsible not only for the administration of the royal estates which, as was said earlier, covered a third of the Hohenzollern dominions, and for meeting the needs of the army for food, transport and in other ways; their duties embraced a range of tasks so numerous as to affect the lives of everyone in the monarchy and for the discharge of which they were endowed with rights of justice. These rights were defined in 1749 as covering "all disputes concerned with political, economic and other questions affecting the public interest."[5] They also included the right to try all offences committed by the *Kammern*'s officials, against whose misdemeanours the public had in consequence no redress.

Notwithstanding the great differences between the ways in which government was organized in France and in Prussia, in matters of justice the abuses and the reactions to them had many points in common. The different kinds of justice that existed in both countries led to continual quarrels over rights of jurisdiction, and in consequence to delays in settling civil disputes and in bringing criminals to trial. These delays were augmented by other causes, some peculiar to France or to Prussia, some common to both countries.[6] In Prussia as in France there were continual complaints that the judges and advocates dragged out cases in order to increase their incomes from the fees paid by the litigants. In Prussia as in France cases could remain unsettled for decades, lifetimes and even generations, so that the Prussians, like the French, described them as "immortal". In both countries it was maintained that the judges were biased and incompetent, and in the second if not in the first of these respects the defects of the Prussian judges before the latter half of the eighteenth century must have been a great deal worse than those of the French, not only in the *Kammern* for reasons that will appear presently, but in the *Regierungen* where, as late as 1749, there were some who could "barely read or write".[7] Again in both countries there were constant complaints about the multiplicity of royal edicts which conflicted one with another and with existing customs in the various provinces, so that, as the Prussians said in words more or less identical with those used in France, they "obscured everyone's conception and understanding"[8] of what was, or was not, legally permissible.

Frederick William I was deluged with petitions from people who, with or without reason, complained of unjust treatment. His ideas on how to deal with this situation were, however, primitive in the extreme. He saw the laziness, greed and stupidity of the advocates and judges as principally to blame for it. He held judges to be the most useless people in the world[9] and treated them accordingly, even, as was shown earlier, to the extent of hitting on the head and knocking out the teeth of those who gave judgments he disliked. In the interests of economy he reduced the judges' salaries,[10] thus increasing their dependence on fees and bribes. When he discovered people with what he described as "a good head" he employed them in the administration, relegating the "dumme Teufel", or blockheads, to the judicial posts.[11] At the same time he continually expressed his rage at the way in which, as he said, cases "were endlessly dragged out, and were either not settled at all or were settled very slowly at a great cost in time and money, and by judgments that were never enforced".[12] His ideas of what constituted justice seem not to have gone beyond the notions that there ought to be one law throughout the land (*ein Landrecht vor's ganze Land*),[13] that a man should not be robbed of his rightful property, and that no case should last for longer than a year.

The achievement of these objectives, however, presented great difficulties which Frederick William I's temperament and limited intelligence were not calculated to overcome. Except for nationalizing criminal justice by providing that all serious crimes should be tried in Berlin, and by the king personally should he so choose, instead of being tried in the various provinces by lawyers commonly under the control of the local nobility, he made no progress towards remedying the existing abuses – a fact he himself admitted in his Testament Politique when he said, "As far as justice is concerned I have done everything I could to ensure that it is fair and quick, but unfortunately I have not succeeded and have been unable to make it so."[14] The judicial reforms for which Prussia became famous in the eighteenth century date from the reign of his son and owed their conception and execution in the first place to the minister of justice and later grand chancellor, Samuel von Cocceji.

Of all Frederick's ministers and generals, Cocceji is the only one to have escaped the anonymity to which the royal autocracy consigned the others, whose names remain unknown to the general reader and are familiar only to specialists. He was born in 1679, the son of a Bremen bourgeois who had been a professor of law in various Dutch and German universities and had ended his career at Frankfurt on the Oder where his sons were educated. As was common in Germany at the time, he combined an academic career with service to the government, holding alternately university chairs and posts in the administration, a pattern later followed by his famous son. Frederick William I rewarded him for his services by raising him into the nobility. His son Samuel was a man of enormous learning in the theory and practice of the law. He combined phenomenal energy with great administrative ability, a high degree of political acumen and a skill in handling people, notably the King himself. He won Frederick's trust to a greater extent than did any other minister with the possible exception of von Hagen, and could speak his mind more freely to his capricious and irascible royal master, and influence his views and policy further, than could any other of Frederick's servants.

From an early age he had been aware of the abuses in the Prussian system of justice and had set himself to consider the means of remedying them. Though he had held various important posts under Frederick William I he had been unable to prevail against that monarch's prejudices. His chance came with Frederick the Great's accession and with the conclusion in 1745 of the wars that ended with Prussia's acquisition of Silesia.

In a number of memoranda which he wrote after that date he set out the prerequisites of an effective system of justice as he understood it. As early as 1743 he had stressed that "the essential point on which everything else turns is that the judges should receive adequate salaries". "There could never," he said, be any proper justice "without learned, experienced and honest" judges who were properly paid and in consequence not forced in order to make a living to depend on fees or bribes from the litigants, or on other practices incompatible with the fair and competent discharge of their functions.[15] The lack of adequate salaries and often indeed of any salaries at all was, he reiterated, the "Hauptverhinderung" – the principal obstacle – in the way of a good administration of justice.[16]

But besides this obstacle he also saw another which seemed to him almost equally important. This was the so-called *Kammerjustiz* – the justice exercised by the *Kammern* – which he not only disliked on principle, seeing it as a usurpation of the rights of the ordinary courts whose supremacy he wished to establish,[17] but because in the existing circumstances it provided no kind of justice at all. The *Kammer* in Magdeburg, he noted on one occasion, had pointed out that to the members of the public it was a matter of indifference whether they were subject to the *Kammerjustiz* or to the justice of the *Regierungen.* Justice was justice, the *Kammer* said, by whatever court it was administered. This, Cocceji admitted, might be so, but the *Kammer* was not in a position to administer justice of any sort. At this time each *Kammer* appears to have had under its control a staff of getting on for 2,000 people,[18] but the Magdeburg *Kammer* (and there is no reason to suppose that the situation elsewhere was significantly different) had only one man responsible for justice. He was overburdened with work and, as Cocceji put it, if he were ill-intentioned or ignorant "*so sind die Parteien ohne Hoffnung verloren*" – the parties to the dispute are lost without hope.[19] Many statements to the same effect were made by other people.

Frederick the Great, however, was never prepared to consider abolishing the *Kammerjustiz,* a point of view in which he was supported by the ministers in the General Directory who maintained, rightly in the view of Otto Hintze, that they, and the *Kammern* subordinated to them, could not discharge their functions without it.[20] Cocceji in consequence concentrated his efforts on the reform of the ordinary courts and on establishing precisely the cases over which they, as distinct from the *Kammern*, had rights of jurisdiction.

Like his father, Frederick the Great at the beginning of his reign was principally disturbed by the time taken to settle legal disputes and the frequent failures to settle them at all. This, he said, was ruining the country. Despite all the cabinet orders issued on the subject there was, he maintained, nothing that deserved the name of justice in his dominions.[21]

Cocceji therefore began his reforms by clearing up the backlog of unsettled cases in every province in turn – a task which took a number of years to complete and involved enormous journeys over atrocious roads at a time when he was in his middle sixties and often in poor health. With the aid of a staff of five or six able young men, two of whom, von Carmer and von Jahriges, subsequently succeeded him as grand chancellor, he drew up a code of procedure which he wrote on the spot when he had reached his first destination, Pomerania,[22] and which he proceeded to apply there and later elsewhere. In Pomerania he and the team under his direction achieved a success which he reported to Frederick the Great in the following words: "All of the 1,600 old trials which were pending before the courts in Stettin during 1747 have been settled [and] of the 684 new trials only 183 are left."[23]

Similar successes were achieved later in the other provinces. In order to prevent a recurrence of the delays, the *Regierungen* were instructed to submit lists at short intervals of the numbers of cases settled, pending, or sent on appeal, and it was laid down that one of the ministers of justice in Berlin, or his representative, should inspect every higher court in every province at least once every three years and if possible more often.

Cocceji diminished the numbers of courts by abolishing some and amalgamating others. He established a regular *Instanzenzug,* or process of appeals, which could never exceed three instances[24] and which limited the cases in which appeals were permissible. He diminished the numbers of judges not only by reducing the number of courts but by dismissing – at a cost in hardship apparently open to dispute[25] – the superfluous and inefficient members of the courts that remained. By these and other means – which excluded financial help from the King who maintained that he lacked the money, but included contributions from the nobility of the various provinces who had been the most vocal protestors against the existing abuses – he was able to increase the judges' salaries. He ensured that no judges should serve without payment; that no individual judge should be able to increase his income by means of fees from the litigants; and that every judge should receive a fixed salary which, it has been estimated, was on an average more than double what those in receipt of payment had received before.[26]

Finally he set about creating a procedure to ensure that the judges should possess the necessary degree of ability, honesty and knowledge of the law. The aspirants to judicial posts were subject to a long period of academic and practical training which, since the state did not subsidize it, was rarely open to young men from poor families. This training began with study in the law faculty of a university and extended after that for some four or five years of apprenticeship in the courts of justice, combined with further study. At the end of his apprenticeship the candidate was required to take a final examination which included the greatly feared *Probe relation* – an ordeal which allowed him a few days in which to go through the files of a case pending before the courts and then required him to defend his judgment on it before a panel of judges, established as a permanent commission in 1755, who were drawn from the appeal courts in Berlin.[27] Though in the appointment of judges in the higher courts preference, other things being equal, was given to nobles, other things commonly were far from equal, with the result, as shown earlier, that in the latter part of the eighteenth century the number of bourgeois greatly exceeded that of nobles.

By all these means Cocceji, who died in 1755, laid the foundations of a national system of justice that proved increasingly capable of removing many of those evils of which the French complained but were unable to remedy. His successes were nevertheless limited, partly by the resistance of Frederick the Great to some of his projects, partly by contemporary attitudes towards absolutism, many of which he himself shared, though his successors among the elite body of lawyers he created increasingly ceased to do so, and partly by social circumstances beyond the power of anyone to alter significantly.

Although Frederick persistently refused to abolish the *Kammerjustiz* against which Cocceji had protested, he admitted that its scope was unduly large and imprecise and its administration defective.[28] In the course of time steps were taken to remedy these defects. On various occasions, most notably by the edict of 1749,[29] instructions were drawn up to fix the rights of jurisdiction of the *Kammern* on the one hand and of the ordinary courts on the other. From the 1760s onwards attempts were made to improve the quality of the judges, their conditions of work, and in general, principally it seems through the initiative of von Hagen, to apply to the *Kammerjustiz* principles similar to those which Cocceji had applied to the ordinary courts.[30]

Cocceji had repeatedly insisted, as he put it in October 1748,[31] that a proper administration of justice depended primarily (*hauptsächlich*) on the judges in the courts of first instance – that is, in the courts in the towns, and in the villages of the royal domains. (He might also have added, though on this occasion he did not do so, in the villages subject to the manorial courts.) Experience had shown, he said, that "most of the judges in the inferior courts are bad men who seek to enrich themselves by the ruin of the people". Frederick the Great endorsed his belief that it was essential that the higher courts should control their activities and continually keep an eye on them.

The ability of the higher courts to do this was plainly limited. Some more or less continuous progress nevertheless seems to have been made. The rights of justice exercised by the *Domänenpächter* were removed from them at the end of the 1760s and entrusted to judges appointed by the crown.[32] The rights of the private landlords were diminished.

It is often assumed that the landlords in Prussia exercised a power over their peasants similar to that enjoyed by their Russian counterparts. The Prussian peasant, it is said, was a subject of the manor and not of the state – a belief to which the eighteenth-century terminology lent support, for the German translation for "subject" is "*Untertan*" and this was the word which not only the king applied to the inhabitants of his dominions but which the landlord always applied to the peasants on his estates. No sentence has been more commonly repeated in German works up to the present day than that the royal authority stopped at the gates of the manor.

This statement is plainly untrue in the matter of justice as in various other matters. However harshly the peasant was treated, and however difficult legal redress may have been for him, the landlord could not punish him for a criminal offence, and in civil cases he had a right of appeal from the decisions of the manorial court, where in any case, from the beginning of the 1770s, the state required the landlords to employ qualified judges whom they were forbidden to dismiss without the consent of the *Regierungen*.[33] How much safeguard this provided is open to question. Doubtless, too, it is true that the peasant often if not commonly dared not risk offending his lord by appealing against him. The nineteen volumes of documents relating to Prussian administration in the eighteenth century which have hitherto been published nevertheless afford abundant testimony to the fact that he often did so. The author of a careful investigation into the legal relations between landlords and peasants in East Prussia concluded that, though it is hard to say how things worked out in practice, and though in the primitive conditions of the time it was difficult for the authorities to exercise effective control, still, as far as can be seen from the documents, towards the end of the eighteenth century the peasants became increasingly able to enforce their rights and more and more efforts were made to ensure justice to the individual peasant.[34]

What in fact Frederick the Great aimed at and to a large extent achieved by his judicial reforms was an administration of justice which met the needs of absolutism while leaving intact – as far as was possible and in his intentions completely – the *Ständegesellschaft* on which absolutism depended for its *raison d'être*. The absolute monarchs needed those conditions described by Adam Smith which were quoted earlier – a fact of which Frederick the Great was always conscious and which towards the end of his life he expressed in his determination to codify the law. The code, he maintained, must be written in German and in simple language which everyone could understand. He saw it as a means which would prevent all unnecessary legal complications and delays and which would in consequence remove an "incubus" from his people so that "we may have more clever merchants, industrialists and artists who will be of use to the state".[35] This project, for which even Frederick William I had seen the need and to which Cocceji, though fruitlessly, had devoted several years of his life, was finally embarked on in 1780 under the direction of the Grand Chancellor von Carmer with the aid of Svarez who was his principal coadjutor and who did most of the work.

This code was completed twelve years later, though the horror aroused at that time by the execution of Louis XVI caused various of its provisions to be expunged as too liberal, and delayed its publication. It was first published in 1794, not under the title of *Allgemeines Gesetzbuch* as had originally been intended, but under that of *Allgemeines Landrecht*, which for various technical reasons was less objectionable to the conservative defenders of provincial liberties.[36] The passages that were expunged were nevertheless very few and were concerned principally with the limitations Svarez had wished to impose on the rights of the king to interfere with the course of justice.[37] The vast majority of the provisions remained in the form in which Svarez had drafted them. Whatever may be said against them, the manner in which they were set out remains a remarkable testimony to the clarity, precision and powers of logical argument of which the Prussian judiciary, as a result of Cocceji's reforms, had become capable by the end of the eighteenth century.

These merits notwithstanding, the fact nevertheless remains that in Prussia even by the end of the century the administration of justice (not to mention the law that was administered) was not just by the standards of the French Enlightenment or by those of later ages; for Prussia (to use the term commonly invoked in this connection) was by then not a *Rechtsstaat*, or a state in which the government is subject to the law, but remained an autocracy. Everyone with any knowledge of Frederick the Great's reign is aware of his remarks in his Testaments Politiques that in the courts it is the law that should speak while the monarch remains silent. The qualifications that were placed on this pronouncement are, however, less familiar.

In the first place this statement applied only to civil and not to criminal cases. In all cases of serious crimes, whether they arose in the civil or in the military courts, the king was the final judge. He could override the judgments given in the courts and annul, reduce or increase the penalties. As the president of one *Regierung* put it at the end of Frederick the Great's reign: "All judgments in criminal cases of any importance in the Prussian states derive their validity from confirmation or alterations made, at choice, either by the ministry of justice or by the king himself."[38]

And not only this: Frederick's dictum, even though applicable only to civil cases, did not prevent him from adding that it was his duty to see that the courts discharged their functions properly. He was adamant that he had the right to hear appeals from any of his subjects if, in his view, there was a *prima facie* reason for believing that they had been unfairly treated. In such cases he appointed a commission which commonly contained or was composed of army officers, in whose good judgment and integrity he always, like his father, placed a greater trust than the judges in general inspired in him.

The consequences of these proceedings were admittedly less disruptive than in the days of Frederick William I. Increasingly means were found for limiting the right to petition and large numbers of the petitions were in fact dismissed.[39] Frederick's mistrust of the judges, however, which he inherited from his father and which increased with age, together with his conviction that it was his duty to protect the weak against the strong and that he alone could do so, made it seem impossible to him that he should abandon his right to hear petitions and in consequence to issue directions to the courts, if not, as in the case of Müller Arnold (see Appendix to this chapter), to overturn their decisions.

Though his tolerance is proverbial, it was confined to permitting only the discussion or practice of beliefs in which he saw no danger to his regime. He would suffer no criticism of his policy which seemed calculated to interfere with its execution. If he did not suppress political opposition it was because none existed, for no ideology hostile to his own was formulated during his reign. The rights of justice which he insisted on retaining cannot have failed to produce, and in a number of individual instances can be shown to have done so, arbitrary if not blatantly unjust decisions in both civil and criminal cases.[40]

We lack the evidence to estimate how common such cases were. For the purposes of the present argument, however, what happened is less significant than what was believed to have happened, and the belief widely held among the articulate sections of the population, and among historians of later generations, was that Frederick's reform of the judicial system, and the creation during his reign of an increasingly uncorrupt, competent judiciary, were among his greatest achievements. Many instances of this belief could be cited. For example, the judge and later professor Eberty, who was referred to earlier, when he became an apprentice in the *Kammergericht* in Berlin, found it "something grand and wonderful to belong to the body of Prussian judges which at that time [the beginning of the 1830s] showed itself worthy of the fame which it enjoyed throughout the world".[41] Similarly Hardenberg when, after the collapse of 1806, he wrote his famous *Rigaer Denkschrift*, in which he could hardly find a good word for the existing Prussian establishment, admitted that the Prussian judges received a better training than did those in any other state.[42]

A more eloquent tribute to Frederick's achievements in the sphere of justice and also – by the standards of the French Enlightenment and of later ages – a more surprising one, was provided by Svarez. For Svarez was a member of the judiciary at the time of the Müller Arnold scandal. He cannot have failed to be aware that it was a "*Justizkatastrophe*" – a "judicial catastrophe" – the term applied to it at the time by one of the judges concerned and used by German historians from that day onwards. In the lectures, however, which he gave to the crown prince in the winter of 1791/92 Svarez totally overlooked this miscarriage of justice – which became a *cause célèbre* throughout Europe – as well as the circumstances which had made it possible and of which it was only a uniquely glaring abuse. On the contrary, he launched into a paean of praise to Frederick the Great as the just ruler *par excellence*. Since he was dedicated to his profession and to the service of the Prussian State, and was without any aspirations to wealth or social status,[43] he can have had no ulterior motives for speaking as he did.

What seems just to one age in the matter of law and its administration, as has been said, may not seem so to other ages in the same country, or to other countries in the same age, even if they have a comparable social structure. Prussian justice in the reign of Frederick the Great has been accorded at different times and in different places both unqualified praise and unqualified abuse.[44] Tocqueville may perhaps be reckoned as impartial a judge as one is likely to find. When he was preparing his work on the Ancien Régime he decided to look at conditions in Germany during the period which concerned him in France. His investigations were somewhat superficial but they led him to study the *Allgemeines Landrecht* on which he wrote a short dissertation, under the title "Code du Grand Frédéric," as a footnote to chapter I of Book II of his *Ancien Régime*.

He rightly saw the *Allgemeines Landrecht* as incorporating Frederick's principles. He described it, as indeed it was seen by its authors, as "a real constitution, in the sense one gives to that word. Its purpose is not only to define the relations between the citizens with each other, but the relations of the citizens with the state. It is at one and the same time a civil code, a criminal code and a charter. It is based, or rather appears to be based, on a certain number of general principles, expressed in a highly philosophical and abstract form, which resemble in many respects those which fill the Declaration of the Rights of Man in the [French] constitution of 1791."[45] The resemblance between the two documents, he continued however, stopped at this point. In other respects he saw the *Allgemeines Landrecht* as principally distinguished by its endorsement of the société d'ordres, of an unlimited autocracy, and of an extreme degree of centralization "bordering on socialism".

APPENDIX

THE FAMOUS SCANDALS IN FRANCE AND PRUSSIA
IN THE SECOND HALF OF THE EIGHTEENTH CENTURY;
THE CASES OF JEAN CALAS AND OF THE MILLER ARNOLD.

When a regime is overthrown by war or revolution the natural instinct of those who want to understand why this happened is to look for the vices, and particularly the moral vices, that may be held responsible for the victim's catastrophe. The vices of the judicial system in France commonly, and sometimes in an exaggerated form, figured high on the list of grievances which contemporaries in other countries believed had led the French people to revolt. By contrast, the Prussian system of justice at the end of the eighteenth century inspired admiration not only in Prussia herself but also in other countries, in spite of its abuses and scandals. These, however, were overlooked, and by some German writers are still seen merely as the defects from which even the best of human institutions suffer in the earlier phases of their development. This point of view did not come under serious attack until imperial Germany, of which Prussia was the founder, was defeated, dismembered and discredited in the two world wars of the present century. Then schools of thought arose which judged defects previously glossed over as minor ones to be of fundamental importance and symptomatic of the vices of the regime in general.

The purpose of the present account is not to attempt an assessment of the merits or otherwise of these different points of view. It aims only to describe the two most famous *causes célèbres*, when justice was shown to have miscarried in the second half of the eighteenth century both in France and in Prussia, and to do so because of the light thereby thrown on the difference between the autocracies in these two countries.

In France in the second half of the eighteenth century the great scandal, comparable, it has been maintained, to the Dreyfus case,[1] was that of the Calas family referred to earlier. In 1761 Jean Calas, a Protestant cloth merchant of Toulouse, was accused of having killed his son, Marc Antoine, on the grounds, which may or may not have been justified, that the latter was on the point of becoming converted to Catholicism.

The Protestants in France at this time were a sect, comparable to the Jews, who were deprived of civil rights. The laws against them, however, were not strictly enforced and in Toulouse they commonly mixed on good terms with their Catholic neighbours. Hostility to them nevertheless remained only dormant, and the fact that Calas was a Protestant and his son possibly contemplating conversion to Catholicism raised presumptions of his guilt which might not have arisen otherwise, although in many respects the case was far from exceptional.

Jean Calas, then in his early sixties, was tried for murder by the *parlement* of Toulouse. He was first tortured in order to extract a confession from him, which he persistently refused to make, and afterwards condemned to death by the customary procedure, that is, his limbs were first broken by the executioner with an iron bar and thereafter he was placed "facing up on the wheel so long as it will please God to give him life", though the executioner was unofficially permitted, after two hours, to put an end to his agony by strangling him. Throughout these proceedings until he died, Calas continued to protest that he was innocent, thereby exciting some degree of admiration even from the crowd of sadistic spectators. Voltaire, as was said earlier, made the case famous by collecting enough evidence to prove before the king's council that Calas was in fact innocent, and by procuring compensation for his family.

Various other Protestants at this time were condemned to similar penalties for crimes they had not committed. To Voltaire and the other *Philosophes* these occurrences symbolized not only the inhumanity of the magistrates in the *parlements* – "those ferocious beasts", as they said, "whose tongues are drenched with human blood",[2] but the intolerance of the Roman Catholic Church and its members. Intolerant these certainly were, though they were becoming progressively less so. Neither their intolerance, however, nor the inhumanity of the magistrates, would have sufficed to condemn so many innocent people to torture and death – for more Catholics than Protestants suffered this fate[3] – had it not been for the inadequacy of criminal procedure in France at the time, which allowed a person who lacked the protection of powerful friends to be accused on the basis of evidence never subjected to proper examination and gave the defendant no adequate means of defence. The Calas case, to which there were many other parallels, became a *cause célèbre* only because of the part which Voltaire played in it.

The more rigorous procedure in the Prussian courts, the abolition of torture in most and of the death penalty in many cases, appear, as far as is known and except in the army, to have prevented the brutalities from which Calas and many others suffered in France. They also prevented comparable miscarriages of justice. They were nevertheless responsible for others of a different kind of which the most famous, that of Müller Arnold,[4] though unique in some respects was typical in others. Since this case is less familiar and less easily intelligible to readers in the English-speaking world and is open to various different interpretations, it requires a description more detailed than that given to the Calas case.

Arnold was what, in the terminology of the time, was known as an

Erbbauer, that is, his status was comparable to the landowning peasant's in France. He was said to own his mill, and did so in the sense that he could sell, bequeath, or otherwise dispose of it as he wished, but he nevertheless paid dues or rent for it to the lord of the manor, or *Gutsherr*, on whose estate it was situated and to whose jurisdiction he was subject.

This lord of the manor was a certain Graf von Schmettau, whose estate was contiguous with that of a Herr von Gersdorff, the local *Landrat*. Arnold's mill was worked by the water from a stream that ran through both estates into the Oder, which formed the eastern boundary of von Schmettau's estate. Arnold complained that he was unable to pay his rent to von Schmettau because von Gersdorff had built a carp-pond which deprived him of water. Von Schmettau had him up before his manorial court which dismissed his excuses as invalid. In 1774 Arnold then appealed to the local *Regierung* (the provincial court of justice for the Neumark) in Küstrin. The *Regierung* pointed out that Arnold had no case against von Schmettau but could, if he wished, bring a case against von Gersdorff. This, however, he never attempted to do. Since he nevertheless persisted in refusing to pay his rent, von Schmettau after an interval of several years took possession of the mill and put it up to auction. Von Gersdorff bought it for 600 thaler and then sold it, in 1779, to a widow of the name Pöchlin.

It was at the time of the auction that Arnold and his wife, who seems to have been the moving spirit in the affair, set about petitioning the King. Their first attempt, when Frederick was making one of his periodic tours through the district, was abortive. According, however, to the President of the *Regierung*, Graf Finck von Finckenstein, they had a powerful acquaintance, to whom Frau Arnold had once done a service, who financed for them a trip to Potsdam. There they succeeded in getting a petition to the King who appointed a commission of two men to examine the matter.

The man in charge of this examination was the commander of the local garrison, Colonel von Heuking, with whom Frederick associated one of the judges in the *Regierung* called Neumann. From the start Neumann and von Heuking were unable to agree, since Neumann maintained that no decision could be reached until a case had been brought against von Gersdorff, while von Heuking insisted that it was his and Neumann's duty to examine for themselves whether or not von Gersdorff's carp-pond had deprived Arnold's mill of water. In the event von Heuking concluded that Arnold's complaints were justified and wrote a report in this sense to the King without Neumann's agreement.

When he had received von Heuking's report Frederick, convinced after his usual fashion that the judges were in league with the nobility to oppress the peasants, flew into a rage, and wrote to the *Regierung* what one of the judges there described as "the most terrible cabinet order which ever issued from . . . the mouth of this monarch". It was transmitted in writing by one of the cabinet secretaries and threatened all the judges with dismissal as "unworthy of the King's service and bread". In accordance with its instructions the *Regierung* proceeded to re-examine the case but came to the same conclusion it had reached before.

Frederick then ordered that the case should be referred to the *Kammergericht* in Berlin – at that time the supreme court of appeal for various provinces, the Neumark included. The judges in the department of the *Kammergericht* that dealt with civil cases supported the judgment of the *Regierung* in Küstrin.

This enraged Frederick further. He summoned the Grand Chancellor, von Fürst, and the judges in the *Kammergericht* concerned. He hurled abuses at them, calling them scoundrels, rogues, and swindlers. He then proceeded to dictate his orders to them. When in the course of the dicatation he referred to the *Kammergericht* as the *Tribunal* (then the court of appeal for the province of East Prussia), von Fürst felt obliged to correct him, whereat he shouted, "Marsch. Seine Stelle ist schon vergeben" ("March. Your post has already been given to someone else"), and ordered him out of the room.

The upshot of the affair was that the Arnolds got their mill back and a number of people were turned out of their jobs – not only the Grand Chancellor von Fürst, but the President of the *Regierung* Finck von Finckenstein, the *Landrat* von Gersdorff, three judges from the *Kammergericht* and four from the *Regierung*. Frederick believed, though without any valid reason, that these last seven judges bore a particularly large responsibility for the judgment against Arnold. In consequence he ordered them to be imprisoned for a year and to pay out of their own pockets the compensation due to the Arnolds for the losses they had suffered. Since the functioning of their mill depended on the state of wind and weather and a number of years had elapsed since they first claimed that they had been unable to work it, there seemed no means of assessing the sum due to them and they were allowed to put a figure on this themselves, though the government later reduced it.

That the Müller Arnold case was a "judicial catastrophe" by any standards is plain, since from the start there was overwhelming evidence that the Arnolds were liars. Particularly, a mill situated between theirs and von Gersdorff's carp-pond had never ceased to work and the purchasers of Arnold's mill found no difficulty in operating it or in paying their rent. For these reasons the judgment in the Arnold case was reversed immediately after Frederick the Great's death.

To some later historians, however, and to the judges at the time, particularly to the minister of justice von Zedlitz, the case was catastrophic principally because of the imprisonment of the seven judges on a criminal charge of having perverted the law in the landowners' interests. The judges, von Zedlitz pointed out, had not been tried for and were not guilty of any crime. The worst that could be said against them was that they had been misled by the arguments against Arnold. Even had this been so, however, which von Zedlitz denied, to be mistaken in such a matter was not a criminal act.

The position in fact was, as Frederick himself never ordinarily denied, that though in any individual case he had the right to decide what penalty, if any, should be imposed on a person convicted of a criminal offence, he did not have the right to decide (whatever means may have been open to him to influence the decision)[5] whether or not a particular offence constituted a crime. This was a matter for the courts to determine.

In the Arnold case, however, which in this respect was exceptional though otherwise not so, he refused to recognize any limits to his right to interfere with the course of the law. All he could see was that von Heuking was more likely to have been right than any law-court because, as he put it, "I believe an honourable soldier who has honour in his blood more than all your lawyers and laws." Whatever the lawyers might say, he maintained, to deprive a poor and innocent peasant of his means of livelihood must be a crime.

The judgment in the Arnold case was a consequence of this attitude, of the fear which Frederick inspired when he was in a rage, and of his power to dismiss any of his officials at will, the judges included, without compensation or pension. This combination of circumstances bred in the judges of the *Kammergericht* a spirit of subservience and fear which, it is generally admitted, caused them to lose their heads and fail to make a proper use of the evidence available to them.[6] According to one modern historian, Eberhard Schmidt, writing in 1962,[7] Frederick repeatedly put to the judges questions of a general kind such as "can one ask a miller to pay his rent when he has no water, and so cannot work his mill, and so cannot earn anything? Is that just?" The judges were so terrified that they could only answer "No". Finck von Finckenstein's version, though it leads to the same conclusion, is somewhat different and *prima facie* more plausible. According to him, one of the judges (having apparently been asked some such question as this) observed that the case the King was postulating was not the same as the one under discussion, whereat the King shouted at him, "Shut up, you scum (*Halts Maul, Canaille*), it *is* the same case."

Not all the judges showed the degree of subservience which the conditions in which they had to work were calculated to breed in them. The imprisoned judges, when offered their freedom if they would confess their guilt, refused to admit that they were guilty. Von Zedlitz in particular showed a remarkable degree of courage. In an attempt to save the seven judges from imprisonment he wrote Frederick a long memorandum in which he set out all the principal evidence which disproved the Arnolds' assertions. He concluded with the words, "I have kept my duty before my eyes and now lay the fate of these unfortunates, as well as my own, in your majesty's royal power and grace. I await with the deepest submission your majesty's decision whether a criminal verdict shall be pronounced." When Frederick insisted that this should be done, and sent the order to imprison the seven judges to von Zedlitz for implementation, the latter did not, as was customary, countersign it. He had expected to lose his job. By this time, however, Frederick, although he would never admit that he had been mistaken, had begun to have qualms about his actions. He did not dismiss von Zedlitz, who retained his office till his death.

The immediate results of the Müller Arnold affair were in various respects curious. Among its other consequences, the administration of justice in the Neumark was temporarily thrown into confusion, for with the dismissal of the President of the *Regierung,* and with four of the five other judges in prison, only one judge was left to cope with all the work, which was far beyond the capacity of a single man. Further, in the words of one of the imprisoned judges of the *Regierung,* "the peasant laid down his flail and the workman his tools. All got ready for the journey to Berlin. The palace was besieged with petitioners . . . everyone screamed about injustice." In general, social relations as well as the course of justice suffered considerable disruption.

By a curious irony Frederick the Great, who in the present century has gone down to history (admittedly not without justice) as the monarch who, above all others, strove to preserve, and indeed to increase, the privileges of the nobility, was seen at the end of his life, and not only in Prussia, as the champion of the peasant against the landlord and of the weak against the strong. In an essay which he wrote in 1948 Rudolf Stadelmann described how, when in 1780 a Prussian merchant ship arrived in Lisbon, the master, once his nationality became known, was besieged by a crowd whose members sank on their knees, stretched out their hands to him and cried, "Glory to the King of Prussia, praise to the strict enforcement of justice. Long live the just King."[8]

V

The attempts to increase wealth, welfare and national power

(a) THE RELATIONSHIP OF WEALTH AND POWER

In most countries on the continent of Europe in the eighteenth century, though there were small numbers of very rich families and others which were able to achieve varying degrees of affluence, the vast majority of people lived in extreme poverty. No government in those days, however, possessed the means that became available later for redistributing wealth, nor, had this possibility existed, would there have been enough wealth, particularly in the second half of the century when the population in all countries began to increase rapidly, to provide everyone with what Necker described as the "minimum vital". This could only be achieved by a growth in wealth.

The absolute monarchs, as was said earlier, always accepted in theory that it was their duty to promote the welfare of the mass of their subjects. They were never in principle indifferent to the problem of destitution, for their Christian upbringing, and increasingly a sense of their own interests, alike precluded such an attitude, however ignorant or indifferent they may have been in practice to the conditions in which the bulk of the population lived. Even those monarchs, however, who, like Frederick William I and Frederick the Great in Prussia, were neither ignorant nor indifferent, could not dissociate the interests of the mass of the people from those of the state which demanded a constant preoccupation with war – a preoccupation which, however unfortunate its consequences, was inescapable given the predatory world in which these rulers lived; and success in war, like the alleviation of poverty, depended on wealth.

The eighteenth century was an age in which rational thinking, in the ways to be described presently, gained increasing currency, and as it did so it changed the formerly accepted standards which prescribed that one should fight for the glory and dynastic interests of the monarch whom one served, for one's religious beliefs, and for the pleasure and prestige of fighting itself, regardless of the material consequences. Admittedly these reasons for going to war continued to evoke emotion and to command respect, particularly in France, but they did so to a diminishing extent. By the 1780s one German writer,[1] in attempting to describe the progress of civilization his generation had witnessed, noted that in, as he called them, the preceding ages of barbarism, when nations were preoccupied solely with warlike adventures, even war was not as yet the science it had become by his day; that is, a pursuit which required not merely courage, but also knowledge, skill and planning, and whose purpose was to increase or maintain the power and prosperity of the state.

Plainly, at any given moment the pursuit of power and the pursuit of prosperity were likely to be mutually exclusive, since power demanded expenditure for military purposes which accounted for nearly three-quarters of government revenue in every major country and hence involved, among other things, a high level of taxation which reduced the general standard of living. In the long run, however, these two objectives seemed inextricably linked, since not only did power depend on wealth; wealth, and indeed mere existence, were always insecure without power to defend them. The Prussians had better reasons than had the western nations to be conscious of this state of affairs because of their experiences in the Thirty Years War when Prussia had been one of the principal disaster areas, as it was to be again in the Seven Years War of 1756 to 1763 and after Napoleon's invasion in 1806. In all the major European countries, nevertheless, the success of governments turned, and increasingly seemed to turn, on maintaining a balance between the long- and short-term interests dictated by the relationship of power and wealth.

When absolutism was in its prime the domestic policies adopted in pursuit of this objective were those commonly described as mercantilist. Since the term mercantilism has, however, been given a great variety of meanings and has even been declared to be a "non-existent entity",[2] its use is a source of confusion. The present account must be concerned with the ideas that were held in governing circles in France and Prussia about how power and prosperity might best be combined, with the ways in which these ideas were pursued, and with the degree of success achieved.

(b) THE PROMOTION OF TRADE AND MANUFACTURES

When absolutism was in its heyday in France and Prussia, the governments of both these states, by comparison with the most advanced contemporary models, ruled over economically underdeveloped communities in which approximately the same proportion of the population – upwards of 80 per cent – were peasants. The model that first excited their admiration was Holland, whose relative degree of power and prosperity was attributable to her foreign and imperial trades. Foreign trade, and manufactures as a means to it if not in their own right, seemed in consequence the key to wealth.

The principal exponent of this point of view in France was Colbert, who was Louis XIV's most influential minister during the earlier years of his reign but whose way of thinking was nevertheless more in harmony with that of the Prussian than of the French monarchs. In 1680 Colbert wrote to Louis that "in regard to expenditure I beg your Majesty to permit me only to say that in war as in peace he has never consulted the amount of money available in determining his expenditures, a thing which is so extraordinary that assuredly there is no precedent for it".[1] This was a way of proceeding by no means extraordinary to any Bourbon, but alien to the eighteenth-century Hohenzollerns. Because of his rational approach to the problems of creating wealth, and to the relationship between wealth and war, Colbert would have found a spiritually more congenial home in Prussia than he found in France, where religious intolerance, culminating in the persecution of the Huguenots, and the pursuit of military glory regardless of the economic consequences, reflected ideas that were becoming increasingly outmoded and were alien to his convictions and temperament.

He was far from hostile to war if he thought it would yield material benefits, and supported Louis' attack on the Dutch in 1672 on these grounds. "If the King", he wrote, "conquers all the provinces subject to and forming part of the states of the United Provinces of the Netherlands, their commerce becoming the commerce of the subjects of the King, there would be nothing more to desire, and if afterwards His Majesty, examining what would be most advantageous to do for the commerce of his old and new subjects, thought it for the good of his service to divide the advantages of this commerce by cutting down a part of the Dutch so as to transfer it into the hands of the French, it would be easy to find the necessary expedients to which the new subjects would be obliged to submit."[2] As shown, however, by his remarks in 1680 quoted above, he shared the Hohenzollerns' calculating attitudes. He saw war as justifiable only as a means to increasing or preserving the wealth of the state.

His principal biographer, C.W.Cole, described him as cold, ruthless, authoritarian, without pity, and fanatically devoted to work in the service of his master – in fact more akin to the type of successful Prussian official in the eighteenth century than to that of the French, at least in the later stages of the Ancien Régime. As has often been pointed out, he neither developed nor had access to anything that can be called an economic theory. His views on how to manage the economy were those long sanctified in the west by conventional wisdom which he attempted to apply on a national scale and to whose application he brought an enormous capacity for work and organizing ability. No modern authority challenges the judgment made on him by Adam Smith, who described him as "a man of probity, of great industry and knowledge of detail, of great experience and acuteness in the examination of public accounts and of abilities, in short, in every way fitted for introducing methods of good order into the collection and expenditure of public revenue".[3] Adam Smith nevertheless went on to say that he was "a laborious and plodding man of business who had been accustomed to regulate the different departments of public offices, and to establish the necessary checks and controls . . . " He assumed that the French economy should be managed after this fashion and that the individual, particularly individual merchants and manufacturers whose activities principally concerned him, were essentially selfish, short-sighted and incapable of promoting the national interest unless directed and controlled by the government.

These assumptions and the actions to which they led were later attacked by the Physiocrats, and after them by Adam Smith, but were less inappropriate to the conditions of France in the reign of Louis XIV and, in an even greater degree, to those in Prussia throughout most of the eighteenth century, than these critics supposed.

As Colbert saw things, the strength of the state depended on its finances, and these on the sums that could be raised in taxes whose collection would be impossible if there were a shortage of bullion to mint into coin.[4] In an age in which credit facilities and the use of paper money were still in their infancy, the government was forced to rely on bullion to pay for most of the services it needed. Neither direct nor indirect taxes could be collected in money, unless the peasants and other producers with commodities to sell could find purchasers who would pay them in money. Taxation, in other words, was dependent on trade, which a shortage of coin frequently brought to a halt.

Above all things to Colbert, and equally to Frederick the Great, it seemed in consequence essential to have a favourable balance of trade as a means to increasing the supply of bullion. Colbert further supposed (not surprisingly in the period of economic stagnation that began in the middle of the seventeenth century and lasted till the end of the first quarter of the eighteenth) that the amount of bullion in Europe and of international trade were more or less fixed quantities, so that one nation's gain was another nation's loss. Economic policy thus involved economic warfare. It was always, if not primarily, directed, by means of tariffs and embargoes, to diminishing the importation of such commodities as seemed inessential or could be produced at home and to increasing exports, and production as a means to exports.

In France though not in Prussia, great opportunities for promoting these objectives were offered by the possibility of establishing trading stations or colonies in America, in the West Indies, in Asia, and in Africa which could supply the western colonies with slaves. For colonies could provide the mother country with a captive market for her manufactured goods, and could produce raw materials, such as sugar and coffee, which could not be grown in Europe and which the mother country could re-export at a profit to other European states.

In France the means used to further these projects commonly stopped short of government ownership but nevertheless involved a high degree of state control over all business activities. Control over these activities was indeed nothing new. It had been exercised by the guilds and other corporate bodies dating from before the days of absolutism. Colbert and his successors, however, extended it and applied it on a national scale.

The government decided what branches of existing trade and manufactures deserved particular encouragement and what new ones it was desirable to establish. It tempted or bribed in foreign workers and entrepreneurs – though on a much smaller scale than in Prussia – who possessed skills which the native population lacked. It rewarded the favoured entrepreneurs, whether native or foreign, with every kind of privilege, particularly subsidies and monopolistic rights. It issued regulations to safeguard the quality of the goods produced, particularly in the luxury industries which, in France as in Prussia, were seen as the most lucrative source of exports; it fixed hours and conditions of work. In France it used the guilds, and indeed increased their number, as a means, together with an army of government inspectors, of ensuring that all these regulations were observed. The edicts relating to manufactures that were issued in France between 1666 and 1730 are said to fill four quarto volumes of 2,200 pages each, plus three supplementary volumes. In his classic work on mercantilism, Heckscher maintained that "an effort of this magnitude in the realm of industrial production could scarcely have been equalled in other periods or countries".[5] C.W.Cole expressed the same opinion in even stronger terms: "From 1683", he wrote, "to the inauguration of the five year plan by the Soviet government in Russia, no conscious and directed effort to develop a nation's industrial life was so prolonged, so thorough, so permeating, so far-reaching as that of Colbert."[6]

Heckscher, however, hardly concerned himself with Prussia and Cole did not do so at all. There can be no doubt that the degree of government control over trade and manufactures in that country was far greater than in France and that the Prussian government, moreover, was always more concerned with agricultural production than Colbert had been.

Colbert was certainly not indifferent to the fate of the peasants. He wished, as he once put it, to secure for them "as much relief as the expenses of the state may permit",[7] to reduce the burden of taxation on them and to make its incidence more equitable. He deplored the practice of selling the peasant's property, including the tools and animals on which he depended for his livelihood, when he failed to pay his taxes. Above all he sought to prevent scarcity and famine by controlling the grain trade.

His policy in all these matters, however, was more negative than positive. He strove to increase trade and manufactures by the methods described, and to educate the business community so that it could compete with the best contemporary models. The idea, however, always present to the minds of the Hohenzollerns, that similar endeavours should be applied to the cultivation of the land, never seems to have occurred to him, nor, had it done so, would he have had the means for putting it into effect.[8]

The degree of success Colbert achieved has long been a matter of debate. The fashionable view among French historians at present seems, like Heckscher's, to be that he achieved virtually no success at all.[9] The obstacles in the way of realizing his vision have often been enumerated and are obvious to hindsight; for the vast apparatus of controls he developed inevitably led to corruption and evasion on a large scale in a country where the bulk of the population was illiterate and where honest and competent officials were hard to find. These abuses, moreover, were greatly increased by the sale of offices which the needs of war demanded. Almost every office concerned with enforcing Colbert's regulations, including the offices in the guilds, was put up for sale, and a traffic in industrial privileges developed which is epitomized in the case of a certain Madame de Rosemain who was imprisoned in the Bastille for engaging in these practices. As Heckscher tells the story,[10] she suggested at her trial "that if all the other people guilty of her offences were put into prison several Bastilles would fail to contain them. The chief of the Paris police then informed the minister concerned that there was hardly a name at court that did not figure on her lists, and he therefore suggested hushing the matter up to avoid too great a scandal."

In the conditions that existed in France in Colbert's day these were inevitable consequences of his system. To say, however, that it achieved virtually no success is to assume that some other system, or the lack of one, would have worked if not better at least no worse – an assumption that is unprovable and indeed dubious; for Colbert established many new industries and new techniques;[11] for better or for worse[12] he brought the French luxury industries to a pitch of perfection unequalled at the time, and established an enduring traditon of excellence; he laid the foundations of an overseas empire and of a merchant navy to meet its needs;[13] he created a formidable royal navy. Most of these enterprises foundered in Louis XIV's wars, but they were resurrected in the eighteenth century and flourished until they were destroyed again, temporarily during the Seven Years War and finally by the revolutionary and Napoleonic wars.

Before the final debacle, however, which annihilated the French empire, the French navy and the French imperial trades after the Revolution, French foreign trade and, though to a smaller extent, French manufactures showed a remarkable increase in the eighteenth century despite the intermittent disasters caused by the wars. In Bordeaux, for example, which had become the largest French port by the end of the Ancien Régime, the value of foreign trade has been estimated by one leading authority, François Crouzet, at twenty times the size it had been at Louis XIV's death.[14] In general, foreign trade is estimated to have increased by 500 per cent in the same period and the colonial trades by double this figure.[15] The rate of growth of industry and manufactures, though less impressive, has been judged more or less comparable to that in England at the time, though it started from a much lower base and showed fewer potentialities for development.[16]

To what extent the government's regulations benefited or impeded the growth of wealth in France in the eighteenth century is a matter of dispute[17] and impossible to estimate. That wealth increased among certain groups in the population – among the successful merchants, slave-owners, manufacturers and financiers as well as among the nobles who married those of their daughters on whom they could bestow large dowries – is indisputable. With the growth of the population, on the other hand, real wages fell.[18] Necker, in the existing circumstances doubtless rightly, assumed it to be impossible that the unskilled worker would ever be able to earn more than enough to keep himself and his family alive, and without the government control of the grain trade not even that.[19]

The wealth, moreover, which the growth of trade and manufactures fostered, did not fertilize the countryside for reasons and with consequences that must be considered later. In spite of the great increase in the rural population, agricultural production by 1789 had only regained the level it had reached at Louis XIV's accession,[20] so that rural poverty, so far from diminishing, increased. Finally, in spite of her economic achievements, France's international status continuously declined throughout the eighteenth century because her ambitions to establish an empire superior to that of the British, as well as to remain the dominant power in Europe, were greater than the resources available to her government could meet.

The responsibility for this, however, cannot be ascribed to Colbert's system, for neither he nor his successors were ever securely, if at all, in control of policy. The French government frequently pursued policies and engaged in practices which Colbert condemned, so that it is not possible to disentangle the results of his endeavours from those of the misguided foreign adventures, and the financial maladministration with its ramifying consequences, which formed the framework within which his system had to operate.

The fact nevertheless remains that while this system lasted, it produced, after the first few years of its ascendancy, neither of the conditions it was designed to fulfil, since French power diminished internationally, and except among the fortunate minority where the increases were sometimes spectacular, prosperity in the sense of consumption per head also declined.

The policy of stimulating the growth of trade and industry which was pursued by the eighteenth-century Hohenzollerns with the same objectives as Colbert's began in very different circumstances. Conditions in Prussia at the accession of Frederick William I – the first Hohenzollern to pursue systematically the task of increasing wealth – were primitive beyond comparison with any that existed in the west; for the Thirty Years War, together with the famines and epidemics that accompanied and succeeded it, had reduced the population by huge proportions, which cannot be exactly estimated but which in the Hohenzollern dominions east of the Elbe may have amounted to between 60 and 70 per cent.[21] Not only were great stretches of the countryside laid waste; many towns were largely destroyed together with the skills they had fostered; for these were handed down from father to son and vanished with the generations that had acquired them. Magdeburg, for example, which had had between 20,000 and 26,000 inhabitants in 1618, had only 2,464 in 1644 – a number which had risen to 8,000 after nearly half a century but even by 1745 was slightly below the level reached before the Thirty Years War started.[22] The town of Brandenburg which had had 1,144 houses in 1618 had only 527 in 1648; Frankfurt on the Oder had had 13,000 inhabitants in 1618 but only just over 2,000 in 1653.[23] Famine and epidemics, moreover, continued to take their toll long after the

Thirty Years War had come to an end. Over one-third of the population of East Prussia died from them in 1709 to 1710.[24] Even in 1700, before this calamity, the number of inhabitants per square kilometer in the Hohenzollern dominions east of the Elbe amounted to only about 38 per cent of those in France,[25] herself at this time the victim of widespread famine and epidemics.

Not only the capital and the techniques necessary to overcome the disasters in Prussia were lacking but also, and more significantly, the psychological prerequisites. Misery on the scale experienced had destroyed in the bulk of the population all desire except that of keeping alive by the simplest means that presented themselves, frequently by robbery, or by begging which for many had become a regular way of life.

It was to finding a cure for these conditions that Frederick William I applied himself under the inspiration of the Pietists and that his son did so after him though without his religious motives. To Colbert, moved by the example of the Dutch, the principal need had seemed to be to increase trade, and particularly international trade, with the aid of a colonial empire, "it being certain both by common sense and natural reasoning, and by the experience of our neighbours", as Louis XIV once put it at Colbert's instigation, "that the profit infinitely exceeds the toil and trouble that is necessary to penetrate to countries so distant."[26] The possibility of access to this source of wealth was, however, closed to the Prussians, to whom in consequence the problems of economic policy presented themselves somewhat differently.

To Frederick the Great, who had studied the writings of Colbertists in his youth, a favourable balance of trade seemed a vital necessity. He wished, as did Colbert, to make his country as far as possible self-sufficient in all the necessities for life and war with a surplus of commodities for export. In pursuit of these objectives, however, an increase in the volume of foreign trade always seemed to him less important than an increase in production, including agricultural production to which Colbert had been relatively indifferent. In consequence he always rated the manufacturer higher than the merchant who was not also a producer, because manufactures gave employment to larger numbers than did trade. Like his father he wished to set his people to work, to teach them new skills and to educate them in, as he said, "moral habits"[27] – that is, in the virtues of thrift and industry.

Long before his accession, at the end of the seventeenth century, Louis XIV's miguided religious policies had greatly aided these endeavours. The number of Huguenots who emigrated from France as a result of Louis' persecution is uncertain. According to a careful estimate made in 1952 it was probably about 200,000, of whom some 30,000 went to Germany and two-thirds of these to Prussia. By the end of the century the Huguenots formed about 16 per cent of the population of the Hohenzollern dominions, and since they included a large number of artisans an even higher proportion of the population of Berlin.[28]

Among the Huguenots were the richest and most industrious artisans in France, but the emigrants came from every walk of life and included nobles and peasants as well as urban workers. They brought with them a great variety of skills – military, industrial, agricultural and intellectual – as well as those attitudes towards work, discipline and self-improvement which the Thirty Years War had largely destroyed in Prussia. It cannot have been without significance that Frederick William I was brought up by a Huguenot tutor, with whom his relations were far from happy, and who does not appear to have got any kind of academic knowledge into his head, but who is nevertheless said to have imbued him with a belief in cleanliness and sobriety and the Calvinists' harsh dedication to a life of work devoid of all those pleasures of the intellect and the senses for which the French court was famous,[29] and which most German princes, his own father included, aspired to cultivate.

One of Frederick William I's first acts on his accession was to abolish the luxury industries in Berlin which had catered for the court and to replace them by the notorious *Lagerhaus,* an institution whose principal purpose was to combine the manufacture of uniforms for the army with work for the population of Berlin. The money to found the *Lagerhaus* was originally put up – more or less under compulsion – by the court financier Andreas Kraut, but it was taken over by the government in 1724 and became, in the words of its principal historian, "more or less of a state socialist organization"[30] and the largest supplier of cloth in the country. The demands of the army may well have equalled if not exceeded all the other demands combined, for the officers and men received new uniforms every year and the population in the countryside, if not in the towns, was dressed in its cast-offs.[31] The *Lagerhaus* controlled wages by paying more than private employers could afford, and recouped itself by charging the members of the court and other civilian consumers the prices it chose. It unloaded its defective products onto the Jews in the Neumark who were forced to accept them under pain of expulsion. By the standards that became fashionable three-quarters of a century later it was a highly inefficient organization.[32] It was nevertheless characteristic of the methods of promoting industrial growth which the eighteenth-century Hohenzollerns pursued with the ambivalent results that must be considered presently.

Frederick the Great was determined to promote manufactures to the greatest extent compatible with his other aims. Entrepreneurs found in him a natural ally as long as – but only as long as – they were able to carry out his policies successfully. Like Colbert, he was prepared to grant them every kind of privilege, including providing them with the necessary labour.

Like his ancestors, though on a larger scale, he encouraged every foreigner likely to be useful to emigrate to his dominions. Prussian embassies abroad became, in effect, labour exchanges.[33] Transit camps were set up in Hamburg and Frankfurt on the Main in which immigrants were collected and dispatched to the destinations allocated to them by the government, which kept lists of the employers, in the towns and the country, who were in need of labour, and of the qualifications of the applicants.

Though sometimes, as in the case of Saxons when Saxony was occupied during the Seven Years War, the immigrants, like many of the mercenaries in the Prussian army, were brought in by force, commonly they came of their own free will and often with money of their own. To a greater or less extent, however, all were subsidized by the government, which offered them many privileges – money, for example, to discharge debts they had contracted in their country of origin or to pay the officials there for permission to leave; money for the journey; free lodging in the towns until work was allocated to them; timber to build a house, implements, seed and animals if they were established in the country; above all tax-exemptions and freedom from military service for varying periods up to three generations. Altogether, it has been estimated, 250,000 immigrants were settled in Prussia – though at a cost of vast and unforeseen difficulties and hardships[34] – between the end of the Seven Years War, when the total population amounted to approximately four million, and the death of Frederick the Great.

The government also saw to it, by means involving greater or lesser degrees of compulsion, that the entrepreneurs were provided with the necessary supplies of native labour. Workers were procured from the orphanages, the workhouses, even the prisons and, except in war, from the huge numbers of soldiers and their wives and children; for the soldier could not live from the half-pay he received in peace and was therefore forced, while remaining subject to military discipline, to work in the fields or the factories. Since the size of the Prussian standing army at Frederick the Great's death is commonly reckoned at about 171,000,[35] if one were to allow three to four people capable of work to a family, the military contribution to the labour force must have been of an order of between half to three-quarters of a million.

During the period of economic stringency that followed the Seven Years War the government was unable to find entrepreneurs of a type and with the capital that seemed necessary, and took over an increasing number of industries itself – the steel and iron industry in Eberswald, the clock and china manufactures in Berlin, the paperworks in Speckshausen and many others.[36] It also established many trading monopolies under its own control – notably the tobacco monopoly, the coffee monopoly, the timber monopoly, the state bank, the *Seehandlung.*[37]

Pressed as it was after 1763 to do what it could to repair the colossal amount of war damage, while at the same time maintaining the army in the same proportion to the population as previously, the government engaged in many of these enterprises primarily in order to raise money at the consumers' expense. The government's revenue, it has been estimated, was three times larger at Frederick's death than it had been at his accession,[38] partly because of higher yields from the royal domains but partly because of the profits of the state monopolies and increases in the rates of indirect taxation.

The taxes and the monopolies increasingly exasperated the business communities which, though impotent politically, influenced the officials who came into contact with them. In 1766, for example, a member of the General Directory, by the name of Ursinus, who had had considerable dealings with the business world, was deputed to draw up a report on the economy, then in a state of crisis. He seized the occasion to point out what seemed to him the errors of the government's policy. Particularly he criticized the tariffs which the government – in an attempt to control the trades of central and eastern Europe and between these areas and the west – placed on foreign goods passing along the Oder and along those stretches of the Elbe which it controlled. He pointed out that the government monopolies were doing the public the greatest damage by forcing it to pay exorbitant prices and were impeding the growth of commerce and manufactures.

Frederick the Great wrote in his own hand in the margin of this memorandum that he was amazed at its impertinence. "The malice and corruption of its author", he said, "deserve exemplary punishment, otherwise I shall never bring this scum [*Canaille*, i.e. the ministers of the General Directory] into a proper degree of subordination." In consequence Ursinus was put into prison, ostensibly on a charge of bribery.[39]

Though Frederick always emphasized that he wished to rule over a prosperous people, when faced with the choice between increasing wealth and maintaining the conditions he saw as necessary to security, he never hesitated. His reactions to Ursinus' criticism were comparable to those which the protests of Hamburg evoked from him three years later. At this time Hamburg was the principal entrepôt for French colonial products which Hamburg merchants distributed to central and eastern Europe. The Hamburg government complained bitterly of the obstacles which the Prussian government placed on its transit trade. These were obstacles, it said, from which it not only suffered itself, but which harmed the Prussians equally. Advocates of the virtues of free trade before Adam Smith had proclaimed them, the Hamburgers argued, among other points, that in order to enforce their tariffs the Prussians were obliged to employ thousands of customs officials who might otherwise have been engaged in productive work; that their policies discouraged from entering the country foreigners who would otherwise have bought Prussian commodities, and that, in general, the extent of a country's favourable balance of trade was no indication of its prosperity.[40] The Prussians replied to these harangues that the Hamburgers' assertions would doubtless be true if the only point at issue were "the welfare of the whole human race"; no state, however, could be expected to sacrifice itself for such a cause. They could not, they said, abandon their policies without jeopardizing their principal sources of revenue, the employment of their people and the means by which they maintained their position as the most important military state.[41]

In this argument it is plain that the two sides started from different assumptions about the principal tasks of government – assumptions whose validity is not a matter of fact but of opinion. For this reason, among others, the balance-sheet of Frederick's successes and failures in his attempt to promote power and plenty is hard to draw up and has been drawn up very differently by different writers at different times.

Since the end of the Second World War it has become fashionable to point to the many mistakes and misapprehensions of which he was plainly guilty in the matters here under discussion, as well as in others. Though he was capable, for example, of choosing and supporting men of ability, energy and integrity, he can hardly be said in general to have been a good judge of character and was often taken in by charlatans. As Christian Garve, who knew him well, remarked in a work which he wrote in 1798 and called "Fragments relating to the spirit, the character and the government of Frederick the Great",[42] Frederick always wanted things done in a hurry, and at minimum cost. He was unable to distinguish between dishonesty and genuine mistakes and was impressed by people who put forward grandiose ideas with confidence. He combined ignorance with suspicion – the best recipe, in Garve's view, for being cheated.

That Frederick was often cheated is beyond dispute. For this and other reasons many of his enterprises failed in the shorter or the longer term.[43] His attempts, for example, to foster the production of luxury commodities for export were unsuccessful because the Prussians could not compete in this sphere with the more sophisticated foreigners, and Prussian musical clocks, china and brocades could not find sufficient purchasers either at home or abroad.

On the other hand, production in general increased greatly in his reign, principally in the textile industries of wool, linen, cotton and silk, though the last foundered after his death. He nursed a body of skilled workers into existence which, though very small by modern standards, was far from insignificant by the standards of his day. According to one eminent modern authority the Hohenzollern dominions contained 165,000 skilled workers in 1786[44] – a figure not incompatible with the conclusions of one of Frederick's principal ministers, Ewald von Herzberg, who, reckoning at a conservative estimate four persons to a family, maintained that Prussian manufactures in the last years of Frederick's life were providing subsistence for between 8 and 9 per cent of the population.[45] As a manufacturing nation, von Herzberg said, the dominions of the Prussian monarchy came perhaps "immediately after France, England and Holland, those countries which for two centuries have had the almost exclusive monopoly of manufactures, commerce and navigation while the Prussians only began to play a part in them at the end of the last century and the beginning of this one".[46]

Before the end of his life and increasingly after his death, Frederick's principles and practices came into disrepute for a variety of reasons – partly for those already described, partly because of the example of Britain, the most successful of the European states in terms of both power and wealth, where economic life was least subject to government control, partly because of Adam Smith's formulation of an economic theory which condemned all the presuppositions on which Frederick's policy was based and revolutionized thinking, particularly in Prussia, to an extent achieved by no other economist before Marx in the present century.

The writings of the Physiocrats, who started the attacks on the dirigiste policies of absolutism, did not excite much enthusiasm in Prussia but those of Adam Smith did. As Alexander von der Marwitz, the younger and cleverer brother of the more famous Karl August Ludwig, wrote to Rachel Varnhagen in 1811 – after having with much uncongenial labour made the experiment himself – it was essential to study Adam Smith seriously "because next to Napoleon he is now the most powerful monarch in Europe".[47]

This (though Alexander personally found Adam Smith detestable) was the view of a new age. Judged by the standards of Colbert which he himself, broadly speaking, had accepted, Frederick, by comparison with Louis XIV and his successors, had been highly successful in his attempt to hold the balance between power and plenty. To quote his own words, he had raised Prussia "out of the dust", both militarily and economically. That he did so is beyond dispute whatever judgments may be made on the cost of the achievement and the consequences for Germany and Europe that followed from it.

(c) AGRICULTURE AND THE ATTEMPTS AT REFORM

(1) *The French experience*

The French peasants, it was said earlier, are commonly believed to have owned about 30 per cent of the land of France, though ownership is not a term which can properly be applied to the conditions on which they held it and which subjected them to the payment, in money, kind or services, of a great variety of feudal dues. Ownership today would not be thought compatible with being the "vassal" (to use the eighteenth-century term) of a seigneur who had the right to hunt over one's property, who could require one to bake one's bread in his oven and grind one's corn in his mill, and who, if one sold the property, could claim up to 16 per cent of its value and, if he wished, buy it back from the purchaser whether or not the latter was willing to part with it.[1] Many provisions, in fact, restricted the way in which the peasant could use and dispose of his land, but subject to these he could leave, sell, bequeath or mortgage it as he wished. He was not *adscriptus glebae*, or tied to the soil as were many peasants in eastern and east-central Europe, and for this reason the French, and the English, who have followed them, have commonly called him a free man, although the peasants in Germany in a comparable position are described by German historians as serfs.

The French peasants are believed to have constituted some 85 per cent[2] of the population, but since they "owned" less than a third of the cultivated land, very few, and an increasingly smaller number as the population increased, owned enough to support a family. A considerable proportion, though one that varied greatly from area to area, owned no land at all.[3] Whether landless, however, or owning enough, or more than enough, from which to live, or in some position between these two extremes, they not only cultivated virtually all the land of France that had been brought under cultivation; they were responsible, in the greater part of the country, for the way in which the land was cultivated.

In the French seigneuries (and the proverb *nulle terre sans seigneur* still broadly corresponded to the facts), the property was commonly divided into two parts. One part, known as the *domaine utile* or *mouvance*, consisted of land which the peasant was said to own where the rights of the seigneur were confined to the exaction of feudal dues. In the other part, known as the *domaine proche*, the land, except for such portions of it (for example, the gardens) as the seigneur reserved for his own use, was let out on various terms – sometimes to tenants in return for rent in money or kind, but most commonly to *métayers*, or share-croppers. Two-thirds or more of the cultivated land of France is said to have been worked by share-cropping[4] – a system whereby the landlord and the tenant shared the produce between them by means of a bargain which took a variety of different forms, but under which, without any transactions in money, the share-cropper did the work and the landlord provided a varying proportion of the buildings, animals, implements and seed.[5] This system, in the form it assumed in eighteenth-century France, was universally condemned by contemporaries with any knowledge of the requirements of efficient agriculture, notably Arthur Young, Turgot and Lavoisier. Arthur Young described it as a "miserable system that perpetuates poverty and excludes instruction".[6] Turgot inveighed against it at length, maintaining that it gave the landlord no control over the share-cropper who, "accustomed to the most miserable kind of life, has neither the hope nor the desire of a better one", and who farmed inefficiently for this reason and also because, "if his harvest fails, the landlord will be obliged to feed him for fear of seeing his land abandoned."[7]

One of the consequences of the arrangements between landlord and tenant in France was that a large part of the land was cultivated in small or very small units. Large farms, as is well known, were relatively rare, except in certain areas of northern France.[8] This was true even, indeed if one may believe Robert Forster particularly, on the large estates, of which, though with some exaggeration, he saw the estate of the Duc de Saulx-Tavanes as typical, and which he described in detail.[9] This Duke, besides property in Normandy, owned over 8,000 acres in Burgundy, in addition to the 20,000 acres in his *mouvance* from which he collected feudal dues. Of these 8,000 acres some 5,000 were woodland, but the rest consisted of meadows and arable land which the Duke let out in plots that were rarely larger than fifteen acres and were commonly less than one.

The kinds of people responsible for cultivating the land in France, and the terms on which they did so, were in fact *sui generis* among the major

European countries. Except in the neighbourhood of Paris, and in parts of Normandy and Flanders, there was in France no equivalent to the prosperous English tenant farmer who worked up to several hundred acres with paid labour, or to the yeomen and gentlemen owner-occupiers who did the same. Nor was there any equivalent to the *Gutsherrschaft* and *geschlossene Dörfer*, which prevailed in the Hohenzollern dominions east of the Elbe and in other parts of eastern and east-central Europe.

In France, for the greater part, the land was cultivated by the uninstructed, unsupervised labour of illiterate, poverty-stricken peasants. Much of the agriculture was subsistence agriculture. Of the land which the peasants were said to own, for example, less than 15 per cent produced for the market.[10] A high proportion of the peasantry, in Quesnay's words, "sell nothing . . . buy nothing and are of no use to other men . . . they are occupied solely in providing, miserably and with difficulty, for their own needs".[11]

The poverty of the bulk of the French peasantry in the century before the Revolution has been a byword from Louis XIV's day onwards among contemporaries and historians of later ages, although both have commonly assumed that the French peasant was better off than his counterparts in eastern and central Europe. Poverty and prosperity are, however, relative terms whose meaning changes from age to age, from place to place and from group to group.

It is not possible to demonstrate statistically the extent and degree of peasant poverty in eighteenth-century France. Enough information, however, has been provided by knowledgeable contemporary observers and by students in later ages to give us a good idea of the answer to these questions.

The subject was one to which Arthur Young, accepted by the French in the 1790s as the best authority on the subject,[12] continually recurred in the notes which he made during his travels in France between 1786 and 1790. Though he admitted that in various parts of the country he had found many peasants in comfortable circumstances and some who were reputed rich, in general his descriptions were catalogues of misery. In the Dordogne, for example, he noted that "all the country girls and women are without shoes or stockings and the ploughmen at their work have neither sabots nor stockings to their feet. This is a poverty that strikes at the roots of national prosperity".[13] On numbers of other occasions he found "the husbandry poor and the people miserable" or in "the lowest poverty". "An Englishman who has not travelled", he wrote in July 1789, "cannot imagine the figure made by infinitely the greater part of the countrywomen in France; it speaks at the first sight [of] hard and severe labour. I am inclined to think that they work harder than the men, and this united with the more miserable labour of bringing a new race of slaves into the world, destroys absolutely all symmetry of person and every feminine appearance. To what are we to attribute this difference in the manners of the lower people in the two kingdoms?" (i.e., England and France). Arthur Young answered this question in one word, which he wrote in capital letters – GOVERNMENT.

A similar picture, though a more sombre one because it emerges from official documents with less rhetoric and more precise facts than Arthur Young provided, appears in the memoranda which Turgot wrote when he was *intendant* in the Limousin. The Limousin, it is true, was a poor province, though not markedly more so, in Turgot's view, than the other parts of France where share-cropping prevailed.

Turgot described the peasants in this province as living in an "excès de la misère", or, as he put it on another occasion, "au dernier degré de la misère" – a misery which he measured by calculating that after the payment of their dues and taxes the peasants were left, at the most, with 25 to 30 livres per head per annum (say just over £1 sterling at the current rate of exchange). Often they did not have that much. Turgot was careful to add that when he spoke of 25 to 30 livres he did not mean this amount in money, for the peasant frequently had no money except what he got from the sale of his produce to pay his state taxes. Turgot meant the value, reckoned in money, of the individual peasant's total consumption supposing he were fortunate enough to consume this much, which was often not the case.[14] When, Turgot pointed out, the share-cropper was unable to keep himself alive the landlord was forced to help him if he wished his land to be cultivated. In fact the landlord who, if a noble, was in the greater part of France immune from the *taille*,[15] was forced to contribute to, if not to assume the whole burden of, the share-cropper's quota. In Turgot's experience, however, the landlord who was himself usually in financial difficulties, did not extend his help beyond the point necessary to prevent the share-cropper from dying of hunger.[16]

This judgment on the misery in which the bulk of the French peasants lived is confirmed by other contemporaries as able and meticulous as Turgot and with an experience equal if not superior to his. Lavoisier, for example, who had an estate in the Orléanais, wrote, in the course of describing his experiments there, that if one were concerned with improving the "languishing agriculture such as exists in the greater part of the French provinces", what was most distressing was "that there remained at the end of the year practically nothing to the unfortunate cultivator, who thought himself lucky if he could lead a miserable, squalid existence".[17]

The social and political, as distinct from the purely humanitarian, aspects of this state of affairs were never fully realized in France until after the middle of the eighteenth century, and only then because, as the Marquis de Mirabeau said, England's "splendour"[18] – her rise as an imperial power and the wealth of her upper classes – seemed attributable to her (by continental standards) remarkably flourishing agriculture; for it was from the 1760s onwards that the so-called English agricultural revolution – in fact more a cumulative process of evolution than a revolution – first dawned on the consciousness of the other major countries of Europe.

The nature of this revolution has been the subject of many books and cannot be discussed in detail here. Its essential feature is often held to have been the introduction of enclosures – the creation, that is, of the farm in individual ownership and the abandonment of the communal system of agriculture. Under this system in France all the members of the village community, the seigneur included, held their land in strips in the open fields and were subject to what came to be known as the *"servitudes collectives"* – a collective bondage which required everyone, in accordance with the decisions of the village assembly, to plough, sow and harvest the same crops at the same time. The beasts of the village were also pastured in common – on the uncultivated common lands, in the woods, on the stubble fields after the harvest and on the meadows after the hay had been cut. Needless to say, these arrangements caused any disease among animals to develop like wildfire into epidemics universal throughout the neighbourhood. They also had the result, to quote the words of one of their eloquent modern defenders, who prized the community spirit which he maintained they engendered, that "one did not tolerate without recrimination" any man-ifestation of individual initiative.[19]

Enclosures facilitated individual initiative, though without the necessary degree of enterprise, skill and capital they could produce results that were no better and might even be worse than those yielded by the old form of agriculture. As Arthur Young observed, "The marvellous folly is that in nine-tenths of all the enclosures of France the system of management is precisely the same as in the open fields . . . Sologne is enclosed yet it is the most miserable province in France."[20]

It was not in fact the enclosures as such which were the clue to the success of English agriculture. They were vital (although on occasion the improvements could occur without them) because of the scope they afforded to experiment and better management, and to changes of which the most significant was the abandonment of the fallow, or rather the introduction of convertible agriculture which made the fallow unnecessary.

Under the old system the greater part of the cultivated land was devoted to grain production – France, Lavoisier once observed, could for the greater part be considered *"une grande fabrique de blé "* – a large grain factory. Since grain, however, exhausts the soil more than any other crop, the method adopted to mitigate this misfortune was to leave one out of every two or one out of every three fields fallow. The result was a shortage of pasture, and hence of animals, and hence of manure, for lack of which the yield of the acreage under grain diminished.

Very large quantities of grain were needed because bread was the staple diet of the bulk of the population – a state of affairs that was exacerbated by the lack of other forms of food, unobtainable because of the amount of land which the cultivation of grain demanded for the reasons described. It was these conditions which the French called "le cercle vicieux de la jachère" – the vicious circle of the fallow land.

At the end of the Middle Ages the English had begun to find a way out of it which they followed at a markedly increasing pace in the eighteenth century. They created artificial meadows; on the fallow they planted crops such as clover, lucerne and the proverbial turnip. These fertilized the soil and yielded heavy crops which provided feed for the animals in the winter. The animals in consequence increased in numbers and quality and provided more manure.

In England the eighteenth century, and particularly its second half, was the great age of enclosures, though the movement had started much earlier. The suffering which it was long supposed to have caused by driving small farmers and cottagers off the land has turned out to be almost entirely a myth,[21] for though the numbers of poor grew in England as elsewhere this was not because of a fall in the opportunities for work on the land – which enclosures in fact increased – but because of a rise in population greater than either the land or the growing industries could support.

The benefits which the improved agriculture conferred on the English nation and on its successful farmers and landowners were a source of amazed admiration in other countries. Large amounts of hitherto unculti-vated land in England were brought under cultivation, not only because of the abolition of the fallow but by the enclosure of common and waste. The yield per acre under grain increased by 10 per cent.[22] Whereas in France there was commonly a yield of four or five to one of seed, in England the yield rose to ten to one.[23] In France Necker estimated that the net return on capital invested in an estate was only 2½ per cent unless the owner were prepared to give assiduous attention to his property;[24] Lavoisier maintained that even if he did so he could not expect as much as 5 per cent.[25] In England, by contrast, the return appears to have been very much larger.[26] The Duc de Saulx-Tavanes, for all his 8,000 acres in Burgundy, and his feudal dues from 20,000 more, had a gross income in 1788 equivalent to less than £5,000 sterling p.a.[27] By English ducal standards he was a poor man. How, the French and equally the Prussians asked, had the British achieved their agricultural miracle?

The most famous group of French thinkers to devote themselves to this question were the Physiocrats, the founders of the science of economics, of whom Adam Smith said that "their system with all its imperfections is perhaps the nearest approximation to the truth that has yet been published".[28] The founders of this school, or "sect" as their contemporaries called it, were that strangely-assorted couple, François Quesnay and the Marquis de Mirabeau, known from the title of one of his books as "l'ami des hommes" and the father of the Mirabeau of revolutionary fame. Quesnay, the dominating intellect, was the son of what then counted as a prosperous peasant family. He managed to get himself educated, became doctor to Madame de Pompadour and ended his life as a noble with several seigneuries. Mirabeau was an impecunious provincial country gentleman filled with hatred of the state, its financial practices and their consequences – its taxes, its sale of offices and noble status, and its financiers. He cherished an idealized vision of the feudal past, which had existed before the emergence of absolutism. Notwithstanding the difference in their outlook (for Quesnay put his faith in enlightened despotism), these two invented the model of a capitalist economy which they assumed would be compatible with the continued existence of the société d'ordres.[29]

The Physiocrats' basic concept was that of the *"produit net"* which may, very broadly, be interpreted as follows: the productivity of the land, they said, depends to a large extent on the capital that is sunk in it. As Turgot once put it: "It is only by heavy investment that the land can be made to yield its richest products and provide a large income."[30] Farm implements and animals, to cite the most obvious examples, must be bought in sufficient quantities; farm buildings must be erected and kept in repair; a proportion of the harvest must be set aside to provide seed for the next harvest; if the landowner or tenant farmer employs labour on the land, the labourers must be paid a wage sufficient to enable them to live and bring up a family.[31] In any given year when these and all other necessary expenses have been met from the gross yield of the land, what remains is the *produit net*. The *produit net* in the Physiocrats' view of things was the sum which was available to the crown and the landowners to spend as they saw fit.

The Physiocrats, in other words, were not revolutionaries who wished to deprive the possessing classes of their wealth. On the contrary, their object was to open the eyes of the possessing classes to their real interests, which they saw as indissolubly linked with those of the peasants – as Quesnay once put it in one of his "Maximes Générales" and wrote in large capital letters: "POOR PEASANTS, A POOR KINGDOM".[32] The burden of their argument was that the government and the possessing classes were killing the goose that laid the golden eggs because they took from the land *more* than the *produit net*.

Far too much, the Physiocrats maintained, was being squeezed out of the peasants in taxes; far too little was being ploughed back into the land by people with money to invest. As a result the yield of the land must diminish and the peasant be plunged more and more deeply into a poverty from which there was no means of escape. This, the Physiocrats said prophetically, was a suicidal way of proceeding which must ultimately lead the whole nation to disaster unless those in authority could be brought to see the folly of their ways.

In general the economic theory of the Physiocrats is irrelevant to the present discussion, which can be concerned only with the impetus it gave to the projects for agricultural reform – projects that became a major preoccupation in government and intellectual circles in the second half of the eighteenth century.

The Physiocrats held many ideas on this subject which were open to debate, which were impracticable in the existing circumstances, and of which some were even absurd and widely seen to be so.[33] When they stressed, however, that the poverty of French agriculture was a result of lack of investment, they expressed an indisputable truth that was widely recognized.

Arthur Young, confident, as he said, "that I have not been guilty of the least exaggeration", maintained that the amount of capital invested on an average per acre in England was more than three times that invested in France.[34] Lavoisier, independently and a year or so earlier, had reached approximately the same conclusion.[35]

As Quesnay always insisted, agricultural improvement, if it were to occur at all, must come from the initiative of people of some substance. "One needs", he said, "wealth in order to produce wealth. A farmer whose fortune has been destroyed by hail, or by the loss of his animals from disease, or by taxes or for other reasons, cannot afford the expense which agriculture requires ... the poverty into which he has fallen necessarily keeps him in poverty, without the means to exercise his profession or to establish his children."[36]

To Quesnay as to many others, including Necker who was not a Physiocrat,[37] the widespread poverty in the French countryside was principally due to the weight and arbitrariness of the state taxes. "In the conditions of uncertainty, in which the arbitrary *taille* keeps the peasant", Quesnay asserted, "he can hope for nothing from his work. He does not even dare to work for fear that the gain which it will be supposed he will derive from it will subject him to increased taxes.... Given the existing arbitrariness every peasant ... will be sure that if he increases his production he will draw on himself an inordinate surcharge ... which will ruin him."[38]

At the same time, however, Quesnay stressed, as did Turgot, the psychological attitudes inimical to change which poverty and suspicion bred among their victims. "The ignorance of this section of society", Turgot said when speaking of the mass of the poverty-stricken, "its habit of living from day to day without thought of the future; the indifference and kind of apathy of these men in whom continual misery has almost extinguished desire by removing from them even the idea of a better life; the sort of vague mistrust of a people which fears everything because it understands nothing; which does not imagine one can confer on it a benefit which it has never envisaged, and which has become incredulous as a result of having been deceived – what obstacles will the best thought-out project not find in the crude mentality of this class of men? And [by] what means [can one] overcome them? And what if success depends on the cooperation of these same men?"[39]

To some extent it plainly did. There were, for example, many occasions when peasants who saw their communal rights menaced by landlords' attempts to enclose their meadows banded together, sometimes under the leadership of local officials and even of local seigneurs, to pull the fences down.[40]

But peasant opposition (in any case before the Revolution never unanimous, for the interests of the "laboureur" – the peasant with a substantial amount of land and animals to cultivate it – differed widely from those of the "manouvrier" who had neither) was by no means the only obstacle to reform. The most formidable obstacles may well have been those which Lavoisier encountered on the estate which he bought in 1778 between Blois and Vendôme.

Lavoisier, who as a tax-farmer was executed under the Terror, was a man of outstanding intellect, who laid the foundations of modern chemistry and has been acclaimed one of the greatest scientists of his century. But he was also a man of practical interests and ability, who devoted ten years to modernizing his property. He set out his experiences, as a preliminary to writing a book on the subject, in a lecture which he gave in 1788 to the Paris Society of Agriculture,[41] and he preached the same gospel on many other occasions.

Like the other French agronomists he stressed the need for investment. "No capital, no animals," he said, "no animals, no manure; no manure, no harvest";[42] but he did not suppose this was all that was required. "When, he wrote, "one has not brought oneself to reflect on these matters, when one has not observed work on the land at first hand, nothing seems easier than to restore a failing agriculture, and one persuades oneself that all one needs is animals and money." This, he discovered, was not so. One needed knowledge, experience, an open mind, a capacity to work, to observe precisely, to learn by trial and error and to keep accurate records. All these attributes, he noted, were wholly lacking among the landowners in his district, and the failure to develop them, there and elsewhere, was encouraged by other and easier ways of making money.

In England more could be learned from successful farming than from investing in government stock. In France, because of its perpetual financial difficulties, the government in the second half of the eighteenth century was forced to borrow at much higher rates of interest than those the British government offered and to engage in operations which permitted ingenious speculators to realize enormous profits.[43] People with money to invest preferred this kind of investment, from which if they were fortunate they could get much larger returns, than any attempt to reform the agriculture on their estates would have yielded them, even in the best of circumstances, and even after decades of effort.[44] Taking all these circumstances into account, Lavoisier concluded that the process of agricultural reform must necessarily be slow because it involved overcoming prejudices "which a long interval of time alone can destroy".

Prejudices of one sort or another, but all of them hostile to change, filled the heads of the greater part of the population from the poorer peasants at the bottom of the social scale to the richer noble landowners at the top, who, whether or not they were as misguided as the Duc de Saulx-Tavanes, who refused to spend a sou on his estates except for unavoidable repairs, were essentially traditionalists. Land, and particularly a seigneurie with its rights to feudal dues, was for them primarily a source of prestige, from which they naturally wished to draw as large an income as they could, though only by conventional methods. A willingness to take risks and a commercial spirit, widely prevalent in England, were, if we may believe Arthur Young and many American historians writing today, largely absent in France.

Arthur Young, as was shown earlier, attributed the generally miserable condition of French agriculture to the institutions of government, and this was a common view for which there is much to be said. The extreme arbitrariness of the taxation (due partly to the fact that the taxes were too heavy given the inadequate means of assessing and collecting them)[45] was plainly a disincentive; so was the *dîme* or tithe, which was payable in kind by all landowners, whether nobles or commoners, to the church, or in certain cases (the so-called *dîme enféodée*) to the seigneur. This was reckoned by some to be the heaviest of the burdens on the land,[46] and Arthur Young maintained that it would have prevented an agricultural revolution in England had it existed there in the same form.[47] The feudal dues were an obstacle to reform in the cases of both the seigneur and the vassal,[48] and were often a heavy burden on the latter, though they varied so greatly from district to district and even from seigneurie to seigneurie that there is no means of estimating their average yield to the seigneur, or their cost to the peasant, not to mention the impossibility of measuring many of them in money terms[49]. Remove all these disincentives to enterprise and change, it was argued, and agriculture would flourish in France as it did in England. The judgment, however, is not justified by the facts; for when the Revolution removed these particular disincentives the increase in agricultural production proceeded at a snail's pace, even if with less serious economic consequences than used to be supposed;[50] for it is easier to destroy institutions than the ways of behaving which have both caused and been fostered by them.

It would be not only fruitless to speculate on what steps the French government might have taken in the second half of the eighteenth century to mitigate agricultural poverty and distress; it is difficult even to imagine them, so deeply was the greater part of every section of society imbued with suspicion of change and with the desire to preserve such practices hallowed by custom as it hoped to manipulate to its own benefit. Though there were landowners, for example, anxious to enclose their meadows and thus protect them from the depredations of the beasts of other villagers, there were also landowners who wished to preserve the existing conditions. These were seigneurs with herds of animals and more or less unlimited customary grazing rights in their own and other villages.[51] Though the richer peasants generally were in favour of enclosing the commons, the poorer ones were not, and were always hostile to any attempts to curtail their rights of pasture on the stubble fields after the harvest and thus to the enclosure of the arable land. This in any case presented peculiar difficulties because the strips in the open fields were usually only accessible by traversing other strips, so that attempts at enclosure promoted innumerable disputes and lawsuits.[52] There was, in fact, no projected reform that did not raise opposition from some quarter and that some local authority was not prepared to support.

The obstacles to reform, as Marc Bloch pointed out, were not the legendary consequence of a class struggle between a rich and greedy nobility and a poverty-stricken peasantry. Such a belief, as Marc Bloch put it, and as has already been shown, attributes to the nobility "a class consciousness it was far from possessing",[53] and the same could be said of the peasantry. Life in the countryside in France in the second half of the eighteenth century seems to have been often if not commonly a more or less continuous state of war, much as Balzac later described it in *Les Paysans*, between a variety of hostile groups that fought each other within as well as across the legal boundaries that separated the estates.

Within the government itself there were many ministers and officials passionately convinced of the need for reform who did their best to promote it. But they had to contend not only with the difficulties already described but with a type of government calculated to frustrate the formulation of any long-term policy, and an administrative structure that made it extremely difficult to carry out any agreed policy at all.

Ministers came and went in accordance with the royal whims and the cliques at court that inspired them, and had no provincial officials at their command who could exercise an undisputed authority. The only provincial officials who had not bought their offices and were therefore directly under the royal control were the *intendants*. Though their training was a legal one and therefore not calculated to equip them to deal with agricultural problems, many familiarized themselves with these and acquired a wide knowledge of them. Not all, however, did so.[54] Though a considerable number stayed for twenty, or even occasionally thirty or more years in the same post, others stayed for only two or three and then moved to another *intendance*, or, in the case of the more able and ambitious – for the post was the gateway to the *contrôle-générale* – were merely birds of passage.[55]

Their staff consisted of people they paid and appointed themselves, who were relatively few, and of that curious type of officials known as *subdélégués* whose principal function was to collect the information the *intendant* needed to reach his decisions. Originally the *subdélégués* had bought their offices, but after the death of Louis XIV they were chosen by the *intendant* himself, from whom, however, they did not receive a salary. They subsisted from the sums he paid them for particular services, and, for the rest, from the profits of some venal office unconnected with their work for him. Though often efficient and devoted in their service to him, and sometimes agronomists with a strong interest in reform, inevitably there were cases where their other interests or occupations took precedence over their loyalty to the *intendance*.[56]

The *intendants'* staff in fact did not itself constitute an official hierarchy, still less form a part of a national one. The decisions of the *intendants* themselves, moreover, were continually, and as the difficulties accumulated increasingly, challenged by the various local bodies whose members had bought their offices. Particularly they were challenged by the *parlements*, and "with a ferocity", it has been said, "it would be hard to exaggerate".[57]

The attitude to agrarian reform in the *parlements* was less universally hostile than it has often been painted. It varied greatly from one *parlement* to another and among the magistrates in any single *parlement* there were those who were convinced by the new ideas and filled their libraries with books on agriculture. Collectively, however, they usually fought to preserve the old institutions and to uphold the sanctity of custom.[58]

Local government thus became a battleground for a variety of authorities with ill-defined powers and no clearly established relation to each other. In his massive account of the peasants in northern Burgundy, Saint-Jacob gives concrete instance after instance of the impotence of the *intendants*, theoretically in charge of affairs, to deal with the vital problems of local administration. "Who was there", Saint-Jacob asked, "to regulate agrarian conditions?" The only answer is nobody.[59]

The government did what it could by way of persuasion. It stimulated the foundation of agricultural societies which proliferated throughout the kingdom. These, however, were concerned more with theory than with practice and Arthur Young was not the only one to believe (as he said of the society which Turgot set up in the Limousin) that the "evils [were] too radically fixed" to be cured by such means. "This society", he wrote of Turgot's, "does like other societies. They meet, converse, offer premiums and publish nonsense. This is not of much consequence, for the people instead of reading their memoirs, are not able to read at all. But they can *see*, and if a farm was established in that good cultivation which they ought to copy, something would be presented from which they *might* learn."[60] To set up model farms throughout the countryside was, however, plainly not a practicable proposition.

Some progress, nevertheless, was made and more, it has been shown, than Arthur Young allowed for. There is evidence that an increasing number of rich proprietors were beginning to develop Lavoisier's ways of thinking and to make intelligently thought-out attempts to improve the cultivation of their estates.[61] As Lavoisier, however, emphasized, agricultural reform could only be achieved slowly. In England it had been the work of centuries. It would indeed have been surprising if the French had managed to achieve it on an extensive scale in the few decades that intervened between the spread of the Physiocrats' gospel and the outbreak of the Revolution. How much success might have been achieved had the Revolution not occurred is an unanswerable question.

Lefebvre maintained that France had a social and political revolution because she failed to have an agricultural one. This judgment may easily be misleading. Peasant misery as great as that in France has often existed for centuries in countries where peasant revolts have not overthrown the government, and in any case, as Lefebvre himself admitted,[62] the revolts in France would not have assumed the magnitude they did had the government not disintegrated before they started. On the other hand, it is beyond dispute that revolution on the scale of the one in France would not have been possible without massive peasant support.

(2) *The Prussian experience*

In western Europe from the eighteenth century onwards, it has always been assumed that the conditions of the Prussian peasant were substantially worse than those of the French because the latter was a free man whereas the Prussian was a serf. Since serfdom, however, is a legal not an economic category, it does not follow that those who fall within it are necessarily worse off than those who do not – the victims of the Irish famine in the middle of the nineteenth century, for example, were not serfs – but, in any case, the belief that the Prussian peasant differed from the French by virtue of his serfdom is a doubtful one, based on a confusion over the meaning of words.

In English, French and Russian there is only one word for serfdom, but in German there are a great many[1] which are used to describe the condition of people who did not necessarily have more than one characteristic in common – that of owing dues and services to, and being subject to the jurisdiction of, some overlord (or several overlords), by virtue of their birth, or of holding land over which an overlord had rights.

The peasants in Germany, according to the German historians (and the English writers have accepted their terminology as they have accepted that of the French in the case of France), were not freed from the last vestiges of serfdom until after the Revolution of 1848. There were nevertheless many German peasants, particularly in South and West Germany but also to some extent in Prussia, whose legal status was similar to, or even better than, that of the peasants in pre-revolutionary France. Among them were the East Prussian *Kölmer*, who held land up to the value of 20,000 thaler[2] (say between £3,000 and £4,000 sterling at the rate of exchange current at the end of the eighteenth century) and whose sons went into the Prussian army as non-commissioned officers.[3] The *Kölmer* were virtually free landowners in the modern sense of the term, and other peasants with a comparable status existed elsewhere in the Hohenzollern dominions east of the Elbe. In East Prussia these free landowning peasants accounted for 26 per cent or more of the peasantry in the province.[4] In this and other provinces there were also peasants subject to dues and services which French- or English-speaking writers, as distinct from German-, would not see as constituting serfdom.

Neither of these classes of peasants, however, is thought of as typical of Prussia. The typical Prussian peasants east of the Elbe have in common estimation always been those who lived in the condition known as *Erbuntertänigkeit* or hereditary subjection – a condition which in any language would unhesitatingly be described as serfdom. These so-called *erbuntertänige* peasants did not in fact account for the majority of the peasant population in the Hohenzollern dominions east of the Elbe. The proportion which they constituted varied from province to province, but has been estimated on an average at less than half.[5] They included, however, the bulk of the landholding peasantry[6] and from an economic point of view were thus of particular importance.

Unlike various other German words used in and in relation to the eighteenth century which can be translated into English only as serfdom, the term *Erbuntertänigkeit* had a constant, precise meaning which is set out at length in the *Allgemeines Landrecht*.[7] This meaning was a purely legal one without relation to material circumstances. The *erbuntertänige* peasant could be relatively prosperous or he could be destitute. He could hold a small or sizable amount of land and do so on a great variety of different terms – sometimes on a basis described as hereditary (though subject to qualifications that would preclude such a description today); sometimes for a period of years, sometimes at six months' notice, sometimes subject to summary eviction. Often he had only a small plot of garden or no land at all. The types and extent of the various dues and services required of him varied greatly.[8] To say that he lived in a condition of *Erbuntertänigkeit* is merely to say that he was bound by certain legal obligations to his lord in return for certain legal rights. He might not leave the estate without the lord's consent, and if he did so he was guilty of a criminal offence, as was anyone who gave him refuge. He needed the lord's consent (which for various reasons was frequently refused) before he could marry. Subject to certain limitations, which in practice must have been difficult if not impossible to enforce, he had to give such of his children as the lord might demand into service in the lord's household. (This provision, known as *Gesindezwangdienst* was the most conspicuous and disliked of the attributes of servile status.) He owed the lord dues in money, kind, or labour services, or in some combination of them. Together with other categories of peasants, he was subject to the jurisdiction of the manorial court.

The type of serfdom described as *Erbuntertänigkeit* was unknown in the west and was a consequence of the way in which estates were run and labour relations organized in eastern and parts of central and east-central Europe. In Prussia, as in Poland, Russia, Bohemia and other parts of the Habsburg dominions, the distinction which existed in France between the *domaine proche* and the *mouvance* – between the land which the seigneur let out to tenants or share-croppers and the land where he had a right to feudal dues – did not exist. In Prussia and other parts of central and east-central Europe the estate, whether it belonged to the crown, to a town, to a religious foundation or to a private individual, was (apart from certain more or less peripheral undertakings)[9] managed by a single authority. In the case of the *Rittergut* or manor (which in law until 1807 could only belong to a noble except with the king's explicit consent), it was managed by the owner himself or one of his relations, with or without the help of an overseer, or let as a unit,[10] usually to a bourgeois tenant.

The estate itself, as it existed until the transformations which began towards the end of the century, consisted partly of arable land cultivated, as in France, on the open field system in which the lord and the peasants held their land in strips mixed up together; partly of meadows and woods where, again as in France, the beasts of the village were pastured in common in accordance with customary provisions, such as that a peasant might send his beasts as far into the forest as a man's voice would carry when he stood on a certain stone. The land belonging on the lord, however, unlike that in France, was not cultivated by share-croppers or by tenants in return for rent, but by the forced, unpaid labour of his *Untertanen* and their draught animals or, and increasingly as the population grew in the eighteenth century, in return for payment to them in money or kind.[11]

The Prussian noble estate, as the founding father of the studies relating to the emancipation of the *erbuntertänige* peasants, G.F. Knapp, described it, was a "Herrschaftsgebiet" or territory subject to a ruler.[12] It commonly embraced the whole village or several villages. These were the so-called "geschlossene Dörfer", or closed villages, which, as the Prussian officials pointed out, facilitated the problems of administration, particularly in relation to taxation.[13] Unlike the French and other western villages where the rights of jurisdiction and to feudal dues generally belonged to a variety of seigneurs (to the confusion but also to the greater liberty of the inhabitants), in the Prussian villages east of the Elbe these rights were usually united in the power of a single person. The peasants on a noble estate in Prussia constituted what was known as the *gutsherrlicher Verband*,[14] or association of people concerned with the cultivation of the estate, and were described as the lord's *Untertanen* or subjects. In return for the services they gave him he was legally obliged, though often in terms that were ill-defined and incapable of enforcement,[15] to afford them help and protection in adversity. In practice as well as in theory he was responsible for their taxes and if they failed to pay them he had to make good the deficit. The peasants on the estates of the Prussian nobility were in consequence, it is usually maintained, not directly but only in the second instance the subjects of the crown. In a phrase that has been continually repeated up to the present day, the authority of the crown stopped at the gates of the manor.

For reasons some of which have already been given, this statement is open to question and becomes increasingly more so the later the period in the eighteenth century to which it is applied. It is based on the belief that, though to all intents and purposes the town officials were appointed and controlled by the crown, there were no royal officials with a right to interfere in the internal affairs of the private estates, apart from the official known as the *Landrat*; and since, or so it is maintained, the *Landrat* was always a land-owning noble, elected in every *Kreis*, or administrative district, by his fellow noble landowners from among their number, he could be relied on to protect their interests against any attempted interference by the government.

It is plainly untrue, however, that the *Landrat* was just the nobles' mouthpiece. Their right to elect him, when they possessed and could exercise it, was merely the right to put forward two or three names from which the king chose one. But this right was often limited or even non-existent. In the reign of Frederick the Great there were provinces where the King appointed *Landräte* without consulting the local nobility at all.[16] There were other provinces where on a number of occasions he interfered with or overrode the nobles' choice.[17] He dismissed *Landräte* whom, with or without reason, he found incompetent or otherwise unsuitable.[18] There was never any question that the *Landrat* was responsible and subordinated to the local *Kammer*, which paid a part of his meagre salary (usually the equivalent of between £30 and £80 per annum) while the *Kreis* and other sources provided the rest.[19]

The *Landrat* was thus the link between the government and the local nobility. He had a foot in both camps. He was not, as many accounts might lead one to suppose, the nobles' representative in the way in which, say, a modern trades-union leader represents the workers in a particular branch of industry. The crown saw in him an instrument which, however defective, was doubtless the best available for controlling, at the minimum cost in money and friction, what went on within the private estates. It emerges plainly from the documents that the royal intention – whatever the degree of failure or success achieved in practice – was to educate a group of noble landowners to discharge certain essential tasks of local government. As that remarkable administrator, the Minister of State, von Hagen, put it on one occasion, the *Landrat* was of the greatest importance to the whole monarchy, since he alone could provide supervision and protection in the countryside and the *Kammern* themselves had, apart from him, no one on whom to rely there.[20]

The *Landrat*'s most important functions were concerned with the collection of the taxes, with providing for the needs of the troops moved through his district in peace or war, with regulating the relations between peasants and landowners and with educating both to cultivate their land efficiently.

He was responsible for ensuring that the direct taxes were justly apportioned among and punctually paid by the peasants, that accurate accounts were kept of each individual's payments and that the money was duly delivered to the *Kreis* and from the *Kreis* to the provincial treasury.

When troops were moved through his district he had to consult with the commanding officer about the line of march; to arrange for billets; to ensure that there was a supply of horses to meet any needs of the cavalry for replacement, that there was adequate forage for all the army horses and that transport for it was provided by the peasants, who were entitled to a special payment for this service, which it was also his duty to see that they got.

His instructions always assigned him a great variety of duties in connection with the relation of lord and serf and particularly with the duty of preventing what was known as *Bauernlegen* – that is, the incorporation in the lord's demesne of peasant holdings from which the peasant had been evicted or which for any other reason had fallen vacant; for in Frederick the Great's day it was always believed that the efficiency of the army and the amount raised in taxes depended on the existence of a substantial landholding peasantry.

Failure to fulfil a number of these functions, and particularly those relating to the army and to taxation, were increasingly likely to come to light and to land the *Landrat* in trouble if not in prison. All his functions, in so far as he discharged them, limited the sovereignty of the *Gutsherr* over his estate.

Particularly in the earlier years of Frederick's reign, however, and doubtless to a considerable extent throughout the whole of it, there were many of his functions which the *Landrat* did not fulfil, as is plain from the number of complaints to this effect, not to mention the recorded sins of omission or commission for which individual *Landräte* were found guilty and punished. This is hardly surprising, not only because of the huge range of duties with which the *Landrat* was burdened – the government deluged him with instructions and demands for information on every aspect of village life[21] – but also because of the kind of people who filled the office before, and presumably, if to a diminishing extent, even after, the reforms that were set in train from 1763 onwards. In a memorandum which he wrote in 1769[22] von Hagen observed that only exceptionally had the *Landräte* been given any serious education in youth, or learned the law of the land or even a proper use of the pen. From such glimpses of their behaviour as are available in sufficient detail to give one an idea of how they conducted themselves, they may well have been violent, undisciplined, corrupt and, as von Hagen put it, "unwissende Leute" – ignorant people.[23]

Throughout the reign of Frederick the Great, but particularly after 1763, the government set itself to remedy this situation by a liberal use of the stick and the carrot. The various *Kammern* were instructed in 1766 and on subsequent occasions to send the crown reports, at increasingly frequent intervals, on the conduct of the *Landräte* in the *Kreise* subject to them.[24] It was continually emphasized, and in 1766 specifically promised, that a *Landrat* who carried out his duties efficiently would be eligible for a high position in the government – the presidency of a *Kammer* or a post in the General Directory, carrying with it a high, or relatively high, salary and numerous perquisites.[25] In 1770 von Hagen proposed that the best *Landräte* in every province should be sent for six months to attend the discussions in the General Directory,[26] so that, presumably, they might acquaint themselves with the nature of administration at the highest level and with the relation between national and local problems. In the same year it was made obligatory for every *Landrat* to pass an examination before his appointment was confirmed.[27] It is significant of the state of affairs at this juncture that a number of prospective *Landräte* tried to get out of the obligation by means of a variety of ingenious excuses. The government was, however, adamant, though it must be admitted that, to start with at any rate, the examiners were prepared to take an extremely lenient view of the candidates' capacities or lack of them.

By all these means, which he pursued with energy, though with how much immediate success remains to be investigated, Frederick set himself to build up what he himself described as a "school of people"[28] skilled in conducting the affairs of primitive agricultural communities at village level. Frederick was never in doubt about the kind of men he wanted as *Landräte* – steady, sensible men of ripe years, as he said, of generally acknowledged good reputation and capable of inspiring trust in the *Kreis*.[29] Characteristically he assumed that an army officer was most likely to meet these requirements.

As a prominent landowner in the district where he held office, the *Landrat* naturally sympathized with the views of his fellow landowners. On the other hand, he was also a servant of the crown, which could reward or punish him according to his success or failure in furthering its policies. Though we do not at present know enough to assess at all precisely the results of Frederick's attempts to create a cadre of efficient gentlemen farmers, it is not possible to doubt that he achieved some degree of success, or that he sowed the seed from which sprang that type of nineteenth-century *Landrat* which Fontane portrayed in his *Effi Briest* – Effi's husband, the Baron von Instetten, whose austere, unremitting dedication to duty, and ambition to rise in the official hierarchy, led him to neglect his wife and to domestic disaster though to professional success.

German historians, doubtless rightly, insist that Frederick William I and Frederick the Great devoted more attention to the details of agriculture than did any other German or, for that matter, European rulers in the eighteenth century, notwithstanding the increasing importance which this subject came to assume in crowned heads. Frederick not only invested in the land sums of government money far beyond the capacity of individuals – in settling colonists, reclaiming waste, draining swamps, building canals; he continually engaged in experiments on the farms of the royal demesne which, long before Arthur Young expressed a similar idea, he hoped would serve as a model for other landowners. Not only did the *Landrat*'s instructions always require him to educate both lord and peasant in the principles, so far as they were then known, of efficient farm management; by the end of the reign the members of the *Kammern* were sometimes if not commonly required before they took their final examination to serve a period of apprenticeship on one of the royal farms.

The attitude that came to prevail, at least among the more efficient *Kammer* presidents, may be illustrated by the story of how he began his official career which is told by Theodor von Schön, the drafter of the famous edict of October 1807 which freed the Prussian peasants from the personal obligations of serfdom. Schön, who was born in 1773 in Gumbinnen on the eastern frontier of East Prussia, decided, after studying for three years at the University of Königsberg, to embark on a career in the bureaucracy. He went, as he tells us in his autobiography,[30] to see the head of the East and West Prussian *Kammern*, Freiherr Friederich Leopold von Schrötter, himself an intimate friend of Kant and of other famous professors in

Königsberg. In order to impress this eminent and elderly official (who had begun his career some thirty or so years earlier as an army officer during the Seven Years War), the young Schön explained that he had read Adam Smith, Arthur Young and various other writers on economic and agricultural matters. Von Schrötter replied: "But you don't know how the *Schultze* [headman] keeps order in the village or the proper way of reaping and sowing," and sent him for a year to a royal farm to get practical experience.

The various efforts to improve the cultivation of the land in the last forty years of Frederick the Great's reign certainly yielded some returns[31] but such as were nevertheless inadequate to meet recognized needs. The Prussians in the second half of the eighteenth century were exposed, like the French, to changes in material circumstances and to new currents of thought which affected the whole of Christian Europe. Among the most significant of these was the great growth in population which occurred throughout the continent, but which in Prussia, one of the most sparsely populated regions at the accession of Frederick William I, was greater than in any western country. In the old Prussian provinces – that is, leaving out of account the gains from the conquered territories – it doubled between 1740 and the beginning of the nineteenth century.[32] As a consequence of this, but also for other reasons – the general rise in prices and the increased demand from western countries, particularly England, for imported grain – the price of grain in Prussia rose steeply, and more quickly than that of other commodities. Real wages, however, fell. This benefited certain classes of people, particularly the landowners who produced for the market, but in general meant an increase in poverty. At the same time, the burden of maintaining large armed forces pressed increasingly heavily on the Prussian government, as on the other governments in countries that were major military powers, and led it to the search for new sources of wealth. In Prussia as elsewhere, a reformed agriculture, in particular, seemed capable of meeting this need.

In the first half of the eighteenth century the Prussian kings never neglected agriculture as the French kings had done, and in the course of the century they evolved an administration more capable of promoting improvement than anything that existed in France. Until after the middle of the century, however, they directed their efforts to making the existing system work as efficiently as possible in circumstances of the greatest difficulties – for in most of their provinces the soil was proverbially among the worst in Europe.[33] Only after the end of the Seven Years War did it gradually emerge that what was needed was not a wider diffusion of conventional wisdom but radical changes in the system itself – in the methods of cultivation and in the relations between landlord and peasant.

Whether the eighteenth-century Prussian peasant should be judged more miserable than the French is an unanswerable question since misery is not measurable. The degree of its intensity is governed not only by material circumstances but also by the relation these bear to expectations and other attitudes of mind. If only material circumstances are in question, however, it must be doubtful whether, in general, the misery was worse in Prussia than in France.

In the agrarian communities of the eighteenth century, with their lack of transport facilities and their provincial barriers, it was extremely difficult to move grain from the surplus to the deficit areas even when, which may often not have been the case, the country as a whole produced enough to feed the population. Though it was rare for the harvest to be universally bad, the problem of local scarcity if not famine was perennial, for a relatively small drop, or even the prospect of one, in the yield of the harvest was enough to induce producers to hoard, and purchasers to buy in excessive quantities in the hope of profit, so that prices were driven up beyond the point which the poor could afford, and not only in the towns but also in the countryside where, in Prussia as in France, the great majority of the peasantry did not hold enough land to support a family.

Though for reasons that no one can fully explain there were no major famines in France in the eighteenth century as there had been in the seventeenth, there was continual and often serious scarcity, which the French government tried to mitigate with conspicuous lack of success. Its attempts were described in two volumes of some 700 pages by an American scholar in 1976.[34] His work is a chronicle of disputes over policy and conflicts in practice among a multitude of different officials; of what he described as "perpetual" bread riots; of misery on occasions so extreme that "people ate grass like animals"; and of "whole families dying of hunger".[35]

The German writers who at the end of the last and the beginning of the present century dealt with the comparable problems in Prussia[36] set out to glorify the achievements of the founding fathers of Prussian absolutism and this bias makes their conclusions suspect. It nevertheless seems unlikely that food shortages as serious, widespread and frequent as those in France occurred in the Hohenzollern dominions because of the means taken to prevent them, including the accumulation of buffer stocks.

This practice as an insurance against scarcity or famine stretches from the earliest times to the wars of the present century. In the eighteenth century the French attempted to pursue it, but by their usual means of working through agents who proved incompetent or dishonest.[37] In Prussia, as in modern industrial states in war, the purchase, control and distribution of stocks was a government undertaking.

Frederick the Great aimed at holding supplies of grain and flour (principally the latter)[38] which would be sufficient to meet any likely demands over a period of eighteen months, and which he distributed in depots throughout the country. By these means he presumed he would be able to control prices, and though he does not appear to have achieved as much as he maintained in his Testaments Politiques, he achieved a considerable degree of success.[39] The editors of the volumes in the *Acta Borussica* concerned with this subject sometimes gave him more credit than

147

seems plausible. They may well have been right, however, when they claimed that he developed his stock policy to "a degree of perfection achieved by no other state in modern times".[40]

In general, in fact, the Prussian administration was better adapted than was the French to discover and deal with actual or impending disaster – notably in France there was no equivalent to the chain of command that stretched in Prussia from the *Landräte* in the villages to the *Kammern* in the provinces and from the *Kammern* to the ministries in Berlin and the cabinet in Potsdam. In consequence, though we lack enough information to speak with certainty, it seems highly likely that the Prussian peasant ran less risk of dying from hunger than did the French peasant.

The mere prevention of death from hunger, however, as has been shown, ceased to be the only goal of agricultural policy, in Prussia as in France. In Germany the humanitarian ideas of the Enlightenment and the new economics came to dominate the thinking in the Universities of Göttingen and Königsberg where the officials in the higher ranks of the Prussian bureaucracy usually completed their education. Humanity and economics preached the same moral in Prussia as in France – that methods of cultivation and relations between lord and peasant must be changed as a means to increasing happiness, wealth and national power.

After the end of the Seven Years War the Prussians became as much impressed by the English achievements as were the French. Frederick the Great sent officials to England to study English agriculture and Englishmen were on occasion prevailed upon to come to Prussia to manage royal or private estates.[41] This experiment met with little or no success and could hardly have done otherwise given the meagre salaries offered by the parsimonious Prussian government and the (by British standards) poor Prussian landowners.

In any event, however, and this was the major problem, the abandonment of the open-field system, the enclosure of arable and common land, and the introduction of convertible agriculture could only be achieved by overriding existing custom; and this, as in France, provoked resistance from every quarter – from most private landowners and the tenants of the royal domains as well as, and even more tenaciously, from the peasants.

As one of the young Prussian officials whom Frederick sent to England reported when he came home, and in words similar to those used by Marc Bloch when describing the difficulties of abolishing the cummunal system of agriculture in France, the power of the English landlords was much greater than that of the landlords in the absolute monarchies where the old agricultural practices prevailed; for the English landowners dominated the Parliament and in the period when enclosures were most frequent, they were introduced by law. In Prussia, by contrast, as in France, the peasants had rights derived from custom or written agreements which the governments were often unwilling and in any case, like the landowners, usually impotent to override. The members of the village community in Prussia, for example, as in France, formed a legal corporation[42] with the right, which they appear to have frequently exercised, to sue the landlords if they contravened these customs and agreements.

That the Prussian noble landowners, like most other groups in a position to behave similarly, in general squeezed out of their peasants as much as they could manage to get, seems beyond dispute. In so doing, however, they created great difficulties for themselves, making the running of an estate a frustrating and by the new standards an increasingly inefficient enterprise. Since the peasants were inarticulate their mentality has remained obscure. There was nevertheless one eighteenth-century writer, the Breslau professor Christian Garve, who set himself to describe it and did so with considerable psychological insight.[43] The peasants, he pointed out, formed the lowest class of society and were comparable only to the Jews in the extent to which they were exposed to arbitrary and unjust treatment. They were in consequence generally suspicious and recalcitrant. Though not, Garve maintained, inclined to revolt (there were in fact in the eighteenth century no peasant revolts in the Prussian provinces apart from Silesia where Garve nevertheless lived), they carried on a continuous secret war with the landlord, cheating him whenever and in every way they could. They were not an enemy whom the lord had cause to fear (as they were in Russia) but they were not willing subjects either. The adjective which Garve thought described them best was "tückisch", the meaning of which he devoted some space to explaining. To say that the peasant was "tückisch" was to say that he was distinguished by a peculiar kind of obstinacy in his relations with those in authority. He was totally deaf to any suggestion, however plausible, which they might make to him even though in other circumstances he was capable of appreciating its plausibility. The lawyers, Garve said, who were concerned with legal cases in which peasants were involved found it hard to make out whether the stubbornness with which they clung to preposterous ideas was the result of blindness or deliberate malice. Whole villages could sometimes show this quality and behave, as Garve put it, like the lunatics who are victims of *idées fixes* which it is impossible to combat by argument or demonstration. German agricultural histories show many cases of peasants who reacted in this way to any suggested alterations in existing practices.[44]

Well might Garve observe that managing the peasants was the hardest task on a large estate, though he maintained that it was one of which certain exceptional landlords were capable by virtue of what he called their "moral qualities", that is, a continuous attention to the job and those personal attributes, not excluding harshness, which in this kind of society could command respect.

H.A. Graf von Borcke was evidently a landlord of this kind. A former general and the son of a field marshal in the Prussian army, he described the improvements he had made, in the reign of Frederick the Great, on one (and the favourite) of his three estates. When he took the estate over, he said, there had been 36 miserable cows, but at the time he wrote there were 200 well-nourished ones. He enclosed land for the growing of clover; the amount of available manure and the yield of the land under grain greatly increased; he took waste land into cultivation. All this required more labour but he found, he said, no difficulty in getting it as conditions on his estate were known to be good. The labour, however, was serf-labour. The newcomers, as he put it "gaben sich unterthänig" – gave themselves into serfdom.[45]

On this estate in Pomerania (a province where the conditions of the peasantry were among the worst) there could plainly exist a patriarchal relationship between lord and serf, and it is possible to cite a number of comparable instances elsewhere[46] though we do not know how numerous they were. Any belief that they were widespread, however, is obviously refuted by what must surely be one of the most extraordinary episodes in the history of any eighteenth-century nobility – the speculation in *Rittergüter*, or noble estates, which began in the third quarter of the century and reached its peak after Frederick the Great's death in the fifteen years or so before Jena in 1806. It was made possible on the one hand by the rise in the price of grain and hence of estates, and on the other by the facilities for credit which Frederick the Great had created for the benefit of noble landowners in order to enable them to repair the damage caused by the Seven Years War.[47]

The resulting phenomenon was compared by contemporaries to the speculation in Dutch bulbs, the first notorious example of its kind, which occurred in Holland in the early seventeenth century and drove up the price of tulip bulbs to more than the value of their weight in gold.[48] In East Prussia a similar speculative mania in relation to land had the result that scarcely an estate did not change hands between 1790 and 1805.[49] Two hundred and fifteen, or 24 per cent of the total, did so in the two years before Jena.[50] In all the Hohenzollern provinces east of the Elbe there were individual cases of astronomical rises in the price of estates accompanied by changes in ownership. As one contemporary put it: "There have been estates which have belonged to a single family for two or three hundred years which have [recently] changed hands three, four or six times."[51] Such changes could occur as frequently as five times in four years or even more often. It was said that at dinner-parties in Königsberg they could pass from hand to hand several times in the course of the meal.[52]

The landowners bought estates with borrowed money in order to sell at a profit which they then invested in other estates until inevitably, though not until after Jena, the bubble burst. Since the peasants who were tied to the land were sold with it, this procedure, given the scale on which it occurred, made a mockery of the notion that the landowner's attitude to his serfs was that of a father to his children.

At the same time, the belief that the serfs being unwilling were also inefficient workers gained increasing currency, particularly in the Universities of Göttingen and Königsberg and among the higher officials who had studied there. "That freedom of person and property beget prosperity", von Schrötter said, "is demonstrated in every East Prussian village where there are both serfs and free peasants."[53] "The single word ownership", observed the writer of a prize essay who was not otherwise noted for his liberal beliefs,[54] "will prove so powerful that [at the sound of it] millions of peasants will awake as out of a sleep." The last word was said by the famous agronomist, A.L. Thaer. Born in Hanover in 1752, he studied English agriculture on which, at the end of the eighteenth century, he wrote a work which made a great impression. In 1804 Hardenberg prevailed on him to settle in Prussia where he was given an estate on which he set up an institute for the study of agriculture. A few years later he published in four volumes his *Principles of Rational Agriculture* which became a classic and was translated into many languages. On the question of serfdom he observed that it was generally reckoned that a plough-team worked by free labour, and with the draught animals owned by the landlord, could do twice as much work as a serf team. The work, moreover, was better done. "One can", he said "see at a glance and even from a long distance, which fields have been cultivated by serf and which by free labour".[55]

There thus arose in Prussia, as there did in France, a body of opinion obsessed with the need for agricultural reform though the problems in the two countries differed in a number of respects, as did the attitudes of mind in relation to them. In both countries, nevertheless, the impetus to reform was, broadly speaking, inspired by the same body of ideas and came from the same groups of people – intellectuals and their apostles among ministers and officials who formed only a minute proportion of the population.

In each country reform demanded measures bound to arouse resistance among both peasants and landowners, for however much the members of either group might complain about existing conditions, they were for the greater part unaccustomed to thinking, and often incapable even of imagining, that methods of production could be radically changed, or that social relations could be so either, except to the extent of removing from them whatever aspects seemed objectionable to this, that or the other discontented group. Knapp described the Prussian peasants as saying, "Wir haben immer einen Herrn gehabt und wollen einen behalten" – "We have always had a lord and want to keep one."[56] Professor G.V. Taylor's sample of the *cahiers de doléances* drawn up for the Estates General reveals that in the rural areas in France only 1 per cent wanted to abolish serfdom and only 11 per cent seigneurial jurisdiction.[57]

In these circumstances, as German historians are increasingly pointing out in relation to Prussia,[58] the necessary agricultural reforms, if they were to come at all, could only be imposed from above since there was no majority in favour of them. The same could doubtless have been said of France (where they did not come), if this solution had not been ruled out by the collapse of the government, which in any event had developed an interest in agricultural matters much later than had the Prussian and possessed no such administrative machinery for dealing with them as the Prussian kings evolved in the course of the eighteenth century.

PART THREE

I

The Enlightenment as a movement
for social and political change:
the common assumptions

The eighteenth century in general, but in France particularly its second half, is commonly known as the age of Enlightenment – *le siècle des Lumières, das Zeitalter der Aufklärung* – and it was indeed an age in which, among the educated, it seemed that a new light had been shed on man's thinking about the arts and sciences, about his personal and social relations, about the purpose of his existence, and about the kind of social and political institutions required to realize it. What were the sources and the nature of this illumination?

This question has been the subject of many books. The fact nevertheless remains that the Enlightenment considered as a movement for social and political change can no more be given a precise, unequivocal meaning than can liberalism, socialism or any other body of ideas that has been invoked to describe the thinking of an age on social and political matters.

Admittedly there were propositions which anyone with a claim to be called enlightened had to accept and others which he had to deny. This nevertheless left wide scope for divergencies of opinion, as well as shifts in attitudes as the century progressed. Those usually seen as representatives of the Enlightenment differed greatly one from another in their views on many matters, and could do so to the point where their claims to illumination were disputed by their contemporaries as well as by the writers of later generations and different nations.

Christian Wolff, for example, who died aged seventy-five in 1754, was seen throughout much of his life, and has continued to seem to many German writers,[1] as the principal founding-father of the Enlightenment in Germany and the Habsburg dominions. To Voltaire, however, as was shown earlier, he was merely another system-builder[2] – a term of abuse among the French *Philosophes* used to describe thinkers who deduced conclusions logically from premises which they did not attempt to test against the facts. In Voltaire's view, which has been endorsed by modern writers, and which he finally induced Frederick the Great to accept, Wolff was not even a good system-builder, but just another German pedant.[3]

Among the acknowledged prophets of the French Enlightenment there were also the disputable cases, notably Montesquieu. Was Montesquieu sufficiently enlightened to count among the illuminated? Most of his great contemporaries thought so, as have many later writers, including his most recent English biographer.[4] He was plainly enlightened, however that adjective is understood, by virtue of his repudiation of medieval attitudes to law, crime, punishment and the position of the church in the state. To the twentieth century in the west his claim may seem particularly strong because of his respect for human dignity and his remarkable insight into the kinds of circumstances that destroy it. On the other hand he was a defender of the société d'ordres and thus came to seem to some of his contemporaries, to some leaders during the Revolution, and to various eminent historians of the present century, an advocate of social institutions dating from "les siècles gothiques et barbares" which had preceded the age of Enlightenment.[5]

Comparable or even more teasing problems have beset the attempts, still being pursued in Germany,[6] to fit the eighteenth-century European absolutisms into categories of the enlightened and the unenlightened. Frederick the Great, in particular, has been commonly, and by all the famous German historians of the nineteenth-century was always, described as the enlightened despot *par excellence.*[7] Yet, though he was a great admirer of the French *Philosophes* and was himself admired by a number of them, his arbitrary behaviour and form of autocracy caused others, notably Rousseau and d'Alembert, to conclude that enlightenment and despotism – and it was impossible to doubt that he was a despot – were contradictions in terms.[8] Even Kant, who described the eighteenth-century as the "age of the Enlightenment or the century of Frederick"[9], saw Frederick's attitude as typified in the phrase "argue as much as you want and over whatever you want, but obey". Kant found this, as he described it, surprising and paradoxical statement a proof of the fact that though the century of Frederick was an enlightened century, Prussia was far from being an unqualifiedly enlightened state.

The present account cannot be concerned with these problems of classification and definition. Its aim is to consider the great changes in the way people came to look on social and political problems – changes which, though far from universally accepted, nevertheless increasingly prevailed, or had lip-service paid to them, in governing circles, and among the groups which were in a position to influence these and which Necker described loosely as "public opinion".

To Necker public opinion in France was a new and strange phenomenon to which there appears to have been nothing comparable in Prussia until after the death of Frederick the Great. Necker described it as an "invisible power without money, without police, without an army", which could nevertheless exercise a powerful influence on policy.[10] He attributed its origins to the progress – that is, the increasingly wide dissemination of the ideas – of the Enlightenment (*les Lumières*), which he saw as having drawn together, in contradistinction to earlier times, "the men who are governed and those who govern", so that "ministers have become actors in the theatre of the world".

Like other people when they speak of public opinion, Necker did not explain, and doubtless could not have explained precisely, what groups he had in mind. Plainly, however, they were the educated, whose ways of thinking the German historian Groethuysen set himself to analyse in an attempt to account for the new attitudes to life and the world which developed in the eighteenth-century.[11] Groethuysen described these changes as "among the most important that have ever occurred in the course of history".

As Groethuysen saw things, and other central and eastern European thinkers have judged them similarly,[12] these were changes in the attitudes towards religion. Groethuysen examined them in relation to France because it was in that country during the Revolution that they found the expression which shook the world. What concerned him were not the ideas of the great thinkers which have preoccupied most writers on the Enlightenment, but the beliefs which, as he supposed, came to be accepted more or less without reflection, and because they corresponded to the needs of life, by people whom he called bourgeois, although it is plain that the *Weltanschauung* he described was widely diffused among the educated, regardless of their social or legal status. He himself, in fact, used the terms "bourgeois" and "educated layman" interchangeably.

What Groethuysen found significant was not primarily the emergence of deism and atheism, notorious though these were, for their adherents constituted, even among the educated, only a small minority; it was the changed role played by religion in the thinking of the educated who remained professing Christians, and particularly the attitude of these Christians, including many in holy orders, to what had hitherto been the key concepts in the doctrines of all the Christian churches – the concepts of God, sin and death.

In the ages of faith, or, as Voltaire called them, the ages of fanaticism, the Christian churches had taught that man was born evil because he was descended from Adam with whom evil had come into the world. Man was sinful, weak and ignorant but God was good, all-powerful and omniscient. Life on earth was a period of painful probation leading in the hereafter either to eternal bliss or to eternal damnation. It was dominated by the shadow of death which reduced all human values to nothingness. "L'empire de la mort", in Bossuet's words,[13] was stronger than life. "It shattered, crushed, destroyed, annihilated everything – greatness, power, dominion, kings, emperors, rulers, the great and the small".[14] No one could defend himself against it. It was proof of God's omnipotence.

It was proof of His mercy that among the members of sinful humanity he bestowed on some (though by methods of selection over which the Catholic and the Protestant Churches and the sects within them differed) the grace which ensured salvation. His mercy was not questioned even by people who, like Pascal, recognized that he manifested this quality after a fashion at variance with the usual human interpretation of it. "For what", Pascal asked, "is more contrary to the rules of our miserable justice than to damn eternally a child, who has no will, for a sin in which he appears to have so small a part, and which was committed six thousand years before he was born?" Pascal nevertheless concluded that here were mysteries beyond our comprehension. "We cannot understand why we should be a prey to misery and death. We must be guilty for otherwise life would be unintelligible".[15]

Human beings find it hard to accept that life is unintelligible and the churches provided them with a means for believing otherwise. The Roman Catholic Church, in particular, though concerned with the needs of the educated for rational expositions of its gospel, appealed also to the emotions, to the love of ceremonial, and to the myths and miracles in which primitive peoples find explanations that satisfy them. It adjusted its preaching and practices to the needs of men in different social circumstances and with different levels of education. Its teaching embraced the whole of life. It taught the why and the wherefore of everything. Children, Bossuet said, learned the language of the church as they learned to talk, without knowing how.[16]

The churches laid down the limits within which, in the fields of art and learning, man might exercise his creative and critical faculties. They prescribed the rules of conduct to be observed in personal, social, economic and political relations. In France, for example, until the Revolution, the Roman Catholic Church prohibited usury, or the lending of money at interest (while nevertheless sanctioning practices which largely served the same purpose). By this means, backed up by the power of the state, it interfered in the conduct of business affairs while attempting to mould the attitudes towards them. It upheld the power of the absolute monarch whom it saw as God's representative on earth, and thus lent its sanction to a particular form of government. In the sphere of social relations it preached that inequality of wealth and status were ordained of God and that each walk of life had its particular duties, as well as its particular vices and temptations, so that one sinned or lived virtuously as it were "*standesgemäß*", or according to one's station. As one Catholic preacher put it: "It has been established that before we were born the Lord traced for each of us the plan of our destiny and, so to say, our road to eternity, and that among the multiplicity of roads, which correspond to the different conditions of society, there is only one which is ours and by means of which God has willed to lead us to salvation".[17]

At the end of the seventeenth century and throughout the eighteenth all the fundamental Christian beliefs here described, and the social, economic and political conditions which they sanctioned, were subjected to a slow but accelerating process of erosion, which to some extent affected even the teaching of the churches themselves, as Groethuysen demonstrated by examining the sermons of the popular preachers in France and noting their changed attitudes to the concepts of God, sin and death. A similar transformation occurred in Protestant Prussia, though considerably earlier than in France. German writers, for example, have seen it as one of the principal claims to enlightenment of Christian Wolff, who never repudiated the Lutheran faith, that he believed that man's natural reason, without the aid of revelation, could distinguish good from evil; that he advocated the pursuit of happiness in this world, and that instead of the God of Luther, Calvin and the Jansenists who arbitrarily, by human standards, consigned men to heaven or hell, he held the vision of a God who was the embodiment of reason.[18]

Though the churches never relinquished their belief in divine revelation as the basis of their teaching, the degree of capacity for adjustment which they showed in the eighteenth century, together with the inevitable persistence of old values, ensured that even among the educated, and even in France, though to a much greater extent in Prussia, Enlightenment and Christianity were not necessarily incompatible, although, and particularly in France, they could easily prove to be so.

Increasingly as the eighteenth century progressed, the churches failed to stem the tide of secularization, so that large areas of human activity were loosened from or prised out of their control – in the arts and sciences and in the conduct of government and social relations.

For the purposes of the present discussion, among the most significant aspects of the thinking of the Enlightenment, however that term is understood, was the repudiation of the belief in original sin. "They shout at us," Voltaire said, "that human nature is essentially perverse, that man is born a child of the devil and wicked. Nothing is stupider; for you, my friend, who preach to me that all the world is born perverse warn me that you, too, are born so, and that I should beware of you as of a fox or crocodile. 'Oh no!', you say, 'I am regenerate because I am neither a heretic nor an infidel."[19] Voltaire professed himself unconvinced that his friend, and other self-satisfied believers in the Roman Catholic faith, were necessarily more regenerate than heretics or non-Christians. The truth was, Voltaire said, that "man is not born wicked but becomes so as he becomes ill", through infection, ill-treatment, bad government or bad education. Moral actions, in Voltaire's view, were not actions in accordance with a divinely prescribed rule of conduct but those which reason could show promoted peace and happiness. This, as a general proposition, was the guide to social and political action which the enlightened adopted. Happiness was the goal to be pursued; reason the means to and the justification of it.

What constituted happiness was understood very differently by different people in different countries and at different dates in the eighteenth century. In France, among the *Philosophes* and their disciples in the salons and the academies, it was the subject of continual but inconclusive debate.[20] At least, however, all those with a claim to be enlightened could reach some measure of agreement about the conditions which precluded it and the need to change them.

Frederick the Great defined reason as "la pensée" – the ability to think –

"the faculty", as he said, "of combining ideas which distinguishes man from the animals". In this sense reason had not been absent in the ages of faith. No one could accuse the medieval theologians of having failed to employ it in justification of their beliefs. In the eighteenth century, however, it was put to new purposes and acquired a new meaning.

Reason, in the sense given to it by Frederick, was seen in the ages of faith as natural to man but subordinate to revelation. It was a tool granted to him in order that he might understand the nature of the beliefs which the churches expounded. To the enlightened, by contrast, it no longer seemed the servant of revelation but an autonomous means by which man could extend the boundaries of his knowledge, not only of the physical universe but also of how social and political institutions worked and could be improved. It required that in considering these, the ends to be pursued should be deliberately considered in conjunction with the means available for achieving them. It thus repudiated a belief in the sanctity of custom and in the necessary virtue of traditional practices. Especially in Prussia, but also increasingly in France, an enlightened policy was a policy directed to achieving with the maximum efficiency ends which seemed self-evidently desirable and therefore in accordance with reason.

The great generation of French *Philosophes* associated with the *Encyclopédie* derived their inspiration from the natural sciences, whose methods of procedure were described by Diderot, the *Encyclopédie*'s principal editor (in a formulation which, admittedly, modern scientists would no longer wholly accept) as "observations of nature, reflection and experiment. Observation gathers the facts, reflection combines them, experiment verifies the results of the combination".[21]

This pronouncement left out of account that the facts, in the natural or social sciences, do not speak for themselves. No investigation of them can start except on the basis of some hypothesis for which the investigator has no proof. When the *Philosophes* came to pronounce on social and political matters they do not seem to have been aware of this truth, even though Voltaire, Hume and others were prepared to admit that, as Voltaire put it, "we can never know completely anything really elementary or absolutely primary".[22] Only too frequently, however, they assumed that "reason" provided them with the suppositions from which their arguments started. Though, for example, the desirability of happiness may seem obvious to many people, this proposition is incapable of scientific proof, as is equally Voltaire's assertion that man is not born wicked but only becomes so through force of circumstances. In consequence the so-called "age of reason" produced a huge variety of often mutually exclusive remedies, based on hypotheses no more capable of proof than those of the schoolmen, for what were seen as social and political evils.

For all this, nevertheless, there was widespread agreement among the enlightened about which the worst of these evils were. They were evils which plainly caused unhappiness – notably poverty, disease, crime, civil disorder and disturbance, war (though some otherwise enlightened also saw this as a source of virtue), tyranny (in the sense of power exercised arbitrarily and cruelly without regard to human dignity and suffering)[23] lack of freedom from various forms of oppression, and particularly from the denial of freedom of worship, speech and writing.

The enlightened saw the essential causes of these evils in what they commonly described as "superstition" (the attitude, for example, of the blacksmith's apprentice who, when his bellows failed to work, assumed them to be bewitched instead of looking to see if they had a hole in them) and in the belief that things were good merely because they were old. They found the principal obstacle to the spread of rational attitudes and behaviour in the teaching and practices of the churches. The history of the Christian churches had hitherto been one of continual disputes among different sects, each of which, when it gained the support of the state, persecuted the others. By enlightened standards everywhere, these disputes were absurd and their results disastrous. The enlightened, however much they might otherwise disagree, were united in their desire for religious toleration and also for the right, in general, to the free expression of opinion. As that protagonist of the late Prussian Enlightenment, Friedrich Nicolai, put it in 1783 – one year before Kant, whose philosophy he misunderstood and disliked, expressed the same sentiments in a more famous work – it is essential "that free discussion of every matter should be allowed without any qualification". "Every man has a natural right to follow his convictions in matters of conscience." "Opinions, above all religious opinions, must never be subject to compulsion."[24]

In this matter the enlightened proclaimed their belief in what in the present century are described as human rights, and they did so in many other respects as well, most significantly, perhaps, in their attitude to crime and punishment, which, in Montesquieu's view, "are of more interest to the human race than anything else in the world."[25]

In the ages of faith crime and sin were synonymous. The ruler, after the fashion of Frederick William I described earlier, believed that in determining what constituted crime and how it should be punished he should fulfil the will of God. "When one punished one atoned, in a sense, the crime in the eyes of God. Punishments therefore could not be too severe".[26] Practices in conformity with this view prevailed, as was shown earlier, in France till the Revolution. But the doctrines of the Enlightenment condemned them. Montesquieu spoke for the enlightened when he said that the idea that man should avenge God was mistaken. "One must honour God but not avenge Him, for if one were to proceed according to this last idea where would the agonies end? If human laws must avenge an infinite being they will be determined by his infinity and not by the weaknesses, ignorance and caprices of human nature."[27]

The most famous exponent of enlightened ideas on this subject was the Italian, Beccaria, whose *Dei Delliti è delle Pene* – of Crimes and Punishments

– was first published in 1764. Two years later it was translated into French and went through seven editions. Subsequently it was translated into almost every European language. Voltaire hailed Beccaria as a brother and the enlightened in many countries proclaimed him the benefactor of mankind.[28] Seeing "the final object and supreme test of all state activity as the greatest happiness divided among the greatest number", Beccaria concluded that the purpose of the criminal law should be "to prevent the criminal from injuring anew his fellow-citizens and to deter others from committing similar injuries." The severity of the punishment should be no greater than was necessary to outweigh the advantages which the criminal might derive from his crime. "All beyond this is superfluous and consequently tyrannical."

There was in fact no attitude towards social and political questions which the new beliefs in happiness and reason did not undermine. Poverty, for example, which the Roman Catholic Church (though not, admittedly, the Pietists or the Calvinists) had seen as a state of blessedness – the poor were beloved of God – appeared to the enlightened as a source of ignorance and misery.

The need to promote the growth of wealth, on social grounds as well as on those of power politics, became a major concern. It provided the inspiration of the mercantilists whom the German historians in consequence assign to the period of the Enlightenment though the French do not.[29] To the French, and to some of their English-speaking supporters,[30] it is the Physiocrats, the opponents of the mercantilists and the founders of the science of economics, who count among the enlightened. To their contemporaries they were the "philosophes économistes". For the purposes of the present argument, however, this problem of classification is less important than the fact which Marc Bloch emphasized when he said: "All the economic thinking of the eighteenth century was dominated by preoccupation with production."[31]

To the enlightened the promotion of wealth, of knowledge and of freedom (however freedom was understood and it was understood in many different senses) were all interconnected needs whose pursuit was necessary to happiness and justified by reason; and this belief, however variously interpreted, and however different the means proposed for implementing it, necessarily altered the attitudes to how government should be conducted and society organized.

An essential and continually emphasized prerequisite of happiness, for example, was believed to be security of life and property, stressed equally in France and Prussia. This security was held to depend on an administration of justice conducted by judges with the necessary knowledge and training, whose judgments the ruler could not override, and on laws formulated with the requisite skill, so that they were clear, precise, and consistent. Like brutal punishments and religious persecution, arbitrary justice, and arbitrary government in general, were equated with tyranny and barbarism.

The antithesis of arbitrary government was seen as the rule of law, and law itself as discoverable by "reason". Civil liberty, it was continually asserted, consisted in not being forced to do anything which the law did not enjoin. As Montesquieu put it in a famous phrase, where there was arbitrariness there could be no liberty, so that in the best governed state a man "who had been [justly] condemned to death was freer [i.e. enjoyed a greater degree of civil liberty][32] than did the Pasha in Turkey."

Arbitrary government appeared incompatible with national wealth. No opinion was more common than that which Mercier de la Rivière expressed when he said: "Arbitrary despotism, because it destroys the rights of property, is totally destructive of plenty. It annihilates industry; it dries up the source of all wealth throughout the whole area which it dominates."[33]

Individual initiative was seen as the motive power in the creation of wealth. Given a properly devised and justly administered system of law the individual should be free – wholly in the opinion of the Physiocrats, subject to certain limitations in the opinion of others[34] – to pursue his own interests untrammelled by corporate or state interference.

All these ideas struck at the roots of the société d'ordres even when their proponents were unaware of or unwilling to admit the fact. The preoccupation with wealth and also with its distribution – for increasingly extremes of wealth and poverty came to seem not only morally wrong but a hindrance to economic growth – led in the course of time to attacks on the corporative organizations in trade, manufactures and agriculture, on the privileges of the nobility, and on privilege (in the sense defined earlier) in general.

They struck not only at the ideology of absolutism as held in France in the reign of Louis XIV, who came to see it as one of his primary duties to preserve the purity of the faith and thus, by persecuting the Huguenots, drove many of his subjects with the greatest economic skills into the service of foreign governments; they also struck at the roots of absolutism itself, including the form of it which existed in Prussia.

The ideas in relation to God and to absolute monarchy moved in harmony. Just as it came to be proclaimed that God embodied reason, so it was equally supposed – for absolutism was the institution of the ancien régimes to which everyone clung most tenaciously – that ways could be found for ensuring that the absolute monarch did the same. The Physiocrats envisaged what they called "le despotisme légal", though they never concerned themselves with the means by which this idea could be translated into practice. Their vision, admittedly repudiated by many of their French colleagues, has been epitomized in an apocryphal account of a conversation between Quesnay and the Dauphin.[35]

"What", the Dauphin asked, "would you do if you were king?"
Quesnay: "Nothing."
The Dauphin: "Then who would govern?"
Quesnay: "The law."

Similar ideas inspired the Prussians. The compilers of the *Allgemeines*

Landrecht, more practical than the French who held the same views, attempted, with the consent of Frederick the Great just before his death, to combine absolutism with the rule of law as defined earlier. The first version of the *Allgemeines Landrecht* contained the provisions that no law should have binding force until passed by a permanent legal commission, and that no *Machtspruch* should be legally valid. Both these provisions were, however, expunged, as having revolutionary implications, from the final version issued in 1794.[36] Absolutism in fact, as Rousseau and d'Alembert saw, was by its nature incompatible with most of the essential ideas of enlightened thinking.

Many of the ideas which have been here described as common to all who claimed to be enlightened, were, as I have said, capable of different interpretations. But even when this was not so, the attempts to put them into practice, which usually involved coercion, showed them to be mutually incompatible. That noted enlightened despot, for example, the Emperor Joseph II, could see no way of giving a greater degree of freedom to the peasants except by arbitrary actions of various kinds, particularly against the landlords' property-rights, actions which he prescribed, to use the phrase current at the time, by a *Federstrich*, or stroke of the pen. To Svarez, the principal architect of the Prussian *Allgemeines Landrecht*, it seemed that no proof was needed of the uncertainty and instability for which these procedures were responsible and "what an unfortunate influence this uncertainty had on the welfare of the country generally".[37]

Svarez' master, that other noted enlightened despot, Frederick the Great, by contrast, though he condemned serfdom as strongly as did Joseph II, was prepared to tolerate it, and Svarez, if with some misgivings, to go along with him, so as to preserve law, order and the security of existing property-rights on which they supposed the power of the state depended.

For all the different interpretations, nevertheless, which could be put on the principal ideas of the Enlightenment, and their incompatibility one with another in many cases, the general assumptions which all people with a claim to be enlightened were prepared to accept found, before the Revolution, no opponents of a stature comparable to that of the great French *Philosophes*. However widespread conservative thinking may have been, it was intellectually unfashionable to express it, and the enlightened ideas appear in France, and in Prussia after a certain time-lag, to have influenced the actions of people in power,[38] and at least large sections of educated opinion, sufficiently to justify Groethuysen's assertion that in the second half of the eighteenth century people spoke a language that would have been unintelligible to their forefathers.

It is no more possible to describe, in the order of their importance, the causes responsible for these new ways of thinking than it is to do so in the comparable cases in other ages. The belief that the explanation lies in terms of changes in the modes of production is plainly inadequate, not only because the modes of production did not change significantly, but because the propounders of the new ideas, and the audiences to which they principally appealed, were not the producing sections of the community, but the intellectuals, the people with intellectual aspirations, and officials who saw in the new gospel an answer to the practical problems of government, which arose to a large extent from the pressure of international competition.

The growth of wealth among the upper classes, the spread of education, the increased circulation of books and newspapers were plainly important factors, as were the increased, although by modern standards meagre, concentrations of people in towns. The Enlightenment was a European phenomenon but France, and in France Paris, a city of some 600,000 inhabitants, was its fountainhead. "Our talents and men of brains", Goethe once said, though his view of the significance of this phenomenon changed, "are scattered over the whole of Germany . . . so that personal contacts and personal exchanges of thought may be considered rarities. But now consider a city like Paris where the highest talents of a great kindom are all assembled in one spot."[39] He regretted that he had not shared in this experience.

Neither the French *Philosophes* nor the German *Aufklärer* were revolutionaries. They saw their function as merely that of clearing away the rubble of centuries. In fact, however, their ideas, putting in question as they did the virtue of all existing institutions and the validity of the beliefs on which they rested, were not only profoundly revolutionary; they set in train a way of thinking that foreshadowed a state of permanent revolution, as d'Alembert saw at the time. "If ", he said, "one examines carefully the midpoint of the century in which we live, the events which excite us or at any rate occupy our minds, our customs, our achievements, and even our diversions, it is difficult not to see that in some respects a very remarkable change in our ideas is taking place, a change whose rapidity seems to promise an even greater transformation to come. Time alone will tell what will be the goal, the nature, and the limits of this revolution, whose shortcomings and merits will be better known to posterity than to us."[40]

II

The Enlightenment and the breakdown
of the consensus in France

In France in the second half of the eighteenth century there developed increasingly a mood of frustration and discontent with the existing organization of government and society that expressed itself in the collective attitudes of almost every major and minor institution as well as in those of large numbers of individuals. There was, in fact, a progressive breakdown in the consensus which is necessary if any regime is to maintain itself.

This hostility to the social and political system manifested itself in a great variety of different ways, for every group had its particular grievances and every head its mixture of ideas. As Voltaire put it, "There was a civil war in every soul," and he was not the only one to say so. The Comte de Ségur, for example, expressed the same idea when he commented on the extraordinary mixture ("le mélange le plus extraordinaire") of beliefs that inspired the young people of his generation and that "inevitably led to a confusion that penetrated as far as the centre of the court". Everyone wanted "to repair the old edifice", but brought to this task so much enlightenment that they ended by "creating a conflagration".[1]

It was common to propose and even introduce reforms that were enlightened in some respects but retrograde in others; to see the existing abuses as due to the abandonment of standards professed (though not observed) in an idealized past, or alternatively to believe (though without any programme or organization for translating the beliefs into action) that the whole social and political system should be overthrown and replaced by something new.

This last idea was widely expressed by very different kinds of people with very different visions of the sort of society that was desirable. Rousseau, for example, maintained that "now we only see people who complain of their existence".[2] Believing that man had two primary emotions, the desire for self-preservation and well-being and horror at the sight of suffering, he himself felt a profound pity for the oppressed. It seemed to him necessary to "clear the air" and scrap all the old institutions.[3] Similar views were held by the chancellor Maupeou. Harsh, ambitious, unscrupulous and avaricious, generally reviled for his arbitrary and despotic actions, and by the *Philosophes* for his lack of culture, he nevertheless strove to improve the administration of justice and brought, although on different grounds, indictments against the existing regime that were as strong as Rousseau's. Though he claimed there was nothing he could do about it, he agreed with the memorandum presented to him in 1763 by his subordinate Lebrun, later third consul after Brumaire, who maintained that no reforms were possible as long as one continued in the old rut, and that the only remedy lay in changes brought about by the people – that is, by revolution, although this was not what he said or doubtless meant.[4]

Many years after he retired, in 1788, Maupeou wrote to Louis XVI that the nation lacked any fixed principles to serve as rallying points for the allegiance of the population. There was only "a vague desire for independence, a spirit of licence", a sense of the burdens imposed by the administration without awareness of its benefits. "Hence the complaints always on the point of bursting out, the eternal condemnation [of the government] ... which is nearly always absurd ... the hatred of the instruments of public power ... the continual tendency towards the fragmentation of desires which if united would make for the strength and prosperity of the monarchy. The people, almost everywhere left to itself, sees in the government only the force which restrains and represses it."[5]

A comparable picture had been drawn by d'Argenson, the descendant of a family ennobled in 1375,[6] who was nevertheless a member of the *robe* and was secretary of state for foreign affairs from 1744 to 1747. In his *Considérations sur le Gouvernement de la France*, which he wrote in 1737 but which was first published in Amsterdam in 1765, he observed that all the organs of government constituted "a chaos of rules, obstructions and contradictions" uninformed by any principles.[7]

The most eloquent and famous of all the testimonies to the general discontent which were expressed by people occupying posts of high authority, was the *Mémoire sur les Municipalités*, written in 1775 by Dupont de Nemours under Turgot's instructions. This stressed, as d'Argenson had done, the lack of any principles in the conduct of government. French society, it pointed out, "was composed of various orders without unity [among themselves] so that everyone is occupied exclusively with his own interest". Families consisted of individuals with duties to each other and to society, but they were very badly informed about the former and wholly ignorant of the latter. They looked on the authorities' demand for taxes which were necessary to the maintenance of public order "as the law of the strongest which there is no other reason to obey except the impossibility of resistance. Hence everyone tries to cheat the authorities and push the burden onto his neighbours." One might say, this mémoire argued, that the king was at war with his people, "and in this kind of war ... no one has any interest in supporting the government. Anyone who does so is viewed with suspicion. There is no public spirit because there is no point of common interest that is visible and known."[8]

How is this state of affairs to be accounted for and why did it prove impossible to remedy? These are not the kind of questions that can ever be answered unequivocally. It nevertheless seems clear that the defeats in war, and the failure of Louis XIV's ambitions as a young man to make France the dominant power not only in Europe but in the colonized world, played a large part in undermining confidence in France's social and political structure. The prestige of the government suffered when, after much loss of life and suffering, it failed to achieve its military objectives, as happened at the end of Louis XIV's reign and again under his successor during the war of the Austrian succession of 1740 to 1748. Far worse humiliations were experienced as a result of the series of cataclysmic defeats, and the loss of most of the French overseas empire, that occurred during the Seven Years War of 1756 to 1763.

It has rarely if ever happened, even in later centuries, that governments which have added significantly to their wealth or territories by military conquest have failed to win the support of their subjects, or that governments which have suffered the opposite fate have managed to keep it. The psychological effects in France of the Seven Years War could hardly be better described than they were by Ségur when he wrote: "The wound which this defeat inflicted on the national *amour propre* was vital and profound. The illusions of hope had gained for the King in his youth the title of the well-beloved. Having been defeated, he lost it. People change with their fortunes. They love, despise or hate authority according to the good it does them, and often they bestow without measure their admiration on success and their scorn on failure."[9]

In the hierarchical societies of the eighteenth century the subordinate was apt to feel for his superior an admiration that could even amount to hero-worship because of the esteem (unless precluded by personal vices) that was attached to birth and rank. These sentiments, however, could easily change to envy and hatred if the regime were discredited by failure and at the same time open to attack on ideological grounds.

Enlightened ideas, in some form or another, appear to have penetrated the minds of most French people, though in greatly varying degrees of bowdlerization or distortion and though invoked in support of widely different courses of action. In ways and with results that must be considered presently, they influenced the actions of the *parlements* – those bastions of conservatism as they are generally and not unjustifiably seen; they became widespread in the army and in large sections of the nobility, particularly, if one may believe Guy Chaussinand-Nogaret, among the poorer nobility.[10] The general mood of discontent spread to the lowest strata of the population – to the urban workers, and to the peasants, whose common propensity to violence assumed a different form, in the latter part of the eighteenth century when they attacked the seigneurs, from that which had distinguished it in the seventeenth century when they had attacked the government's tax-collectors. The reasons for this change of attitude have been only imperfectly examined. Plainly, however, as the churches grew emptier and the village pubs fuller, the influence of new ideas, mixed up as they were with old ones, played an important part.[11]

A whole series of ministers, often highly enlightened and humane, continually attempted, from the middle of the eighteenth century, to introduce reforms. As Rousseau put it: "on raccommodait sans cesse"[12] – one was continually trying to improve things piece-meal – to remedy the defects in the system of government finance and taxation; to remove the obstacles to increasing production; to create a more just, less inegalitarian society unified in an effort to promote national prosperity and power.

It has recently been pointed out that the burden of the royal taxes was less onerous in the eighteenth century than it had been in the seventeenth, given the increase in production which, however inadequate, was nevertheless substantial, the rise in prices and the growth in populations.[13] This fact, however, is of no significance if what is at issue is popular beliefs as distinct from statistics. Everyone supposed that the taxes were getting heavier as new ones were added to the old,[14] and particularly the nobility believed this as their immunities were increasingly eroded. Few subjects can have been more widely discussed in government and educated circles or given rise to a larger literature. The animosities were fuelled by the military failures, by the conspicuous waste, by the wealth of the financiers, by the extravagance of the court and, particularly among many ministers and officials, by the enlightened principles in favour of rational administration and protection of the weak against the strong. As many royal edicts and orders in council testify, these principles came to take an equal place with, if not precedence over, the attitudes which had prevailed under Louis XIV, when the government had striven to increase the royal revenues at any cost.

A whole succession of reforming ministers attempted to lighten the burden of direct taxation borne by the peasants by pushing as much of it as possible onto the nobility. Though the nobles (or noble land in the *pays de taille réelle*) continued to remain immune from the *taille*, they were subject to other taxes, particularly the so-called *vingtièmes*. The *vingtième* was a tax of 5 per cent, theoretically on all sources of income but in fact usually only on land. It was doubled and then tripled in the second half of the eighteenth century and also increased by an additional percentage on every livre paid.[15] Further, the nobles were subject to the so-called *capitation* whose rate was also raised. Though commonly said to have been light there is evidence that it was often not so.[16] Moreover, in addition to all this, the nobles in effect paid the *taille* of their tenants, who took the sums this tax required of them into account when fixing the price of the lease, and often a part or the whole of the *taille* of their share-croppers who would otherwise have starved. Well might that noted revolutionary, the Abbé Sieyès, observe in his famous pamphlet *Qu'est-ce que le Tiers Etat?*,[17] that the introduction of a general tax payable without exemptions, and the abolition of all tax privileges, would be to the nobles' pecuniary advantage – a fact which they themselves had come to accept before the outbreak of the Revolution.

In law the French nobility at the end of the Ancien Régime were subject to a higher rate of direct taxation than were their counterparts in Britain,[18] or, in all probability, in any other nation, but, so we are often told, they managed to avoid payment. Certainly they frequently did so. The Duc d'Orléans, the richest man in the kingdom, is noted for having said that he fixed things with the *intendants* so that he paid no more than the minimum he chose. In matters of direct taxation, however, the situation seems to have been similar to that described earlier in relation to the administration of justice. The rich and powerful nobles could evade their obligations. The poorer nobles were less fortunate.[19]

It seems likely, moreover, that the nobles suffered from inequalities in the distribution of the direct taxes comparable to those among other categories of people. Professor Robert Forster, for example, made a study in 1960 of the estates belonging to the twenty richest nobles in Toulouse[20] (who were nevertheless not rich by English standards since their average net income from land was only about £250 per annum at the current rate of exchange). He discovered that in 1750, when the rate of tax was much lower than it later became, they paid, again on average, 15 per cent of their gross income in direct taxes. Arithmetical averages are, however, misleading in circumstances that varied as greatly as did those in eighteenth-century France. Of these twenty nobles, all of them in comparable circumstances and living in the same neighbourhood, one, whose gross income was £226 per annum paid 20 per cent in direct taxes; another, whose gross income was £141 paid 27 per cent as did a third whose gross income is not recorded. One noble paid as much as 31 per cent. Two paid only 3 per cent.[21]

The object of the reforming ministers was to iron out these and other worse inequalities. The conditions, however, that existed in every country at the time made it impossible to achieve this objective. Particularly no means were available for assessing income derived from business or financial sources, whose owners in consequence escaped direct taxation altogether. Income from land could nevertheless be taxed, though only at a flat rate which was a much more serious burden to the poor than to the rich. Even this kind of tax, however, could not be imposed with any approach to fairness except by means of a *cadastre* or land survey.

In 1763, at the end of the Seven Years War, the government ordered that such a survey should be undertaken, while admitting that "so extensive an operation requires assiduous work extending over several years". It nevertheless ordered that this task should be embarked on in all the lands of the kingdom, even in those "belonging to the domains of the crown, the princes of the blood, the church, the nobles and other privileged persons".[22] This project, however, aroused furious opposition from every class in the population, including the victims of the existing system, who assumed that it was designed to extract more money from them. The rich from whom the government hoped to gain larger payments protested after the fashion common among those who fear that their incomes will be reduced, though with a better excuse than often exists in such circumstances because of the lack of any body of officials in whose skill and honesty one could place any trust.[23] The opposition to the *cadastre*, led by the *parlements* and other sovereign courts, was in fact such that the project had to be dropped. More or less comparable projects[24] were attempted in various administrative districts, but succeeded only in two: in the Limousin when Turgot was *intendant* there and in Paris under Bertier de Sauvigny.[25] Even if the taxes were in general less heavy, and the inequalities in their distribution smaller than in the previous century, these facts were not recognized, and in the new climate of opinion their arbitrariness aroused in many groups a resentment that expressed itself in ways unknown in the past.

An equally, if not a more, serious defect in the French financial system was the one referred to earlier, which deprived the government of control over or even knowledge of its revenue and expenditure as a result of the sale of offices and the analogous arrangements with the tax-farm. In the course of the eighteenth century many *contrôleurs-généraux* came to see that these arrangements were both a cause of waste and an obstacle to the pursuit of any rational foreign, social or economic policy.

A number of *contrôleurs-généraux*, variously seen as liberals like Turgot, as cheats and tyrants like Terray, or as a mediocre parvenu – the term commonly applied to Necker until recent attempts (sometimes exaggerated) have been made to emphasize the humanity of his ideas and the virtues of his policies[26] – strove to mitigate or abolish these anomalies. Necker was the advocate of the most radical changes. He was responsible for a number of edicts designed to bring the various officials concerned with financial matters under closer government control. He abolished (with compensation which nevertheless appears to have been inadequate) a number of venal offices, particularly those of the 48 *receveurs-généraux*, referred to earlier,[27] who handed over to the crown the sums collected in direct taxes. He removed various indirect taxes from the control of the tax-farm and reduced the number of general farmers from 60 to 40.[28]

These attempts to proceed towards a nationalization of the financial system created a storm of opposition. Necker's reforms diminished if they did not annihilate the fortunes of many individuals, disrupted the expectations of families where offices were passed on to sons or near relatives, and in spite of the long-term benefits that would have flowed from them produced no immediate financial return. On the contrary, it appeared that their result must be an immediate financial loss. The crown, it was shown earlier, depended wholly for its short-term loans on the financiers who had bought their offices and on the tax-farm which was also a source of long-term loans. How was it to manage in the situation which Necker was endeavouring to create? As Joli de Fleury, who succeeded Necker in 1781, put it, "The people who lend their money want a richer guarantor." They would not trust the crown.[29] As Calonne said in 1783: "It is thus – and I could cite many other examples – that these operations, allegedly designed for economy, and these badly conceived suppressions, often leave behind them only the infuriating effects of useless innovation, of private fortunes overturned without any increase in the state's revenues, of reimbursement charges on the royal treasury and, what is still worse, of public confidence damaged by charges which must inevitably shake it."[30] As a result of all these protests Necker was dismissed from office and most of his measures reversed. They were not reconsidered till the eve of the Revolution.

The attempts to reform the administration of justice, as was shown earlier, failed equally, as did those to bring about an agricultural revolution. The same fate overtook the many projects to abolish the innumerable tolls and customs duties to which French internal trade was subjected. These projects dated from the days of Colbert, but were pursued with increasing vigour after the end of the Seven Years War – that watershed in attitudes towards rationalizing administration and increasing production.

These tolls and duties had originally been levied as a result of legal bargains between the crown and the individuals or authorities concerned. Though the fruits of a few remained in private hands, the bulk were taken over by the General Farm which developed an increasing efficiency in collecting them, though at a proportionate cost in harassment and financial loss to merchants and producers. Like the direct taxes, these indirect taxes had under Louis XIV and later been imposed and increased merely in order to add to the crown's revenues, regardless of the economic consequences. From the middle of the eighteenth century onwards, however, increasing numbers of ministers and officials came to see that this was a self-defeating procedure. As one observer wrote in 1786: "Although English merchandise is subject [on importation] to duties of 10% or 12%, England can supply nearly all the provinces of the [French] kingdom more cheaply than can our own industry. Our goods are subject to customs duties which prevent them from meeting English competition. It costs from 10% to 12% to send silk from Lyon to Brittany, and it costs as much to send Flemish products into the interior of the kingdom. – The cloth of Languedoc arrives in Paris and Brittany only after having paid 15% or 16% in duties and expenses."[31]

The projects, however, to abolish this state of affairs and to turn France into a free trade area foundered on the same rocks as did the other attempted reforms: the protests of the beneficiaries of the existing system and the immediate loss of revenue which reducing or abolishing the internal trade barriers would have caused, designed though these measures were to stimulate production and thus increase revenue in the future. As L'Averdy, a magistrate in the Paris *parlement* who later became *contrôleur-général*, observed in 1764: "To gain the support of the people is doubtless necessary; to reduce the taxes is the road to follow; to change their nature and form is a means; to proceed against the financiers a crowning one. But, Monsieur, at the moment bankruptcy would be the result of any one of these measures and a fortiori of all three in conjunction. You do not understand how extreme are the ills from which France suffers. It is easy to talk of the need to change . . . the taxes. But who is to do this? Where are the people trained to introduce this new order of things? . . . Proceed against the financiers and the government contractors and there won't be a penny tomorrow. Are they not the people with all the money?"[32]

France in the eighteenth century thus found herself increasingly unable to maintain her predominant position in Europe and as a colonial power, and the more or less continuous attempts to bring about reforms which would have enabled her to mobilize her resources and reverse this situation, and which in any case the enlightened advocated in the name of justice and humanity, proved abortive. How does one account for these failures?

It has long been customary to lay the blame for them on the selfishness of those, particularly the nobility, who were, or were supposed to be, the beneficiaries of the regime. These indictments are doubtless often justified but useless as an explanation, since selfishness among privileged groups, particularly in the kind of societies that existed in the eighteenth century, is a common feature of political life. The problem is how to overcome it sufficiently in times when drastic reforms are essential.

The most powerful and intractable of the groups with which the reforming ministers had to contend were the twelve *parlements*. They are commonly said to have represented the nobility, but this statement is plainly inexact. The nobles were divided by huge differences of wealth (those at the bottom of the scale had incomes of a few pounds a year, those at the top incomes of tens or even hundreds of thousands), and their style of life, education and manners varied accordingly. They were also divided by status and by the advantages or otherwise, and degree of esteem, attached to it. There were nobles for life only, first, second, third and fourth generation nobles, and so on up to the families who had been noble in 1400 and had the right to be presented at court. All these categories of nobles, in addition to the privileges which belonged to any noble as such, had their own particular privileges which were often a bone of contention among them.[33] The nobles were further divided among a great variety of different occupations and professions, many of which were often hostile to each other and some of which, particularly that of the ennobled financiers, were a principal object of the *parlements'* attacks. What sense has the term representation when applied to a group composed of people so diverse, so riven by dissensions, and no more capable of acting in concert than would be the members of any arbitrarily selected category – say redheads or people with green eyes – unless, as such, they became the object of attack?[34] In any case, the magistrates of the *parlements* bought their offices. Before they could enter on their functions they needed the consent of the crown and of the *parlement* concerned, but in no modern sense of the term representation can they be said to have represented any body except that in which they worked.

They nevertheless claimed to represent the people and, whatever their actions or motives, may be said to have done so in the sense that they frequently protested against practices that were generally harmful and recognized to be so by wide sections of opinion. As d'Argenson put it in 1752: "They are the only organ possessed by the people which is capable of making itself heard."[35]

They saw themselves as the guardians of the so-called "fundamental laws", or, in other words, of what was seen as the constitution, although as this was neither written down nor defined by any clear precedents it was capable of a variety of different interpretations and was a continual subject of disputes on which there was no arbiter to adjudicate.

The ideologies which inspired the *parlements* have been admirably described in a recent work, *Le Conseil du Roi sous Louis XV*, by Michel Antoine. He points out that though they always proclaimed themselves the defenders of absolutism, the *parlements* increasingly developed doctrines and practices calculated to destroy it. They never denied the King's right to make law but nevertheless claimed that it was for them to decide which royal edicts and other orders were constitutionally valid and which were not. As it was put in 1763: "Your august predecessors, Sire, . . . realized that they were men, and as such subject to error and uncertainty. In order to avoid uncertainty they not only believed that no changes in the law should ever be permitted except after the most careful examination . . . but they also laid down fundamental principles in which they declared that they and their successors would never make any changes. These two precautions were of the greatest wisdom, but it was necessary to ensure their success. The preservation of the law had to be entrusted to men capable of fulfilling with good faith and courage the duties it imposed. These men are the magistrates . . ."[36]

In pursuit of these principles, the *parlements* embarked on a war with the crown on the grounds that it had violated the constitution and, in the terminology of Montesquieu, was changing from monarchy into despotism. Lawyers trained in a system of law whose principles had remained unchanged since the evolution of the doctrine of absolutism in the sixteenth and seventeenth centuries,[37] and thus by their education and professional ethos authoritarians and traditionalists, they were collectively hostile to the *Philosophes*, though their members were far from necessarily so as individuals. They banned the first edition of the *Encyclopédie*, Helvetius' *De L'Esprit* and many other famous works of the Enlightenment. They upheld the existing administration of justice with all its abuses, as described earlier, and the barbarous punishments inflicted on Calas and many others. For all this, nevertheless, they condemned many practices which had been tolerated in the past and which were equally condemned by all those who claimed to be enlightened.

They put forward claims to resist the royal authority and to uphold the rights of the people – claims which were contrary to hitherto accepted theory and had never been expressed in the days of Louis XIV.[38] For all the conservatism, in fact, of which they are often and justifiably accused, it is plain that, after their fashion, they, too, were influenced by the new ideas.

The quarrels between the crown and the *parlements* reached a climax in the years 1750 to 1770 over a large range of matters, notably over the (as they claimed illegitimate) practice by which the crown bypassed their authority by issuing orders in council which did not have to be submitted to them.[39] Above all, however, they protested against the imposition of new taxes, against the arbitrary assessment of the taxes generally, against the general financial mismanagement, against the lack of any fixed procedure for relating expenditure to revenue, against the profits of the tax-farm and the extravagance of the court. However retrograde they may have been in other respects, in these matters, as Cardinal Bernis observed, "The *parlements'* opposition derives its strength from the support of public opinion."[40]

When the crown refused to listen to their protests the *parlements*, individually or collectively, went on strike – that is, they declined, together with the courts dependent on them, to discharge their judicial functions, and the administration of justice came to a full stop. This, as may well be imagined, threatened the country, in Michel Antoine's words, with chaos.

In consequence, in 1770 the chancellor Maupeou arrested the magistrates who refused to resume their duties, exiled them to the provinces where many were forced to live in conditions of extreme hardship, and finally dismissed them with highly inadequate compensation,[41] replacing them by a new machinery of justice in which the sale of offices, and the right to refuse to register the royal edicts, were forbidden.

However many and uncertain the various interpretations of the law and the constitution, these actions were plainly both illegal and unconstitutional and raised a storm of protest which expressed itself, among other ways, in a vast pamphlet literature, much of which the government failed to suppress. As one contemporary put it: "However long the nation had been accustomed to yield to the yoke imposed upon it, because this yoke had never had the force of law but only of practice, the nation, from attachment to the king, had always given way. But in this affair, ashamed to see itself treated as a slave, and despotism erected into law, it raised its head and proclaimed itself a free people."[42]

It did not in fact do so. The opposition to Maupeou gradually subsided. Nevertheless, for reasons that remain somewhat uncertain but among which the outcries against despotism seem undoubtedly to have played a part, Louis XV on his accession in 1774 restored the *parlements*, though subject to the conditions that they should confine their protests to remonstrances only and that they should not go on strike – provisions which they observed till 1786.[43]

It has often been maintained that the recall of the *parlements* was a disastrous decision which made revolution inescapable. This belief, however, is hardly plausible. It was not held even by Flammermont, who wrote the fullest account of the subject in 1883 and believed that Louis' action was, as he put it, the "greatest mistake". Flammermont nevertheless concluded that as a cause of the Revolution it was irrelevant.[44]

Apart from any other reason, the *parlements*' opposition even at its worst (and so greatly had Maupeou's actions alarmed them that they showed none for twelve years), was only negative. In 1756 they claimed, contrary to all precedent, that far from being unrelated institutions, responsible only in their respective areas of jurisdiction, they constituted, as they put it, "the separate classes of a single body, animated by the same spirit, nourished by the same principles, devoted to the same object".[45] They nevertheless proved incapable of acting in concert.[46] The opinion which d'Argenson once expressed, that they might have become the leaders of a revolution against what he called the worst government in Europe,[47] was plainly absurd. They neither could nor claimed to decide policy. This was a task for the government which, however, lacked the means to discharge it adequately, or, even in the absence of the *parlements*' opposition, to get its orders obeyed.

A prime minister in the modern sense of the term was impossible under absolutism. At best there could be a "first minister" who enjoyed the royal favour and dominated his colleagues. Many such existed in France in the eighteenth century. His position was, however, always precarious and at the mercy of the fears and whims of the cliques at court and the royal mistresses who influenced or determined the policy of two weak kings in succession. This situation could only be overcome in the more or less unlikely circumstances that came to exist in Prussia after 1806 (and were repeated under Bismarck) when a weak and indecisive monarch was prepared to delegate his power more or less completely to men of strength and vision such as Stein and Hardenberg. Stein and Hardenberg, moreover, had at their disposal an administrative machine and a loyal army, both of which in France were largely lacking.

It is true that in the course of the eighteenth century in France there were increasing attempts to abolish the sale of offices and to replace their holders by paid servants of the crown. Particularly, as has been shown, both Maupeou and Necker strove to achieve this. Within the bureaux of the ministers, chosen though these largely were from among people who had begun their careers by the purchase of an office, there developed a class of permanent employees with the mentality of civil servants, and certain institutions, for example the *ponts et chaussées*, came to be staffed exclusively by "fonctionnaires" or government servants in the modern sense. One might, in fact, say that before the end of the Ancien Régime the embryo of a modern civil service had come into existence.[48]

It nevertheless remains true that the commanding heights in the administration of justice and finance were still largely held by people who had bought their offices, which they ran partly as private undertakings and partly on behalf of the crown, or by semi-private organizations such as the tax-farm. Much of the provincial administration was also in the hands of people in comparable positions.

The provinces were subjected to the control of a multitude of venal officials whose spheres of operation were continually in dispute, who were related one to another by no chain of command and who were perpetually at loggerheads. As Tocqueville put it: "There existed in France under the Ancien Régime all kinds of authorities which varied to infinity and none of which had any fixed and well-recognized limits, with the result that the sphere of action of everyone was always common to various others."[49]

Those writers who at various times have claimed that the Revolution might have been averted if this, that, or the other minister – particularly Turgot but more recently Necker – had not been ousted from power, might well pause to consider what practical difficulties would have faced such a person had he remained in office. Those who have blamed the nobility for their selfish refusal to surrender their privileges might profitably ask themselves what sacrifices, precisely, might have saved the day.

Tocqueville pointed out in one of his most illuminating chapters – chapter VI of Book III, not commonly cited – that France was an atomized society. For decades before the Revolution it had been continually subjected to those "raccommodements" of which Rousseau spoke, and this was particularly true after 1787 when a further attempt was made to reform the administration of justice, and provincial assemblies were set up in every *village département* and province to facilitate a less arbitrary distribution of the taxes.[50] These continual changes, introduced by royal edicts which constantly referred to the abuses of the existing regime, affected the lives and mental attitudes of everyone from the peasants upwards, and produced, in Tocqueville's words, "a greater state of perturbation" among the population at large "than had ever been seen in the history of a great nation".[51]

In addition, the allegiance of the army became increasingly problematic. Though war was denounced by many *Philosophes* and their disciples – by no one in perhaps more sincere and moving terms than by Necker[52] – the military profession, in France as in Prussia, remained the most prestigious, and the military virtues – courage, honour, self-sacrifice, the capacity to endure hardship and death with fortitude – commanded the highest respect and evoked the emotions which de Gaulle expressed when he spoke of "cette destination de misère, cette vocation de sacrifices, depuis que le monde est le monde."[53]

The French army had acquitted itself very badly between 1756 and 1763. The disaster of these war years inspired in military as in other circles a desire for reforms whose introduction in the military system laid the foundations for Napoleon's victories.[54] The reformers' belief, however, in the "armée pure et dure" led them to despise the pursuit and enjoyment of wealth and to attack the court favourites and the nouveaux-riches nobles, who were able to procure themselves commissions, and to sustain the expenses of military life, which were beyond the means of the poor provincial nobility, who saw themselves, and were seen by the reformers, as the repository of the military virtues.

The military reforms in the last years of the Ancien Régime were technically remarkable[55] but socially disastrous. The *Loi Ségur* referred to earlier set noble against noble and fomented a widespread sense of injustice. As Sénac de Meilhan (*intendant* of Hainault with aspirations to the *contrôle-général*, but of recent noble origin) put it, the *Loi Ségur* "humiliated the magistrates, the rich and a crowd of honourable families" who were unable "de faire ses preuves" (i.e., to give proof of the necessary number of noble ancestors) and were despised henceforth by other members of their estate who had one or two more generations of nobility to their credit.[56]

The absurdities and injustices of the Ancien Régime, in fact, infiltrated the army in which all the national grievances came to be reflected. By 1790 the minister of war, La Tour Du-Pin, observed that the number of seditious or mutinous regiments was increasing daily.[57]

Torn by conflicting ideologies and thus without any ideology at all; lacking any effective means for formulating policy or for carrying it out; without support from any of the major groups in the population and faced with the hostility of many, which the army could not be relied on to control, the government, when confronted with a slump, a series of bad harvests and a financial crisis, could only abdicate, for summoning the Estates General was in effect an abdication – an abandoning to the representatives of the people the solution of those problems with which the monarch, his ministers and his administration were unable to cope. The Ancien Régime in France, in other words, had fallen to pieces before the revolutionaries attacked it.

III
The Enlightenment in Prussia

(a) THE BUILD-UP OF THE CONSENSUS, 1740–1786

As was said earlier, by the standards of many French *Philosophes*, Frederick the Great's Prussia was not enlightened at all, and to some Prussians themselves it seemed so only with qualifications. To Lessing, a Saxon by birth but for the best part of thirty years a Prussian by adoption, even the qualifications were absent, though in this matter at the time his was a voice crying in the wilderness. "Don't talk to me", he wrote from Hamburg in 1769, "of your freedom of thought and publication in Berlin. It consists only of the freedom to publish as many idiotic attacks on religion as one wants – a freedom of which any honest man would be ashamed to avail himself. But just let anyone try to write about other things in Berlin . . . let him attempt to speak the truth to the distinguished rabble at court, to stand up for the rights of the subject, to raise his voice against despotism as now happens in France and Denmark, and you will realize which country, up to the present day, is the most slavish in Europe."[1]

However open, nevertheless, Frederick's government may have been to the accusation that it was not enlightened, his own thinking and actions in many ways belied the charge, by the standards of the Enlightenment described earlier, because of his encouragement of free speculation on all matters other than his own actions and form of government, because of his belief in religious toleration (which he expressed in the famous words: "Hier muß ein jeder nach seiner Façon selig werden"[2] – here everyone must be allowed to go to heaven in his own way) and because of his respect for reason in the sense of believing that the state should be organized in accordance with a rationally thought-out plan in which ends and means were considered in conjunction.

This is not to say, on the other hand, that he was what would commonly be described as a reasonable man, since his legally untrammelled power, combined with his highly irascible, capricious, and often vindictive temperament continually, and increasingly as he grew older, led him to yield to whims and prejudices, and to commit injustices, of which many more cases could be cited than those of Ursinus and Müller Arnold already mentioned.

For all this, nevertheless, he endeavoured to the best of his ability, misguided though his actions often were, to organize his government in accordance with principles which, though he did not seek to apply them in a doctrinaire way, he always consciously directed to achieving his principal objective – the maintenance of his power internationally, including, as far as the two seemed compatible, those psychological and material conditions on which, in the long run, it rested. For in the predatory world in which he lived, and in which he was no more, but only more successfully, aggressive than most other rulers, military defeat, as the future was to show, meant an end to such welfare and happiness among his subjects as, in the cynicism of his old age, he believed that life on earth permitted.

The difference in the meaning which Enlightenment had for him and for the prophets of the Enlightenment in France, was well illustrated recently by a German historian[3] when he noted that to the Physiocrats, those *Philosophes économistes*, the common good depended on allowing the greatest possible freedom to the individual. To Frederick, by contrast, the interests of the state and those of the individual were indissolubly bound together, and if at any moment the two appeared to conflict, the individual must be sacrificed for the benefit of the community.

The idea that the individual as such had certain inalienable rights, for example those expressed in France in the Declaration of the Rights of Man of 17 August 1789, was alien to his thinking. In theory, he subscribed to many of the principles which this document set out, notably that "property is a sacred and inviolable right" of which "no one may be deprived . . . unless a legally established public necessity obviously requires it"; that "no one should be accused, arrested, or detained except in cases determined by law"; that "no one should be disquieted because of his opinions, even religious ones, provided their manifestation does not disturb the public order established by law". His acceptance of these doctrines, however, together with their qualifications, was due to his conviction that no state could flourish unless they were observed. The state over which he ruled nevertheless remained an autocracy based on a *Ständegesellschaft* – facts which led Tocqueville to say of what he called "le code du grand Frédéric" (i.e., the *Allgemeines Landrecht*) that "sous cette tête toute moderne nous allons voir apparaître un corps tout gothique", which he proceeded to label a monstrosity.[4]

The complaints in France against the abuses of justice, the weight and arbitrariness of the taxes, the extravagance of the rich, the miseries of the poor, and the social and political abuses generally, owed their origins to the disasters of Louis XIV's last years and reached their apogee in the second half of the eighteenth century. The writers in the age of the French Enlightenment formulated the ideas in whose name the old order was destroyed. Towards the end of the Ancien Régime, admittedly, they may be said to have entered the establishment like a Trojan horse[5] – Voltaire, for example, was made a member of the French Academy in 1778. Most of the famous *Philosophes*, however, Voltaire included, had passed a large part of their lives menaced by the censor and by imprisonment. Their doctrines never influenced the curricula in the schools and universities, and only partially and spasmodically received official recognition.

The ideology of the Prussian Enlightenment, by contrast, as it was described by the nineteenth-century German historians who saw in Frederick the Great the enlightened despot *par excellence* was the ideology of the King himself, which in social and political matters he derived partly from the principles of his father, notwithstanding the early hostility between them, and partly from that leading luminary of the early German Enlightenment, Christian Wolff.

Wolff, as was shown earlier, was regarded as the greatest philosopher in central Europe for much of his life, and his pupils were scattered throughout the Prussian universities and others in the German-speaking world; so that the Enlightenment as understood by Frederick, in so far as it was concerned with social and political affairs, was not, as in France, an ideology of protest, but the official ideology taught in the universities and, until like all ideologies it was overtaken by events, accepted by the bulk of educated people.

The works of Christian Wolff were always published with a picture of him set against a background of the sun, the symbol of Enlightenment, breaking through the clouds.[6] Meticulously orderly in his work and the regulation of his domestic affairs (he accounted for every penny), proud of his European reputation, his professorial status, and the title of Freiherr by which Frederick the Great raised him into the nobility, he was arrogant, authoritarian and a believer in authoritarianism. His *Politik*, of which the last edition was published in 1736, was a manual for monarchs, the purpose of which was, as he put it, "to establish on a thorough basis how a state should be constructed on this earth". Taking men as he assumed them to be, and reason (which he equated with natural law) as he understood it, he was a believer, like many of his contemporaries, in the contract theory of government. Reason, he concluded, demonstrated that the state must have come into existence by the agreement of the population to subject themselves to its authority in order that they might enjoy security and protection, and progress towards perfection – ends which, as he supposed, the state alone was capable of promoting. The functions of the state, as he understood them, were commonly described by nineteenth-century historians as those of the *Wohlfahrtsstaat*, or welfare state, and though the material circumstances of the time, and the nature of its thinking which they conditioned, gave to the term welfare a sense different from its present one – in eighteenth-century Prussia it was the group and not the individual that was the state's essential concern – still the two conceptions had points in common. Both saw the individual as a creature necessarily dependent on and owing obligations to his fellow men, and as the member of various groups, of which the lowest was the family and the pinnacle the state, whose duty was to ensure a decent life for everyone, though this assumption did not involve any belief in equality of wealth, esteem or legal rights, but was based on acceptance of the *Ständesgesellschaft*.

To Wolff and his disciples who dominated the teaching in the universities, in which the government controlled the appointments, the state was all-powerful and the source of all rights. Everyone owed it unquestioning obedience. In its tasks of promoting welfare, materially and morally, it had the right to interfere in every aspect of national and personal life, though since it owed its existence to man and not to God, and man's specific attribute was reason, it was assumed that it had no right to require adherence to any particular form of religious belief or to limit freedom of thought in religious and philosophical matters.

The obligations of the subject (the *Untertan*, not envisaged as a *Staatsbürger* or citizen) were seen by Wolff as being due to the state and not to the monarch, although in fact this distinction was meaningless; for though Wolff, in accordance with the theories prevalent at the time, recognized that there were different forms of government, he held absolutism to be the best; and though he was forced to admit that there might be bad rulers, he assumed (for he was often far from consistent) that the will of the ruler expressed the needs of the state and was subject to no limits. There was no place in this doctrine for the idea of fundamental law as expressed, however imprecisely, by the French *parlements*, or for any bodies with the right to question the actions of the government. As Tocqueville observed of the *Allgemeines Landrecht*, and as has sometimes also been observed of Wolff's beliefs, the Enlightenment as he expounded it in relation to social and political matters had certain affinities with socialism, though also many features incompatible with it. His doctrines, however, advocated a more complete autocracy than any propounded at the time in the west.

Seeing in mathematics the queen of the sciences and in the syllogistic form of argument the only path to truth, he was contemptuous of the methods of empirical investigation dear to the hearts of the French *Philosophes*. He was totally lacking in the subtlety and intellectual sophistication that distinguished the great prophets of the French Enlightenment, but was nevertheless the founding father of the German.

What has been said here previously is sufficient to show how faithfully, in broad outline, Frederick followed Wolff's precepts. These nevertheless came to seem increasingly open to question as, after the end of the Seven Years War, the level of education and experience rose in the bureaucracy, as new ideas filtered in from the west, and as a discriminating reading public developed which, small though it was – one of the leading figures of the later Prussian Enlightenment, Nicolai, put the numbers of the highly educated at only 20,000 in a population of 5½ million[7] – included many prominent figures in government and society.

Here was fertile soil for criticism in which Frederick sowed the seeds when, in the endeavour to make good the vast damage caused by the Seven Years War and at the same time to maintain an army four times as large as a state with the population of the Hohenzollern dominions might be expected to support,[8] he resorted to misguided and unpopular economic measures.

The dirigisme of his economic policy inevitably created many enemies in the business community, as had Colbert's in France. A member of the Academy of Sciences in East Berlin[9] has recently described at length the mistakes he made, the interests he outraged, the charlatans who bamboozled him and the doubts engendered among high officials even though they could only criticize him at their peril. His pressing need for money led him greatly to increase indirect taxation, and to do so by employing officials from the French tax-farm, though on terms less favourable than the tax-farmers got in France, because he assumed they possessed more highly developed techniques than any that existed in Prussia. These proceedings were, needless to say, a cause of bitter complaint to the consumers, and outraged the Prussian officials whose functions the Frenchmen usurped.

None of this, however, led to the formulation of a revolutionary ideology, let alone to revolutionary action, either during Frederick's lifetime or for two decades afterwards, and even then only with qualifications, because his achievements seemed by far to outweigh his faults.

His personality had a charismatic effect on many people besides the peasants who formed the great majority of his subjects. Not for nothing had he led peasant armies in many battles. Though he habitually wrote in French and spoke what he called a servants' German, he could talk to the peasants in Plattdeutsch.[10] When he toured the crown domains he would discuss agricultural matters with the royal tenants, showing a remarkably detailed (if sometimes inaccurate) knowledge of the neighbourhood and its problems.[11]

Proverbially, in every *Ständegesellschaft* the peasants felt sentiments for the monarch comparable to those they felt in Prussia for *der alte Fritz*. Frederick's charisma, however, which certainly owed nothing to the pomp and ceremony of ordinary monarchies, also captured the imagination of many of the educated even when, like Ludwig von der Marwitz, they were critical of the kind of state he had created. In later life Marwitz told the story, apparently without any sense that his early enthusiasm had been misplaced, of his first meeting with the King when he was a child. This occurred when Frederick, on one of his periodic tours through the provinces, came into the neighbourhood of the Marwitz estate at Friedersdorf in the Mark of Brandenburg. An old woman held the small Ludwig up until he was on a level with a window of the royal carriage. "I was", Marwitz said, "only a foot or so [eine Elle] away from the King and I felt as if I were looking at God. I kept thinking that he would speak to me, but I was not afraid. I had merely an indescribable feeling of awe."[12] In a less exaggerated and emotional manner than that in which Marwitz was accustomed to express himself, many other people felt the same.

The later generation of the so-called *Aufklärer*, or enlightened – the circle constituted by the publicist Nikolai, Moses Mendelssohn, Lessing, Svarez and others – though they never, in their views on government and society,[13] wholly severed their connection with their Wolffian origins, held views on these matters that differed in certain important respects from Wolff's.

Particularly, the word "Menschheit" was continually on their lips, by which they meant humanity in the sense of a Christian love of one's neighbour, a recognition that all men shared qualities in common, and a belief that these common human qualities should be "the principal yardstick in the determination of priorities".

From these assumptions followed a number of opinions hardly compatible with the existing organization of government and society. The later *Aufklärer*, while not questioning that the interests of the State must take precedence over those of the individual, were the first to complain of the *mechanischer Staat* or *Maschinenstaat*, in which people were seen as cogs in a machine – as means to an end instead of ends in themselves. Man, they maintained, had a value as a human being superior to his value as a subject.

Like most of the French *Philosophes* they believed that careers should be open to talent, and were therefore critical of all legally guaranteed privileges, including particularly the privileges of the nobility, though they were prepared to welcome as associates any individual nobles who shared their views and who did not go in for frenchified airs and graces, which seemed to them incompatible with decent human behaviour and true Enlightenment. They deplored serfdom, were in favour of emancipating the Jews and, in general, desired many changes of a liberal nature.

They based their hopes (and they included a high proportion of officials among their number)[14] for a more humane society, purged of the defects of the existing one, on the development of those attitudes which the Enlightenment since its earliest days had always attempted to foster: on a rational approach to the problems of life and government, and particularly on a recognition that ideas and practices hallowed by custom must be subjected to the test of reason. These attitudes, they assumed, could be developed by a growth of knowledge, and better and more widespread education.

They were perfectly aware that in Prussia there was no freedom of speech in matters of politics, but since during Frederick the Great's reign they were free to preach their gospel without interference from the state they were willing to leave politics alone.

They did not doubt that Frederick had been guilty of grave mistakes and injustices but they were prepared to excuse him – in the Müller Arnold case, for example, because of what seemed to them his essentially just intentions, and in the case of the debasement of the coinage during the Seven Years War, which they recognized as a means of cheating the public, on the grounds that he had no alternative – an argument which it would be difficult to refute.

They saw that the Prussian state was far from perfect but they thought it superior to other contemporary states, apart from Britain, until the British government attempted to deny the American colonists their freedom. Particularly they thought it superior to the French, which they stigmatized as a despotism, while denying that their own form of government could be so described. Svarez gave this point of view a typical expression when in his lectures to the crown prince, later Frederick William III, he ascribed the French Revolution to "the confusion in the finances, the heavy weight of excessive taxes, the extravagance of the court, the mistresses and the favourites, the arbitrary and despotic actions taken against the persons, the freedom and the property of individual citizens by ambitious and greedy ministers under the supervision of a negligent monarch".[15] "These", he said, were "the true and only causes of the Revolution", not the opinions of the *Philosophes*, to whom it was commonly ascribed, but whose views, he admitted, determined the course it took.

Svarez' judgment appears to have been widely accepted. One German historian, for example, discovered a number of essays written for the *Abitur*[16] – the qualifying examination for entrance to the universities. In the schools which prepared candidates for this examination there was instruction in current affairs. From these essays it emerged that all their young authors believed that Prussia was a free country; all thought that the French Revolution had been caused by the despotism of Louis XV and the weakness of Louis XVI; all thought that the French people were ground down by taxes; one ascribed the burden of debt to Marie Antoinette's extravagance.[17]

From all this one might reasonably conclude that one of the principal reasons why the criticisms of the later *Aufklärer* never developed into public protest was their belief in the superiority of Prussia to other states, not only militarily, but because in the reign of Frederick the Great, as they saw things, her system of justice had been fairer, direct taxes less burdensome and more equitably distributed, a greater concern shown there than elsewhere for the general welfare, and a higher degree of freedom of thought permitted in the subjects that seemed to them of first importance. Nicolai, for example, observed on one occasion[18] that what had changed his attitude to Frederick, whom previously he had judged unfavourably, was the way in which Frederick had prevented famine in the famine years of the early 1770s. The misery in Prussia, in these years, Nicolai said, had certainly been very great but was not to be compared with that in other and richer countries, many of whose subjects had emigrated into Prussia to escape starvation.[19]

These attitudes were reinforced by the emphasis laid on obedience and dedication to the service of the state which was inculcated by the educational system and by the all-pervading military spirit which, because of the enormous size of the army, penetrated the whole society,[20] including the bureaucracy, where many high officials had started their careers as army officers or were the scions of military families.

They were reinforced further by the actions Frederick took to secure the support or at least the acquiescence of those groups without which his military power could not be maintained – the nobility and the peasants.

The Prussian army in Frederick's day was composed of native conscripts and a high proportion of mercenaries.[21] The tactics of the time, which as Frederick developed them became the admiration of Europe, required that the soldiers should function as automata; for according to his principles "battles are won by fire-superiority", and the maximum fire-power was achieved by advancing lines of men of whom nothing was required except blind obedience and steadfastness in the face of death. These tactics allowed no scope for initiative or intelligence. Even aiming at the enemy was forbidden because it slowed down the rate of fire.[22] In these circumstances, and also because of the propensity of the mercenaries to desert, the army could only be brought to fulfil its functions by means of a notoriously brutal discipline,[23] which caused the soldier, it was often said, to fear his officers more than he feared the enemy.

As for the peasants, in spite of the harsh life which was their lot, and the brutalities to which they were exposed in the army and often as civilians, there were no peasant revolts in Prussia in the eighteenth century, except in Silesia on rare occasions when they were easily put down by the army. Such revolts were nevertheless endemic in other parts of central and eastern Europe, and in Russia and Bohemia in the 1770s reached the proportions of a civil war. Even in France, which is often held to have been immune from them, they exploded in 1774 into the so-called "guerre des farines", in which large bands of rioters, sometimes composed of as many as 15,000 people, pillaged the bakeries and markets.[24]

The relative docility of the Prussian peasants in the eighteenth century is a phenomenon which has never been explained. Partly, no doubt, the reason for it must lie in the peasant's inability to imagine a different and better future, which he came to do later as a result of the spread of new ideas and the example of other countries. Plainly, however, this is not the whole explanation, for if it were there would not have been the great revolts, notably that of Pugachev in Russia, in countries where the ideas of the French Revolution, and the attempts which Napoleon made to implement them in the European states he conquered, still lay in an unimaginable future.

In the absence of any serious analysis one can only hazard the guess that a considerable responsibility for the absence of peasant risings in Prussia must be attributed to the actions of Frederick's government – particularly to its insistence that direct taxation must never be raised (for what provoked the peasant more than anything else was an increase in his obligations) and its stock-policy that prevented large-scale famine. It seems also highly likely that, among the officials concerned with the administration of local government described earlier, some combination of competence and fear of the royal displeasure was sufficient to prevent the worst outrages which were committed by the landlords in Poland, Russia and parts of the Habsburg dominions, and which drove the peasants to desperation.

As for the nobles, to Frederick they always seemed the principal bulwark of his regime. He continually maintained (absurdly as it seemed to later generations) that education in a noble household bred in them a sense of honour which the bourgeoisie by its nature lacked. They provided the officers on which the efficiency of the army primarily depended, and alone (in his view) possessed the qualities which were required to control the countryside, the principal sector of the economy.

Because the nobility seemed to him essential, he allowed the nobles an increasing degree of power, notwithstanding his harshness to such of their individual members as did not, in his view, fulfil their duty to the state in their capacity as army offficers, as civil servants or as landowners.

He tried to ensure that in their capacity as landlords they did not exploit their peasants, but he was not prepared to push his attempts in this matter beyond the limits it appeared that the landlords would tolerate. He made no serious attempt to abolish serfdom on the private estates, greatly though he deprecated it. Nor did he attempt, as did the French government, to subject the nobles to direct taxation in those provinces where they possessed a long-standing immunity, or even to deprive them of their many privileges in relation to indirect taxation. In order to help noble landowners in difficulties, particularly after the disaster of the Seven Years War, he created the credit institutes, or *Landschaften*, already referred to. In most, if not all, of the eastern provinces these institutes were managed by the local nobles, though they were usually presided over by a high government official. By these means and by the continued existence in most *Kreise*, or administrative districts, of a representative body of nobles dating from before the days of absolutism, the Prussian nobility retained, collectively, a degree of local self-government which did not exist in eighteenth-century France.[25]

For all this, nevertheless, as individuals the Prussian nobles lacked many of the freedoms – for example the right to foreign travel – enjoyed by the richer nobles in France; they were exposed to greater risks of humiliating punishments; they were even, though how often it is impossible to say, subject to inquisitions into their personal lives which no French grandee would have tolerated. Fontane, for example, tells the story of a certain General von Prittwitz, who possessed a fine property which he proceeded to develop with the aid of his rich wife's money. While he was in the process of building himself a grand new house, Frederick came into the neighbour-hood and observed what was going on. "Ah," he said, "so you are living it up." Von Prittwitz took the hint and put the roof over the ground floor.[26]

By a combination of means, in fact, Frederick assured himself the support or the acquiescence of the groups in the community which might otherwise have caused trouble. He did so by concessions in some cases, by fear in others and, perhaps most significantly, by fostering and channelling the growth of an ideology favourable to his regime, which was disseminated by the schools, the universities and the Lutheran church, in all of which appointments were controlled or supervised by the state.

So strong was the belief in the virtues of the Frederician regime, in spite of the criticisms of it that began to develop at the end of Frederick's life, that the censorship was hardly if ever invoked to suppress dissident opinion. When, for example, in 1759 Nicolai asked the Censor for Philosophical Works to prohibit the publication of a book to which he took exception, the

Censor replied that he was suprised that anyone should want to censor anything since such a suggestion had not been made to him for years.[27]

Fichte once said (though in defence of ends other than Frederick's) that "if you want to do anything with men you must mould them so that they are unable to want anything except what you will that they should want".[28] Some situation approximating to this appears to have been created in Prussia during Frederick's lifetime. It can be seen in the attitude of even the most upright and conscientious who, when required to take action of which they disapproved, felt they must submit, even if occasionally with protest. This was the line which von Zedlitz took in the Müller Arnold affair and on other occasions. It was the line which Svarez took in the reign of Frederick William II after the French Revolution had caused that monarch to find some of the provisions in the original version of the *Allgemeines Landrecht* too liberal. Svarez volunteered to expunge the passages to which he attached most importance because the man entrusted with the task was intellectually incapable of it.[29] It was the line which Kant took when, again in the reign of Frederick William II, the free discussion of religious questions, permitted by Frederick the Great, was forbidden. A cabinet order of 1794 declared various of Kant's writings to be derogatory to the Christian religion, whereat Kant declared that in future he would keep silent on the subject. A note was subsequently found among his papers in which he said: "To withdraw or deny one's convictions is base, but silence in such a case as this is the subject's duty."[30]

Such a conception of the subject's duty and its origins in "the working on men's minds and hearts",[31] as Wilhelm von Humboldt later put it, so that they were willing to accept the state's tutelage in moral and material matters, seemed to the reformers after 1806 destructive of the rights of human beings to develop their capacities to the full. This, however, was never Frederick's view. The Enlightenment as he understood it, and to the best of his ability translated it into practice, produced, by the standards of the times, a high degree of consensus. In Prussia it was a unifying force while in France it was a disruptive one.

(b) THE LEGACY IN THE PERIOD OF REFORM

The criticisms of Frederick the Great's regime which had begun in the last decades of his reign were reinforced and added to by the events that followed his death. His successor, Frederick William II, who ruled from 1786 to 1797, was a man without *esprit de suite*, capacity for work or talent. During his reign, absolutism began to exhibit in Prussia many of the characteristics which, more often then not, had distinguished it in every other country in which it had become established – the rule by favourites, including mistresses (absent from the Prussian scene in the two previous reigns); the lack of coherent policy in foreign or internal affairs; an unsupervised bureaucracy that developed an increasing tendency to arbitrariness, red-tape and the multiplication of minutes and memoranda – that *Vielschreiberei* of which Stein continually complained. Above all, Frederick William II's reign was the occasion for an extravagance which dissipated Frederick the Great's war reserve. Frederick, as was shown earlier, reckoned on accumulating a supply of bullion sufficient to pay for a four years' war. When he died in 1786 he left in his war reserve 52 million thaler – a sum equivalent to nearly three times his annual revenue at the end of his life. Eleven years later, on the death of Frederick William II, the war reserve was empty and there were 40 million thaler of debts[1] – a state of affairs which his successor, Frederick William III, was able to mitigate but far from wholly to reverse, and which, at a time when the French Revolution and Napoleonic armies were conquering Europe, was largely responsible for the vacillating foreign policy and military unpreparedness that led to the disasters of Jena and Auerstedt.

Doubts about Prussia's social and political institutions increased rapidly after Frederick's death, and particularly after 1797 when Frederick William III, who had been educated by Svarez, succeeded to the throne. Many of the projects later embodied in the legislation of the reform movement had already been advocated in the nine years before Jena.[2] Various commissions were set up to consider ways of reducing the nobles' privileges; of abolishing the internal tolls and customs barriers; of reorganizing the central government, particularly so as to permit the financial position to be brought more easily and exactly under review; of changing conditions in the army so as to reduce the number of mercenaries and abolish the brutal punishments; and, above all, of putting an end to serfdom. These ideas reflected a new ideology inspired partly by the French Revolution but, to an even greater extent, by the works of Adam Smith.

The theories of Adam Smith first became a subject of serious study in the 1790s among the professors and their students in the University of Göttingen[3] which, though it was in Hanover, a possession of the British monarchs, was frequented by many young men from Prussia and other German states (notably by Stein and Hardenberg) who later rose to high positions in the Prussian universities and government.

Adam Smith's theories, which preached the virtues of free trade and free enterprise, were totally hostile to the kind of government and social structure which existed in Prussia, and to the corporate and state control applied there to commerce, industry and agriculture. They represented an attack on absolutism and the *Ständegesellschaft* comparable to that later directed against capitalism by Marx. A number of German professors abandoned the role of servants of the state, hitherto adopted in the universities, and became "political professors" who preached not, admittedly, revolution but the need for drastic changes in the existing social system. Whether or not they accepted all Adam Smith's views, they made future leaders in the worlds of power and learning familiar with them.

From Göttingen Adam Smith's doctrines penetrated into Königsberg, sometimes described, because of its close trading relations with England, as the gateway through which English ideas entered Prussia. In Königsberg, and later throughout Germany, Adam Smith's principal expositor was a certain Professor Kraus who in his youth had studied in Göttingen. Kraus exercised an enormous influence not merely on his students but throughout the whole province of East Prussia, which assumed a particular importance in Prussian history because after Napoleon occupied Berlin in 1807 the court was established in Königsberg for the best part of two crucial years.

In the University of Königsberg, Kant and Kraus were the great attractions. Their lectures were attended by many members of the aristocracy as well as by officers from the Königsberg garrison. Because of the intimate association which had always existed in Prussia between the universities and the government, the leading figures of the reform movement, which began in 1807, had all been exposed to, and in varying degrees had accepted, Adam Smith's doctrines. The Germans even paid these the tribute, never accorded to them in England, of inventing an abstract noun – *Smithianismus* – to describe them. Stein's one-time friend and collaborator, Freiherr von Vincke, who later became head of the administration of Westphalia and began the industrialization of the Ruhr,[4] referred to Adam Smith as "der göttliche Smith" – "the divine Smith".[5] Others made pilgrimages to his tomb. There was in fact no major country, including his own, where Adam Smith received as much honour, or exercised so direct an influence on affairs, as he did in Prussia between 1807 and 1848.

This, however, is not to deny that many of Adam Smith's apostles combined their belief in his gospel with ideas inherited from the Frederician past. Still less is it to minimize the importance of the ideology which grew up in opposition to it and of which the two Marwitz brothers, particularly the elder, were noted exponents during the period of reform. To Alexander, the younger and cleverer, Adam Smith was a narrow-minded but, within his limited sphere, a sharp-witted man who, regardless of all other ideas and ignorant of the forces that determined man's destiny, saw in an economy based on trade the salvation for every nation no matter what its circumstances. To Adam Smith, as Alexander interpreted him, the whole art of government lay in allowing people to do what they wanted. "He takes his stand", Alexander wrote "on private interest. That something higher than this is required by the state – which must steer the desire for material achievement in a quite different direction from that pursued by a person who wants only vulgar enjoyment – of this he has no conception."[6]

The elder Marwitz, Ludwig, shared in this matter his brother's views. A large landowner and an army officer who became a general, he was the more famous of the two brothers because he was that rare phenomenon – a member of the aristocracy who threatened the government with rebellion,[7] albeit with a scarcely credible degree of ineptitude.

To Ludwig von der Marwitz a money economy was anathema – that is, an economy in which all goods and services were exchanged for money and which created a society in which power and status, if not directly dependent on money, were impossible without it. As late as 1820 Marwitz could maintain that though money was necessary in the towns, except for the purposes of paying taxes it was unnecessary in the countryside. He himself, admittedly, had a money income, but by the standards of the nobles in France and England whose families, like his, had connections with the court, it was extremely small. He reckoned that when he attained his majority he had per annum "over 1,500 thaler to spend"[8] (that is, allowing 10 thaler to the £ sterling, £150), but he owned around 2,000 or more acres of land, with a population of some 200 people subject to his jurisdiction,[9] and he lived in a house so large that when a child was being born in one part of it the people in the other parts were unaware that such an event was in progress.

In his youth in the 1790s Marwitz had spent the best part of two months in England,[10] which seemed to him a model country, particularly because of the absence of that envy which he found conspicuous in Prussia at the time, because of the willingness of all people to accept their station in life, and because of the deference shown by the lower classes to the upper. Marwitz and many others lamented that respect for birth and authority had been banished from the Prussian social scene by means of the infection that had spread from France.[11]

Marwitz, needless to say, was wholly ignorant of the circumstances which had made English society into the kind he admired. He assumed that it was England's preservation of her ancient customs that was responsible for her successful resistance to Napoleon – a point of view he expressed forcibly in the protest which he drafted and which was signed by twenty-one other nobles and sent to the King in May 1811, threatening revolt against Hardenberg's innovations. This document has survived, together with the furious comments which Hardenberg wrote in the margin to the effect, among other things, that Britain's ability to stand up to the French was not due to her unwillingness to change, or to the legal privileges of her nobility which were non-existent, and that Marwitz, whom he ordered to be sent to Spandau, was talking criminal nonsense.[12]

The noble landowners who, like Marwitz, clung to the *Ständegesellschaft*, or even harked back to the days before absolutism had imposed bureaucracy upon it, are always claimed, and doubtless rightly, to have been the majority. Between 1806, however, and the final defeat of Napoleon, they were economically and psychologically in a weak position. They were unable to prevent irreversible changes which laid the foundations of Prussia's future supremacy in Europe.

The people in favour of drastic change were only a tiny minority. Since political parties, as they came to exist under constitutional governments with representative assemblies, were impossible under absolutism, the reformers lacked any political organization. They differed widely in their ideas and often became divided by bitter quarrels. As Clausewitz once observed of

Frederick William III's trusted cabinet councillor, Beyme, whom Stein and Hardenberg pursued and ousted from power with venom, but who was nevertheless one of the first to insist on the liberation of the serfs,[13] he held democratic and the most illiberal opinions mixed up together in such a way that first one and then the other found expression.[14] A similar judgment could be made on most of the other reformers.

All the leaders of the reform party – Stein, Hardenberg, Altenstein, Schön, Wilhelm von Humboldt among the civilians, Scharnhorst, Gneisenau, Boyen among the military, to mention only the best known – were nevertheless in agreement on various important matters. All were profoundly convinced of the need for change in conformity with the new *Zeitgeist*, the neglect of which they saw as the cause of Prussia's downfall. All wished in some way or another to associate the people with the government so as to create a community-sense and patriotism, the absence of which Turgot and others had deplored in France some thirty years earlier. The belief in the benefits that would follow from setting the individual free from the shackles imposed on him by the state and the corporative society was expressed *ad nauseam*. In the instructions issued to the local officials in 1817, for example, it was said that "everyone should be allowed, within the limits of the law, to develop his natural inclinations, his capacities and his energies, morally and physically, and that all existing obstacles in the way of this development should be removed as quickly as possible by legal means".[15]

These visions of an ideal society, free, prosperous and united, like other Utopian visions did not in fact materialize. In the English-speaking world the Prussian reform movement that started in 1807 is commonly assumed to have failed. The work most familiar to English readers, which was written by an émigré from Hitler's Germany, is entitled *The Failure of the Prussian Reform Movement, 1807-1819*.[16] It is indeed beyond dispute that the movement did fail in a number of respects, judged not only by the standards that prevailed in the west at the time and later, but also by those of its principal leaders. The belief in free enterprise as a panacea for all ills, in spite of the achievements for which it was responsible, proved unjustified. The hope that the government could be reorganized so as to permit the major groups in the population to participate in it, at a local and national level, failed equally, except in the towns.[17] In spite of Frederick William III's numerous promises to grant a constitution and representative government, no attempt to implement these promises was made for almost half a century, and meanwhile Prussia became a police-state, in which democrats and liberals were persecuted for their opinions to a degree unknown in the reign of Frederick the Great, who, though he possessed the means to silence criticism and doubtless would have used them had he thought it necessary, was never faced with the necessity, because in his day no ideology hostile to his own ever found organized expression.

For all this, the reform movement achieved in many respects a high degree of success. In the famous words of Frederick William III's wife, that

"Königin Luise" long beloved of the Prussian people because of her beauty, her wisdom, and the fortitude she showed during the French occupation: "Divine providence has unmistakably introduced new world conditions, and a new order of things must be brought into being, since the old one has outlived itself."[18] Had the Prussians not recognized this fact they could not have attained the position of power they reached in the course of the nineteenth century.

The reforms which were achieved were, as has been shown, for the greater part such as had been seen as necessary before 1806. The upheavals, however, which their introduction would have caused, the divergence of opinion about the lengths to which it would be practicable to proceed, the vested interests and administrative difficulties that blocked the way, ensured that very little was accomplished.[19] Nothing substantial could in fact be accomplished except by means of a dictatorship which Frederick William III was intellectually and temperamentally incapable of exercising. As Ludwig von der Marwitz once observed of him, when faced with a difficult decision his instinct was always "ausweichen" – to evade it.

What changed this situation was the total defeat of Prussia by Napoleon in the battles of Jena and Auerstedt in 1806, and Frederick William III's willingness, in the desperate situation in which he then found himself, to allow first Hardenberg, then Stein (at Beyme's instigation), then Hardenberg again for a considerable number of years, to exercise in effect the position of dictator.

The magnitude of the Prussian defeat and its disastrous consequences have long faded from, if they were even present to, the consciousness of the west. On 10 October 1806 two Prussian armies, one outnumbered by three to one but the other considerably larger than the French, were not merely defeated; they were put to a wild, wholly disorganized flight as a result of the new French tactics which totally demoralized them.[20]

The French pushed up north, capturing one inadequately defended fortress after another, including the great fortress at Magdeburg, subsequently incorporated in the French puppet kingdom of Westphalia. Napoleon entered Berlin on October 27. Being at that time at war with Russia, which was Prussia's ally, he quartered 600,000 troops in East Prussia, requiring the inhabitants to supply them. After the Russian defeat at Friedland, Prussia was forced to sign peace with Napoleon at Tilsit in July 1807. She was required to surrender all the Polish territories she had acquired by the three partitions of Poland and all her provinces west of the Elbe. Her population was reduced from 10½ to 4½ million. In addition she was subjected to a huge indemnity and required to maintain 10,000 French troops in various garrisons until it was paid, though they were in fact withdrawn a year later because of the demands of the war in Spain.

The misery caused by these events, though a phenomenon familiar to the present century, exceeded anything at that time known in the west as a consequence of foreign occupation. The Napoleonic blockade cut off

Prussian exports to England and ruined many exporters of grain and timber from the Baltic ports. East Prussia suffered more than any other province because she became a principal theatre of war in 1807, and later the route which the *grande armée* traversed for the attack on Russia in 1812. All the Prussian provinces, however, which Napoleon left to the Hohenzollerns suffered heavily from the weight of the indemnity and from the demands which the French continually made for draught animals, forage and labour. It has been reckoned that, taking all things together, the French in the two years after Jena exacted from the depleted Prussian territories a sum equivalent to about sixteen times the Prussian government's annual revenue before the invasion.[21]

The indebted landlords were unable to pay the interest they owed on their loans from the credit institutes. These put their properties up for sale but in the circumstances could find few purchasers and as a result much land went to waste. Thousands of peasant holdings were ruined by the French requisitions. Thousands of businesses went bankrupt. In East Prussia the animal population fell to between 2 and 5 per cent of its pre-war level.[22] Of the 5,846 children born in Berlin, 4,300 died in infancy.[23] The French plenipotentiary said on one occasion that no foreign occupation had ever pressed so heavily on any country.[24] As Clausewitz put it: "The bankruptcies here are endless ... what was achieved in this sandy waste throughout centuries in the way of prosperity, culture and trade, will now be destroyed in perhaps a decade."[25]

In these circumstances the changes long envisaged came to seem a necessity, not only for the reasons which had hitherto moved their advocates, but as the only means of promoting the country's recovery and paying off the French indemnity. In the words of Gerhard Ritter, Stein's principal biographer, economic freedom, by virtue of the energies it was expected to release, seemed the only remedy for all the damage.[26]

This is not the place in which to recount in any detail the various reforms which were proposed, carried out, introduced in a modified form or wholly abandoned. Many and some excellent books have been written on this subject.[27] The purpose of the present account is merely to show in broad outline the extent to which the reform movement altered, or failed to alter, the nature of Prussian society and government, and the links that connected the achievements and the failures with the Frederician past.

The most immediately and obviously successful reforms were those in the military sphere. They were put in train by the military reorganization commission which was set up in July 1808 under the chairmanship of Scharnhorst, and which came to include, among its more famous members, Gneisenau, Boyen, Grolman and, in effect, Clausewitz who, though he was not officially a member of the commission, was *chef de cabinet* to Scharnhorst. All these men were officers who had seen the need for reform before 1806 and were among the few who had distinguished themselves in that calamitous year.

They realized, as had the French military reformers who paved the way for Napoleon, and as Clausewitz was later to emphasize in his book *On War*, that "the nature of armies is determined by the nature of the civilization in which they exist."[28] Napoleon's victories drove home to them the fact, of which they were already aware, that troops who are treated like human beings and trained to use their reason can be capable of feats impossible for men beaten by a brutal discipline into fulfilling the functions of automata. Between 1807 and 1813 the structure and tactics of the Prussian army were totally reorganized. The limit of 42,000 men which the French had set on its size was overcome by the so-called Krumper system under which recruits were called up for short periods of service and then released, so that though the number of 42,000 was not exceeded there was a large trained reserve. By the time of Napoleon's retreat from Russia the Prussian army had become as efficient as the French and the proportion of the Prussian population under arms was enormously larger than France had been able to achieve after the *levée en masse* of 1793[29] when the mobilization of native Frenchmen reached its peak. The military and the civil reformers worked in conjunction, seeing the reforms in the army on the one hand, and those in the state and society on the other, as different aspects of the same process they both desired to further – the transformation of the ways of life and government so as to give scope to the energies, the talents and the sense of patriotism which they believed were latent in the population.

Of all the measures taken in relation to civil life the first and most important was the edict of 9 October 1807 – the famous so-called "Oktoberedikt" which Schön drafted and described as Prussia's *habeas corpus*. This edict abolished *Erbuntertänigkeit* and gave the peasants their personal freedom. The preamble stated that it was both an obligatory demand of justice, and necessary to any well-ordered economy, that all the obstacles should be removed which prevented the individual from attaining such a degree of well-being as his abilities permitted.[30] Article 10 accordingly declared that *Erbuntertänigkeit* should cease to exist for all men, women and children not later than 11 November 1810, though this by no means disposed of the problem of serfdom since it related only to the obligations which were held to fall on the peasants personally – particularly, it liberated them from bondage to the soil and from the obligation to give their children into the lord's service and to obtain his consent before they could marry.[31] It left for future settlement what should be done about the dues and services attached to peasant land and about the obligations owed by peasants with little or no land who continued to work on an estate.[32]

The edict of October 1807 also destroyed the legal barriers which had hitherto separated the three principal estates – the nobles, the bourgeoisie and the peasants – from each other. Henceforth no occupations, trades or professions, including particularly the ownership of land, were closed or reserved to any particular group of persons. Nobles might engage in trade; bourgeois or successful peasants, if they could afford to do so, might buy what had hitherto been noble land. Careers, in other words, were, in law, thrown open to talent in accordance with the principles of Adam Smith; and also in accordance with these principles, the monopolies of the guilds were abolished and, in the course of time, the government monopolies. Though the provincial liberties were not eliminated to the same extent as in France they were nevertheless curtailed. The provincial tariffs were replaced by a single tariff enforceable at the state frontiers – the famous tariff of 1818, which the one-time doyen of British economic historians, J.H. Clapham, described as "immeasurably the wisest and most scientific tariff then existing among the greater powers". [33]

Though with certain exceptions, the *Ständegesellschaft* as it had existed before 1806 thus came to an end in Prussia as it had done in France during the Revolution. Absolutism admittedly continued in Prussia, which remained without a constitution or a representative assembly until 1850, but still it was a different sort of absolutism from that which had existed in the reign of Frederick the Great; for the royal cabinet was abolished – that kitchen cabinet which in Frederick's day had consisted of secretaries (later elevated to the rank of cabinet councillors) who, while remaining without responsibility, came to exercise an increasing influence under his two weak successors. Henceforward the ministers of the various departments of state assumed the degree of authority they enjoyed under other absolutisms. [34] These new arrangements, combined with the creation in 1817 of the *Staatsrat*, [35] or council of state, without whose consent the king theoretically could not, and in practice did not, issue any laws, deprived the crown of so much power that it is customary to say that the royal autocracy was replaced by an autocracy of bureaucrats. This, however, is plainly an exaggeration, since the king retained the right to appoint and dismiss the ministers, as well as to intrigue against them behind their backs, and in fact nominated most of the members of the council of state, so that he was still in a position to determine the broad lines of policy.

While Prussia thus remained an absolutism, though one of a different kind, so, too, the nobility regained the prestige it had enjoyed before the French Revolution, though here also with a difference. While a great name, if combined with wealth and high position, still endowed its owner with the power of patronage, as commonly happened in all nineteenth-century societies, after the issue of the edict of 1807 the nobles had increasingly to compete with bourgeois in the state service and in the ownership of land. Nobles, for example, who had previously been accustomed to be admitted to the schools and universities on privileged terms, now lost these advantages. The schools which trained students for entrance to the universities refused the requests of counts and dukes that their sons might be excused the study of Greek, and even when these exalted fathers appealed to the Ministry of Education their demands were almost invariably turned down. [36] By the middle of the nineteenth century nearly 43 per cent of the *Rittergüter*, or former noble estates, were in the hands of bourgeois. [37] The owners of these estates, however, whatever their origins, continued to enjoy most of the privileges – the hunting rights, the powers of justice and many of the tax immunities[38] which had belonged to a *Rittergut* in the eighteenth century.

It was the persistence of these attributes of absolutism and the *Ständegesellschaft*, the persecution of those who protested against them, and the misery suffered as a result of the change-over from a feudal to a capitalist agriculture, that have led to the assertion that the reform movement was a failure. This assertion overlooks the economic achievements, which were of profound significance, since they formed the basis of Prussia's future power in central Europe.

Here it is possible to describe only, and even so in no more than broad outline, the most important of these achievements, the gradual abolition of serfdom, which overshadowed the other reforms in importance not merely because it affected directly the lives of the largest number of people, but because it was an essential if not a sufficient cause of the development of Prussia's industrial strength.

The emancipation of the peasants, of which the edict of 1807 was only the first step, was accomplished by means of a series of further edicts whose implementation took virtually half a century. The process was begun in the most unfavourable circumstances imaginable, after the end of a peculiarly destructive war, when both the state and the business community (whose wealth, it was supposed, would flow into the countryside) lacked the capital to ease the transition from a communal to a capitalistic form of agriculture.

This transition presented problems of the utmost complexity, combined as it was with the need to dismantle the old communal system of agriculture and with the division of the commons. The edict of 1807 had only given the peasant his personal freedom. It had said nothing about the land which the landholding peasant cultivated for his own use and in return for which he owed dues and services to the lord who owned it.

To free the peasants from these dues and services unconditionally seemed to all the reformers an act of illegitimate confiscation. However much they might disagree about the terms of the compensation and the way in which they should be carried out, no one doubted that the landlord must be compensated. Since the landholding peasants had commonly little or no money, if they were to compensate the landlords they could do so only by the surrender of land. Though, however, in the past the landowners had usually wanted more land, and had resented the provisions against *Bauernlegen*, or acquiring peasant holdings to add to their demesne, additional land was of no benefit to a man who could not afford paid labour, or to equip his farm with the draught animals and implements which had belonged to the serfs but which they had used for the lord's benefit.

Broadly speaking, this problem was essentially: on the one hand how to leave the landholding peasant with enough land on which to live, whose productivity he was expected to increase because of the incentive to work with which freedom, it was supposed, would endow him. But, on the other hand, this objective had to be achieved without creating such difficulties for the landlord that he, too, could not profit from the benefits which the use of free labour were expected to entail. To subscribe to these principles was, however, one thing; to implement them quite another.

In the event the edict which finally laid down the guidelines for the compensation due from the peasants, and which was followed till 1850, was the edict, or so-called "Declaration", of 1816. It dealt with only one category of peasants and by no means with all of them.[39] This category consisted of peasants without hereditary rights to their holdings who were, as it was said, *spannfähig* – that is, possessed a team or teams of draught animals and were thus substantial landholders. They were required, according to their terms of tenure, to surrender either one-half or one-third of the land they had hitherto cultivated for their own use, in order to own the remainder free of every kind of obligation. All other categories of peasants were excluded from the "Declaration", though comparable provisions were made in 1821 in relation to the numerous peasants with so-called "better rights of possession" [40] i.e., peasants who "owned" their land on terms similar to those on which the French peasant "owned" his.

The application of the Declaration of 1816 gave rise to enormous administrative problems. The details had to be worked out in every province separately, in accordance with laws and customs with which the *Allgemeines Landrecht* had not been concerned, and ultimately in relation to each *Rittergut*.[41] A whole army of officials had to be employed in this work, and many of them, occupying as they did relatively humble posts in the official hierarchy, and ignorant as they commonly were of the particular conditions with which they had to deal, came under the dominance of the principal local landowners, who in any case, after the peace, acquired an increasing influence on the king and hence on the ministers.

The result was that the Declaration of 1816 was drafted and implemented in such a way as to permit an almost infinite variety of combinations between redemption payments in various forms and the continued use of serf labour. The landlords, or those with sufficient skill and power, were enabled to acquire as much land as they could manage to cultivate, while hanging on to as much serf labour as suited them, for as long as this seemed more acceptable than free, paid labour.[42]

The nobles (or more accurately the owners of *Rittergüter*, who increasingly after 1807 came to include bourgeois) are always seen as the beneficiaries of the emancipation, and the peasants as the victims, since large numbers of peasants were unable to keep themselves afloat in the new conditions, and in the absence of the protection which the landlords had been required to give them under the old regime, but from which the Declaration of 1816 absolved them.

Broadly speaking, this judgment is undeniable but nevertheless needs some qualifying, for in the first place, a class of prosperous peasant farmers succeeded in establishing itself, even though at the cost of great hardship and with much less help from the state than the owners of the *Rittergüter* obtained,[43] and in the second place, when one says that the owners of *Rittergüter* were the principal beneficiaries one needs to remember that thousands of the noble landowning families who were in existence before Jena went under in the cataclysms that followed, or during the period shortly after the end of the Napoleonic wars when grain prices fell, and foreign markets, particularly the English, were closed to imports of Prussian grain. Many in any case lacked the ability as well as the means to adapt to the new conditions.

Those who prospered were the tough and efficient, who were willing and able to follow the principle of the famous agronomist Thaer and to introduce a modern capitalist agriculture, which came to prevail over large areas of Prussia although accompanied by many small and inefficient holdings.[44] As Clausewitz once put it in a work he wrote in the 1820s: "We can all remember from our youth the hordes of servants, the pomp, the liveries, the clothes, the domestic untensils, without which a noble household thought it could not exist. Only in the most recent times do we see the nobles running their estates in an industrial way."[45]

The Prussians, in fact, brought about an agricultural revolution on a scale unequalled at the time by any other major continental country. They did so, nevertheless, at a price of upheavals of a magnitude not generally realized in the west. In the two decades after the end of the Napoleonic wars, notwithstanding all the changes in ownership that had occurred in the previous eight years, the greater part of the existing property changed hands.[46] Hardship, insecurity and often ruin was the fate of many landowners and destitution the fate of many peasants.

There was, however, another side to this picture. The amount of land under cultivation increased remarkably, partly because of the divisions of the commons and partly because of the taking in of marginal land, principally by peasants. The amount of work they put into this, together with the improvements on the large estates, ensured that the average yield of land under cultivation did not fall.[47]

In the years between 1815 and 1848, however, the peasant population grew at a rate greater than the land could support,[48] and many peasants could with difficulty, if at all, keep body and soul together. Such unfortunates, if they did not remain in this unhappy condition in the countryside, either emigrated or drifted into the towns where they provided cheap labour for the developing industries. The government did its utmost to foster these, particularly by promoting that technical education for which Prussia later became famous, but also by other forms of state intervention such as loans and financing the cost of foreign travel for entrepreneurs likely to benefit from the experience of the more highly industrialized countries.[49] For though the Prussian government continued to believe in free enterprise, it did not, as in the case of agriculture, attempt to apply this belief dogmatically, but sought to create the conditions, materially and psychologically, in which those who were capable of standing on their own feet should be given the best chance of doing so. By 1835 these efforts had so far succeeded that Prussia had reached the position where a number of the products of her industries had begun to oust those of Britain and France from their foreign markets.[50]

The Prussia that emerged from the period of the reforms was in many ways a different Prussia from that of Frederick the Great's day, particularly because the welfare state as he had understood it, based on a *Ständegesell-schaft*, had given place to a free enterprise economy based on equality before the law where all economic transactions were concerned. The Frederician legacy is nevertheless obvious.

Though Frederick's policies, and he himself at the end of his life, became discredited, this was a temporary phenomenon. His achievements, as the principal architect of Prussia's international status, and of a system of justice better, it was supposed, than any in Europe, became a legend that was widely though not universally accepted.[51] In any event it was beyond dispute that Prussia's remarkable achievements in the wars of liberation against Napoleon – the fact that she was the only major German state that refused to be incorporated in the Napoleonic empire, and that she provided the leadership and the great majority of the troops that Germany contributed to Napoleon's defeat – were due to the degree of consensus which had been built up during his reign, even though between 1806 and 1815 it was disrupted, if not, as it turned out, to a material extent, by quislings in high circles.

Many of the attitudes, institutions and practices to which this consensus owed its origins therefore persisted, particularly the prestige of the nobility and the army, together with the authoritarianism and the inability to stand up to it which they fostered, and on which much emphasis has recently been laid. The story was doubtless typical which Marwitz told of the events which occurred in 1798 during the paying of homage to Frederick William III after his accession. Among those present were two representatives of Frankfurt an der Oder, of whom one was a professor. The other began a speech about the people's rights against the crown which was greeted with applause by some and with protests from others. Suddenly a certain Major von Bredow said in a voice of thunder: "Shut up, you infamous scoundrel. Otherwise, as sure as I live, I'll take you and throw you out of the window." Marwitz noted that von Bredow was known to be a man of his word and observed with satisfaction that the speaker, having turned as white as a sheet, subsided into a mouselike silence.[52]

As in the eighteenth century, so after 1806, the reforms were introduced by autocratic means – by "revolution from above" in the stock phrase – and could not have been otherwise. Hardenberg's famous remark, which he made in a memorandum (the *Rigaer Denkschrift*) in 1807, that what was needed was "democratic principles in a monarchical government", was so much nonsense. Democracy, or constitutional government of any kind, was incompatible with the reforms which he believed to be necessary and a number of which were in fact set in train, since the great majority in every group had no desire for them.

During and after the period of reform Prussia retained what Madame de Staël, who visited Berlin in 1803, described as its Janus face – the world of the army on the one hand, civil society on the other; the prejudices of the nobility combined with a philosophic spirit which, in the more distinguished walks of life, transcended social barriers.[53]

In Frederick's day Prussia had come to possess the most powerful military machine east of the Rhine; she was also economically the most progressive state and intellectually, apart from Weimar, the most distinguished. Her bureaucracy, whatever its faults, was the best organized and the least corrupt in the major countries on the Continent of Europe. It was also probably – although in relation to such a disorderly age the statement could hardly be substantiated – the one most capable of exacting obedience. All these attributes Prussia retained, and in some cases increased, in the new climate of the nineteenth century. Ludwig von Gerlach, who was born in 1795, died in 1877 and occupied a number of high positions in the law, observed in his diary in 1815 that a certain Madame Schüll, as he called her, had said to him there was no reason why one should not trust the government since "we have a god-fearing king, a loyal army and sound finances, so all must be well". Just like a woman, Ludwig von Gerlach commented, but he nevertheless found the opinion just.[54]

The last two attributes, though hardly the first, were Frederick's legacy. Though in his later years he failed to see the shape of things to come, and like most other very successful men in their old age did not wish to have his handiwork changed, still he had never been unqualifiedly a conservative, after the fashion, say, of the princes of the blood in France on the eve of the Revolution, or the bulk of his subjects before 1806. His regime was a unique mixture of the old and the new, as was, though after a different fashion, the regime which followed it.

Conclusion

This book has attempted to compare two countries which, notwithstanding the great differences between them, had many points in common: for both were military powers of the first rank; both were ruled by absolute monarchs; and in both society took the form, to which there was never an exact equivalent in England, which the French call a *société d'ordres* and the Germans a *Ständegesellschaft*. The purpose of the present comparison, first undertaken by Tocqueville, was to examine the nature of government and society in these two cases and the circumstances which caused them to change.

In France the attempts at change reached a sudden and violent climax in revolution. In Prussia the kind of changes seen as necessary in France were, subject to the qualifications mentioned earlier, introduced – and with more success in the economic sphere than the French Revolution achieved – by means of reforms undertaken by the government itself. In both countries, though in these different ways, the legal barriers were breached which divided what the French revolutionaries, and the Marxists after them, called "feudal" society, from what is now commonly called "bourgeois" society.

Admittedly, as was said earlier, the use of the term "feudalism" in this context is open to objections though capable of defence. The term "bourgeois" is imprecise. So-called bourgeois society has throughout the long period of its existence been subject to a process of continuous evolution. Both in France and in Prussia it first appeared in communities that were overwhelmingly agrarian. Its major prophet, Adam Smith, published his *Wealth of Nations* in 1776 before one can speak, even in England, of an industrial revolution. The ideals which for long inspired the members of the bourgeoisie were not those of a capitalist society in the Marxist sense. For the capitalist, as defined in volume I of *Das Kapital*, profit was the sole objective. "It is only in so far as the appropriation of more wealth in the abstract becomes the sole motive of [a man's] operations that he functions as a capitalist."[1] The capitalist buys goods for £100 and sells them for £110, and with his £110 he starts the process afresh, and so on *ad infinitum*.

This way of proceeding found no favour in either France or Prussia in the periods here under discussion. In an analysis based on contemporary newspapers, a German historian, writing in 1925,[2] described the way in

199

which the bourgeois (in the sense of a person who was neither a noble, nor a peasant, nor an urban worker) saw his specific attributes and contrasted them with those of the noble. The bourgeois felt that he was distinguished by the fact that he worked. He owed his position to his own efforts and not to inheritance. From his youth on he had been taught that industriousness was the greatest virtue. As a member of the middle class (*Mittelstand*) he experienced neither the extremity of need which destroyed feeling nor the refined sensuality of the noble which weakened it. He was an individualist and a free man who determined his own destiny; a rational man but also a compassionate one. Unlike the noble, he was not conditioned by custom and bound to the past, but carried within him the seeds of a future which he presumed would be one of progress towards a more moral, more rational and generally more prosperous society. He had only contempt for the pursuit of wealth as an end in itself. As one periodical put it in 1793: "Wealth can make one happier and increase the joys of life, but it does not make one nobler." Marx's capitalist would have been anathema to him, as he was at the beginning of the present century to the famous German economist and sociologist, Werner Sombart.[3] Labrousse painted a similar picture of the French business world as it existed up to the Revolution – and indeed beyond – when he complained that there was no question of putting the profits of enterprise into the spiral of increasing production.[4]

Nevertheless, in spite of all the changes which bourgeois society has undergone, two attributes have always been held to distinguish it, whatever traditions or practices it may have inherited from the past or developed in periods later than those considered here. In the first place it was a society in which the state was what the Germans called a *Rechtsstaat* – that is, a state in which theoretically all the actions of the government, as well as those of private individuals, were subject to precisely defined laws administered by qualified judges, who could not be dismissed nor their judgment set aside for political reasons.[5] In this respect bourgeois society was distinguished from the société d'ordres, in which decisions on matters of justice were held ultimately to rest with the monarch, and in which justice could be administered, though it was so to an increasingly diminishing extent as the ideas of the Enlightenment gained currency, by such institutions as the *Chambres de Justice* described earlier.

In the second place (and to some schools of thought this was the most important matter), in bourgeois society all economic transactions took place between people who were equal before the law as distinct from being conducted, as in the société d'ordres, by the members of groups each endowed with different rights, so that, to mention again only one of the examples cited earlier, the purchaser of a French seigneurie paid a heavy tax on it if he were a commoner but not if he were a noble.

The French Revolution, because of the radical changes it brought about, the ideological wars to which it led, and its utopian visions (which failed to materialize) had an impact on Europe comparable only to that of the Russian

Revolution in the present century. Its causes in consequence cannot fail to be a matter of major concern to anyone interested in the course of European history.

The most famous of the writers to devote his attention to this subject was Tocqueville, whose *Ancien Régime et la Révolution* was first published over a century and a quarter ago, in 1856. It is still universally held in honour in France and prescribed reading for students – a situation which has been made possible because many of the major judgments to which Tocqueville committed himself in some parts of this work he qualified or contradicted in others, so that he can be quoted, like the Bible, in support of widely different points of view.

For all this, no writers have seriously concerned themselves with a point he found essential to his argument. He expressed it in the last sentence of chapter IV of Book I of his *Ancien Régime* where he observed that "anyone who has only seen and studied France will never, I venture to say, understand the French Revolution". He realized that many of the circumstances that had undermined the French Ancien Régime were common to other European countries, and in consequence asked himself why the Revolution should have broken out in France and not elsewhere. He himself attempted to answer this question by spending a considerable time in Germany studying German history. It was impossible for him, however, to bring this enterprise to a successful conclusion because he lacked most of the essential information which was only accumulated in the hundred or more years after his death.

The attempt which has been made here to pursue his line of enquiry leads essentially to the conclusion that the French failure to make, except by revolution, the reforms that seemed necessary to promote economic growth and military power, and the greater degree of success achieved by the Prussians through reforms imposed from above, must be attributed primarily to the differences in the nature of the government in these two countries, and to the mentality of their ruling classes, which the governments concerned did much to mould.

We have seen that both in theory and in practice the institution of absolutism differed greatly in France and Prussia but was also similar in a number of respects, including its exposure to the risk of incompetent rulers – a risk which became increasingly dangerous the wider and more complicated the tasks of government became. The workings of heredity being what they are, it was not to be expected that a monarch would have talent or vision above the average, and given the kind of upbringing to which he was subjected in France and many other countries, his capacity for dealing with practical affairs was likely to be below the average among educated people whose fortunes to a greater or less extent turned on their own efforts.

The eighteenth-century Hohenzollerns were the exceptions. They were the least disputable of historical accidents. Much time and thought have been expended in considering whether the great events in history were accidental, avoidable, or a likely if not inevitable outcome of the circumstances of the time. No argument could maintain that in 1713, when Frederick William I came to the throne, Prussia was predestined to dominate Germany. Had he and his son been monarchs of a more common type, it is not to be imagined that the barren, disunited Prussian provinces could have been welded into a sufficient degree of unity to permit the military achievements of Frederick the Great or the domestic ones which were their prerequisite, including the creation, by contemporary standards, of an efficient bureaucracy.

Tocqueville concluded that in France it was the bureaucracy, without which absolutism could not function, that destroyed the société d'ordres, on whose existence nevertheless the absolute monarchs saw their position as depending. A similar state of affairs existed in Prussia though there its consequences were different. The French bureaucracy, or more accurately the various organs of government which can only with many qualifications be so described, disintegrated because of the need, which they were unable to meet, for greater economic growth, particularly in agriculture, and for larger government revenues. The Revolution was the consequence, not the cause, of this disintegration. In Prussia, by contrast, the bureaucracy was not divided, as were the French organs of government, into a large number of more or less autonomous and continually warring groups. Whatever quarrels, rivalries and injustices may have gone on behind the scenes, it was a single organization, with a clear chain of command, whose tentacles stretched over all the Hohenzollern dominions. However conservative and obstructionist some of its members may have been, there developed among many others, principally through the efforts of Cocceji and Hagen,[6] both of whom enjoyed the complete trust of the King, a high degree of professional skill and expertise. In consequence, when calamity descended there were men who, with the King's consent, were not only capable of taking over control; they were able to pick from the members of the General Directory and other bodies highly efficient assistants who shared their views.[7] Without this team of trained men the task of reform would have been impossible.

The example of the French Revolution filled all the more or less unfortunate in Prussia with hopes of a better future they had not previously envisaged. Considerable numbers of artisans and peasants rose in spontaneous, though generally small and isolated, movements of revolt.[8] The nobles became the object of widespread abuse and contempt. At least one writer of repute has seen all this as proof of a potentially revolutionary situation in Prussia.[9] Any such danger, however, if it existed, was held in check by the army and the bureaucracy.

No German historian has ever doubted that in Prussia, which was ultimately to weld Germany into a nation, the state was created by the standing army and by the bureaucracy which first became necessary to meet the army's needs. Because of the disasters of the two world wars of the present century, it has become fashionable in and outside Germany to search the past for historical causes of these disasters, and in consequence the bureaucracy, especially in its formative period in the eighteenth century, has been the subject of much abuse.

Professor Hans Rosenberg, in particular, has emphasized the boots and doormat attitudes which the eighteenth-century Hohenzollerns fostered among their servants, and which spread downwards throughout the population. He has stressed how recruitment, the examinations notwithstanding, was determined by patronage, those in high positions giving posts to their friends and relations, with the result that many incompetents held high office; how the state service was one of the best ways of making money, and how the ambition of the bourgeois bureaucrat was always to imitate the way of life of the noble.[10] A great deal of evidence can be and has been adduced in support of these assertions which nevertheless need qualifying if they are judged by eighteenth-century standards and not by those which prevail in the western democracies today.

That a spirit of military subordination was introduced into the Prussian bureaucracy in the eighteenth century to an extent that prevailed nowhere else does not seem open to question, but that patronage was a feature peculiar to the Prussian scene is certainly untrue, and that it was used there with a more than common degree of discrimination seems highly likely. That more money could be made out of the state service than by other means was a common phenomenon in the eighteenth century and was certainly much more conspicuous in France and other countries than it was in Prussia. There is, in fact, another side to the picture which these indictments paint.

It can be seen, for example, in the words of Freiherr von Schrötter, who, when he retired from his official post in 1808, said that he himself and his work were related to each other like body and soul.[11] An equally eloquent and more comprehensive testimony to the way in which public officials could see their functions was provided by Friederich von Raumer who, though he began his career in the bureaucracy, and as a young man was very successful in it, decided he would prefer to devote himself to writing history. Hardenberg did his best to dissuade him. "You are," he said, "a first-class administrator. How do you know you will be a first-class historian?"[12] Friederich von Raumer nevertheless left the state service for the academic life. In 1812 when he was already a professor in Breslau, he wrote to Hardenberg as follows:

In our state neither the nobility nor the bourgeoisie, nor the peasantry, nor the province, is an effective body. There are...hardly any forces, let alone counterforces. The officials of state have hitherto up to a certain point been a substitute for representative assembly. They have been a substitute for a constitution itself. Only in these large bodies is there unity and determination. If they were broken up I can see in our state only isolated groups and individuals.

In the bureaucracy a spirit was created which made people ashamed of behaving badly and sustained them by a sense of honour. One man restrained the other; one man educated the other. The young man saw in front of him a noble sphere of action and a fine goal for his activity. The head of the office, if he was efficient, was in command, but as in a free state, and not as a tyrant. His insight and his reasons became freely accepted laws.[13]

Von Raumer was in a position to know. He may nevertheless have exaggerated. If he did so, and to what extent, are questions that have hitherto remained unanswered. But at least we have no proof that Richard Cobden was wrong when, on visiting Prussia in 1830, he said that this was the best administered country in Europe.[14]

The notion that the Prussian reform movement was led by and to the ultimate benefit of the nobility hardly stands up to examination. Admittedly, the heads of the government in Prussia during the period of reform were all nobles, and Hardenberg himself, who was a Hanoverian by birth, but had entered the Prussian service in the early 1790s and was, by Prussian standards, a rich man,[15] adopted the airs and habits of a *grand seigneur* on the French model – one of the reasons, no doubt, why the Germans have always held him in less esteem than Stein, who was in power for a much shorter period and accomplished less. These nobles at the pinnacle of power, however, may be seen merely as a small group, such as every ruling class throws up in times of social crisis, which recognized the need for change. The bulk of their friends, colleagues and assistants, who produced many of the ideas and were responsible for carrying them out, were either bourgeois in law before 1806 or came from very recently ennobled families.

Theodor von Schön, for example, who drafted the Octoberedikt of 1807 and spent the greater part of his life as Oberpräsident, or regional controller, of East and West Prussia, where he exercised enormous power and was responsible for the rehabilitation of these provinces, was the son of a *Domänenpächter*, or tenant of the royal demesne – an office always held by bourgeois until the end of the eighteenth century. Merckel and Sack who held comparable positions with comparable distinctions, the former in Silesia and the latter in Pomerania (where a statue was erected in his honour in Stettin), were both born bourgeois. Kunth, who together with Maasen and Motz was responsible for the tariff of 1818 already referred to, began his career as tutor to Wilhelm and Alexander von Humboldt. Maasen, the fourth of thirteen children, was the son of a tax-collector. Motz, made minister of finance in 1825, came from a well-to-do bourgeois family. Beuth, who held a number of important official posts, and was principally responsible for the beginnings of technical education in Prussia, was the son of a doctor.[16] This list could be greatly extended, and were it to include the senior army officers would show the same picture. Scharnhorst, Gneisenau, Grolman, Yorck von Wartenburg and Clausewitz, to mention only the most famous, were none of them of noble origin.[17]

These are indisputable facts. It is nevertheless often maintained that the bourgeois who rose to high positions and were themselves ennobled, desired nothing so much as to integrate themselves into the nobility, so that for all the opportunities which the edict of 1907 opened to the bourgeoisie, the old aristocratic attitudes to life still prevailed. This is a crude summary of a complicated situation.

In Prussia as elsewhere the idea of what constituted a bourgeois and what a noble way of life changed in the course of time as well as varying from individual to individual and from group to group. It is nevertheless plain that there were many bourgeois to whom the noble as they imagined him excited a degree of admiration amounting to *Schwärmerei*. Christian Garve expressed sentiments of this sort when he said that the nobles (or more accurately, it seems clear, those among them whom the French always described as "les grands") were distinguished by their dignity, their self-confidence, their ability to please without being affected, to talk fluently without being prolix, by being able to adjust themselves to any circumstances in which they might find themselves, by never showing embarrassment, and yet at the same time by their awareness, when in the company of their own kind, of belonging to a group superior to all other groups.[18] Similar ideas, expressed with greater subtlety, inspired the writings of Stendhal and Balzac in France. The attitude of all these writers was nevertheless ambivalent, for however much the behaviour and style of life of the noble fascinated them, they subscribed to the belief in honesty and the other sterling virtues which they saw as typical of the bourgeoisie in its upper reaches. The noble, for his part, was forced to emulate many of these virtues if he wished to preserve his status and the wealth necessary to sustain it. He became progressively *verbürgerlicht* or *embourgeoisé*. In Prussia he had long been so to a greater extent than his French counterparts. After the reforms which started in 1807 the inefficient goats in the nobility, to borrow Professor Rosenberg's phrase, were weeded from the efficient sheep.[19] The latter, though except in Silesia they did not engage in industry, took, in Clausewitz's words, to running their estates in an industrial way. They, together with the bourgeois owners of *Rittergüter*, became a class of entrepreneurs, comparable to those in industry. By this means they long ensured their survival together with the military and authoritarian traditions for which they had always stood.

Notes

ABBREVIATIONS: *AB: Acta Borussica, ABB: Acta Borussica Behördenorganisation; A.H.R.: American Historical Review; ALR: Allgemeines Landrecht für die Preußischen Staten 1794; Annales E.S.C.: Annales Economies Sociétés Civilisations; E.H.R. English Historical Review; Ec.H.R.: Economic History Review; FBPG: Forschungen zur Brandenbürgischen-Preußischen Geschichte; F.H.S.: French Historical Studies; H.J.: Historical Journal; H.Z. Historische Zeitung, V.J.S.W.: Vierteljahrschrift fur Sözial- und Wirtschaftsgeschichte.*

Notes: pages 1-15

Introduction

1 See particularly Marc Bloch's summary, in the concluding chapters of his *Société Féodale*, of the essential characteristics of feudalism as he understood it. Some of these characteristics persisted long after the end of the age which he himself labelled feudal. In his foreword he maintained that one could without compunction use the word feudal in relation to these later ages provided one explained exactly what one meant by the term. In this sense see also Otto Brunner in his 'Feudalismus: Ein Beitrag zur Begriffsgeschichte', published in 1958 by Die Akademie der Wissenschaften und der Literatur.

2 Particularly the confusion between public and private functions, the persistence of serfdom in some form or another in the countryside and the corporative organization in the towns, the absence of equality before the law and the other attributes of the 'société d'ordres' discussed below.

3 See particularly A. Daumard and F. Furet, *Structures et Relations Sociales à Paris au XVIII*e* Siècle*, Paris 1961, and Jean Sentou, *Fortunes et Groupes Sociaux à Toulouse*, Paris 1969.

4 Marcel Garaud, *Historie Générale du Droit Privé de 1789 à 1804*, v.2, *La Révolution et la Propriété Foncière*, Paris 1959, pp.169ff.

5 See G.V.Taylor, 'Types of Capitalism in Eighteenth Century France' in *E.H.R.* 79, July 1964.

6 See, e.g., C. Carrière, *Négociants Marseillais au XVIII*e* Siècle*, Marseille 1973. Carrière notes that though writers, ministers and officials continually complained about the obstacles to trade – the tariff barriers, tolls, different weights and measures, etc. – which Necker once described as 'monstrueux aux yeux de la raison', the merchants themselves, so far from finding them monstrous, accepted them and accommodated themselves to them.

7 This was true of C.G. Svarez, the principal architect of the *Allgemeines Landrecht*, and of C.F. Beyme, the beloved cabinet councillor of Frederick William III.

8 R. Mandrou, *Louis XIV en son Temps*, in the series *Peuples et Civilisations*, Paris 1973.

PART ONE

I The société d'ordres or Ständegesellschaft

1 Lefebvre's preface to E.Dumont *Souvenirs sur Mirabeau* (new edition), ed. J. Bénetruy, Paris 1951.

2 For a not unusual use of this word see e.g. Mirabeau, speech in the Constituent Assembly, 16 June 1789 (*Archives Parlementaires*, vol. 8, p.125), in which, in considering the meanings attached to the word 'peuple', he says that one of the meanings given to it is 'ce que les aristocrates, *tant nobles que roturiers* [author's italics], appellent insolement canaille'. The term was in fact one of abuse applied to anyone of substance to whom the writer or speaker objected.

3 See A.J. Tudesq, *Les Grands Notables en France, 1840-1849*, Paris 1964.

4 See Braudel and Labrousse, *Histoire Economique et Sociale de la France*, Vol. 2 (1660-1789), Paris 1970.

5 See M. Reinhard, 'Elite et noblesse dans la seconde moitié du XVIII*e* siècle', in *Revue d'Histoire Moderne et Contemporaine*, vols. 3 to 4, 1956 to 1957.

6 See *Allgemeines Landrecht für die preußischen Staaten von 1794*, introduction by H. Hattenhauer, Frankfurt a/M. and Berlin 1970 (hereafter *ALR*).

7 For a statement of these functions as late as 1766 by the Paris *parlement*, see R. Mousnier, *Les Institutions de la France sous la Monarchie Absolue*, I, Paris 1974, pp. 39-40.

8 Mirabeau, *Archives Parlementaires*, vol. 8, p.110.

9 *ALR*, II, 7, Para. 1.

10 *ALR*, II, 8.

11 The absence of further discussion on the nobility is, however, attributable to the fact that the nobles' privileges were based on the different laws and customs of the provinces in which they lived, and the *ALR* was not concerned with these.

12 See e.g. *ABB*, VIII, doc. 31, p.46. Cocceji to Frederick the Great, 5.xii.48: 'Your Royal Majesty could not believe how difficult it is to find the kind of presidents your Majesty desires.'

13 This figure is not invariably cited. Other and much lower figures are sometimes given. This discrepancy is presumably a consequence of the many different kinds of nobles that existed in France under the Ancien Régime. There were nobles for life only, first, second, third and fourth generation nobles; 'nobles chevaleresques' who could prove that their families had been noble in AD 1400, 'nobles d'ancienne extraction' who could prove the same in relation to 1500, etc. All these categories of nobles had different legal rights, and the circumstances in which nobility was transmissible also varied greatly. Obviously any estimate of the total number of nobles must depend on which of these categories the writer chooses to exclude – but never specifies.

14 See B. Hyslop, *L'Apanage de Philippe Egalité*, Paris 1965.

15 See Jean Meyer, *La Noblesse Bretonne*, Paris 1972.

16 See Martini, 'Die Adelsfrage in Preußen 1806', in *V.J.S.W.* Beiheft 35, pp. 70-77.

17 See R. Koselleck, *Preußen zwischen Reform und Revolution*, Stuttgart 1967, pp.80-81.

18 See K. Hinze, *Die Arbeiterfrage zu Beginn des modernen Kapitalismus in Brandenburg-Preußen*, Berlin 1963, p.223.

19 See G.T. Matthews, *The Royal General Farms in Eighteenth-Century France*, New York 1958, pp.86 ff.

20 Felix Eberty, *Jugenderinnerungen eines alten Berliners*, Berlin 1878, p.95.

21 See Montesquieu, *De L'Esprit des Lois*, Book V, Ch.IX, 'Les terres nobles auront des privilèges, comme les personnes'.

22 For Rabaud de Saint-Etienne's views on this subject see particularly his *Considérations sur les Intérêts du Tiers-Etat*, in *Précis de l'Histoire de la Révolution Française*, ed. Boissy d'Anglas, Paris 1827, pp.43 ff.

23 D. Gerhard, *Ständische Vertretungen in Europa im 17. und 18. Jahrhundert*, Göttingen 1969, p.31.

24 E. Fehrenbach, *Traditionale Gesellschaft und Revolutionäres Recht*, Göttingen 1974,

pp.40 ff.

25 Flammermont, p. 645, Maupeou's Mémoire to Louis XVI, 1788.

26 C.G. Svarez, *Vorträge über Recht und Staat*, ed. H. Conrad and G. Kleinheyer, Cologne and Opladen 1960, pp.482 and 485.

27 *Archives Parlementaires*, vol. 8, p.110.

28 *Archives Parlementaires*, vol. 10, p.39.

29 E. Fehrenbach, *op. cit.*, p.60.

30 See F. Crouzet, 'Angleterre et France au XVIIIᵉ Siècle', *Annales E.S.C.* 1966, vol. 21(i), p.701, and M. Levy-Leboyer, *Les Banques Européenes et l'Industrialisation Internationale dans la Première Moitié du XIXᵉ Siècle*, Paris 1964, p.29: 'La Révolution a été une catastrophe nationale' as far as production was concerned.

II The ideology of absolutism in France and Prussia

1 See the useful article by Rudolf Vierhaus, entitled 'Absolutismus', in *Sowjetsystem und demokratische Gesellschaft, Eine vergleichende Enzyklopädie*, Vol. I, Freiburg, Basel, Wien, 1966.

2 See O. Hintze, *Staat und Verfassung*, vol. I of *Gesammelte Abhandlungen*, Göttingen 1962, p.122.

3 See F. L. Carsten, *Princes and Parliaments in Germany*, Oxford 1959, pp.429 ff.

4 Quoted by Michel Antoine, *Le Conseil du Roi sous le Règne de Louis XV*, Paris 1970, p.9.

5 See M. Bloch, *Les Rois Thaumaturges*, Strasbourg and Paris 1924, pp. 224 ff.

6 *Ibid*, p.399.

7 See P. Schwartz, *Der erste Kulturkampf in Preußen um Kirche und Schule*, Berlin 1925, pp.1 ff.

8 On the principal events of Wolff's life and on his political ideas, see W. Frauendienst, 'Christian Wolff als Staatsdenker', *Historische Studien*, Heft 171, Berlin 1927.

9 See Part Two, ch. II (b) below.

10 C. Hinrichs, *Friedrich Wilhelm I, König in Preußen, Jugend und Aufstieg*, Hamburg 1941, pp. 37-38.

11 Frauendienst, *op. cit.*, p.51.

12 *Ibid*, p.54.

13 This story is told by Thomas Mann in his *Friedrich und die große Koalition*, Berlin 1916.

14 See *Der aufgeklärte Absolutismus*, ed. K.O. Freiherr von Aretin, Cologne 1974, a collection of essays on enlightened absolutism in which France is not so much as mentioned.

15 R. Mousnier, *Fureurs paysannes*, Paris 1967.

16 *Mémoires de Louis XIV*, ed. J. Lognon,

Paris 1927, p.136.

17 *Siècle de Louis XIV*, ed. R. Groos, Paris 1947, p.4.

18 Testament Politique, 1768, ed. G.B. Volz, Berlin 1920, pp. 11 and 194.

19 E. von Meier, *Die Reform der Verwaltungsorganisation unter Stein und Hardenberg*, 2nd (posthumous) edition, ed. F. Thimme, Munich/Leipzig 1912, p.25.

20 Mousnier, *Fureurs Paysannes*, (n. 15 above) p. 17.

21 See ch. I, n. 6 above.

22 U.-J. Heuer, *Allgemeines Landrecht und Klassenkampf*, East Berlin 1960, p.113.

23 See H. Möller, *Aufklärung in Preußen*, Berlin 1974, p. 565. Also R. Ibekken, *Preußen 1807-1813*, Cologne and Berlin 1970, p.18.

24 Testament Politique, 1768, p.200.

25 The office of first minister existed officially during the minority of Louis XV (see M. Antoine, *Le Conseil* . . ., p. 202) but not at any other time. However, many ministers, generally *contrôleurs généraux*, had the principal say in determining policy – Colbert, Choiseul, Turgot, Necker, Calonne, to name only some of the more famous. They were nevertheless always liable to be overriden, if not dismissed, as a result of intrigues at court.

26 *Mémoires de Louis XIV, op. cit.*, p.33.

27 R. Mousnier and F. Hartung, 'Quelques Problèmes concernant la Monarchie Absolue', in *Relazioni del Congresso Internazionale di Scienze Storiche vol. IV, Storia Moderna*, Rome 1955.

28 See S. Skalweit, 'Frankreich und Friedrich der Große. Der Aufstieg Preußens in der öffentlichen Meinung des Ancien Régime', in *Bonne Historische Forschungen*, Bonn 1952, Vol. I *passim*.

29 See Part Three, ch. III (a) below.

30 The Physiocrats proclaimed themselves the advocates of 'le despotisme légal' but distinguished this from despotism as described by Montesquieu which they called 'le despotisme arbitraire'. They described this hardly less eloquently than had Montesquieu himself and with more insight into how it worked. See Le Mercier de la Rivière, 'L'ordre naturel et essentiel des sociétés politiques', published in *Collection des Economistes et des Réformateurs Sociaux de la France*, ed. E. Depitre, Paris 1910, pp.131 ff.

31 *Mémoires de Louis XIV*, p.16.

32 *Ibid*, p.137.

33 *De L'Esprit des Lois*, Book VI, ch. II.

34 See A. Kamp, 'Friedrich Wilhelm I und das preußische Beamtentum', in *Forschungen zur Brandenburgischen-Preußischen Geschichte* (hereafter *FBPG*) XXX, 1918.

35 See the case of Müller Arnold in the appendix to Part Three, ch. IV below.

36 Testament Politique, 1752, p.31.

37 See K. Hinze, *Die Arbeiterfrage* . . ., *op. cit., passim*.

38 Testament Politique, 1768, p.129: 'J'en ai toujours usé envers elle (la noblesse) avec distinction et considération.'

39 C. Duffy, *The Army of Frederick the Great*, Newton Abbot 1974, p.46.

40 For the gradual and increasingly drastic steps which Frederick took to ensure that these injunctions were obeyed, see particularly *Acta Borussica Behördenorganisation*, Vol. VI (2), doc. 418; VII, pp. 31, 47, 436, 459; VIII, pp. 749, 791; IX, pp. 775-76; XIII, pp. 107, 181. That so many orders had to be issued is a proof (as was often noted in the texts) that they were not obeyed. It seems nevertheless significant that Graf Lehndorff in his memoirs continually referred to his passionate desire to visit France and England, yet did not question that he could not do so without the royal consent – which he never got. This prohibition applied to the whole population (see *ABB*, XVI (1), p.259, circular to the General Directory and to all *Kriegs- und Domänenkammern*, 15. ix .1775).

41 The most famous instance of this is the case of von Katte, in the reign of Frederick William I (there were other cases in the reign of Frederick the Great though the present writer does not know how many). Von Katte was the friend and fellow-officer of Frederick the Great when he was crown prince, and conspired with him to escape from Prussia to England. Von Katte was condemned by court martial to life imprisonment, but Frederick William I overrode this judgment and ordered his execution, which Frederick was made to watch. The most vivid description of this episode, of von Katte's character, and of the reactions of his family to his fate, is given by Th. Fontane, *Wanderungen durch die Mark Brandenburg* in his *Sämtliche Werke*, ed. W. Keitel, vol. I, Munich 1966, pp. 831-36.

42 The most notable instances, though there are many others, are those that occurred in the course of the Müller Arnold case, described in the Appendix to Part II, ch. IV below.

43 *Mémoires de Louis XIV*, p.28.

44 To give only a few examples among an enormous number that could be cited, see the diary of Graf Lehndorff, *Dreißig Jahre am Hofe Friedrichs des Großen*, ed. K.E. Schmidt-Lötzen, 3 vols, Gotha 1907-13; the account by Koser (in 'Friedrich der Große und die preußischen Universitäten', in *FBPG*, XVII,

1904) of his treatment of a university professor – Frederick often appointed and even examined professors himself – who claimed to have read Locke but when questioned by the King turned out not to have done so; his treatment of Christian Garve, whom he always summoned to see him when he went to Breslau and to whom he delivered diatribes on the bourgeois vices of cowardice and lack of a sense of honour, though Garve was acutely conscious of being a bourgeois himself (see C. Garve, *Fragmente zur Schilderung des Geistes, des Charakters, und die Regierung Friedrichs des Zweyten*, Zweyter Theil, Breslau 1798).

45 This fragment was found by W. Naudé and published in *FBPG*, XV, 1902 ('Denkwürdigkeiten des Ministers Grafen von der Schulenburg').

46 Of these, one of the most arresting examples (though never seen as such by German historians) is the grovelling attitude to the government shown by most of the 21 nobles who supported Marwitz in his threatened revolt against Hardenberg in 1811. Hardenberg deprived them of their posts in the government and of their pensions. Particularly Obermarschall von Massow excelled himself in providing implausible excuses and in begging that his job and pension might be restored to him, since otherwise he would be unable to pay his servants or provide for his innocent children. His letter is transcribed by F. Meusel in vol. II, part 1, pp. 30 ff. of his life of Marwitz, Berlin 1908-13 (cf. below Part Three, ch. III (b), n.7).

47 *Mémoires de Louis XIV, op. cit.*, Introduction.

48 *Ibid.*, p.149.

49 *Ibid.*, p.288.

50 *Ibid.*, pp.80 ff.

51 *Ibid.*, p.287: Projet de Harangue, written by Louis in his own hand in 1710.

52 In *L'Administration des Finances de la France* in *Oeuvres Complètes*, ed. Baron de Staël, Paris 1812, vol. IV, p.65.

53 See *Louis XIV et Vingt Millions de Français* (Paris 1965) by Pierre Goubert, who nevertheless could not altogether rid himself of admiration for Louis, and *Louis XIV en son Temps*, in which Robert Mandrou, *op. cit.*, set himself to destroy the legend that Louis' reign was the most brilliant and remarkable of the Ancien Régime – a legend, as he said, disseminated throughout the years by school textbooks on which generations of French children were brought up.

54 E. Lavisse, *Histoire de France*, Paris 1908, vol. VIII (1), p.272.

55 Goubert, *Louis XIV . . .*, p.167.

56 Mandrou, *op. cit.*, p.310.

57 The bad harvests of these years were caused in the first place by climatic conditions which did not recur until the eve of the Revolution, but they cannot alone have been responsible for famines on the enormous scale that occurred. As Professor Goubert points out, in order to understand these tragic phenomena one has to be aware that the great majority of French people, even in the countryside, had to buy their bread, which became impossible with the rise in prices caused by scarcity. He nevertheless admits that all their small savings had been eaten away by taxation. Taxation too, it would seem, must have reduced production, because those who produced grain had to sell it to pay their taxes, often presumably at the expense of the next year's seed. Natural calamities in grain-growing communities in the 18th century were always liable to produce famine, and did so on a large scale in many countries in central Europe in the early 1770s. They could, however, be averted by government action, as they were in Prussia. See Part Two, ch. V(c)(1) below.

58 See *Mémoires de Louis XIV, op. cit.*, Introduction p.9.

59 These were published by G.B. Volz under the title *Die politischen Testamente Friedrichs des Großen*, Berlin 1920.

60 Testament Politique, 1768, p.177.

61 *Exposé du Gouvernement Prussien*, Volz, p.244.

62 Testament Politique, 1768, p.230.

63 *Ibid.*, p.160.

64 See Duffy, *op. cit.*, p.22.

65 *Exposé du Gouvernement Prussien*, p.243.

66 G.F. Knapp, *Die Bauernbefreiung*, 2 vols, Munich/Leipzig 1927, vol. II, p.73.

67 *ABB*, VII, p.574.

68 *Acta Borussica Getreidehandelspolitik*, vol. IV, p.122.

69 Quoted in Koser, *Geschichte Friedrichs des Großen*, p.545.

70 On this see, particularly, O. Büsch, *Militärsystem und Sozialleben im alten Preußen*, Berlin 1962.

71 See G. Ritter, *Staatskunst und Kriegshandwerk* (3rd edition), Munich 1965, vol. I, pp.13 ff. and *passim*. Whatever the judgment on Ritter's general argument, his defence of Frederick the Great against the charge of militarism amounts to no more than saying that Frederick was a realist who saw as clearly as Clausewitz was to see later that the circumstances that make for success in war cannot be divorced from the circumstances of

civilian life.
72 Testament Politique, 1768, p.111.
73 *Ibid.*, p.229.
74 *Ibid.*, pp.220-21.
75 F. Meinecke, *Die Idee der Staatsräson*, Munich 1960, p.395.

PART TWO
*I The bureaucracies'
tasks in France and Prussia,
and the conditioning circumstances*

1 Eberty, *op. cit.* p.75.
2 Le Mercier de la Rivière, *op. cit.*, p.131. This point is also made by Rousseau in his *De l'Inégalité Parmi les Hommes* (Editions sociales), Paris 1954, p.139.
3 L. Namier, *Revolution of the Intellectuals.*
4 See Part Two, ch. II below.
5 T. Winkler, *Johann Gottfried Frey und die Entstehung der preußischen Selbstverwaltung*, Stuttgart 1957, p.71.
6 *The Wealth of Nations*, ed. E. Cannon, London 1950, Vol. II, pp.395-96.
7 For the fervour with which the doctrines of Adam Smith were adopted in Prussia see Part Three, ch. II below.
8 See R. Darnton, *The Business of the Enlightenment: A publishing History of the Encyclopédie, 1775-1800*, Cambridge, Mass. 1979, *passim*, particularly p.286, on how small an appeal the *Encyclopédie* had for the commercial and industrial bourgeoisie.
9 See the last chapter of Tocqueville's *Ancien Régime* entitled 'Comment la Révolution est sortie d'elle-même de ce qui précède'.
10 M. Antoine, *Le Conseil . . .*, *op. cit.*, p.634.
11 Quoted by H. Rosenberg, *Bureaucracy, Aristocracy and Autocracy: The Prussian Experience 1660-1815*, Cambridge, Mass. 1958, p.161.
12 *Ancien Régime*, p.127.
13 *ABB*, VI(1); Einleitende Darstellung.
14 R. L. de V. Marquis d'Argenson, *Considérations sur le Gouvernement Ancien et Présent de la France*, Amsterdam 1765, p.13.
15 Quoted by H. Berger, 'Friedrich der Große als Kolonisator' in *Giessener Studien*, vol. VIII, Giessen 1896.

*II The composition of the
bureaucracies*

(a) THE FRENCH EXPERIENCE
1 See François Bluche, 'L'Origine Sociale

des Secrétaires d'Etat de Louis XIV', in *XVIIIᵉ Siècle*, 1ᵉʳ trimestre, 1959, nos. 42-43.
2 For a discussion of the meaning of this term see François Bluche, *Les Magistrats du Parlement de Paris au XVIIIᵉ Siècle*, Paris 1960, p.131.
3 See M. Antoine, *Le Conseil*, pp. 571 ff.
4 See Bluche, *Les Magistrats . . .*, Part I, ch. II.
5 Bluche, 'L'Origine Sociale des Secrétaires d'Etat', p. 8.
6 Quoted by M. Marion, *Dictionnaire des Institutions de la France au XVIIᵉ et XVIIIᵉ Siècles*, Paris 1968, under 'Ministre'.
7 See R. Mousnier, *La Vénalité des Offices sous Henri IV et Louis XIII*, Rouen n.d., p. 58.
8 *Ibid.*, p. 496.
9 R. Mousnier, *Fureurs Paysannes*, p. 27.
10 Alexis de Tocqueville, *Oeuvres Complètes*, vol. 2, ed. J.P. Mayer, 3rd edition, Paris 1952. 'L'Ancien Régime et la Révolution', p. 132. Alternatively, Tocqueville may simply have been ignorant of the facts, as he often was. Certainly this was so when he said, on p. 109 of the same work, that the king's council was not composed of *grands seigneurs* but of persons of low or mediocre birth. The council at the end of the Ancien Régime in fact contained many *grands seigneurs* (see M. Antoine, *op. cit.*, p. 200).
11 Tocqueville's great-grandfather was the famous Malesherbes (Chrétien-Guillaume Lamoignon de Malesherbes), guillotined 1794, at one time first president of the *Cour des Aides* in Paris and government censor, noted for the tolerance he showed to the *Philosophes* (see P. Grosclaude, *Malesherbes. Témoin et Interprète de son Temps*, Paris 1962).
12 For the library collected by Chrétien François de Lamoignon in the 17th century, see Bluche, *Les Magistrats . . .*, p. 290.
13 See Bluche, *Les Magistrats . . .*, pp. 88 ff., and p. 92 (where he shows that the proportion of magistrates who came from the 'noblesse chevaleresque' and the 'noblesse d'ancienne extraction' was approximately the same as that in the nobility as a whole), as well as the table following p. 94 (which shows the noble origins of those magistrates who entered the *parlement* between 1716 and 1770).
14 See Bluche, 'Les Honneurs de la Cour', in *Les Cahiers Nobles*, Paris 1957.
15 *ALR*, II, 9, para. 19.
16 Strictly speaking, some of these dues were 'feudal' and others 'seigneurial', but in practice they were commonly confused. See Marion, *Dictionnaire*, under 'Féodalité'.
17 I.e. by so-called *rentes constituées*, a form of loan extremely common between indi-

viduals, in which the creditor (in order to evade the prohibition on lending money at interest which existed till the Revolution) gave the debtor a sum in perpetuity in return for an annual payment in money or kind and the right to seize the latter's property if the payments were not made (see R. Forster, *The Nobility of Toulouse in the Eighteenth Century*, Baltimore 1960, p. 106, and Goubert, *L'Ancien Régime*, Paris 1969, vol. I, p. 127).

18 See Mousnier, *Vénalité des Offices*, pp. 505-06.

19 Marion, *Dictionnaire*, under 'Noblesse'.

20 See Mousnier, *Vénalité des Offices*. For a short account see his *Assassination of Henry IV*, trans. J. Spencer, London 1973.

21 The office-holder did not own his office in the sense in which the seigneur owned his feudal dues, since the office remained in law the property of the crown, the holder having only a right *to* it as distinct from *in* it. Though, however, the king could suppress offices, it was always recognized that he could only do so by repaying the holders the capital they had invested in them. Even in the second half of the eighteenth century, however, when the government became increasingly unwilling to treat its creditors with the dishonesty which had characterized its dealings in the days of Louis XVI, this assumption by no means safeguarded the office-holders completely, as was demonstrated when Maupeou dissolved the *parlements* in 1771 (see J. Flammermont, *Le Chancelier Maupeou et les Parlements*, Paris 1883). Further, the rights of the office-holder to sell his office were frequently limited, notably in the case of offices in the *parlements*, by the necessity of finding a purchaser who fulfilled a number of requirements and was acceptable to his colleagues.

22 Necker, *Oeuvres Complètes*, published by M. le Baron de Staël, Paris 1809-21, vol. V, pp. 365 ff.

23 Figure given by M. Göhring, 'Die Ämterkäuflichkeit im Ancien Régime', *Historische Studien*, Heft 346, Berlin 1938, p. 262. This otherwise carefully documented work does not, unfortunately, say how this figure of 51,000 was arrived at.

24 Göhring, *op. cit.*, p. 164, quotes Colbert as saying that 'peut-estre toutes les terres du royaume estimées suivant leur juste valeur ne pourroient pas payer le prix de toutes les charges de judicature et des finances'.

25 G.V. Taylor, in his article 'Non-capitalist Wealth and the Origins of the French Revolution', in *AHR*, January 1967, concludes that a sum 'far above 600 million livres' was invested in offices. Göhring gives the same figure, though whether these two assessments come from the same or a different source is not clear. At the end of the Ancien Régime the annual revenue of the French government was between 500 and 600 million livres. See also Marion, *Dictionnaire* . . ., under 'Offices'.

26 Quoted by Gohring, *op. cit.*, p. 181, and by Marion, *Dictionnaire*. . . .

27 See the two highly illuminating articles by D.D. Bien, 'La réaction aristocratique avant 1789', in *Annales E.S.C.*, vol. 29 for January/February and March/April 1974.

28 *Ibid.* According to Bien, 266 people became *Secrétaires* in the Paris chancellery between 1774 and 1789. They came from many different walks of life – merchants, municipal officials, financiers, doctors, lawyers, even on occasions prosperous peasants, as well as nobles with less than four generations of nobility.

29 See Yves Durand, *Les Fermiers Généraux au XVIIIᵉ Siècle*, Paris 1971, p. 295.

30 Quoted by Bluche in *Les Magistrats* . . ., p.66.

31 See Bluche, 'L'Origine Sociale des Secrétaires d'Etat de Louis XIV', *op. cit.;* also 'L'Origine du Personnel Ministériel Français au XVIIIᵉ Siècle', in *Bulletin de la Société d'Histoire Moderne*, 1957. In these two articles Bluche points out that whereas in the reign of Louis XVI the ministers were on an average third-generation nobles, between 1718 and 1789 over 74 per cent possessed nobility older than this (38 per cent were nobles of the seventh genetration or more and 25 per cent of the tenth generation or more). As against this, however, the most important post in the government, that of *contrôleur-général*, continued frequently to be held by people from recently ennobled families. Of the 25 *contrôleurs-généraux* between 1718 and 1789, nine were only second-generation nobles and one, Necker, being a foreigner and a Protestant, was never granted noble status but remained a commoner.

32 See Bien (as in n. 27 above).

33 Bluche, *Les Magistrats* . . ., p. 109.

34 Tocqueville, *op. cit.*, quoted by Lefebvre in his Introduction, p. 21.

35 Quoted by Yves Durand, *op. cit.*, p. 300.

36 See M. Antoine, *Le Conseil* . . ., p. 212.

37 *Ibid.*, Book I, ch. III.

38 Bésenval, *Mémoires*, ed. Ségur, Paris 1805, III, p. 69.

39 See E. von Bodelschwingh, *Leben des Freiherrn von Vincke*, Berlin 1853, p. 262, which describes the difficulty Vincke had in getting Blücher to attend a meeting of civil

servants, all of whom he called 'Federfüchsern'.

40 Bluche, *Les Magistrats* . . ., p. 305.

(b) THE PRUSSIAN EXPERIENCE

1 *ABB*, III, pp. 441 ff.
2 See Part Two, ch. IV (c) below.
3 H. Rosenberg, *Bureaucracy* . . ., p. 68.
4 See O. Hintze, 'Der Beamtenstand', in
Soziologie und Geschichte, vol. II of *Gesammelte
Abhandlungen*, Göttingen 1967; also Rosenberg, *op. cit.*, ch. 3.
5 On Hille (Christoph Werner) see *ABB*, V,
pp. 135-38 and 198-99; C. Hinrichs,
Preußentum und Pietismus, Göttingen 1971, p.
319. The quotation from Hille is taken from
F. Mehring, *Die Lessinglegende*, 3rd ed., Berlin
1953, p. 150.
6 For these and other statements relating to
the Pietists, see Hinrichs, as in n. 5 above.
7 See W. Gericke, *Glaubenszeugnisse und
Konfessionspolitik der brandenbürgischen Herr-
scher bis zur preußischen Union 1540 bis 1815*,
Bielefeld 1977, p. 61. He points out that by
these words Frederick William did not understand that he himself had deserved God's
favour because of his good actions. On the
contrary, he admitted that he was a bad man
(*ein böser Mensch*) and if he behaved well one
day immediately afterwards relapsed into bad
behaviour. 'This,' he said, 'I know well but I
can't help it.' What he meant was that he
believed himself to be one of the elect among
sinners who were predestined to salvation by
the grace of God.
8 See, for example, Lehndorff, *op. cit.*, in
which Lehndorff refers to a large number of
such cases. See also F. Meusel, *op. cit.*, vol. I,
p. 175. The mother-in-law of that outstanding denouncer of the bourgeois *Weltanschauung*, Ludwig von der Marwitz, was a
bourgeoise.
9 *ALR*, II, 9, para. 3.
10 *ABB*, XIII, Cabinet order of 20. iii. 1763.
11 Quoted by O. Hintze, 'Die Hohenzollern und der Adel', in *Regierung und Verwaltung*, vol. III of *Gesammelte Abhandlungen*,
Göttingen 1967.
12 Theodor Fontane, *Der Stechlin*, Gold-
manns Gelbe Taschenbücher, Munich n.d.,
p. 265.
13 H.C. Johnson, *Frederick the Great and his
Officials*, New Haven 1975, p. 245. On the
Prussian bureaucracy in the eighteenth century see particularly the articles by W. Dorn in
Political Science Quarterly, vols. 46 and 47,
1931 and 1932; and Rosenberg, *op. cit.* For
the evolution of the king's cabinet, see H.
Hüffer, 'Die Beamten des alteren preußi-

schen Kabinetts', in *FBPG*, V, part I, 1892.
14 H. C. Johnson, *op. cit.*, p. 259, and see
Part Two, ch. IV (c) below.
15 H. Hüffer (as in n. 13 above). On
Eichel's influence in general, see *ABB*, VI (1),
Hintze's Einleitende Darstellung, p. 117.
16 Notably Lombard and Beyme, the particular objects of Stein's and Hardenberg's
attacks.
17 See E. M. Arndt, *Wanderungen und
Wandelungen mit dem Reichsfreiherrn von [sic]
Stein*, Berlin 1858, *passim;* and E. M. Arndt,
Erinnerungen aus dem aüsseren Leben, Leipzig
1840. For other illuminating examples, see
Hans Hattenhauer's description, in the introduction to the 1970 edition of the *ALR*, p. 17,
of the relations between Graf Carmer, and
the two, by origin, petits bourgeois Svarez and
Klein. All three lived as well as worked
together, when they were producing the *ALR*.
See also H. Moller, *op. cit.*, for the composition of the *Mittwochsgesellschaft*.
18 Otto von Bismarck, *Gedanken und Erinnerungen*, 3 volumes in one, Stuttgart and
Berlin n.d. (Cotta'sche Buchhandlung), p. 41.
19 See *ABB*, XV, p. 252.
20 See H. N. Preradovich, *Die Führungs-
schichte in Oesterreich und Preußen 1804 bis
1918*, Wiesbaden 1955, p. 160. He notes that
the normal method of progression, presumably also true of the second half of the
eighteenth century, was from peasant or
artisan, via the university, to Lutheran pastor,
and then into the bureaucracy, though sometimes, but more rarely, from the families of
merchants or *Domänenpächter*. No analyses
appear to have made, comparable to those
relating to France, of the ways in which one
rose to power in Prussia in the eighteenth
century.
21 C. Duffy, *op. cit.*, p. 27. See also Peter
Baumgart, 'Zur Geschichte der kurmärkischen Stände im 17. und 18. Jahrhundert', in
*Veröffentlichungen des Max-Planck-Instituts für
Geschichte*, 27, Göttingen 1969, p. 141.
22 On this see, for example, P. Paret, *Yorck
and the Era of Prussian Reform 1807-1815*,
Princeton 1966; G. H. Pertz and H. Delbrück, *Das Leben des Feldmarschalls Grafen
Neithard von Gneisenau*, 5 vols, Berlin 1864-
80, vol. I; Th. Fontane, *Wanderungen durch die
Mark Brandenburg*, vol. II, pp. 109 ff. (the case
of Wilhelmi, later Wilhelm von Anhalt).
23 *ALR*, II, 10.
24 On the position of the *Eximirte*, see R.
Koselleck, *Preußen zwischen Reform und Revolution*, pp. 89 ff. For a precise definition
of the term in the reign of Frederick the
Great and the legal difficulties which could

arise over a person's right to the status, see *ABB*, XVI (1), doc. 253.

25 See Friedrich von Raumer, *Lebenserin-nerungen und Briefwechsel*, Leipzig 1861.

26 See Hüffer, *op. cit.*

27 See H. Schoeps, *Aus den Jahren preußischer Not und Erneuerung, Tagebücher der Geb rüder Gerlach*, Berlin 1963.

28 See particularly the judgment of Madame de Staël, in *De l'Allemagne*, ed. Comtesse de Pange, 2 vols, Paris 1958, vol. I, pp. 210 ff.

29 See H. Möller, *op. cit.*

30 J. P. Eckermann, *Gespräche mit Goethe*, ed. F. Bergemann, Wiesbaden 1955, p. 289.

31 R. Darnton, *The Business of the Enlightenment . . .*, p. 299.

32 C. Garve, *Versuche über verschiedene Gegenstände aus der Moral, der Literatur und dem gesellschaftlichen Leben*, Breslau 1802, vol. I, pp. 306-07.

33 See J. Schultze, 'Die Auseinandersetzung zwischen Adel und Bürgerstand, 1773-1806', in *Historische Studien*, vols. 161-64, Heft 163, 1925.

34 Molière, *Le Bourgeois Gentilhomme*, Act I, scene II.

35 See Manfred Neuman, 'Diderot und das "siècle des lumières", in Wilhelm von Humboldt's Pariser Tagebuchern (1797-1799)' in *Thèmes et Figures du Siècle des Lumières*, Geneva 1980.

36 See Clausewitz, 'Die Deutschen und die Franzosen', printed in K. Schwartz, *Das Leben des Generals Carl von Clausewitz und der Frau Maria von Clausewitz*, Berlin 1878.

37 Pertz and Delbrück, *op. cit.*, vol. 5, p. 12.

38 *Treitschke's History of Germany in the Nineteeth Century*, trans. by Eden and Cedar Paul, London 1915, vol. I, p. 102.

39 Thomas Mann, *Betrachtungen eines Unpolitischen*, Berlin 1929, p. 80.

III Taxation and government finance

(a) THE FRENCH EXPERIENCE

1 *Projet d'une Dîxme Royale*, ed. E. Coornaert, Paris 1933, p. 25.

2 See M. Marion, *Les Impôts Directs sous l'Ancien Régime*, Paris 1910, document 36, p. 192: 'Mémoire sur la taille envoyée aux intendants par le contrôleur général Orry, février 1732.'

.**3** See Part Three, ch. III below.

4 H. Grange, *Les Idées de Necker*, Paris 1974, p. 38. Grange gives no evidence for this assertion.

5 G. V. Taylor, 'Revolutionary and Non-revolutionary Content of the Cahiers of 1789.

An Interim Report', in *FHS*, vol. VII no. 4, Autumn 1972.

6 See Part Three, ch. II below.

7 G. T. Matthews, *The Royal General Farms in Eighteenth Century France*, New York 1958, p. 88.

8 See M. Marion, *Dictionnaire des Institutions*, under this heading.

9 The term 'financier' in eighteenth-century France did not have the meaning which it has in English today. It meant a person concerned with the financial affairs of the crown and thus excluded, notably, the bankers who dealt with private clients. In his *De l'Administration des Finances de la France* (*Oeuvres, op. cit.*, vol. 5, p. 346), Necker defined it as follows: 'One gives the title of financier in France to the various persons who are charged with the levying of the public revenue whether as receivers, [tax] farmers or "régisseurs" [i.e., people in charge of a Régie]. The same also applies to the treasurers who pay the expenses of the state, to the court bankers who deal with financial affairs relating to foreign countries, and to the various persons who, in return for a commission, advance money to the crown on the security of the more or less distant receipt of the taxes.'

10 See Jean Bouvier and Henry Germain-Marton, *Finances et Financiers del l'Ancien Régime*, in the series *Que sais-je?* (No. 1109), Paris 1964, p. 11.

11 See Yves Durand, *op. cit., passim.*

12 For the business organization and activities of the General Farmers, with which Yves Durand does not deal, see G. T. Matthews, *op. cit.*

13 *The Wealth of Nations*, ed. E. Cannon, 2 vols, London 1950, vol. II, p.333.

14 Turgot, *Oeuvres*, ed. Schelle, Paris 1913-23, vol. II, p.446.

15 Quoted by Marion (as in n. 8 above) under 'Collecte'.

16 Marion, *Les Impôts Directs*, ch. I. Also F. Hincker, *Les Français devant l'Impôt sous L'Ancien Régime*, Paris 1971, p. 60.

17 See circular from one of the *receveurs des tailles* to the collectors, Bordeaux, 27 October 1741, quoted in Marion, *Les Impôts Directs*, doc. 41, p.203.

18 See B. Behrens, 'Nobles, Privileges and Taxes at the End of the Ancien Régime', *Economic History Review*, Second Series, vol. XV, no. 3, 1963, p. 460.

19 Marion, *Les Impôts Directs*, doc. 25, pp. 181-82.

20 P. de Saint-Jacob, *Les Paysans de la Bourgogne du Nord au Dernier Siècle de l'Ancien*

Régime, Paris 1960, pp. 127-28.

21 As in n. 2 above.

22 See P. Mathias and P. O'Brien, 'Taxation in Britain and France, 1715-1810. A Comparison of the Social and Economic Incidence of Taxes Collected for the Central Government' in *Journal of Economic History*, V, no. 3, Winter 1976. They show that throughout the eighteenth century indirect taxes accounted for 50 per cent or more of the tax revenue received by the government in France, but for between 70 per cent and 80 per cent in England.

23 See Marion, *Dictionnaire des Institutions*, under 'Offices'.

24 These devices are described in detail by M. Göhring, *op. cit.*

25 Marion, *Les Impôts Directs*, p. 8.

26 This is not meant to deny that, at least in the second half of the eighteenth century, the wealth of the rich nobility was considerable by comparison with annual government revenue. Had the government been able to seize all this wealth, or a high proportion of it, by means of a wealth tax or surtaxes, this must have gone a long way towards alleviating its problems, at least for a year or so. Such action, however, was wholly inconceivable except by means of revolution (which in any event, when it occurred, provided only a temporary remedy). Short of revolution, action of this sort was out of the question not only because of the impossibility of making accurate assessments, but because of the passionate resistance it would have provoked not just in France – where the nobility may well have been more highly taxed than any other in Europe – but in every country, Britain included. The most that could have been done in France, and that many French ministers, notably Turgot, thought should be done, was to abolish the so-called 'taille arbitraire', and replace it with a land-tax proportionate to the yield of the land and payable by every landholder, regardless of the estate to which he belonged.

27 J. F. Bosher, *French Finances 1770 to 1795*, Cambridge 1970, Part I, chapters 4 and 5.

28 See Bosher, *op. cit.*, pp. 14 and 18-19. Also Marion, *Dictionnaire des Institutions*, under 'Acquits de comptant'.

29 Bosher, *op. cit.*, p. 77.

30 This is Professor Bosher's assumption, the truth of which, however, can hardly be open to doubt. (As Professor Bosher points out, though the most elaborate analyses have been made of the wealth and status of the owners of so-called venal (i.e., purchasable) offices in other spheres of the administration, curiously enough this has not been done for the financiers, except by Yves Durand in the case of the general farmers.)

31 See Bosher, *op. cit.*, Part II, ch. 10, and p. 308.

32 *Ibid.*, p. 6.

33 See Marion, *Dictionnaire des Institutions*, under this heading.

34 Bosher, *op. cit.*, p. 153.

35 Necker published his *compte rendu* just before he resigned from his first ministry. He admitted that his attempts at reorganization had not reached the point where it was possible – without a prodigious labour which he thought unwarranted – to produce anything approaching a complete set of figures. His error, however, does not appear to have come from this but from the fact that his calculations related to what was called an 'ordinary year'. Since in 1781 the most expensive war which France had ever waged – the War of American Independence – was still in progress, this year was as far removed from an 'ordinary year' as could be imagined. Moreover, as his successor Calonne immediately discovered, Necker's 'ordinary year' was a model put together from figures relating to a variety of different years, and not a year that had ever existed.

36 *Oeuvres* (see n. 9 above), vol. IV, p.64.

37 Bosher, *op. cit.*, p.43.

38 *Ibid.*, Preface, p.11.

39 See *Oeuvres* (as in n. 14 above), vol. IV, pp.138 ff.

(b) THE PRUSSIAN EXPERIENCE

1 Testament Politique, 1768, *op. cit.*, p. 126.

2 *Oeuvres Complètes*, ed. J.D.E. Preuss, Berlin 1846, vol. I, p. 234.

3 See *ABB*, VII, p. 617.

4 *Dissertations Lues dans les Séances Publiques de l'Académie des Sciences et Belles-Lettres de Berlin, dans les Années 1780, 1781, 1782 à 1787, par M. de Herzberg, Ministre d'Etat et Membre de l'Académie*, Berlin 1787. Lecture for 1785.

5 The word *Beamte* was always used in the eighteenth century to describe these crown tenants and did not have its modern meaning of civil servant. Civil servants, as in the *Allgemeines Landrecht*, were commonly referred to as *Bedienten*.

6 See A. Zottmann, *Die Wirtschaftspolitik Friedrichs des Großen*, Leipzig and Vienna 1937, pp. 21 ff.

7 A. Smith, *op. cit.*, II, p. 309.

8 See Altenstein's *Rigaer Denkschrift*, printed in G. Winter, *Die Reorganisation des preußischen Staates unter Stein und Hardenberg*,

Leipzig 1931, p. 473; also R. Stein, *Die Umwandlung der Agrarverfassung Ostpreußens*, Königsberg 1933 and 1934, vol. III, p. 325.

9 *ABB*, VI (1), Darstellende Einleitung, p. 149.

10 Adam Smith (see *The Wealth of Nations*, I, p. 408) thought that the Prussian was the only monarchy in Europe to have no debt. In 1807 when, owing to the French seizure of Prussian property and the depredations of the Napoleonic armies, the facilities for borrowing were much more limited than in the time of Frederick the Great, the reformers thought it axiomatic ('versteht sich von selbst', as Hardenberg and Altenstein put it) that the government should borrow as far as possible, with due allowance for interest payments, both at home and abroad.

11 *The Wealth of Nations*, I, 409.

12 *Rigaer Denkschrift*, Winter, *op. cit.*, p. 412.

13 See W. O. Henderson, *Studies in the Economic Policy of Frederick the Great*, London 1963, p. 39.

14 See *ibid.*, particularly the section on the Berlin commercial crisis of 1763.

15 Quoted by F. Fetjö, *Un Habsburg Révolutionnaire, Joseph II*, Paris 1953, pp. 93-94.

16 See, for example, his instructions to the General Directory of 1748, printed in *ABB*, VII.

17 See *FBPG*, XXII, 1909. Marwitz's 'Von dem Instande des Vermögens der Grundbesitzer des platten Landes der Mark Brandenburg und von dem Verhältnis der ihnen jetzt auferlegten Abgaben zu dem ehemaligen'.

18 This is Krug's estimate, quoted by I. Mittenzwei, *Friedrich II von Preußen*, [East] Berlin 1980, p. 141.

19 On this see Lefebvre's foreword to Dumont's *Souvenirs sur Mirabeau*, *op. cit.*

20 Quoted by Mittenzwei (as in n. 18 above), p. 164.

21 See H. Grange, *op. cit.*, pp. 174 ff.

22 Quoted by O. Hintze, *Zur Agrarpolitik Friedrichs des Großen*, in *FBPG*, X 1898, p. 292, n. 2.

23 Instructions to the *Kammer* in Cleves, 1.vii.1748, in *ABB*, VII.

24 See Marion, *Les Impôts Directs*, and *Dictionnaire* under 'Cadastres'.

25 Turgot, *op. cit.*, vol. II, pp. 228 ff.

26 See, e.g., Instructions to the *Landräte* in Magdeburg, 1766, *ABB*, XIV, pp. 142 ff.

27 See *ABB* under 'Contributionswesen'.

28 John Quincy Adams, *Letters from Silesia, 1800-1801*, London 1804, p. 318.

29 *Archives Nationales*, K 879, 78-79.

30 The account of this episode, together with the correspondence between the Fiscal General and Eichel concerning it, is given in *ABB*, IX, pp. 1 ff. For the functions of the Fiscal General see p. XX below.

31 One outstanding case in point is that of the Oberpräsident Domhardt, head of three *Kammern* in East and West Prussia. He is described by H. Rosenberg, *Bureaucracy*, p. 162, as 'an administrator of eminent quality' and by W. Hubatsch (*Frederick the Great*, London and New York 1973, p. 96) as 'an exceptionally gifted administrator'. He was, however, accused of amassing a large fortune by a variety of illegal means, including cheating the customs (see *ABB*, XVI (1), p. 146). Frederick observed of these accusations that he did not suppose all of them were true but that doubtless some were. No action, however, appears to have been taken against Domhardt who was one of the very few civilian officials whom Frederick ennobled.

The honesty of Ernst Wilhelm von Schlabrendorff, Minister for Silesia from 1755 until his death in 1770, seems less certain than Hans Rosenberg supposed, even though he was always on the look-out for crooks. Schlabrendorff, too, was a man of great energy and efficiency. Frederick, however, (admittedly suspicious of almost everyone), accused him of taking army bribes from army-contractors (see *AB Getreidehandelspolitik*, IV, p. 66) and of other forms of cheating (see *ABB*, XV, pp. 220-21. Instructions for von Hoym, Schlabrendorff's successor). Evidently, however, Frederick judged him indispensable, as he did Domhardt.

32 J. Ziekursch, *Hundert Jahre schlesischer Agrargeschichte*, Breslau 1927, p. 69.

33 See, for example, *ABB*, XVI (1), pp. 98 and 272. For the best general account of these arrangements see O. Hintze's Einleitende Darstellung in *ABB*, VI (1), pp. 182 ff.

34 Among the documents in the *ABB* is a large number of instructions to the *Landräte* in different provinces.

35 These are the words ('das Fiskalat entwickelte sich ... zu einer riesigen Behörde') of Eberhard Schmidt in 'Kammergericht und Rechtsstaat' in *Schriftenreihe der juristischen Gesellschaft*, Berlin 1968, p. 26. All the volumes in the *ABB* contain a great deal of information on the activities of the fiscals.

36 See, e.g., *ABB*, VI (2), p. 445.

37 See H. Friedberg, 'Friedrich der Große und der Prozeß Goerne', in *H.Z.*, vol. 65, 1890.

38 See *Mitteldeutsche Lebensbilder*, Magdeburg 1928, vol. 3, p. 47.

39 Testament Politique, 1768, Volz, *op. cit.*, p. 112.

40 The reason for this assertion is as follows: in both Prussia and France the vast majority of the population – between 80 and 90 per cent – consisted of peasants and most of them in both countries were living in extreme poverty. Whether, on an average, the consumption of the French peasants was higher than that of the Prussian is impossible to estimate. Turgot maintained that most French peasants were living in the greatest possible state of misery – an assertion confirmed by Olwyn Hutton's *The Poor in Eighteenth Century France*, Oxford 1974. Though the legal position of a high proportion of the Prussian peasantry was worse than that of the French, this does not necessarily mean that their consumption was less. For reasons to be discussed later it seems not improbable that fewer actually starved. In any event, however, though the material standard of life of the peasantry in the two countries cannot be accurately assessed or compared, the difference between the two can hardly have been large enough to warrant the assertion that average income or consumption per head in the two countries was markedly different among the overwhelming mass of the population.

41 French government revenue at the end of the Ancien Régime is usually reckoned at between 500 and 600 million livres per annum. The rate of exchange was 23 livres to the £ sterling. Prussian government revenue at Frederick the Great's death was apparently (see Zottmann, *op. cit.*, pp. 21 ff.) between 20 and 23 million thaler. The rate of exchange was 10 thaler to the £ sterling.

42 *The Wealth of Nations*, II, pp. 190-91.

43 F. Crouzet, 'Angleterre et France au XVIIIᵉ Siècle,' *op. cit.*

44 Lombard, quoted by A. Naudé, 'Der preußische Staatsschatz unter König Friedrich Wilhelm II und seine Erschöpfung', in *FBPG*, V, Part I, 1892, p. 203.

IV The administration of justice

(a) THE NATURE OF THE PROBLEM

1 See W. F. Church, 'The Decline of the French Jurists as Political Theorists, 1660-1789,' in *F.H.S.*, vol. 5, 1967-68.

2 Quoted by Marion in the article on 'Justice' in his *Dictionnaire des Institutions*.

3 Quoted by M. Antoine, *Le Conseil*, p. 513.

4 *A.L.R.*, II 17.1, para. 18.

5 Eberhard Schmidt, 'Die Justizpolitik Friedrichs des Großen,' in *Heidelberg Jahr-*

bücher, VI, 1962, p. 97.

6 See L. Radzinowicz, *A History of the English Criminal Law*, London 1948, vol. I, pp. 287-88.

7 Lamoignon did not in fact have the title of chancellor but that of *garde des sceaux*. This office was not irremoveable like that of the chancellor, but was often a substitute for it.

8 *ABB*, VI (1), 115 ff.

9 See J. Flammermont, *op. cit.*, p. 4 ff.

10 O. Hintze, 'Preußens Entwicklung zum Rechtstaat', in *Regierung und Verwaltung*, vol. III of *Gesammelte Abhandlungen*, Göttingen 1967.

11 These are the words of Maupeou in his Mémoire to Louis XVI of 1788 transcribed by Flammermont, *op. cit.* (see p. 615).

12 Altenstein's *Rigaer Denkschrift*, printed in Winter, *op. cit.*, p. 502.

13 The words of Johann Gottfried Frey, the head of the police in Königsberg, an intimate friend and collaborator of Stein; see T. Winkler, *op. cit.*

(b) THE FRENCH EXPERIENCE

1 See P. Villard, *Les Justices Seigneuriales dans la Marche*, Paris 1969, pp. 323 ff. Also J. Bastier, *La Féodalité dans la Région de Toulouse 1730-1790*, Paris 1975, pp. 119 ff.

2 Maupeou's Mémoire to Louis XVI, referred to in Part Two, ch. IV (a) above, Flammermont, *op. cit.*, p. 612.

3 P. Villard, *op. cit.*, p. 344.

4 G. V. Taylor, 'Revolutionary and Non-revolutionary Content . . .', *op. cit.*

5 The so-called sovereign courts were, besides the *parlements*, the *Cours des Aides*, the *Cours des Monnaies* and the *Chambres des Comptes*. (See Marion, *Dictionnaire*, and M. Bordes, *L'Administration Provinciale et Municipale en France au XVIIIᵉ Siècle*, Paris 1972.)

6 See Flammermont, *op. cit.*, p 287, n. 1, and Marion, *Le Garde des Sceaux Lamoignon et la Réforme Judiciaire de 1788*, Paris 1905, p. 70. 'Practically no case,' Marion wrote, 'was settled in the inferior courts,' so that 'all plaintiffs and defendants were forced [because the judicial practices of the time required it] to make journeys at a ruinous cost, and were exposed besides to considerable delays because [the Paris *parlement*], whose procedure was in any case slow, was literally overwhelmed by the vast number of cases that flowed into it from every part of the huge area subject to its jurisdiction.'

7 Cases involving direct taxes paid by nobles were dealt with by the *intendants* with appeal to the council (see M. Antoine, *Le Conseil*, p. 402).

8 On all these matters see Marion, *Dictionnaire des Institutions.*

9 Quoted by Marion, *Dictionnaire*, in his article on 'Justice'.

10 Quoted in *Mémoire Inédit du Chancelier d'Aguesseau sur la Reformation de la Justice*, ed. P. Combe, Valence 1928, p. 44.

11 See P. Villard, *op. cit.*, p. 311. He points out that this was because the documents which established a seigneur's right to justice were kept not by the *baillages* or *sénéchaussées* but by the *Bureaux des Finances*.

12 Quoted by Marion, *Dictionnaire*, in his article on 'Justice'.

13 The *procureur général*, who like all other holders of judicial offices had bought his office, was one of those officials known as 'les gens du roi'. He fulfilled in effect the function of public prosecutor.

14 Quoted in *Mémoire Inédit, op. cit.*, p. 31.

15 See Marion, *Le Garde des Sceaux Lamoignon . . .*, p. 69, n. 2.

16 Quoted in *Mémoire inédit, op. cit.*, p. 9.

17 See F. Bluche, *Les Magistrats . . ., op. cit.* On p. 170 Bluche gives the salary of councillors in the *parlement* of Paris between 1758 and 1760. In these three years their total salary was 1,550 livres, but their taxes amounted to 1,595 livres, leaving them with a deficit of 45 livres. Admittedly, as Bluche points out, these were war years when taxes were unusually heavy, but all the same, he adds, and 'even if one excludes periods of crisis, salaries were pretty derisory.'

18 See Marion, *Dictionnaire*, article on 'Justice'.

19 *Mémoire Inédit, op, cit.*, p. 47.

20 Quoted by P. Grosclaude, *op. cit.*, p. 302.

21 Mémoire to Louis XVI; Flammermont, *op. cit.*, p. 645.

22 These words were uttered in the *lit de justice* which demanded the introduction of Maupeou's reforms. They are quoted by P. Combe *Mémoire Inédit, op. cit.*, p. 58.

23 See M. Antoine, *Le Conseil*, Book II, chapter III, sections II and III.

24 Monnerat's case is described in detail in Flammermont, *op. cit.*, pp. 51 ff.

25 See M. Antoine, *Le Conseil*, p. 413.

26 This letter is printed in P. Grosclaude, *Malesherbes et son Temps, Nouveaux Documents Inédits*, Paris 1965, pp. 35-37.

27 Quoted in M. Antoine, *Le Conseil*, p. 421, n. 150.

28 The phrase used by Flammermont, *op. cit.*, p. 286.

29 Marion, *Le Garde des Sceaux Lamoignon . . .*, p. 71.

30 See Flammermont, *op. cit.*, p. 295.

31 *Memoire inédit, op. cit.*, p. 109.

32 Marion, *Le Garde des Sceaux Lamoignon . . .*, p. 6.

33 Arthur Young, *Travels in France*, ed. C. Maxwell, Cambridge 1929, p. 333.

34 Quoted in Radzinowicz, *op. cit.*, vol. I, p. 268.

(c) THE PRUSSIAN EXPERIENCE

1 See O. Hintze, *ABB*, VI(1), Darstellende Einleitung, p. 88.

2 On this see O. Büsch, *op. cit., passim.*

3 Johann Gottfried Frey, 'Gedanken und Meinungen über manches in Dienst', quoted by T. Winkler, *op. cit.*

4 The *intendances* were comparable to the *Kammern* only because the *intendants* were appointed by the crown and had not bought their offices (though admittedly they had bought the offices which made eligibility for an *intendance* possible). Their staffs were not government employees, as were those of the *Kammern*, but were appointed by and responsible to the *intendants* themselves.

5 *ABB*, VIII, p. 366. 'Reglement was für Justizsachen denen Kriegs- und Domänenkammern verbleiben und welche vor die Justizkollegien oder Regierungen gehören'.

6 In Prussia, for example, until 1746 it was possible in certain cases to appeal to the court of the Holy Roman Empire in Wetzlar, which was proverbial for its delays. For the many other causes of delay see H. Weill, *Frederick the Great and Samuel von Cocceji*, Wisconsin 1961, chapter V.

7 See *ABB*, VIII, p. 347, correspondence between Frederick the Great and Cocceji, April to July 1749.

8 *ABB*, VI(2), Landesdesiderien des Herzogthums Magdeburg, 2 August 1740.

9 See *ABB*, VI(1), p. 48.

10 *Ibid.*

11 R. Koser, *Friedrich der Große*, vol. I, p. 323.

12 *ABB*, V(2), 26 September 1737.

13 R. Koser, *op. cit.*, p. 321.

14 Quoted by Eberhard Schmidt in 'Rechtssprüche und Machtsprüche . . .'.

15 See particularly *ABB*, VI(2), p. 615, Cocceji to Frederick the Great, 13 August 1743.

16 *ABB*, VI.(2), p. 841.

17 See H. Weill, *op. cit.*, pp. 67 ff.

18 In May 1748 Frederick the Great ordered all the *Kammern* to return lists of the people 'from the highest to the lowest' who were in their pay. The lists therefore included not only the administrative staff, which was relatively small, but all the people – *Landräte*, tax collectors, excise officials, etc. – who though subject to the authority of the *Kammern* did not work at headquarters. Document 89 of *ABB*, VIII, gives lists for the *Kammern* in the Kurmark, in East Prussia, Lithuania and Pomerania. Though some of these *Kammern* had larger staffs than others, the difference is not significant.

19 *ABB*, VIII, p. 143.

20 For the General Directory's defence of the *Kammerjustiz* see von Hagen in June 1769 (*ABB*, XV, p. 45). For Hintze's see 'Die Entwicklung Preußens zum Rechtsstaat' in *Regierung und Verwaltung, op. cit.*

21 *ABB*, VI(2), p. 841.

22 See Weill, *op. cit.*, p. 42.

23 *Ibid.*, p. 47.

24 For the way in which this system worked at the end of Cocceji's life and as a result of amendments added afterwards, see Weill, *op. cit.*, and Eberhard Schmidt, 'Kammergericht und Rechtsstaat', *op. cit.* Broadly speaking, the three instances were as follows: for peasants, and for bourgeois who were not *Eximirte:*

(1) The lower courts – i.e., courts of the towns, of the *Domänenpächter*, and of the *Gutsherrn*.

(2) The first senate of the *Regierung*

(3) The second senate of the *Regierung*

For nobles, and for bourgeois who were *Eximirte:*

(1) First senate of the *Regierung*

(2) Second senate of the *Regierung*

(3) Supreme court in Berlin

25 Weill, *op. cit.*, p. 119.

26 *Ibid.*, p. 223.

27 *Ibid.*, pp. 132 ff.

28 See *ABB*, VII, p. 650, in which, in 1745, Frederick the Great wrote to the General Directory to complain that the *Kammern* lacked enough time, or indeed any time at all, to deal with judicial matters; that their powers of justice were too wide, and that this situation led to continual complaints from the public and to disputes with the ordinary courts.

29 See *ABB*, VIII, pp. 366 ff.

30 See *ABB*, XV, O. Hintze's introduction; also *ABB*, XII, pp. 192 ff. and 590; *ABB*, XIII, p.524; *ABB*, XIV (instructions to von Carmer when he was made minister of justice for Silesia); *ABB*, XV (von Hagen's proposed reforms of 1769).

31 *ABB*, VIII, pp. 128-29.

32 See O. Hintze's introduction to *ABB*, XV.

33 See F. W. Henning, *Herrschaft und Bauernuntertänigkeit in den ländlichen Bereichen Ostpreußens und des Fürstentums Paderborn vor*

1800, Würzburg 1964, pp. 97 ff.

34 *Ibid.*, p. 104.

35 Quoted by H. Conrad, 'Die geistigen Grundlagen des Allgemeinen Landrechts', in *Arbeitsgemeinschaft für Forschung des Landes Nordrhein-Westfalen*, Heft 77, Cologne and Opladen 1957, p. 13, n. 9.

36 For a full discussion of these objections see U. J. Heuer, *op. cit.*, pp. 233 ff.

37 For an account of the differences between the *Allgemeines Gesetzbuch* and the *Allgemeines Landrecht* see H. Conrad, *op. cit.* The principal passage omitted runs as follows:

'*Machtsprüche* or similar enactments by the higher authorities which are made in contested cases out of relation to legal judgments by the courts are neither lawful nor binding.' Svarez defined the term *Machtspruch* – in common use in the eighteenth century but untranslatable into English – as follows: 'A decision in contested cases which is given without the appropriate legal investigation and judgment is called a *Machtspruch*' (*Vorträge über Recht und Staat*, p. 605).

38 Memorandum by Reichsgraf Finck von Finckenstein on the Müller Arnold case, printed in *Zeitschrift für preußische Geschichte und Landeskunde*, erste Jahrgang 1864, p. 152, n. 6.

39 On this, see Svarez, *Vorträge, op. cit.*, p. 617.

40 The writers who have set out to denigrate Frederick the Great have produced many instances; some, as in F. Mehring's *Lessinglegende*, without any evidence, others, as in U. J. Heuer's *Allgemeines Landrecht und Klassenkampf* supported by chapter and verse. Among those with no intention of grinding this particular axe see e.g. Graf Lehndorff, in his *Dreißig Jahre am Hofe Friedrichs des Großen*, pp. 484 ff.; H. Schnee-Bochum, 'Die Hoffinanziers Friedrichs des Großen' in Schmoller's *Jahrbücher für Gesetzgebung, Verwaltung und Wirtschaft*, 1952, p. 76. This gives instances of Frederick's intervention in the courts to protect the entrepreneurs who enjoyed his favour.

41 F. Eberty, *op. cit.*, p. 63. In idle moments, Eberty said, he amused himself by going through old files in the *Kammergericht*. He found large numbers of cases which suddenly came to an end with no judgment recorded.

42 Winter, *op. cit.*, p. 356.

43 See A. Stölzel, *Carl Gottlieb Svarez*, Berlin 1885, especially p. 189.

44 See n. 40 above. Particularly the East Germans cannot find a good word for him, and will not even allow him the title of 'the

Great'. Even Ingrid Mittenzwei entitles her work on him *Friedrich II von Preußen*, and although she is not wholly unsympathetic to him will not allow him any significant achievements.

45 Tocqueville, *op. cit.*, pp. 268 ff.

APPENDIX CHAPTER IV

1 See D. D. Bien, *The Calas Affair*, Princeton 1960.
2 E. Lavisse, *op. cit.*, vol. VIII (2), p. 342.
3 See Marion, *Le Garde des Sceaux Lamoignon*, pp. 34 ff.
4 There are many different versions, varying in length and quality, of the Müller Arnold affair which no historian concerned with Frederick the Great has felt able to neglect. Most of these versions are drawn, to a greater or less extent, from two contemporary accounts, one written by G.K.F. Bandel and the other by Graf Finck von Finckenstein.

Bandel, the son of a high Prussian official, was appointed to the post of *Regierungsrat* in the Neumärkische *Regierung* in 1774. (In the present account a *Regierungsrat* and a *Kammergerichtsrat* are described as 'judges' since they functioned as such, though the literal translation of *Rat* is 'councillor'.) Bandel was one of the judges whom Frederick imprisoned for his part in the Arnold affair and he wrote his account while he was in prison. It is written clearly and precisely with a remarkable lack of malice or animosity – even against Frederick, whom he spoke of with admiration while nevertheless emphasizing how unreasonable, arbitrary and unjust his decisions on this occasion were. Bandel was evidently a clever and agreeable person who later had a distinguished career. His account is reproduced verbatim with an introduction by F. Graner in *FBPG*, XXXVIII, 1926.

Graf Finck von Finckenstein, described by Graner as an acute and experienced lawyer, was made President of the Neumärkische *Regierung* in 1777, that is, in the middle of the Arnold case. His account – entitled 'History of the case of Arnold v. Gersdorff heard before the Neumärkische *Regierung* and of its consequences' – is fuller and more authoritative than Bandel's because he had access to all the documents, which Bandel had not. It is sober, factual, precise, and provided with a number of explanatory footnotes. Unlike Bandel, however, as we know from other sources, Finckenstein derived from the Arnold affair an intense albeit impotent sense of outrage. Leopold von Gerlach wrote in the early nineteenth century that ever afterwards Finckenstein was opposed to authority 'so dass man ihn ... für die symbolisierte Opposition halten möchte' – one might see him as a symbol of opposition. His history of the Arnold case is published in the *Zeitschrift für preußische Geschichte und Landeskunde*, erste Jahrgang 1864, pp. 133 ff. Unless otherwise stated the following account is based on these two sources.

5 That possibilities of this sort existed is suggested by the case of Ursinus, a high official in the General Directory, referred to in Part Two, ch. V (b).
6 On this see Koser, *Friedrich der Große* vol. II, pp. 541 ff., and the following works by Eberhard Schmidt: 'Kammergericht und Rechtsstadt ...', *op. cit.*; 'Die Justizpolitik Friederichs des Grossen ...', *op. cit.*; Rechtssprüche und Machtsprüche ...', *op. cit.*
7 E. Schmidt, 'Die Justizpolitik ...', *op. cit.*, p. 107.
8 R. Stadelmann, in *Deutschland und Westeuropa. Drei Aufsätze*, Württemberg 1948, p. 27.

V The attempts to increase wealth, welfare and national power

(a) THE RELATIONSHIP OF WEALTH AND POWER
1 J. H. Eberhard, 'Ueber die Zeichen der Aufklärung einer Nation' in *Literarische Chronik*, Bern 1786, vol. 2, pp. 164-65.
2 D. C. Coleman, *The Historical Journal*, vol. 23, 4 December 1980.

(b) THE PROMOTION OF TRADE AND MANUFACTURES
1 Quoted in C. W. Cole, *Colbert and a Century of French Mercantilism*, London/Hamden, Conn. 1964, vol. I, pp. 311-12.
2 *Ibid.*, vol. I, p. 446.
3 *The Wealth of Nations*, II, pp. 161-62.
4 See Cole, vol. I, pp. 336-37.
5 E. F. Heckscher, *Mercantilism*, trans. M. Shapiro, London 1935, vol. 1, pp. 159-60.
6 Cole, *op. cit.*, vol. II, p. 362.
7 *Ibid.*, vol. II, p. 540.
8 See Part Two, ch. V (c) (1) below.
9 See R. Mandrou, *Louis XVI en son Temps*; and P. Goubert, 'Le Temps de Colbert,' in *Histoire Economique et Sociale de la France*, vol. 2, Paris 1970.
10 Heckscher, *op. cit.*, vol. I, p. 170.
11 See Cole, *passim*, particularly vol. II, pp. 552 ff.

12 Worse because the future lay with the industries that catered for a mass market.

13 See Cole, *op. cit.*, vol. I, pp. 468 ff.

14 See *Bordeaux au XVIII*ᵉ *Siècle*, ed. F. G. Pariset, Book II, ch. 2. Professor Crouzet estimates (p.196) that the rate of growth of Bordeaux's foreign trade was about, on average, 4 per cent p.a. between 1715 and 1789.

15 See F. Crouzet, 'Angleterre et France au XVIIIᵉ Siècle', *op. cit.*, pp. 254 ff.; and Labrousse's Survol in *Histoire Economique et Sociale de la France*, vol. 2, p. 700.

16 Crouzet, *ibid.*, notes that French industrial production was considerably larger than the British though (France's population being much bigger) less per head. Britain was a more developed country, more urbanized, more industrialized, much more technically inventive, with a higher income per head. The subsistence economy had virtually disappeared though in France it still existed in 'de vastes régions'.

17 See C. Carrière, *Négociants Marseillais au XVIII*ᵉ *siècle*, Institut historique de Provence, 1974. Carrière (pp. 309 ff.) points out that Colbert's system was, as described by P. Masson in 1896, 'bâtard et incohérent'. He does not believe that it had much effect on the development of Marseille while nevertheless noting Crouzet's point that Bordeaux's great prosperity would have been impossible without the protection afforded by the government to the French trades with the West Indies.

18 See L. Labrousse, *La Crise de l'Economie Française à la Fin de l'Ancien Régime et au Début de la Révolution*, Paris 1943, vol. I, p. XVIII.

19 See H. Grange, *op. cit.*, pp. 92 ff.

20 See Labrousse's Survol, referred to in n. 15 above, p. 696.

21 See F. Lütge, *Deutsche Sozial – und Wirtschaftsgeschichte*, 3rd edition, Berlin, Heidelberg, New York, pp. 334-35.

22 See K. Hinze, *op. cit.*, pp. 24 and 71.

23 *Ibid.*, pp. 24-25.

24 *Ibid.*, p. 29.

25 *Ibid.*, p. 22.

26 Cole, *op. cit.*, vol. I, p. 483.

27 See H. Berger, *Friederich der Große als Kolonisator, op. cit.*

28 See *Journal of Political Economy*, vol. 60, 1952: article by W. C. Scoville on 'The Huguenots and the Diffusion of Technology', pp. 294 ff. and 392 ff.

29 See C. Hinrichs, *op. cit.*, pp. 37 ff. The author of this work was a fervent admirer of Frederick William I but gives an account of Frederick William's relations with his tutor, Jean Philippe Rebeur, of a kind that suggests that this founding father of Prussian absolutism was psychologically abnormal. Learning was a torture to him and his difficulty in attempting it would drive him into the wildest fits of rage, when he would pull off Rebeur's wig or kick him in the stomach. He would then rush to his room and scream: 'The devil take me, when I am grown up I will hang them all and chop off their heads.' On other occasions he would show an inordinate degree of affection for Rebeur. As he himself admitted of his ungovernable rages, 'ich kann nicht anders' (see W. Gericke, *op. cit.*, ch. II (1)).

30 C. Hinrichs, 'Das königliche Lagerhaus in Berlin', in *FBPG*, XLIV, 1932.

31 See O. Büsch, *op. cit.*

32 See W. Treue, *Wirtschaftsgeschichte der Neuzeit*, 3rd edition, Stuttgart 1973, p. 177.

33 K. Hinze, *op. cit.*, p. 73.

34 For the figures of 250,000 see Berger, *op. cit.*, p. 75. For the hardships see K. Hinze, *op. cit.*, particularly pp. 125 ff., in which he describes the unforeseen problems that arose over finding accommodation and building houses for the immigrants.

35 The figure given by P. Paret, *Clausewitz and the State*, New York 1967, p. 25, n. 10. He has taken it from Jany, *Geschichte der preußischen Armee*, 4 vols, 3nd ed., Osnabrück 1967.

36 See H. Rachel, 'Der Merkantilismus in Brandenburg-Preußen' in *FBPG*, XL, 1927, pp. 252 ff.

37 On this see Part Two, ch. III (b) below.

38 See A. Zottmann, *op. cit.*, pp. 21 ff.

39 On this episode see I. Mittenzwei, *Preußen nach dem Siebenjährigen Krieg*, [East] Berlin 1979, pp. 39 ff.

40 See *Quellen zur Geschichte von Hamburgs Handel und Schiffahrt im 17. 18. und 19. Jahrhundert*, ed. E. Baasch, Hamburg 1910, pp. 204-21.

41 *Ibid.*, p. 189.

42 Garve, *Fragmente zur Schilderung des Geistes, . . ., op. cit.*

43 On this see particularly I. Mittenzwei, *op. cit.*, and H. Brunschwig, *La Crise de l'Etat Prussien à la Fin du XVIII*ᵉ *Siècle*, Paris 1947.

44 See Introduction by Otto Büsch to K. Hinze's *Die Arbeiterfrage . . ., op. cit.*

45 *Dissertations Lues dans les Séances Publiques . . ., op. cit.*

46 *Ibid.*, Dissertation of 2 January 1786.

47 Rahel Varnhagen, *Briefwechsel mit Alexander von der Marwitz*, ed. F. Kemp, Munich 1966, p. 93.

(c) AGRICULTURE AND THE ATTEMPTS AT REFORM

(1) THE FRENCH EXPERIENCE

1 See Marion, *Dictionnaire . . .* under the

headings 'Féodalité', 'Retrait', 'Lods et Ventes'.

2 *Histoire Economique et Sociale de la France,* p. 607.

3 See G. Lefebvre, *Etudes sur la Révolution Française,* Paris 1963, pp. 289-90. This proportion varied from 3 per cent at the lowest to 70 per cent at the highest.

4 See R. Forster, 'Obstacles to Agricultural Growth in Eighteenth Century France', in *A.H.R.,* October 1970. Arthur Young thought that share-cropping was practised over ⅞ of France. Lefebvre estimated the proportion to be ¾.

5 See, for example, Arthur Young, *Travels in France,* pp. 296-337, and Turgot, *Oeuvres,* II, pp. 447 ff.

6 Arthur Young, *op. cit.,* p. 16.

7 Turgot, *op. cit.*

8 See, e.g., Lefebvre, *Etudes* ... p. 287; Young, *op. cit.,* p. 297.

9 See R. Forster, *The House of Saulx-Tavanes, Versailles and Burgundy,* Baltimore 1971. That the arrangements of the Duc de Saulx-Tavanes should not be seen as wholly typical seems plain from the account, referred to below, which Lavoisier gave of the neighbourhood where he owned his estates, or of Burgundy (see E. Le Roy Ladurie, 'Révoltes et Contestations Rurales en France de 1675-1788', in *Annales E.S.C.,* vol. 29, Jan.-Feb. 1974, p. 16).

10 Forster, as in n. 4 above.

11 F. Quesnay, article entitled 'Hommes', originally written for the *Encylopédie* but not published. Transcribed in *François Quesnay et la Physiocratie,* 2 vols, Paris 1958, vol. II, pp. 511-73. The words cited are printed on p. 553.

12 See the Introduction to Young's *Travels in France,* edited by C. Maxwell, Cambridge 1929, p. XVII, where it is stated that the Maréchal de Castries, former Minister of the Marine, expressed his astonishment at the extent, accuracy and insight of Young's observations, which he claimed were much greater than his own. When the work was translated into French in 1793 'the Convention ordered 20,000 copies to be printed and distributed gratuitously in each commune.'

13 *Travels* . . ., p. 23.

14 See Turgot, *Oeuvres,* II, p. 451.

15 Re the *taille personelle,* see Part Two, ch. III (a) above.

16 Turgot, *op. cit.,* II, 452 ff.

17 Lavoisier, *Oeuvres,* Paris 1893, vol. II, 'Résultats de quelques expériences d'agriculture et réflexions sur leurs relations avec l'économie politique', p. 821.

18 Quoted in E. Fox-Genovese, *The Origins of Physiocracy,* Ithaca 1976, p. 323.

19 Saint-Jacob, *op. cit.,* p. 78.

20 Young, *op. cit.,* pp. 291-92.

21 See J. D. Chambers and G. C. Mingay, *The Agricultural Revolution 1750 to 1880,* London 1966, p. 84.

22 *Ibid.,* pp. 34-35.

23 *Ibid.*

24 Necker, *Oeuvres Complètes,* V, p. 440.

25 Lavoisier, *op. cit.,* p. 816.

26 See Chambers and Mingay, *op. cit.,* p. 84. They say, 'The landowner's gross return on his investment [on enclosed land] was probably between 15 per cent and 20 per cent but higher where much waste was enclosed.' Both Necker and Lavoisier spoke of a net return so that their figures are not comparable with Chambers' and Mingay's. The latter, however, note that the return from investment in land was 'very much higher than on investment in the Funds.'

27 R. Forster, *Saulx-Tavanes, op. cit.,* p. 104.

28 Quoted by H. Higgs, *The Physiocrats,* London 1897, p. 2.

29 On the relationship between Quesnay and Mirabeau see E. Fox-Genovese, *op. cit.*

30 For Turgot's views on this subject see *Oeuvres, op. cit.,* vol. II, pp. 447 ff.

31 See *François Quesnay et la Physiocratie* (as in n. 11 above), p. 979. See Vol. I of this work, article on 'Le produit net des physiocrates', in which the writer maintains that this concept was never altogether clearly defined, particularly in relation to what was to be understood by an adequate standard of life for the cultivator.

32 *Ibid.,* p. 973.

33 Among those which were contested and impracticable was their belief in complete freedom of enterprise, including freedom for the grain trade, which inevitably proved disastrous when attempts were made to apply it by Bertin and Turgot. Among those that were absurd were the beliefs that land was the sole source of wealth and that the only legitimate tax was a tax on the landed proprietors – the so-called '*impôt unique*' which Voltaire described as the '*impôt inique*'.

34 Young, *op. cit.,* p. 287.

35 See Lavoisier, *Oeuvres, op. cit.,* vol. VI, pp. 347 ff.

36 Article on 'Hommes', as in n. 11 above, p. 540.

37 This was a theme to which Necker continually referred. See, e.g., *Oeuvres,* vol. V, p. 583. 'La population [de la France] est immense mais l'excès et la nature des impôts appauvrissent et découragent les habitants des campagnes.'

38 Article on 'Hommes', *op. cit.*, pp. 540-41 and 604.

39 Turgot, *op. cit.*, II, pp. 34-35.

40 For many examples of these riots, including one led by the seigneur, see Saint-Jacob, *op. cit.*, pp. 370 ff. See Marc Bloch, 'La Lutte pour l'Individualisme Agraire', in *Annales, E.S.C.*, vol. II (1930), p. 530, for a riot in which one of the employees of the *intendant*, the *subdélégué* Faussabry, 'resolutely allied himself to what he himself called "the popular movement".'

41 See Lavoisier, *op. cit.*, vol. II, pp. 812 ff.

42 *Ibid.*, vol. VI, 'Instructions Données par la Noblesse du Baillage de Blois à ses Députés aux Etats Généraux', p. 348.

43 One of the more notorious examples of the profits that could be made out of government loans is provided by the sale of annuities with which Necker largely financed the War of American Independence and of which Herbert Lüthy gives an account in his *La Banque Protestante de France*, vol. 2, Paris 1961, Chapter IV. A man could borrow from his banker the sum required to purchase an annuity and could pay back the capital and the interest within twelve years out of the interest he received from the government. Thereafter, without at any time having expended so much as a sou, he could expect to enjoy the interest for the rest of his life. 'One can understand,' Lüthy observed, 'the craze that developed for this miraculous investment.'

44 Quesnay also inveighed against the high rate of interest as a disincentive to investment in agriculture. See Fox-Genovese, *op. cit.*, p. 241.

45 See Part Two, ch. III (a) above. The inequalities within the various estates seem to have been as great as, if not greater than, those between one estate and another. See part 3, ch. II, below.

46 This was Necker's view. See M. Garaud, *op. cit.*, p. 116, n. 5.

47 See Chambers and Mingay, *op. cit.*, p. 35; also *Quellen zur Geschichte der deutschen Bauernbefreiung*, ed. W. Conze, Göttingen/Berlin 1957, p. 82. This was also Thaers's view (see Part Two, ch. V (c) (2) below).

48 The most famous of all the diatribes against them is Boncerf's *Les Inconvénients des Droits Féodaux*, London 1776, who said of the feudal dues that for only a moderate return they were the cause 'of a thousand embarrassments to the seigneurs and the vassals' (p. 17). See also M. Bloch 'La Lutte pour l'Individualisme Agraire', in *Annales E.S.C.*, vol.

II (1930), p.530, and Arthur Young, *op. cit.*, p. 332.

49 A great variety of different estimates have been made of the amount derived by the seigneurs from their feudal dues in different districts and seigneuries. See, e.g., R. Forster, *Nobility of Toulouse ...*, 'The Provincial noble, a reappraisal', in *A.H.R.*, 68, ii, 1963; A. Soboul, 'La Révolution Française et la Féodalité', in *Revue Historique*, vol. 240, 1968.

50 See C. Heywood, 'The Role of the Peasantry in French Industrialisation 1815-1880', *Economic History Review*, Vol. XXXIV, no. 3, August 1981.

51 See M. Bloch (as in n. 40 above), pp. 334 and 514.

52 *Ibid.*, p. 523.

53 *Ibid.*, p. 513.

54 See A. J. Bourdes, *Agronomie et Agronomes en France au XVIII⁰ Siècle*, Paris 1967, pp. 1377 ff.

55 See V. R. Gruder, *The Royal Provincial Intendants*, Ithaca 1968, Appendix IV.

56 On the *subdélégués* see J. Ricommard, 'Les Subdélégués des Intendants au XVIIIᵉ et au XVIIᵉ Siècles', in *L'Information Historique*, 23-25, 1961-63.

57 See R. Mandrou, *Louis XIV en son Temps*, pp. 97-104.

58 See A. J. Bourdes, *op. cit.*, pp. 1377 ff.

59 Saint-Jacob, *op. cit.*, p. 522.

60 Young, *op. cit.*, p. 20.

61 A. J. Bourdes, *op. cit.*, pp. 1594 ff.

62 G. Lefebvre, *La Grande Peur*, Paris n.d. (Société d'Edition d'Enseignement Supérieur), p. 33.

(2) THE PRUSSIAN EXPERIENCE

1 *Hörigkeit, Eigenbehörigkeit, Leibeigenschaft, Erbuntertänigkeit*, to mention only those in most common use in the eighteenth century.

2 W. Abel, *Geschichte der deutschen Landwirtschaft*, Stuttgart 1962, p. 308.

3 G. F. Knapp, *Die Bauernbefreiung*, vol. I, p. 15.

4 See C. Dipper, *Die Bauernbefreiung in Deutschland*, Stuttgart, Berlin, Cologne, Mainz 1980, who gives this percentage on p. 56. F. W. Henning, *Dienste und Abgaben der Bauern im 18. Jahrhundert*, Stuttgart 1969, p. 8, estimates that the *Kölmer* and other free peasants accounted for about 33 per cent of the non-noble population in the area subject to the control of the *Kammer* in East Prussia and Lithuania.

5 See F. Lütge, *Deutsche Sozial- und Wirtschaftsgeschichte*, 3rd edition, Berlin, Heidelberg, New York 1966, p. 434. R. Koselleck (*Preußen zwischen Reform*, pp. 81-82) puts the proportion of *erbuntertänige* peasants on noble estates at 33 per cent in East Prussia, between 60 per cent and 70 per cent in Pomerania and Silesia, and 50 per cent in the Kurmark.

6 See F. W. Henning, *Herrschaft und Bauernuntertänigkeit...*, p. 328.

7 *ALR*, II, Tit. 7, paras. 87 ff. The most common word for serfdom is *Leibeigenschaft*. It had a variety of more or less imprecise meanings. See, for example, G. F. Knapp (*Grundherrschaft und Rittergut*, Leipzig 1897, pp. 90 ff.) who defined as *Leibeigene* West German peasants who held their land on terms similar to, though apparently less onerous than, those to which many French peasants were subject. These West German peasants, Knapp said, 'were something quite different from the falsely so-called *Leibeigene* of the East, the *Erbuntertanen*'. In the *Allgemeines Landrecht*, by contrast, *Leibeigenschaft* is described (II, Tit. 7, para. 48) not as something less but as something more onerous than *Erbuntertänigkeit*. Here it is said to be 'a kind of personal slavery which has ceased to exist.' In the eighteenth century, *Leibeigenschaft* was very commonly used as a pejorative term in this sense. It has no agreed or precise meaning. Except in the one passage just referred to, it does not appear in the *Allgemeines Landrecht*.

8 Prussian serfdom is a peculiarly confusing subject because of the different categories of serfs and the imprecision of the terminology. Serfs could be classified according to the following criteria:

a) According to the amount of land they held (which bore no necessary relationship to the terms on which they held it). Thus one spoke of *Vollbauern* or full peasants who (see Knapp, *Die Bauernbefreiung*, vol. I, p. 9) usually owned two or two and a half *Hufen*. (One *Hufe* was the amount of arable land plus communal rights to pasture, free firewood, etc., sufficient to support a family. It was thus a measure that varied from province to province.) Similarly one spoke of *Halbbauern* and *Viertelbauern* – half and quarter peasants.

b) According to whether or not they were, as it was said, *spannfähig* – i.e., owned a team or teams of draught animals.

c) According to whether or not they were entitled to a voice in the village community, which depended simply on whether they held land in the open arable fields known as the *Flur*.

d) According to the terms on which they held their land, i.e., whether they had what were known as '*bessere Besitzrechten*' or better rights of possession – viz. hereditary rights – or

whether they came into other categories among which the most common was that of the so-called *Lassiten* or *Lassbauern*, whose holdings were usually not hereditary, but in such cases where they were so described might only be passed on to such of the peasants' sons as the lord himself selected.

e) According to the amount of dues and services required of them. On this see F. W. Henning, *Dienste und Abgaben ...* (as in n. 4 above).

9 H. A. von Borcke, in his *Beschreibung der Stargardischen Wirtschaft in Hinterpommern*, Berlin 1783, says in his description of the labour on his estate that he rented out his sheep. Abel, *Geschichte der deutschen Landwirtschaft*, describes this as a common practice, and in relation to other activities besides sheep farming. The whole of the arable land, however, was never let out as in France.

10 See Knapp, *Die Bauernbefreiung*, vol. I, pp. 2-3.

11 See G. Ipsen, 'Die preußische Bauernbefreiung als Landesaufbau', in *Zeitschrift für Agrargeschichte und Agrarsoziologie*, 2, 1954, p. 32. n. 3; and Henning, *Dienste und Abgaben ...* (as in n. 4), p. 15, who reckons that only 68 per cent of the noble estates in East Prussia employed forced labour services and in only 36 per cent of these did the labour services account for more than 50 per cent of the work.

12 *Die Bauernbefreiung*, vol. I, p. 4.

13 See report from von Hagen, 22.ii.1764, in *ABB*, XIII, pp. 355 ff.

14 The peasants who came within this category included all classes of peasants apart from free peasants, notably the *Kölmer*. See Knapp, *Die Bauernbefreiung*.

15 The lord's legal obligations to the peasants are set out in the *Allgemeines Landrecht*. See K. Spies, *Gutsherr und Untertan in der Mittelmark Brandenburg zu Beginn der Bauernbefreiung*, Berlin 1972, for an analysis of their lack of precision compared with the definition of the obligations of the peasants.

16 See *ABB*, X, pp. 571-72.

17 See *ABB*, IX, pp. 157 and 612; *ABB*, X, pp. 54 and 561.

18 See the case of von Gersdorff referred to in the Appendix to Chapter IV above. See also *ABB*, XV, p.254, for the case of Freiherr von der Reck whom Frederick dismissed because of the disorders in his private life (his 'äußerst derangirten häuslichen Umständen').

19 It is plain that there was little uniformity – though increasing attempts to introduce it – in how much and by whom the *Landrat* was paid. This was a continual source of argument

among all the parties concerned – the *Kammern* in question, the General Directory and the local nobility organized in the *Kreisstände*. A somewhat superficial investigation makes it appear that, generally speaking, the *Landrat* received between 200 and 500 thaler per annum.

20 *ABB*, XV, pp. 113 ff. Correspondence between Frederick the Great, von Hagen and von Derschau, 5.x to 22.xi.1769.

21 A considerable number of these instructions, and of guidelines for the General Directory in their compilation, are printed in the *Acta Borussica*. See particularly *ABB*, VI (2), 278 ff., in Lower Silesia, 19.xii.1741; *ABB*, IX, 437 ff., in East Prussia, 23.viii.1752; *ABB*, XIII, 480 ff., in Cleves-Mark, 22.ix.1764; *ABB*, XIV, 12 ff., General instructions for *Landräte* and *Steuerräte*, 30.iv.1766; *ABB*, XIV, 142 ff., for Magdeburg 1.viii.1766. The *Landrat* was required to travel round his *Kreis*, at least once – sometimes it was said at least twice – a year. (As the reign progressed steps were taken to ensure that the *Kreise* were of a uniform size – neither too large for one man to manage nor too small for a full-time job.) He had to provide the government with a huge miscellany of information: the number of people in the *Kreis*, for example, the number of *Hufen*, the state of the harvest, the crops that were grown. He was responsible for taking steps to prevent, or to mitigate the consequences of, natural disasters such as flood, fires, cattle-disease. He was required to instruct the villagers in a variety of agricultural activities. Most instructions contained a clause to the effect that his most important task was to safeguard the peasant against oppression and, should he be unable to do so, to report the matter to the *Kammer*.

22 *ABB*, XV, p. 119.

23 This is certainly the impression given (though admittedly documents are incomplete) by the behaviour of Herr von Blankensee, a *Landrat* in Pomerania, who conducted a dispute with the local *Kammer*, whose rights of jurisdiction he disputed, which lasted from 1761 to 1767. Later he got into another dispute with the nobility in his *Kreis*. He resigned (apparently for fear of being dismissed) in 1772. This story appears in vols XII, XIII and XV of the *ABB*.

24 See, for example, *ABB*, XIV, p. 382, Order from the General Directory to the presidents of the *Kammern*, 10.xi.67, requiring them to report twice a year on how far the *Landräte* and other local officials had followed the instructions issued to them and which of

them had distinguished themselves by 'orderliness, promptitude, industry, competence, loyalty and application'. See also *ABB*, XV, p. 54, Cabinet orders of 6 and 9.vii.1769, complaining of ignorance and disobedience on the part of the *Landräte*. The General Directory was ordered to instruct the *Kammern* to pay more attention to the behaviour of the *Landräte* and to report to the King every three months on their ability, behaviour and industry.

25 See particularly *ABB*, XIV, Cabinet order to the General Directory, 30.iv.1766.

26 *ABB*, XV, p. 246.

27 *ABB*, XV, p. 251.

28 Quoted by Abel, *Geschichte der deutschen Landwirtschaft*, p. 270.

29 *ABB*, X, p. 444.

30 'Selbstbiographie', in *Aus den Papieren des Ministers und Burggrafen von Magdeburg, Theodor von Schön*, Halle 1875, vol. I, p. 7.

31 See Abel, *Geschichte der deutschen Landwirtschaft*, chapter 7.

32 W. Abel, *Agrarkrisen und Agrar-Konjunktur*, Hamburg and Berlin 1966, pp. 187 ff.

33 A state of affairs that may be illustrated by the fact that the amount of land needed to support a family east of the Elbe was double what it was in west Germany (C. Dipper, *op. cit.*, p. 43).

34 S. L. Kaplan, *Bread, Politics and Political Economy in the Reign of Louis XV*, 2 vols, The Hague 1976.

35 *Ibid.*, pp. 47 and 502.

36 In *A. B. Getreidehandelspolitik*, 4 vols, 1896-1934.

37 See Kaplan, *op. cit., passim*, and particularly pp. 8-9, where he quotes the *fermier général*, Dupin (the owner of Chenonceaux), as having observed that 'most nations have placed themselves on guard against the disastrous effects of dearth and excessive abundance by means of magazines which cause grain to disappear when there is too much and from which it surfaces when it is lacking ... We alone, who have the glory to possess the wisest regulations in the universe on other matters, have remained far behind our neighbours on this one which is nevertheless the most important.'

38 *A. B. Getreidehandelspolitik*, vol. III, p. 173 and vol. IV, p. 53. Frederick kept most of his stocks in flour because if packed in barrels (or so he maintained) it would keep for fifty years, whereas grain quickly goes bad and grain stocks must in consequence be turned over at intervals. Flour also took up less space and saved cost on warehouses.

39 The principal evidence adduced in support of this is that in the famine years of the early seventies there was no famine in Prussia but an influx of people from Bohemia, Poland and various parts of Germany in search of food. See *A. B. Getreidehandelspolitik*, vol. IV, pp. 130 ff.

40 *A. B. Getreidehandelspolitik*, vol. III, p. vi.

41 See P. Habernol, 'Die Versuche Friedrichs des Großen das englische System der Fruchtwechselwirtschaft in Preußen einzuführen', in *Landwirtschaftliche Jahrbücher*, vol. XXIX, Berlin 1900.

42 *ALR*, II, Tit. 7, para. 19, 'Dorfgemeinen haben die Rechte der öffentlichen Corporationen'. See following paragraphs for what these rights were.

43 In *Ueber den Charakter der Bauern und ueber ihr Verhältnis gegen die Gutsherrn und gegen die Regierung*, Breslau 1796.

44 A number, for example, are given by Abel, *op. cit.* (as in n. 2 above).

45 See n. 9 above.

46 Fontane, in his *Wanderungen durch die Mark Brandenburg*, describes several well-run estates. He mentions one or two, but conveys the impression that they were exceptional, where the landlord ill-treated his peasants.

47 These credit institutes, known as *Landschaften*, were introduced in one province after another, the last to receive one being East Prussia which did not get it until 1788, because of Frederick the Great's hostility to the East Prussian nobility on account of their submission to the Russians during the Seven Years War. The *Landschaft*, erected by royal decree and supplied with funds by the government, was an association of the noble landowners of the province, who were collectively responsible for loans granted to their members for agricultural purposes. (See R. Stein, *Die Umwandlung der Agrarverfassung Ostpreußens*, 2 vols, Königsberg 1933/34, vol. I, pp. 524-25, and P. Baumgart, 'Zur Geschichte der kurmärkischen Stände im 17. und 18. Jahrhundert' in *Veröffentlichungen des Max-Planck-Instituts für Geschichte*, vol. 27, Göttingen 1969.)

48 For an account of this episode see W. Sombart, *Der Bourgeois*, Munich/Leipzig 1913, p. 62.

49 R. Stein, *op. cit.*, vol. I, 530.

50 *Ibid.*, vol. I, 531.

51 Abel, *op. cit.* (see n. 2 above), p. 203.

52 W. Görlitz, *Die Junker*, 2nd edition, Glücksburg, Ostsee, 1957.

53 R. Stein, *op. cit.*

54 The writer was Wöllner, Frederick William II's notorious favourite. See R. Stein, *op. cit.*, vol. I, p. 542-43.

55 Quoted by J. Kulischer, 'Leibeigenschaft in Russland und die Agrarverfassung Preußens im 18. Jahrhundert', in *Jahrbücher für Nationalökonomie und Statistik*, vol. 137, Dritte Folge, Jena 1932.

56 Knapp, *Die Bauernbefreiung*, vol. I, p. 88.

57 G. V. Taylor, 'Revolutionary and Non-revolutionary Content of the Cahiers of 1789', Table 3, p. 498.

58 This point is particularly insisted on by R. Koselleck, *Preußen zwischen Reform und Revolution*.

PART THREE

I The Enlightenment as a movement for social and political change: the common assumptions

1 See Eduard Winter, *Der Josephinismus*, [East] Berlin 1962, pp. 30-31. 'Halle became through Wolff's influence the centre of attraction for many of the students of learning in all European countries. From Halle and Leipzig the Enlightenment began its triumphal progress.' See also *Deutsche Literatur*, ed. F. Bruggermann, Reihe Aufklärung, vol. 2, *Das Weltbild der deutschen Aufklärung*, Leipzig 1930, pp. 5 ff.; and W. Frauendienst, *op. cit.*, pp. 21 ff.

2 See Part One, ch. II above.

3 Frauendienst, *op. cit.*, stresses the great influence Wolff exercised on Frederick the Great, who saw his return to Prussia after his exile by Frederick William I as the 'triumph of freedom of thought and reason over barbarism, ignorance and superstition'. For a modern scholar's view of Wolff's philosophy, see L. W. Beck, *Early German Philosophy*, Cambridge, Mass., 1969. Beck observed (p. 267) that he found it 'positively painful to see how little Wolff profited from his reading of Descartes, Leibnitz and Locke.'

4 R. Schackleton, *Montesquieu, A Critical Biography*, Oxford 1961; see also M. Richter, *The Political Thought of Montesquieu*, Cambridge 1977.

5 See Sieyès, *Essai sur les Privilèges*, printed with an Introduction by E. Champion, Paris 1888, and A. Mathiez, 'La Place de Montesquieu', in *Annales Historiques de la Révolution Française*, vol. 7, 1930. Mathiez described Montesquieu as a reactionary, and accused him of having written in *De l'Esprit des Lois* an apology 'du régime féodale dont il est le défenseur déterminé'.

6 See *Der aufgeklärte Absolutismus, op. cit.*

7 See, for example, W. Dilthey, 'Die

deutsche Aufklärung im Staat und in der Akademie', in *Deutsche Rundschau*, vol. 107, 1901, p. 21. 'Kein anderer deutscher Staat war mit den Ideen der Aufklärung so tief verwachsen.'

8 S. Skalweit, *op. cit.*

9 'Was ist Aufklärung?', 1784, in *Schriften*, vol. VIII, Berlin 1912.

10 Necker, *Oeuvres Complètes, op. cit.*, vol. IV, p. 9.

11 B. Groethuysen, *Die Entstehung der bürgerlichen Welt- und Lebensanschauung*, 2 vols, Halle/Saale, 1927, 1930, introduction vol. 1, p. xii.

12 See particularly J. L. Talmon, *The Origins of Totalitarian Democracy*, Jerusalem 1951, and L. Kalakowski, *Religion*, London 1982.

13 See 'Sermon sur la Mort', 1662, in *Bossuet, Textes Choisis et Commentés* par H. Brémont, Paris 1913.

14 This is my translation from Groethuysen's German translation from the 'Discours aux Filles de la Visitation'.

15 Quoted by Groethuysen (in French), vol. I, p. 199.

16 *Ibid.*, vol. I, p. 8.

17 Quoted by Groethuysen (in French), vol. II, p. 199, from a sermon by Bardalou.

18 See Bruggermann and Frauendienst (referred to in n. 1 above); 'Since God,' Wolff declared, 'Who represents the highest form of reason, can never act except in accordance with reason, or lay His wisdom aside, it is not possible that He should bring anything about by miracles that cannot happen naturally' (Bruggermann, p. 11).

19 *Dictionnaire Philosophique*, under 'Méchant'.

20 See R. Mauzi, *L'idée du Bonheur au XVIIIᵉ Siècle*, Paris 1960, and the illuminating review of this by Louis Trénard in *Annales Historiques de la Révolution Française*, vol. 35, 1963.

21 Quoted by A. M. Wilson, *Diderot*, Oxford 1957, p. 190.

22 Quoted by E. Cassirer, *The Philosophy of the Enlightenment*, translated by F.A.C. Koellin and J. P. Pettegrove, Princeton 1951, p. 54.

23 The definition of tyranny in the *Encylopédie* is 'tout gouvernement injustement exercé sans le frein des lois'.

24 Quoted by H. Möller, *op. cit.*, p. 213.

25 *De L'Esprit des Lois*, Book XII, chapter II.

26 Quoted from R. Höhn, *Die Stellung des Strafrichters in den Gesetzen der französischen Revolutionszeit* by L. Radzinowicz, *op. cit.*, p.270, n. 9.

27 *De L'Esprit des Lois*, Book XII, chapter

IV.

28 See L. Radzinowicz, *op. cit.*, pp. 277 ff.

29 See, for example, F. Lütge, *op. cit.*, pp. 404-05.

30 See E. Fox-Genovese, *op. cit.*

31 'La Lutte pour l'Individualisme Agraire', in *Annales E.S.C.*, 1931, p. 333.

32 Montesquieu's ideas on liberty can hardly be said to have been clear. He noted that no word had been given a greater number of different meanings (Book XI, chapter II). He himself spoke of 'Philosophical liberty' (Book XII, chapter II), which he defined as doing what one wanted, or believed that one wanted, to do. Hence it could not exist in any society. In a state governed by laws, he said, liberty was the right to do whatever the laws permitted (Book XI, chapter III). Elsewhere he equated liberty with security, or at least with the citizen's belief that he possessed security. This would appear to have been his essential opinion. Hence his view that liberty was only to be had when those in power, who were always inclined to abuse their power, were prevented from doing so by a division of powers.

33 Le Mercier de la Rivière, *op. cit.*, p. 136.

34 The question of free trade in grain versus the control of the grain trade was a major issue in French politics in the second half of the eighteenth century. The Physiocrats' attempts to remove the controls, and the disasters which followed, discredited Physiocracy (see S. L. Kaplan, *op. cit.*). It is nevertheless significant that the Physiocrats' opponents, notably Necker in an attack on them, asserted that the right to freedom of property and enterprise be subject to a degree of state control sufficient to ensure what he called the '*minimum vital*' to the unskilled workers, whom he saw as subject to the iron law of wages (see H. Grange, *op. cit.*).

35 Quoted by H. Higgs, *op. cit.*, p. 45.

36 See H. Conrad, *op. cit.*, pp. 40 ff.

37 C. G. Svarez, *op. cit.*, p. 614.

38 A typical illustration of this is the changed attitude to the government debt. Until the end of the wars of Louis XIV's reign, as was shown earlier, the government spent its revenues on war and display, regardless of the financial, economic and social consequences; and when its resources were exhausted proclaimed itself bankrupt, defrauded its creditors, and set up a *chambre de justice* to mulct the war-profiteers of their fortunes even though they had acted under its orders or with its connivance. This way of proceeding came to seem increasingly incompatible with the behaviour of a civilized state until Calonne could write to Louis XIV on 9 February 1789, 'may one banish for ever the false and murderous idea that one can save the state by bankruptcy' (*Lettre adressée au Roi*, London 1789). See also G. Chaussinand-Nogaret, *La Noblesse au XVIIIe Siècle*, Paris 1976, for the degree to which the *cahiers* of the nobility revealed how the ideas of the Enlightenment had penetrated the thinking of the nobility.

39 J. P. Eckermann, *op. cit.*, p. 563.

40 Quoted by Cassirer, *op. cit.*, p. 3.

II The Enlightenment and the breakdown of the consensus in France

1 Le Comte de Ségur, *Mémoires, ou Souvenirs et Anecdotes*, Paris 1825, pp. 59-62.

2 J. J. Rousseau, *De L'Inégalité parmi les Hommes*, Editions Sociales, Paris 1954, p. 93.

3 *Ibid.*, p. 64.

4 See J. Flammermont, *op. cit.*, pp. 37-38.

5 The text of this mémoire is printed by Flammermont, *op. cit.*, in an appendix.

6 See F. Bluche, *Les Magistrats . . ., p. 67.*

7 D'Argenson, *Considerations . . .*, p. 11.

8 The text of this mémoire is printed in Schelle's edition of Turgot's works, vol. IV, pp. 568 ff.

9 Ségur, *op. cit.*, pp. 13-15.

10 G. Chaussinand-Nogaret, *op. cit.* Chaussinand-Nogaret, having described at length the great differences in wealth and culture among the nobility, devotes much space to the liberal attitude of the nobles' *cahiers de doléances*. Since, however, these *cahiers* were drawn up in assemblies in which all the nobles in the area had the right to be, and usually were, present in person; since, according to his calculations, a good many fewer than half of them had, at the best, only enough to live in decency as distinct from comfort, and since voting was by majority, it was the opinion of the poor nobles that presumably carried the day – i.e., the opinion of the 11,000 with incomes (at the current rate of exchange) of between £43 and £172 per annum, and the more than 5,000 with incomes varying from something less than £21 per annum to £4 or even £2.

11 See particularly E. Le Roy Ladurie, 'Révoltes et contestations rurales . . .', *op. cit.* Le Roy Ladurie attributes the changed attitudes of the peasants to a variety of causes, notably the weakened hold of the church, the attempts made by some landlords to modernize their property (see Part Two, ch. V (c) (i) above) at the expense of the peasants'

customary rights – but also to the diminishing weight of the direct taxes which he suggests were not felt to be a burden – an assumption contradicted by many contemporary writers in a position to know – particularly Turgot and Necker – and also by Saint-Jacob in his *Les Paysans de la Bourgogne du Nord*, one of the secondary authorities on whom Le Roy Ladurie largely relies.

12 Rousseau, *op. cit.*, p. 128.

13 See F. Hinker, *op. cit.*, p. 41, and E. Le Roy Ladurie, *op. cit.*

14 See the documents transcribed by Marion in his *Les Impôts Directs*, particularly documents 103 and 109.

15 These were the so-called *sols pour livres* or 5 per cent on every livre paid.

16 See F. Bluche, *Les Magistrats.* On p. 170 Bluche gives figures for the sums paid by the councillors in the Paris *parlement* between 1758 and 1760. See also J. Egret, *Louis XV et l'Opposition Parlementaire*, Paris 1970, p. 115, and Marion, *Dictionnaire des Institutions* under 'Sol pour livre'.

17 Third edition, p. 84, n. 1.

18 See B. Behrens, *op. cit.*

19 *Ibid.*

20 R. Forster, *The Nobility in Toulouse . . .*, *op. cit.*

21 In none of the last three cases is the gross income recorded. See Table A, pp. 183 ff.

22 M. Marion, *Les Impôts Directs*, document 103.

23 *Ibid.*, doc. 121, and J. Egret, *op. cit.*, p. 107.

24 These were the so-called *tailles tarifées;* see Marion, *Dictionnaire des Institutions . . .*, *op. cit.*

25 *Ibid.*

26 See particularly H. Grange, *op. cit.;* J. Egret, *Necker: Ministre de Louis XVI*, Paris 1975; J. F. Bosher, *op. cit.*

27 See Part Two, ch. III (a) above.

28 See J. F. Bosher, *op. cit.*, Part 2, chapter 8.

29 *Ibid.*, p. 175.

30 *Ibid.*, p. 179.

31 Quoted by J. F. Bosher, *The Single Duty Project*, London 1964, p. 23.

32 L'Averdy to the Keeper of the Seals, quoted by Egret, *Louis XV . . .*, pp. 131-32.

33 See Egret, 'La Révolution Aristocratique en Franche-Comté et son Echec, 1788-1789', in *Revue d'Histoire Moderne et Contemporaine*, vol. 1-2, 1955, for the quarrels between the nobles with less than a century of noble ancestry and those with more.

34 The assumption that the nobles were a

body united in resistance to reform is one of the many myths that abound in the history of the Ancien Régime. The only occasion when they showed a united resistance – and that only for a very short time – was when they refused to sit together with the representatives of the *Tiers Etat* in the *Assemblée Nationale*. One of the best commentaries on this state of affairs is that of Arthur Young (*op. cit.*, pp. 189-90): 'It is however curious to remark, that if the nobility of other provinces are hunted like those of Franche Comté, of which there is little reason to doubt, that whole order of men undergo a proscription and suffer like sheep, 'without making the least effort to resist attack. This appears marvellous, with a body that have an army with 150,000 men in their hands, for though a part of those troops would certainly disobey their leaders, yet let it be remembered, that out of the 40,000, or possibly 100,000 noblesse of France, they might, if they had intelligence and union among themselves, fill half the ranks of more than half the regiments with men who have fellow-feelings and fellow sufferings with themselves; but no meetings, no associations among them; no union with military men; no taking refuge in the ranks of regiments to defend or avenge their cause; fortunately for France they fall without a struggle and die without a blow.'

35 Quoted in Egret, *Louis XV . . .*, p. 91.
36 Quoted in M. Antoine, *Le Conseil du Roi . . .*, pp. 575-76.
37 See W. F. Church, 'French Jurists as Political Theorists, 1660-1789', in *F.H.S.*, vol. V, 1967-1968.
38 On this see Flammermont, *op. cit.*, p. 51, who observed that it was certain that the *parlements* only had the right to present remonstrances and not to oppose the will of the king when solemnly expressed in a *lit de justice.*
39 On this see M. Antoine, *Le Conseil du Roi . . .*, pp. 580 ff.
40 Quoted by Egret, *Louis XV . . .*, p. 230.
41 On this see Flammermont, *op. cit.*, pp. 519 ff.
42 *Ibid.*, p. 144.
43 Egret, *Louis XV . . .*, p. 226.
44 Flammermont, *op. cit.*, pp. 501 ff.
45 *Ibid.*, p. 126.
46 See Egret, *Louis XV . . .*, p. 257.
47 Quoted by Egret, *ibid.*, p. 231.
48 See R. Mousnier, *Les Institutions. . .*, *op. cit.*, vol. II, pp. 653 ff.
49 Tocqueville, *op. cit.*, vol. II, p. 237.
50 On these see P. Renouvin, *Les Assemblées Provinciales de 1787*, Paris 1921. The *départe-*

ment consisted sometimes of the old *élections*, sometimes of a new administrative unit.
51 Tocqueville, *op. cit.*, p. 242.
52 Particularly by comparison with the rhetoric common among the *Philosophes*, and in other parts of Necker's own writings, what could be more convincing than the following observation (in his 'De l'Administration des Finances,' ch. XLII, *Oeuvres Complètes*, vol. V p. 590): 'I can never remember without a shudder the sight of the following announcement in an estimate for the costs of war,

To be embarked for the colonies 40,000 men
Deduct ⅓ for deaths
[apparently on voyage]   13,333

Remainder   26,667
It is a clerk who wrote this in cold blood.'
53 Quoted by E. G. Léonard, 'La Question Sociale dans l'Armée au XVIIIe Siècle', in *Annales E.S.C.*, April-June 1948.
54 See E. G. Léonard, *L'Armée et ses Problèmes au XVIIIe Siècle*, Paris 1958; also Liddell Hart, *The Ghost of Napoleon*, London 1933.
55 Léonard, *L'Armée et ses Problèmes*, p. 288.
56 Quoted by D. D. Bien, 'La réaction aristocratique . . .', *op. cit.*
57 *Archives Parlementaires*, vol. 17, pp. 640-41.

III The Enlightenment in Prussia

(a) THE BUILD-UP OF CONSENSUS, 1740-1786
1 This famous remark is frequently quoted. See, for example, F. Kopitzsch (ed.), *Aufklärung, Absolutismus und Bürgertum in Deutschland*, Munich 1976, p. 334.
2 This remark, too, is frequently quoted. See, for example, H. Möller, *op. cit.*, p. 90.
3 V. Sellin, 'Friedrich der Große und der aufgeklärte Absolutismus', in *Festschrift für Werner Conze.*
4 Tocqueville, *op. cit.*, vol. II, pp. 268 ff.
5 See R. Darnton, 'Literary Low Life in Pre-revolutionary France', in *Past and Present*, 51, May 1971.
6 See W. Frauendienst, *op. cit.* (as in Part I, ch. 2, n. 8 above), p. 80. For the following account of Wolff's political ideas, see Frauendienst, *passim.*
7 H. Möller, *op. cit.*, p. 253.
8 Adam Smith maintained that a state could support a standing army equivalent in size to 1 per cent of the population. The Prussian army was always equivalent to 4 per cent of the population. See Part 2, ch. V (b).
9 I. Mittenzwei, *Preußen nach Dem Siebenjährigen Krieg. Auseinandersetzung zwischen*

Bürgertum und Staat und die Wirtschaftspolitik, [East] Berlin 1979.

10 See Fontane, *Wanderungen . . ., op. cit.,* vol. I, pp. 388 ff.

11 *Ibid.,* vol. I, pp. 402 ff.

12 *Ibid.,* vol. I, pp. 763 ff. Frederick did not in fact speak to Marwitz but ignored him. This was because, having beckoned the local pastor and asked whose child he was, the pastor replied that he was the son of Herr von der Marwitz of Friedersdorf, and to Frederick's further question if this was the General von der Marwitz the pastor replied no, he was the court chamberlain. Frederick made no comment. He could not endure courtiers.

13 Though they differed on matters of literature from the early *Aufklärer.* On this and what follows see H. Möller, *op. cit.*

14 H. Möller, *op. cit.,* pp. 246 ff. Of the 300 people who wrote for the *Berlinische Monatschrift,* the principal organ of the *Aufklärung* in the last quarter of the eighteenth century, the largest single group (80 members) was composed of professors and schoolteachers, but the second largest (60 members) of bureaucrats in the higher or highest ranks.

15 C.G. Svarez, *op. cit.,* p. 497.

16 This was introduced in 1788. See K. E. Jeismann, *Das preußische Gymnasium in Staat und Gesellschaft,* Stuttgart 1974.

17 This information is provided by P. Schwartz, *op. cit.* Admittedly he says nothing about how large his sample was, so that his conclusions can only be accepted with reservations though *prima facie* they seem plausible.

18 H. Möller, *op. cit.,* p. 332.

19 See *AB Getreidehandelspolitik,* vol. IV, pp. 130 ff. for the immigrants from Saxony, Bohemia, the Palatinate, Württemberg, Poland and Mecklenburg. It nevertheless appears from this account that the amount of grain which Frederick felt himself able to release from stock was less substantial than Nicolai's remarks suggest.

20 For an excellent account of this see O. Büsch, *op. cit.*

21 The number of mercenaries in the Prussian army was very large and was increased by Frederick the Great on the principle, as he put it in his Testament Politique of 1768, that 'useful hard-working people should be guarded as the apple of one's eye, and in wartime recruits should be levied in one's own country only when the bitterest necessity compels.' At the end of the eighteenth century the proportion of mercenaries accounted for about 50 per cent of the

rank and file. See G. Craig, *The Politics of the Prussian Army, 1640-1945,* Oxford 1955, p. 23.

22 See P. Paret, *op. cit.,* pp. 16 ff.

23 *Ibid.,* ch. 2.

24 See Edgar Faure, *La Disgrâce de Turgot,* Paris 1961.

25 See P. Baumgart, *op. cit.*

26 Fontane, *Wanderungen . . ., op. cit.,* vol. II, pp. 127-28.

27 Dilthey, *Gesammelte Schriften,* vol. IV, Leipzig 1921, 'Der Streit Kants mit der Zensur', p. 267.

28 *Reden an die deutsche Nation,* quoted by R. Ibbeken, *op. cit.,* p. 204.

29 See A. Stölzel, *Carl Gottlieb Svarez,* Berlin 1885, p. 394. Stölzel, writing when he did, saw in Svarez' behaviour on this occasion only a further proof of his 'conscientiousness, thoroughness and loyalty'.

30 Dilthey, *op. cit.*

31 W. von Humboldt, 'Ideen zu einem Versuch die Grenzen der Wirksamkeit des Staats zu bestimmen', in *Gesammelte Schriften,* ed. A. Leitzmann, vol. I, Berlin 1903, p. 234.

(b) THE LEGACY IN THE PERIOD OF REFORM

1 See A. Naudé, 'Der preußische Staatschatz unter König Wilhelm II und seine Erschöpfung', in *FPBG,* V (1), 1892.

2 See Otto Hintze, 'Preußische Reformbestrebungen vor 1806', in *Regierung und Verwaltung, op. cit.,* pp. 504-30.

3 See W. Treue, 'Adam Smith in Deutschland', in *Deutschland und Europa,* ed. W. Conze, *Festschrift für Hans Rothfels,* Düsseldorf 1951.

4 See F. Schnabel, *Deutsche Geschichte im Neunzehnten Jahrhundert,* vol. 2, Freiburg 1949, p. 281.

5 E. von Bodelschwingh, *op. cit.,* p. 96.

6 Letter to Rachel Varnhagen, 24 October 1811, printed in *Briefwechsel mit Alexander von der Marwitz, op. cit.*

7 For the best account of this episode see F. Meusel, *Friedrich August Ludwig von der Marwitz,* 2 vols, Berlin 1908-1913, vol. II, part 2, pp. 3 ff.

8 *Ibid.,* vol. I, p. 173.

9 See *FBPG,* XXII, 1909: Marwitz's 'Von dem Instande des Vermögens der Grundbesitzer des platten Landes der Mark Brandenburg und von dem Verhältnis der ihnen jetzt auferlegten Abgaben zu den ehemaligen'.

10 Meusel, *op. cit.,* vol. II, part I, pp. 60 ff.: Marwitz's Tagebuch über die Reise nach England.

11 Marwitz continually referred to the

attacks on the nobility current at the time he wrote, and Meusel confirms his judgment. See e.g. vol. I, p. 41, where he says that in all the children's books prescribed in the schools the noble was portrayed as an uneducated fool, spending his time in hunting and plaguing his peasaɪts. Wilhelm von Humboldt, in his 'Denkschrift über Preußens ständische Verfassung', of February 1819 (*Gesammelte Schriften*, vol. III, Berlin 1904, p. 94), referred to the nobility as a half-dead institution which it was essential that the state should bring back to life. Brandes, in his *Ueber den Einfluß und die Wirkungen des Zeitgeistes auf die höheren Stände Deutschlands*, Hanover 1810, p. 106, observed that after the outbreak of the French Revolution 'There arose in Germany, on the French model, a furious plebeian outcry not only against the privileges of the nobility but against its very existence'. To Brandes this outcry was 'wild, blind, unjust, the work of political agitators'. Kant, in his *Metaphysik der Sitten*, maintained that a hereditary noble was a concept as lacking in reality (*ein Gedankending ohne Realität*) as a hereditary professor (quoted by G. Birsch, 'Zur sozialen und politischen Rolle des deutschen, vornehmlich preußischen Adels am Ende des 18. Jahrhunderts', in *Der Adel vor der Revolution*, ed. R. Vierhaus, Göttingen 1971). Many other testimonies could be cited in proof of the hostility to the nobility – a phenomenon whose scope, origins, consequences and decline seem not to have been analysed.

12 This document, with Hardenberg's marginal comments, is printed in vol. II, part 2 of Meusel's life of Marwitz (*op. cit.*), pp. 3 ff.

13 Every account of the reform movement refers to Stein's and Hardenberg's attacks on Beyme – inspired principally by their dislike of the power he exercised as the principal member of the kitchen cabinet they were determined to destroy. See particularly Gerhard Ritter's *Stein: Eine politische Biographie*, 3rd edition, Stuttgart 1958. For a short account of Beyme's origins and career see the article by Saring in *Jahrbuch für brandenbürgische Landesgeschichte*, 1956.

14 Letter to Gröben, 4-8 January 1818, printed in E. Kessel, 'Zu Boyens Entlassung', *H.Z.*, 1953, vol. 175, p. 47.

15 Quoted by R. Kosellek, 'Staat und Gesellschaft in Preußen, 1815-1848', in *Staat und Gesellschaft in deutschen Vormärz*, ed. W. Conze, Stuttgart 1962, p. 86, n. 24.

16 By W. M. Simon, Ithaca 1955.

17 As a result of Stein's Städteordnung of 1808, revised 1831, which granted self-government to the towns. On this see Kosel-

leck, *op. cit.* (in n. 15 above), and *Preußen zwischen Reform und Revolution, op. cit.*

18 Quoted by O. Hintze, *Die Hohenzollern und ihr Werk*, Berlin 1915, pp. 461-62.

19 See O. Hintze, 'Preußische Reformbestrebungen. . .' (n. 2 above).

20 See P. Paret, *Yorck and the Era of Prussian Reform, op. cit.*, p. 112. For the best outline account of the main events that led up to and followed from the French invasion, see O. Hintze, *Die Hohenzollern* . . .

21 R. Ibbeken, *op. cit.*, p. 92.

22 *Ibid.*

23 *Ibid.* Presumably these figures relate to the years 1806-08 but the author gives no dates.

24 Quoted by O. Hintze, *op. cit.* (in n. 18), pp. 438-39.

25 *Schriften, Aufsätze, Studien, Briefe*, ed. W. Hahlweg, vol. I, Gottingen 1966, p. 639.

26 G. Ritter, *Stein*, p. 219.

27 See particularly the works by R. Koselleck referred to above.

28 See B. H. Liddell-Hart, *op. cit.*, p. 16.

29 The numbers in each case are somewhat uncertain but the discrepancy is so great as to make this unimportant. See, for example, Ibbeken, *op. cit.*, p. 398. He speaks of nearly 300,000 men having been put into the field between 1813 and 1815. M. Reinhardt, in his *Le Grand Carnot*, vol. II, Paris 1952, p. 93, thinks that the number of French troops (after the *Levée en masse*) was unlikely to have exceeded about 700,000. France at that time had a population of about 26 million and Prussia 4½ million or less in 1813.

30 The text of this edict is given by E. R. Huber, *Dokumente zur deutschen Verfassungsgeschichte*, Stuttgart 1961, vol. I, pp. 39-40.

31 For the other obligations deemed to come into this category see Koselleck, *Preußen zwischen Reform und Revolution*, pp. 488-89.

32 To the peasants, as may be imagined, this distinction between personal obligations and obligations attached to the land was apt to seem meaningless and proved totally impossible to introduce in Westphalia when Napoleon tried to impose the Code Napoléon there. See E. Fehrenbach, *op. cit.*, p. 88 ff.

33 J. H. Clapham, *Economic Development of France and Germany*, Cambridge 1936, p. 97. See also Mieck (as in n. 49 below) on this.

34 The ministries were, however, reorganized so that instead of each being responsible for the affairs of a particular province, as well as sometimes for matters affecting the whole kingdom, they became responsible only for the latter.

35 For the composition and functions of the *Staatsrat*, see E. R. Huber, *Deutsche Verfassungsgeschichte seit 1789*, vol. I, Stuttgart 1957, pp. 158 ff.

36 See K. E. Jeismann, *op. cit.*, pp. 358-59.

37 See Koselleck, *Preußen zwischen Reform und Revolution*, pp. 496 ff.

38 *Ibid.*, ch. 3, section 4.

39 See Knapp, *Die Bauernbefreiung*, p.492, for the various categories of *spannfähige* peasants who were omitted.

40 *Ibid.*, ch. V.

41 See Koselleck, *Preußen . . .*, ch. 3, section 4.

42 *Ibid.*, and C. Dipper, *op. cit.*, p. 64, for the creation of a landless proletariat.

43 See Koselleck, 'Staat und Gesellschaft'.

44 See Finck von Finckenstein, *Die Entwickelung der Landwirtschaft*, p. 164 and Appendices pp. 389-91.

45 'Umtriebe', printed in K. Schwartz, *op. cit.*

46 F. Lütge, 'Uber die Auswirkung der Bauernbefreiung in Deutschland', in *Studien zur Sozial- und Wirtschaftsgeschichte*, Stuttgart 1963, p. 198.

47 Finck von Finckenstein, *op. cit.*, p. 96.

48 Koselleck, 'Staat und Gesellschaft . . .', estimated the increase in population – most of it on the land – between 1815 and 1848 at 40 per cent.

49 See I. Mieck, *Preußische Gewerbepolitik in Berlin, 1806-1844*, Berlin 1965, *passim*.

50 *Ibid.*

51 See A. Bussmann, 'Friedrich der Große im Wandel des europäischen Urteils', in *Festschrift für Hans Rothfels* (as in n. 3 above).

52 F. Meusel, *op. cit.*, vol. I, p. 136.

53 Madame de Staël, *op. cit.*, vol. I, p. 227.

54 H. Schoeps, *op. cit.*, p. 169.

Conclusion

1 *Capital*, 3rd edition, ed. Engels, trans. G. Moore and E. Aveling, New York 1967, vol. I, pp. 152-53.

2 J. Schulze, 'Die Auseinandersetzung zwischen Adel und Bürgertum, 1773-1806', in *Historische Studien*, vol. 161-64, Heft 163, 1925.

3 See W. Sombart, *op. cit.* Sombart contrasted what he called 'der Bürger' (which in German means citizen, as in the term *Staatsbürger*, as well as bourgeois), whom he saw as possessing the qualities of a good citizen, with 'der Bourgeois' or Marxist capitalist.

4 Braudel and Labrousse, *op. cit.*, vol. II, p. 708.

5 On this see O. Hintze, 'Preußens Entwicklung . . .', *op. cit.* To Hintze and other German historians the term *Rechtsstaat* did and does not mean constitutional government, although it is so described in German-English dictionaries, including the old and the new two-volume *Langenscheidt*. The word is untranslatable into English except by a periphrasis such as that given above.

6 See H. C. Johnson, *Frederick the Great and his Officials*, New Haven 1975, particularly pp. 210 ff. The remarkable memoranda of Cocceji and Hagen printed in the *Acta Borussica* themselves give sufficient support to Johnson's judgment.

7 On this see, e.g., O. Hintze, *Die Hohenzollern . . .*, p. 446; Raumer, *Lebenserinnerungen . . .*; and the biographies of the principal ministers and officials in the *Allgemeine Deutsche Biographie* and other works.

8 See H. Brunschwig, *La Crise de l'Etat Prussien à la Fin du XVIIIe Siècle*, Paris 1947, pp. 139-41.

9 *Ibid.*; on p. 141 Brunschwig maintains that had all these revolts occurred at the same time, as they did in France, the government would have been unable to suppress them. He overlooks the fact that the government in France had broken down before the revolts of the kind he describes had erupted there.

10 H. Rosenberg, *op. cit.*

11 His own untranslatable words were, 'Der Dienst und mein Gemüt . . .' quoted in E. von Meier, *op. cit.*, p. 135.

12 Raumer, *op. cit.*, vol. I, pp. 165-66.

13 Quoted by E. von Meier, *op. cit.*, pp. 242-43.

14 Quoted by A. Bußmann, 'Eine historische Würdigung Friedrich Wilhelms IV', in *Spiegel der Zeit*, Festgabe für Max Braubach, Münster 1964, p. 714.

15 See H. Hausherr, *Hardenberg*, Graz 1963.

16 These facts are taken from the *Allgemeine Deutsche Biographie* and from a large number of works dealing with the people in question.

17 See P. Paret, *Yorck . . .*, *op. cit.*, p. 243.

18 C. Garve, *Versuche . . .*, *op. cit.*

19 See his 'Die Demokratisierung der Rittergutsbesitzer', in *Festschrift für Hans Herzfeld*, Berlin 1958.

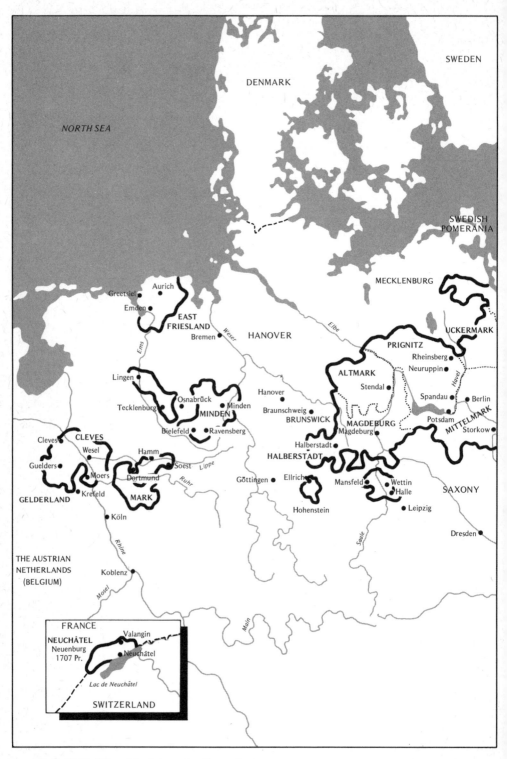

Prussia in 1786: The Administrative Boundaries

RUSSIA

BALTIC SEA

Memel

Tauroggen

Niemen

Tilsit

Königsberg • Insterburg
Gumbinnen

Pregel

Lauenburg

Danzig • Bartenstein • Angerburg

Köslin

EASTERN POMERANIA

Bütow • Elbing • EAST PRUSSIA • LITHUANIA

Kolberg

WEST PRUSSIA

WESTERN POMERANIA

Draheim • Marienwerder

Mockrau

Stettin • Kulm • Graudenz • Neidenburg

Fordon

Schwedt • Bromberg

NEUMARK • DISTRICT OF NETZE • Thorn

Netze

Landsberg • *Warthe* • *Vistula*

Lebus • Küstrin

Frankfurt • Schwiebus

POLAND

Peitz

Cottbus • Glogau

Spree

Wohlau

Liegnitz • Breslau

Oder

SILESIA • Brieg

Oppeln

Neisse • Neisse

BOHEMIA • Glatz • Cosel • Beuthen

Prague

| | Boundaries of Prussia |
| | Provincial boundaries |

0   50   100 Kilometres

0   50 Miles

AUSTRIA   HUNGARY

France in 1789: The Provinces

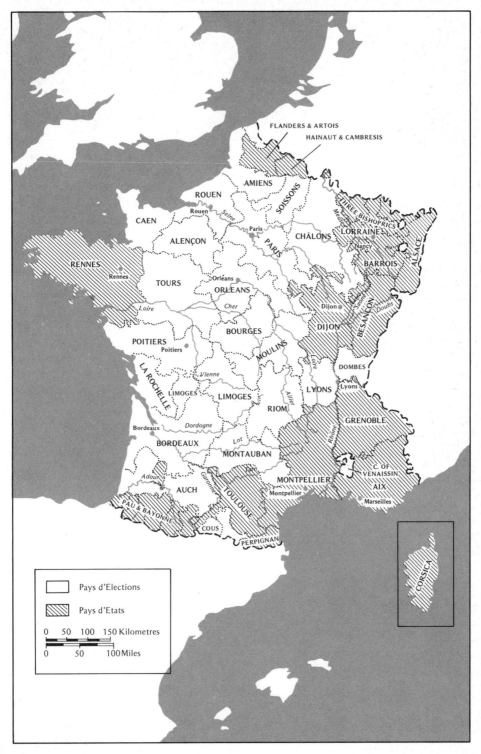

France in 1789: The *Intendances: Pays d'Elections* and *Pays d'Etats*

Bibliography

This bibliography makes no claim to comprehensiveness. It includes only such works as are referred to in the notes or have seemed essential to an understanding of the matters discussed in the text.

ABEL, W., *Geschichte der deutschen Landwirtschaft*, Stuttgart 1962
Agrarkrisen und Agrarkonjunktur, Hamburg and Berlin 1966
Massenararut und Hungerkrisen in vorindustriellen Europa Hamburg 1974
ACTA BORUSSICA, Denkmäler der preußischen Staatsverwaltung im 18 Jahrhundert, published by the preußischen Akademie der Wissenschaft
Die Behördenorganisation, vols. 1-17, Berlin 1892 ff
Die Getreidehandelspolitik und Kriegsmagazinverwaltung, Berlin 1901 ff
ADAMS, John Quincy, *Letters on Silesia*, 1800-1801, London 1804
D'AGESSEAU, *Mémoire Inédit du Chancelier d'Aguesseau sur la Reformation de la Justice*, 1738, ed. P. Combe, Valence 1928
ALLGEMEINES LANDRECHT, Ed. Hans Hattenhauer, Frankfurt a/M and Berlin 1970
ANDREAS, Willy, 'Marwitz und der Staat Friedrichs des Grossen' in *Historische Zeitung* 122 (1920)
ANER, Karl, *Der Aufklärer Friedrich Nicolai*, Giessen 1912
ANTOINE, Michel, *Le Conseil du Roi sous Louis XV*, Paris and Geneva 1970
'La Notion de Subdélegation dans la Monarchie d'Ancien Régime' in *Bibliothèque de l'Ecole des Charles* 132 (July-September 1974)
ARCHIVES PARLEMENTAIRES, Première série 1789-1799, Paris 1879
ARENDT, Hannah, *Rahel Varnhagen*, Munich 1959
ARETIN, K. O. Freiherr von (ed.), *Der aufgeklärte Absolutismus*, Cologne 1974
ARGENSON, R.L. de V. de P., Marquis d', *Mémoires*, Paris 1823
Considérations sur le Gouvernement Ancien et Présent de la France, Amsterdam 1765
ARNDT, E. M., *Erinnerungen aus dem äußeren Leben*, Leipzig 1849
Meine Wanderungen und Wandelungen mit dem Reichsfreiherrn Heinrich Karl Friedrich von [sic] Stein, Berlin 1858
Staat und Vaterland: Eine Auswahl aus seinen politischen Schriften, ed. E. Müsebeck, Munich 1921

BAASCH, E., *Quellen zur Geschichte von Hamburgs Handel und Schiffahrt im 17, 18 und 19 Jahrhundert*, Hamburg 1910
BACZKO, B., *Lumières de l'Utopie*, Payot 1978

BACZKO, Ludwig von, *Versuch einer Geschichte und Beschreibung Königsbergs*, 2nd edition, Königsberg 1804
BARNAVE, Antoine Pierre Joseph Marie, *Introduction à la Révolution Française*, ed. F. Rude, Cahiers des Annales 15, Paris 1960
BASTID, Paul, *Sieyès et sa Penseé*, Paris 1939
BASTIER, J., *La Féodalité au Siècle des Lumières dans la Région de Toulouse*, Paris 1975
BAUMGART, P., *Zur Geschichte der kurmärkischen Stände im 17 und 18 Jahrhundert*, ed. Dietrich Gerhard, publication of the Max-Planck-Institut für Geschichte, Göttingen 1969
BECK, L. W., *Early German Philosophy: Kant and his Predecessors*, Cambridge, Mass. 1969
BERGER, H., *Friedrich der Große als Kolonisator*, Giessen 1896
BESENVAL, Baron de, *Mémoires*, Paris 1805
BIEN, D. D., *The Calas Affair*, Princeton 1960
'La Réaction Aristocratique avant 1789: L'Exemple de l'Armée' in *Annales E.S.C.* 24 (Jan. – Feb, and March – April, 1974)
BISMARCK, Otto von, *Gedanken und Erinnerungen*, Stuttgart and Berlin 1928
BLACKALL, E., *The Emergence of German as a Literary Language*, Cambridge 1959
BLEEK, W., *Von der Kameralausbildung zum Juristenprivileg*, Berlin 1972
BLOCH, Marc, 'La Lutte pour l'Individualisme Agraire' in *Annales E.S.C.* 2 (1930)
Les Rois Thaumaturges, Strasburg and Paris 1924
Les Caractères Originaux de l'Histoire Rurale Française, Paris 1961
Feudal Society, trans. L. A. Manyon, foreword M. M. Postan, London 1961
BLUCHE, François, 'L'Origine Sociale des Secrétaires d'Etat de Louis XIV 1661-1715' in *XVIIe Siècle* 42 – 43 (1959)
'Les Honneurs de la Cour' in *Les Cahiers Nobles*, Paris 1957
Les Magistrats du Parlement de Paris au XVIIIe Siècle, Paris 1960
BLUM, J., *Noble Landowners and Agriculture in Austria 1815-1848*, Baltimore 1948
The End of the Old Order in Rural Europe, Princeton 1978
BODELSCHWINGH, *Leben des Freiherrn von Vincke*
BOISGUILLEBERT, Pierre de, *Le Détail de la France*
BONCERF, *Les Inconvénients des Droits Féodaux*, London 1776
BORDEAUX AU XVIIIe SIÈCLE, Ed. F.-G. Pariset with the collaboration of F. Crouzet and others, Bordeaux 1968
BORDES, M., *L'Administration Provinciale et Municipale en France au XVIIIe Siècle*, Paris 1972

Bibliography

Bosher, J. F., *The Single Duty Project*, London 1964
French Finances 1770-1795, Cambridge 1970

Bourdes, A. J., *Agronomie et Agronomes en France au XVIIIᵉ Siècle*, Paris 1967

Bouvier, J. and Germain-Martin, H. *Finances et Financiers de l'Ancien Régime*, series *Que Sais-Je?*, Paris 1964

Boyen, H. von, *Erinnerungen*, 3 vols., ed. F. Nippold, Leipzig 1889-90

Brandes, E., *Ueber den Einfluß und die Wirkungen des Zeitgeistes auf die höheren Stände Deutschlandes*, Hanover 1810

Briefe eines Schlesischen Grafen an einen Kurländischen Edelmann, Altona 1795

Bruggemann, F., (ed.) *Das Weltbild der deutschen Aufklärung*, Leipzig 1930

Brunner, O., 'Feudalismus: Ein Beitrag zur Begriffsgeschichte' in *Abhandlungen der Geistes- und Sozialwissenschaftlichen Klasse*, Wiesbaden 1958

Brunschwig, H., *La Crise de l'Etat Prussien à la Fin du XVIIIᵉ Siècle*, Paris 1947

Busch, O., *Militärsystem und Sozialleben im allen Preußen*, Berlin 1962

Calonne, Charles Alexandre de, *Lettre Adressée au Roi*, London 1789
Speech to the Assembly of Notables, London 1787

Carre, H.T.G., *La Noblesse de France et l'Opinion Publique au XVIIIᵉ Siècle*, Paris 1920

Carriere, C., *Negociants Marseillais au XVIIIᵉ Siècle*, Marseille 1973

Carsten, F.W., *Princes and Parlements in Germany from the Fifteenth to the Eighteenth Century*, Oxford 1959

Cassirer, E., *Philosophy of the Enlightenment*, trans. F.A.C. Koellin and J.P. Pettegrove, Princeton 1951

Chaussinand-Nogaret, G., *La Noblesse au XVIIIᵉ Siècle*, Paris 1976

Church, W.F., 'The Decline of French Jurists as Political Theorists, 1660-1789' in *French Historical Studies* 3 (1967-8)

Clapham, J.H., *Economic Development of France and Germany 1815-1914*, Cambridge 1936

Cobban, A., *The Myth of the French Revolution*, London 1955
The Social Interpretation of the French Revolution, Cambridge 1964

Combe, P., (ed.) *Mémoire Inédit du Chancelier d'Aguesseau sur la Réforme de la Justice*, Valence 1928

Condorcet, Marquis de, *Esquisse d'un Tableau Historique des Progrès de l'Esprit Humain*, ed. O.H.Prior, Paris 1933

Conrad, H., 'Die Geistigen Grundlagen des Allgemeinen Landrechts für die preußischen Staaten' in *Arbeitsgemeinschaft für Forschung des Landes Nordrhein-Westfalen* 77, Cologne and Opladen 1957
'Rechtsstaatliche Bestrebungen um Absolutismus Preußens und Osterreichs am Ende des 18 Jahrhunderts' in *Arbeitsgemeinschaft für Forschung des Landes Nordrhein-Westfalen* 95, 1961

Coyer, G.F., *La Noblesse Commerçante*, London 1756

Craig, G., *The Politics of the Prussian Army 1640-1945*, Oxford 1955

Crouzet, F., 'Angleterre et France au XVIIIᵉ Siècle: Essai d'Analyse Comparée de Deux Croissances Economiques' in *Annales E.S.C.* 21 (1966)
'Agriculture et Révolution Industrielle: Quelques Réflexions' in *Annales E.S.C.* 22 (1967)

Czybulka, G., *Die Lage der ländlichen Klassen Ostdeutschlands im 18 Jahrhundert*, Brunswick 1949

Dakin, D., *Turgot and the Ancien Régime in France*, London 1939

Dardel, P., *Commerce, Industrie et Navigation à Rouen et au Havre au XVIIIᵉ Siècle*, Rouen 1966

Darnton, R., 'The High-Enlightenment and Low-Life of Literature in Pre-revolutionary France' in *Past & Present* 50-53 (May 1971)
'Trade in the Taboo: The Life of a Clandestine Bookseller in Pre-revolutionary France' in *The Widening Circle*, ed. P. Korshin, Philadelphia 1977
The Business of the Enlightenment: A Publishing History of the Encyclopédie, 1775-1800, Cambridge, Mass. 1979

Daumard, A. and Furet, F., *Structures et Relations Sociales à Paris au XVIIIᵉ Siècle*, Paris 1961

Delbeke, F., *L'Action Politique et Sociale des Avocats au XVIIIᵉ Siècle: Leur Part dans la Préparation de la Révolution Française*, Louvain 1927

Demeter, K., *Das deutsche Offizierkorps in Gesellschaft und Staat 1650-1945*, Frankfurt a/M 1965

Dilthey, W., 'Der Streit Kants mit der Zensur' in *Gesammelte Schriften* 4 (1921)
'Die deutsche Aufklärung im Staat und in der Akademie Friedrichs des Großen' in *Deutsche Rundschau* 107 (1901)

Dipper, C., *Die Bauernbefreiung in Deutschland*, Stuttgart, Cologne, Berlin and Mainz 1980

Dorn, W.L., 'The Prussian Bureaucracy in the 18th Century' in *Political Science Quarterly* 46, 47 (1931, 1932)

Doyle, W., 'The Parlements of France and the Breakdown of the Old Regime 1771-1788' in *French Historical Studies* 6 (1969-1970)

Droz, J., *L'Allemagne et la Révolution Française*, Paris 1949

Duffy, C., *The Army of Frederick the Great*, David & Charles 1974

Dumont, E., *Souvenirs sur Mirabeau*, introduction and notes by J. Bénétray; preface by G. Lefebvre, Paris 1951

Dupont, de Nemours, 'De l'Origine et des Progrès d'une Science Nouvelle, 1768' in *Collections des Economistes et des Réformateurs Sociaux de la France*, ed. A. Dubois, Paris 1910

Durand, Y., *Les Fermiers Généraux au XVIIIᵉ Siècle*, Paris 1971

Eberhardt, J.H.E., 'Ueber die Zeichen der Aufklärung einer Nation, 1783' in *Litterarische Chronek*, Bern 1786

Eberty, F., *Jugenderinnerungen eines alten Berliners*, Berlin 1878

Eckermann, J.P., *Gespräche mit Goethe*, Wiesbaden 1955

Egret, J., *La Pre-Revolution Française*, Paris 1962
'La Révolution Aristocratique en Franche Comté

et son Echec 1788-9' in *Revue d'Histoire Moderne et Contemporaine* 1-2 (1955)
Louis XV et l'Opposition Parlementaire 1715-1774, Paris 1970
Necker: Ministre de Louis XVI, Paris 1975
EISENSTEIN, E.L., 'Who Intervened in 1789' in *American Historical Review* 71 (October 1965)
ENCYCLOPEDIE OU DICTIONNAIRE RAISONE DES SCIENCES, DES ARTS ET DES METIERS, 1751 edition
ENDRES, R., 'Das Armenproblem im Zeitalter des Absolutismus' in *Aufklärung, Absolutismus und Bürgertum*, ed. F Kopitzsch, Munich 1976

FAURE, E., *La Disgrâce de Turgot*, Paris 1961
FEHRENBACH, E., *Traditionale Gesellschaft und revolutionäres Recht*, Göttingen 1974
FETJO, F., *Un Habsburg Révolutionnaire, Joseph II*, Paris 1953
FICHTE, J.G., *Reden an die deutsche Nation*, ed. H. Freyer, Leipzig 1933
FINCK VON FINCKENSTEIN, H.W. Graf, *Die Entwickelung der Landwirtschaft in Preußen und Deutschland 1800-1930*, Wurzburg 1960
FLAMMERMONT, J., *Le Chancelier Maupeou et les Parlements*, Paris 1883
FONTANE, T., *Wanderungen durch die Mark Brandenburg* in *Sämtliche Werke*, ed. W. Keitel, Munich 1966
FORSTER, R., *The Nobility of Toulouse in the Eighteenth Century*, Baltimore 1960
'The Provincial Nobles: A Reappraisal' in *American Historical Review* 68 (2, 1963)
'The Survival of the Nobility during the French Revolution' in *Past and Present* 37 (1967)
'Obstacles to Agricultural Growth in Eighteenth-century France' in *American Historical Review* 75 (October 1970)
The House of Saulx-Tavanes. Versailles and Burgundy 1700-1830, Baltimore and London 1971
FOX-GENOVESE, E., *The Origins of Physiocracy*, Ithaca and London 1976
FRAUENDIENST, W., 'Christian Wolff als Staatsdenker' in *Historische Studien* 171, Berlin 1927
FREDERICK THE GREAT, *Oeuvres*, ed. J.D.-E. Preuss, 28 vols., Berlin 1846 ff
Die Politischen Testamente Friedrichs des Grossen, ed. G.B.Volz, Berlin 1920
FREVILLE, H., *L'Intendance de la Bretagne*, Rennes 1953
FREYMARK, H., *Die Reform der preußischen Handels- und Zollpolitik von 1800-1821 und ihre Bedeutung*, Jena 1898
FRIEDBERG, H., 'Friedrich der Große und der Prozeß Goerne' in *Historische Zeitschrift* 65 (1890)
FURET, F., 'Le Catéchisme de la Révolution Française' in *Annales E.S.C.* (March-April, 1971)
Penser la Révolution Française, Paris 1978
and DAUMARD, A. *Structures et Relations Sociales à Paris*, Paris 1961

GARAUD, M., *Histoire Générale du Droit Privé de 1789 à 1804*. Vol.2: *La Révolution et la Propriété Foncière*, Paris 1959
GARDEN, M., *Lyon et les Lyonnais au XVIIIᵉ Siècle*, Paris 1970
GARVE, C., *Ueber den Charakter der Bauern und ueber ihr Verhältnis gegen die Gutsherrn und gegen die Regierung*, Breslau 1796
Versuche über Veschiedene Gegenstände aus der Moral der Literatur und dem gesellschaftlichen Leben, 5 vols., vol.1, Breslau 1802
Fragmente zur Schilderung des Geistes, des Charakters, und die Regierung Friedrichs des Zweyten, Breslau 1798
GASS, E., *Antoine de Rivarol und der Ausgang der französischen Revolution*, The Hague 1938
GASTON-MARTIN., *Nantes au XVIIIᵉ Siècle*, Paris 1924
GEBHARDT, B., *Handbuch der deutschen Geschichte*. Vol.2: *Von der Reformation bis zum Ende des Absolutism*, ed. H. Grandmann, Stuttgart 1955
Handbuch der deutschen Geschichte. Vol.3: *Von der französischen Revolution bis zum ersten Weltkrieg*, ed. H. Grandmann, Stuttgart 1970
GEMBRUCH, W., *Freiherr vom Stein in Zeitalter der Restauration*, Wiesbaden 1960
GERARD, A., *La Révolution Française: Mythes et Interpretations*, Paris 1970
GODECHOT, J., 'L'Histoire Sociale et Economique de Toulouse au XVIIIᵉ Siècle' in *Annales du Midi* 78 (1966)
La Prise de la Bastille, Paris 1965
GOHRING, M., 'Die Amterkäuflichkeit im Ancien Regime' in *Historische Studien* 344-346 (1938)
GOODWIN, B., 'Social Structure and Economic and Political Attitude to the French Nobility in the Eighteenth Century' in publications of the International Congress in Vienna, 1965
GORLITZ, W., *Die Junker*, 2nd Edition, Glücksburg/Osten 1957
GOUBERT, P., *Beauvais et le Beauvaisis de 1600 à 1730*, Paris 1960
Familles Marchandes sous l'Ancien Régime: Les Danse et les Motte de Beauvais, Paris 1959
'Les Officiers Royaux des Présidiaux, Baillages et Elections dans la Société Française au XVIIIᵉ Siècle' in *XVIIᵉ Siècle* 42-43 (1, 1959)
L'Ancien Régime, Vol.1: *La Société*, Paris 1969; Vol.2: *Les Pouvoirs*, Paris 1973
Les Français ont la Parole, Paris 1964
Louis XIV et Vingt Millions de Français, Paris 1965
GRANER, F., 'Aus der hinterlassenen Papieren des in Müller Arnoldschen Prozeß zur Festungsstrafe Verurteilten neumärkischen Regierungsrat Bandel' in *FBPG* 38 (1926)
GRANGE, H., *Les Idées de Necker*, Paris 1974
GREER, D.M., *The Incidence of the Emigration during the French Revolution*, Cambridge, Mass. 1951
The Incidence of the Terror during the French Revolution, Cambridge, Mass. 1935
GROETHUYSEN, B., *Die Entstehung der Bürgerlichen Welt- und Lebensanschauung in Frankreich*, 2 vols., Halle/Saale 1927, 1930
GROSCLAUDE, P., *Malesherbes: Témoin et Interprète de son Temps* (pt.2: *Nouveaux Documents Inédits*), Paris 1961, 1964
GRUDER, V.R., *The Royal Provincial Intendants*, Ithica 1968
GRUNBERG, C., Die *Bauernbefreiung*, Leipzig 1894

HABERNOL, P., 'Die Versuche Friedrichs des Großen das englische System der Fruchtwechselwirtschaft in Preußen einzuführen' in *Landwirtschaftliche Jahrbücher* 29, Berlin 1900

HARNISCH, H., 'Die Agrarpolitischen Reformmaßnahmen der preußischen Staatsführung in dem Jahrzehnt vor 1806/7' in *Jahrbuch für Wirtschaftsgeschichte* 3 (1977)

HARTWELL, R.M., *Industrial Revolution and Economic Change*, London 1971

HARTUNG, F., *Deutsche Verfassungsgeschichte*, Stuttgart 1950

and MOUSNIER R., 'Quelques Problèmes Concernant la Monarchie Absolue' in *Relazioni, Vol. IV: Storia Moderna*, Comitato Internazionale die Scienze Storiche X Congresso Internazionale di Scienze Storiche, Rome 1955

HAUSHERR, H., *Hardenberg: Eine politische Biographie 1750-1800*, Cologne and Graz 1963

HECKSCHER, E.F., *Mercantilism*, trans. M. Shapiro, 2 vols., London 1935

HENDERSON, W.O., *Studies in the Economic Policy of Frederick the Great*, London 1963
The State and the Industrial Revolution in Prussia 1740-1870, Liverpool 1967

HENNING, F.W., *Herrschaft und Bauernuntertänigkeit*, Wurzburg 1964
Dienste und Abgaben der Bauern im 18 Jahrhundert, Stuttgart 1969
Die Industrialisierung in Deutschland 1800 bis 1914, Paderborn 1973

HERZBERG, E. von, *Dissertations dans les Séances Publiques de l'Académie des Sciences et Belles Lettres de Berlin dans les Années 1780, 1781, 1782 à 1787*, Berlin 1787

HEUER, E.-J., *Allgemeines Landrecht und Klassenkampf*, (East) Berlin 1960

HIGGS, H., *The Physiocrats*, London 1897

HINCKER, F., *Les Français devant l'Impôt sous l'Ancien Régime*, Paris 1971

HINRICHS, C., *Friedrich Wilhelm I. König in Preußen Jugend und Aufstieg*, Hamburg 1941
Preußentum und Pietismus: Der Pietismus in Brandenburg-Preußen als Religiös-Soziale Reformbewegung, Göttingen 1971
'Preußen als historisches Problem' in *Gesammelte Abhandlungen*, ed. G. Ostreich, Berlin 1964
'Das königliche Lagerhaus in Berlin' in *FBPG* 44 (1932)

HINRICHS, E., 'Die Ablösung von Eigentumsrechten zur Diskussion über die droits féodaux in Frankreich am Ende des Ancien Regimes und in der Revolution' in *Eigentum und Verfassung*, ed. R.Vierhaus, Göttingen 1972

HINTZE, O., *Gesammelte Abhandlungen*. Vol.1: *Staat und Verfassung*, Göttingen 1962; vol.2: *Soziologie und Geschichte*, Göttingen 1964; vol.3: *Regierung und Verwaltung*, Göttingen 1967
Die Hohenzollern und ihr Werk, Berlin 1915

HINZE, K., *Die Arbeiterfrage zu Beginn des modernen Kapitalismus in Brandenburg-Preußen*, Berlin 1963

HOLLDACK, H., 'Der Physiokratismus und die absolute Monarchie' in *Historische Zeitschrift* 145 (1931)

HUBER, E.R., *Deutsche Verfassungsgeschichte*. Vol.1: *Reform and Restauration*, Stuttgart 1961
Dokumente zur deutschen Verfassungsgeschichte, Stuttgart 1961

HUFFER, H., 'Die Beamten des älteren preußischen

Kabinetts, 1713-1808' in *FBPG* 5 (1, 1892)

HUTTON, O., *The Poor in Eighteenth Century France*, Oxford 1974

HUMBOLDT, W. von, 'Ideen zu einem Versuch die Grenzen der Wirksamkeit des Staates zu bestimmen' in *Gesammelte Schriften*, ed. A. Leitzmann, vol.1, Berlin 1903
'Wie weit darf sich die Sorgfalt des Staats um das Wohl seiner Bürger erstrecken?' in *Gesammelte Werke*, vol.2, ed. C. Brandes, 1841-52

HYSLOP, B., *A Guide to the General Cahiers of 1789*, Columbia 1936
L'Apanage de Philippe Egalité, Duc d'Orleans, 1785-1791, preface by M. Reinhard, Paris 1965

IBBEKEN, R., *Preußen 1807-1813*, Cologne and Berlin 1970

IPSEN, G., 'Die preußische Bauernbefreiung als Landesaufbau' in *Zeitschrift fur Agrargeschichte und Agrarsoziologie* 2 (1954)

JEISMANN, K.E., *Das preußische Gymnasium in Staat und Gesellschaft*, Stuttgart 1974

JOHNSON, H.C., *Frederick the Great and his Officials*, New Haven and London 1975

KANT, E., *Was ist Aufklärung?*

KAPLAN, S.L., *Bread, Politics and Political Economy in the Reign of Louis XV*, 2 vols., The Hague 1976

KESSEL, E., 'Zur Boyens Entlassung' in *Historische Zeitung* 175 (1953)

KLEIN, E., *Von der Reform zur Restauration: Finanzpolitik und Reformgesetzgebung des preußischen Staatskanzlers Karl August von Hardenberg*, Berlin 1965

KNAPP, G.F., *Die Bauernbefreiung und der Ursprung der Landarbeiter in den alteren Teilen preußens*, 2 vols., Leipzig 1887
Grundherrschaft und Rittergut, Leipzig 1897

KOSELLECK, R., 'Staat und Gesellschaft in Preußen 1815-1848' in *Staat und Gesellschaft in deutschen Vormärz*, ed. W.Conze, Stuttgart 1952
Preußen zwischen Reform und Revolution, Stuttgart 1967

KOSER, R., *König Friedrich der Grosse*, Stuttgart 1893-1903

KULISCHER, J., *Allgemeine Wirtschaftsgeschichte des Mittelalters und der Neuzeit*, Munich 1958
'Leibeigenschaft in Russland und die Agrarverfassung Preußens im 18 Jahrhundert' in *Jahrbücher für Nationalökonomie und Statistik*, vol. 137, part 3, Jena 1932

LABROUSSE, E., *Esquisse des Revenues en France au XVIIIe Siècle*, Paris 1933
La Crise de l'Economie Française à la Fin de l'Ancien Régime et au Début de la Révolution, Paris 1944
and BRAUDEL, F.T. (eds.), *Histoire Economique et Sociale de la France 1660-1789*, Paris 1970-

LACOURT-GAYER, R., *Calonne*, Paris 1963

LANDGREEN, P., 'Gegensatz und Verschmelzung von "alter" und "neuer" Burokratie im Ancien Regime: Ein Vergleich von Frankreich und Preußen' in *Sozialgeschichte Heute*, Festschrift für Hans Rosenberg, Göttingen 1974

LAVISSE, E., *Histoire de France*, vol.8, Paris 1908 and 1909; vol.9, Paris 1910

LAVOISIER, A.-L. de, *Oeuvres*. Vol.2: *Résultats de*

Quelques Expériences d'Agriculture et Reflexions sur leurs Relations avec l'Economie; vol.6: *Instructions données par la Noblesse du Baillage de Blois à ses Députés aux Etats Généraux*, Paris 1893

LEFEBVRE, G., *Quatre-vingt Neuf*, Paris 1939
La Grande Peur, Paris 1932
La Révolution Française in 'Peuples et Civilisations' series, Paris 1951
Etudes sur la Révolution Française, introduction by A. Soboul, Paris 1963
Etudes Orléannaises Contribution à l'Etude des Structures Sociales à la Fin du XVIIe Siècle, Paris 1962

LEHNDORFF, Graf, *30 Jahre am Hofe Friedrichs des Großen*, trans. from the French by L. E. Schmidt-Lotzen, 3 vols., Gotha 1907-13

LIEBEL, H., 'Laissez-faire versus Mercantilism: The Rise of Hamburg and the Hamburg Bourgeoisie against Frederick the Great in the Crisis of 1763' in *Vierteljahrschrift für Sozial- und Wirtschaftsgeschichte*, vol.52, no.2, 1965

LOUIS XIV, *Mémoires*, introduction and notes by J.Lognon, Paris 1927

LUBLINSKYA, A.D., *French Absolutism: The Crucial Phase 1620-1629*, trans. B.Pearce, foreword by J.H.Elliott, Cambridge 1968

LUCAS, C., 'Nobles, bourgeois and the origins of the French Revolution' in *Past and Present* 60 (August 1973)

LUTGE, F., *Deutsche Sozial- und Wirtschaftsgeschichte*, 3rd edition, Berlin, Heidelberg and New York, 1966
'Uber die Auswirkung der Bauernbefreiung in Deutschland' in *Studien zur Sozial- und Wirtschaftsgeschichte. Gesammelte Abhandlungen*, Stuttgart 1963

LUTHY, H., *La Banque Protestante en France de la Révocation de l'Edit de Nantes à la Révolution*, Paris 1959
From Calvin to Rousseau: Tradition and Modernity in French Political Thought from the Reformation to the French Revolution, trans. S.Attanasio, New York and London 1970

MANDROU, R., *La France au XVIIe et XVIIIe Siècles*, Paris 1967
Louis XIV en Son Temps (*Peuples et Civilisations* series), Paris 1973

MANN, G., *Friedrich von Genz*, Zürich 1947

MANN, Thomas, *Betrachtungen eines Unpolitischen*, Berlin 1918
Friedrich und die große Koalition, Sammlung von Schriften zur Zeitgeschichte, Berlin 1915

MANUEL, F.E., *The Prophets of Paris: Turgot, Condorcet, Saint-Simon, Fourier, Comte*, New York 1962

MARION, M., *Dictionnaire des Institutions de la France aux XVIIe et XVIIIe Siècles*, new edition, Paris 1968
Le Garde des Sceaux Lamoignon et la Réforme Judiciaire de 1788, Paris 1905
Les Impôts Directs sous l'Ancien Régime, Paris 1910
Histoire Financière de la France depuis 1715, Paris 1927

MARSEILLES, *Histoire du Commerce de Marseille. Vol.6: de 1660 à 1789*, ed. G.Rambert, Paris 1959

MARTINI, F., 'Die Adelsfrage in Preußen vor 1806' in *Vierteljahrschrift für Sozial- und Wirtschaftsgeschichte*, supplement 35, 1938

MATHIAS, P. and O'BRIEN, P., 'Taxation in Britain and France, 1715-1810: A Comparison of the Social and Economic Incidence of Taxes Collected for the Central Government' in *Journal of Economic History* 5 (3, 1976)

MATHIEZ, A., *La Révolution Française*, 3 vols., Paris 1933

MATTHEWS, G.T., *The Royal General Farms in Eighteenth Century France*, New York 1958

MAUER, H., *Die private Kapitalanlage in Preußen wahrend des 18 Jahrhundert*, ed. E.Wegener, Mannheim, Berlin and Leipzig 1921

MAUZI, R., *L'idée du Bonheur au XVIIIe Siècle*, Paris 1960

MAY, G., *Madame Roland and the Age of Revolution*, New York and London, 1970

MAYER, E.W., *Das Retablissement Ost- und Westpreußens unter der Mitwirkung und Leitung Theodors von Schön*, Jena 1916
'Politische Erfahrungen und Gedanken Theodors von Schön nach 1815' in *Historische Zeitschrift* 117, 1917

MEHRING, F., *Die Lessinglegende*, 3rd edition, Berlin 1953

MEIER, E. von, *Die Reform der Verwaltungsorganisation unter Stein und Hardenberg*, 2nd edition, ed. F.Thimme, Munich and Leipzig 1912

MEINECKE, F., *Das Zeitalter der deutschen Erhebung*, Bielefeld and Leipzig 1906; 6th edition, Göttingen 1957
Die Idee der Staatsräson, Munich 1960

MERCIER DE LA RIVIERE, LE, *L'Ordre Naturel et Essentiel des Sociétés Politiques*, 1767, reprinted with an introduction by E.Depitre in *Collections des Economistes et des Réformateurs Sociaux de la France*, Paris 1910

MEUSEL, F., *Friedrich August Ludwig von der Marwitz*, Berlin 1908 ff

MEYER, J., *La Noblesse Bretonne au XVIIIe Siècle*, Paris 1972
'Un Problème Mal Posé. La Noblesse Pauvre. L'exemple de la Bretagne au XVIIIe Siècle' in *Revue d'Histoire Moderne et Contemporaine* 18 (April–June 1971)

MIECK, I., *Preußische Gewerbepolitik in Berlin 1806-1844*, Berlin 1965

MIRABEAU, Comte de, *Essai sur les Privilèges*, 1789
De la Monarchie Prussienne sous Frédéric le Grand, 7 vols., London 1788

MITTENZWEI, I., *Preußen nach dem siebenjährigen Krieg: Auseinandersetzung zwischen Bürgertum und Staat um die Wirtschaftspolitik*, (East) Berlin 1979
Friedrich II von Preußen, (East) Berlin 1980

MOLLER, E., *Aufklärung in Preußen*, Berlin 1974

MONTESQUIEU, Charles-Louis de Secondat Baron de la Brède et de, *De L'Esprit des Lois*, Classiques Garnier, Paris n.d.

MORNET, D., *Les Origines Intellectuelles de la Révolution Française*, Paris 1954

MOUGEL, F.C., 'La Fortune des Bourbon-Conty 1655-1791' in *Revue d'Histoire Moderne et Contemporaine* 18 (1971)

MOUSNIER, R., *La Vénalité des Offices sous Henri IV et Louis XIII*, Rouen 1945
Fureurs Paysannes, Paris 1967
Les Institutions de la France sous la Monarchie Absolue

vol.1: *Société et Etat*, Paris 1974; vol.2: *Les Organes de l'Etat et la Société*, Paris 1980
L'Assassinat de Henri IV, Paris 1964
MULLER, A., *Elemente der Staatskunst 1808/9*, republished Leipzig 1936

NAUDE, W., 'Denkwürdigkeiten des Ministers Grafen von der Schulenburg' in *FBPG* 15 (1902)
NECKER, J., *Oeuvres Complètes*, published by M. le Baron de Stael, Paris 1820-21
NEUGEBAUER, W., 'Zur neueren Deutung der preußischen Verwaltung im 17 und 18 Jahrundert' in *Jahrbuch für die Geschichte Mittel- und Ostdeutschland* 26, Berlin 1977
NEUMANN, S., 'Die Stufen des Preußischen Konservatismus' in *Historische Studien* 190, Berlin 1930

OLIVIER-MARTIN, J.M., *L'Organisation Corporative de la France*, Paris 1938

PARET, P., *Yorck and the Era of Reform 1807-1815*, Princeton 1966
Clausewitz and the State, New York, London and Toronto 1976
PASCAL, R., *The German Sturm und Drang*, Manchester 1953
PERTZ, G.H. and DELBRUCK, H., *Das Leben des Feldmarschalls Grafen Neilhardt von Gneisenau*, 5 vols., Berlin 1864*ff*
PINLOCHE, A., *La Réforme en l'Education en Allemagne au XVIIIe Siècle*, Paris 1889
PRERADOVICH, H.N. von, *Die Führungsschichten in Oesterreich und Preußen 1804-1918*, Wiesbaden 1955

QUESNAY, F., *François Quesnay et la Physiocratie*. Vol.1: *Etudes, Biographie, Bibliographie*; vol.2: *Textes Annotés*, Institut National d'Etudes Demographiques, Paris 1958

RACHEL, H., 'Der Merkantilismus in Brandenburg Preussen' in *FBPG* 40 (1927) and WALLICH, P. *Berliner Großkaufleute und Kapitalisten*. Vol.2: *Die Zeit des Merkantilismus 1648-1806*, Berlin 1938
RADZINOWICZ, L., *A History of the English Criminal Law*, London 1948
RAUMER, F. von, *Lebenserinnerungen und Briefwechsel*, Leipzig 1861
Ueber die preußische Städteordnung nebst einem Vorworte ueber bürgerliche Freiheit nach französischen und deutschen Begriffen, Leipzig 1828
REINHARD, M., 'Elite et Noblesse dans la Seconde Moitié du XVIIIe Siècle' in *Revue d'Histoire Moderne et Contemporaine* 3-4 (1956-7)
RENOUVIN, P., *Les Assemblées Provinciales de 1787*, Paris 1921
RICHTER, M., *The Political Thought of Montesquieu*, Cambridge 1977
RITTER, G., *Friedrich der Grosse: Ein historisches Profil*, Leipzig 1936
Stein: Eine politische Biographie, 3rd edition, Stuttgart 1958
Staatskunst und Kriegshandwerk, vol.1, 1740-1890, Munich 1965

ROBERTS, J.M. and Cobb, R.C., *French Revolutionary Documents*, Oxford 1966
ROSENBERG, H., *Bureaucracy, Aristocracy and Autocracy: The Prussian Experience 1660-1815*, Cambridge Mass. 1958
'Die Demokratisierung der Rittergutsbesitzerklasse' in *Zur Geschichte und Problematik der Demokratie*, Festgabe für Hans Herzfeld, Berlin 1958
ROTHKRUG, L., *Opposition to Louis XIV*, Princeton 1965
ROUSSEAU, J.J., *De l'Inégalité parmi les Hommes*, editions sociales, Paris 1954

SAINT-ETIENNE, R., de, 'Considérations sur les Intérêts du Tiers-Etat' in *Precis de l'Histoire de la Révolution Française*, ed. Boissy d'Anglais 1827
SAINT-JACOB, P. de, *Les Paysans de la Bourgogne du Nord au Dernier Siècle de l'Ancien Régime*, Paris 1960
SCHELLE, G., *Vincent de Gournay*, Paris 1897
SCHMIDT, E., 'Kammergericht und Rechsstaat' in *Schriftenreihe der juristischen Gesellschaft*, Berlin 1968
'Die Justizpolitik Friedrichs des Großen' in *Heidelberger Jahrbücher* 6, Heidelberg 1962
'Rechtssprüche und Machtsprüche der preußischen Könige der 18 Jahrhunderts' in *Berichte über die Verhandlungen der sächsischen Akademie der Wissenschaften*, vol.95, no.3
SCHMOLLER, G., *Deutsches Städtewesen*, Berlin 1922
SCHNABEL, F., *Deutsche Geschichte im 19 Jahrhundert*, 4 vols., Freiburg im Breisgau 1948–1955
SCHNEE-BOCHUM, H., 'Die Hoffinanciers Friedrich des Großen' in *Schmoller's Jahrbuch für Gesetzgebung, Verwaltung und Volkswirtschaft*, Berlin 1952
SCHOEPS, H.J., *Aus den Jahren preußischer Not und Erneuerung: Tagebücher der Gebrüder Gerlach und ihres Kreises 1805-1820*, Berlin 1963
SCHON, T. von, *Aus den Papieren des Ministers und Burggrafen von Marienburg*, 6 vols., 1878-83
SCHULZE, J., 'Die Auseinandersetzung zwischen Adel und Bürgertum 1773-1806' in *Historische Studien* 163 (161-4,1925)
SCHWARTZ, K., *Leben des Generals Carl von Clausewitz und der Frau Marie von Clausewitz*, Berlin 1878
SCHWARTZ, P., *Der erste Kulturkampf in Preußen um Kirche und Schule*, Berlin 1925
SEGUR, Comte de, *Mémoires ou Souvenirs et Anecdotes*, Paris 1825
SELLIN, V., 'Friedrich der Große und der aufgeklärte Absolutismus' in *Festschrift für Werner Conze*, n.d.
SENAC DE MEILHAN, *Considérations sur les Richesses et le Luxe*, 1787
Des Principes et des Causes de la Révolution Française, 1790
SENTOU, J., *Fortunes et Groupes Sociaux à Toulouse sous La Révolution*, Toulouse 1969
SIEYES, E.J., *Qu'est-ce que le Tiers Etat? Précédé de L'Essai sur les Privilèges*, ed. E Champion, Paris 1888
SKALWEIT, S., 'Frankreich und Friedrich der Große: Der Aufstieg Preußens in der öffentlichen Meinung des Ancien Régimes' in *Bonner Historische Forschungen*, vol.1, Bonn 1952
SMALL, A.W., *The Cameralists: The Pioneers of German Social Polity*, Chicago 1909

SMITH, Adam, *The Wealth of Nations*, 2 vols., ed. E.Cannon, London 1950

SOBOUL, A., *La France à la Veille de la Révolution*, 2 vols., Paris 1966
Paysans, Sans-culottes et Jacobins, Paris 1966
Les Sans-culottes Parisiens en l'An II, Paris 1962

SOMBART, W., *Der Bourgeois*, Munich and Leipzig 1913

STADELMANN, R., *Deutschland und Westeuropa: Drei Aufsätze*, Wurttemberg 1948

STAEL, Madame de, *De l'Allemagne*, 2 vols., ed. Comtesse de Pange, Paris 1958

STEIN, R., *Die Umwandlung der Agrarverfassung Ostpreußens*, 3 vols., vol.1, Jena 1918; vols. 2 and 3, Königsberg 1933-34

STEWART, J.H., *A Documentary Survey of the French Revolution*, 6th edition, New York 1966

STOLZEL, A., *Carl Gottlieb Svarez*, Berlin 1885

SVAREZ, C.G., *Vorträge über Recht und Statt*, ed. H. Conrad and G. Kleinheyer, Cologne and Opladen 1960

TALMON, J.L., *The Origins of Totalitarian Democracy*, Jerusalem 1951

TAYLOR, G.V., 'Noncapitalist Wealth and the Origins of the French Revolution' in *American Historical Review*, January 1967
'Types of Capitalism in 18th century France' in *English Historical Review* 79 (July 1964)
'Revolutionary and Non-revolutionary Content of the Cahiers of 1789: An Interim Report' in *French Historical Studies* 7 (Fall 1972)

THIELEN, P.G., *Karl August von Hardenberg 1750-1822*, Cologne and Berlin 1967

TOCQUEVILLE, A. de, *L'Ancien Régime et la Révolution*, in Vol.2 of *Oeuvres Complètes*, ed. J-P Mayer, introduction by G.Lefebvre, Paris 1952
Preceded by *Etat Social et Politique de la France avant et depuis 1789*

TREITSCHKE, H. von, *History of Germany in the Nineteenth Century*, trans. E. and C. Paul, 7 vols., London 1915-19

TREUE, W., *Wirtschaftsgeschichte der Neuzeit*. Vol.1: *18 und 19 Jahrhundert*, 3rd edition, Stuttgart 1973

TROUSSON, R., (ed.) *Thèmes et Figures du Siècle des Lumières*, Geneva 1980

TUDESQ, A.J., *Les Grand Notables en France 1840-1849*, Paris 1964

TURGOT, A.-R.-J., Baron de l'Aulne, *Oeuvres*, ed. G. Schelle, Paris 1913-23

VARNHAGEN, Rahel, *Briefwechsel mit Alexander von der Marwitz*, ed. F.Kamp, Munich 1966

VAUBAN, S. Seigneur de, *Projet d'une Dixme Royale*, notes and introduction by E.Coornaert, Paris 1933

VIERHAUS, R., 'Ständewesen und Staatsverwaltung' in *Dauer und Wandel der Geschichte*, Festgabe für Kurt von Raumer, Munster 1966

VILLARD, P., *Les Justices Seigneuriales dans la Marche*, Paris 1969

VOLTAIRE, *Le Siècle de Louis XIV*, Paris 1966
Lettres Philosophiques, Paris 1964
Dictionnaire Philosophiques, Paris 1964

WALD, A., 'Die Bauernbefreiung und die Ablösung des Obereigentums – eine Befreiung der Herren?' in *Historische Vierteljahrschrift* 28, 1934

WEILL, H., *Frederick the Great and Samuel von Cocceji*, Madison 1961

WEIS, E., 'Ergebnisse eines Vergleichs der grundherrschaftlichen Strukturen Deutschlands und Frankreichs bis zum Ausgang des 18 Jahrhunderts' in *Vierteljahrschrift für Sozial- und Wirtschaftsgeschichte* 57, 1970

WILSON, A.M., *Diderot*, New York and Oxford 1957

WINKLER, T., *Johann Gottfried Frey und die Entstehung der preußischen Selbstverwaltung*, new edition, foreword by Hans Rothfells, Stuttgart 1957

WINTER, G., *Die Reorganisation des preußischen Staates unter Stein und Hardenberg*, Prussian state archives publication 93, Leipzig 1931

YOUNG, A., *Travels in France during the Years 1787, 1788 and 1789*, ed. C. Maxwell, Cambridge 1929

ZIEKURSCH, J., *Hundert Jahre schlesische Agrargeschichte*, 2nd edition, Breslau 1927
Das Ergebnis der friderizianischen Städteverwaltung und die Städteordnung Steins am Beispiel der schlesischen Stadte dargestellt, Jena 1908

ZOTTMANN, A., *Die Wirtschaftspolitik Friedrichs des Großen*, Leipzig and Vienna 1937

Index

absolutism and absolute monarchs, and bureaucracy, 202; and despotism and totalitarianism, 31; differences between French and Prussian absolutism, 9, 11-12, 32-3, 35, 40, 202; distinguishing vices of, 185, 201; Enlightened and unenlightened absolutism 153, 181; and fundamental law, 179; Hohenzollerns as exceptional, 201-2; and justice, 89-90; limitations in practice, 41; and the nobility, 42, 56; origin of term absolutism, 24; powers attributed to and claimed by absolute monarchs, 25, 29, 41; and semi-divine powers of French Kings, 25; and standing armies, 42; and violation of human rights, 91; and war, 41; and welfare, 116

Adams, John Quincy, 84

agriculture, agricultural revolution and enclosures, 131; agricultural revolution in Prussia, 196; agricultural societies in France, 139; attempts at reform in France, 138-39; communal system of, 131; different methods of organizing agricultural production in Western and Eastern Europe, 141; division of land into small units in France, 129; feudal dues as disincentives to, in France, 137; high rate of interest as disincentive to, in France, 136; hostility to change, in France, 135, 136, 137; hostility to change, in Prussia, 151; importance attached to, by Frederick William I and Frederick the Great, 145-6; *intendants* and, 138; investment and, in France, 134, 136; *Landräte* and, 143; *servitudes collectives* (collective bondage), in France, 132; sharecropping (*métayage*), in France, 129; subsistence farming, in France, 130, 131: note 16; taxes and tithes as disincentives to, in France, 135, 137

Aguessau, Henri François d', Chancellor, 52, 90, 93, 94, 95-6, 99

Alembert, Jean le Rond d', 153, 161, 162

Aligré, Etienne Françoise de, 195

Allgemeines Landrecht, 29, 60, 89, 106-7 109, 141, 161

Altenstein, Freiherr von, 80, 81, 189

Antoine, Michel, 96, 171, 172

Argenson, René Louis de Voyer, Marquis d', 10, 46, 164, 171, 173

armies, Adam Smith on normal ratio between population and size of, 88; cost of, as an incentive to change, 146; nature of, determined by the society in which they exist, 192; significance for the maintenance of internal order, 42. *See also* Armies, French; Armies, Prussian

armies, French, disaffection at the beginning of the Revolution, 175; *Loi Ségur* and, 174-75; Louis XIV and, 38, 58; reforms in, after Seven Years War, 174-75

armies, Prussian, brutal discipline in, 183; conscription for, 19, 59; Frederick the Great and, 60-1, 63-4, 182-3; Frederick William I and, 56-8; militarism and, 182; proportion of mercenaries in, 182: note 21; reforms after 1806, 191-92

Arndt, Ernst Moritz, 63

Arnold, Muller, 107, 108, 111-15, 176, 181, 185

baillages, 92-3, 94

Balzac, Honoré de, 138

Bauernlegen (appropriation of peasant land), 143

Beaumarchais, P.A. Caron de, 52

Beccaria, Cesare, 158-9

Belle-Isle, Duc de, 54-5

Benekendorff, von, 85

Bernis, Abbé de, 54

Bertier de Sauvigny, Louis Jean, Intendant of Paris, 168

Beuth, 204

Beyme, C.F., 63, 189

Bismarck, Otto von, 63, 64, 173

Bloch, Marc, 7, 138, 159

Bluche, François, 52

Blücher, Field Marshal von, 55, 67

Borcke, H.A., Graf von, 149-50

Bossuet, 154, 155

bourgeois, acquisition of noble status in Prussia, 63; attitude of Frederick the Great to, 60; attitude of Frederick William I to, 57, 62; bourgeois and capitalists contrasted, 199; *bourgeois gentilshommes*, 49, 53; bourgeois in high positions in Prussian bureaucracy, 62-3; desire to enter the nobility in France, 9, 54; faking of noble status in France, 54; and *Feudalisierung* (adopting noble attitudes and behaviour), 205; impreciseness of the term, 199, 205; meaning of in France under Louis XIV, 48; means of acquiring noble status in France, 52; numbers of French bourgeois who bought themselves noble status, 1774 to 1789, 52; as owners of *Rittergüter* (noble estates) in Prussia by mid-19th century, 193; part played by, in the Prussian reform movement, 204; predominance of bourgeois values in Prussia, 67; and the Revolution, 7-9; and the *robe*, 49; and sale of offices, 9.v.; specially privileged Prussian bourgeois (the *Eximirte*), 64

bourgeois society, changing meaning of the term, 199; specific characteristics, 200

Boyen, Fieldmarshall Hermann von, 189, 191

Bredow, Major von, 197

Bristol, Lord, 66

bureaucracy, and absolutism, 202; and centralization, 41; and creation of state and nation, 27; bourgeois in high positions in, in Prussia under Frederick the Great, 62-3; bourgeois in high positions in, in Prussia under Frederick William I, 62-3; differences between French and Prussia, 32-3, 202; different attitude of French and Prussian

243

119, 120-1; and colonies, 11, 119, 165; Frederick the Great's study of Colbertism, 123; government trading monopolies in Prussia, 125; growth of French foreign trade in the 18th century, 121; and guilds, 119; and national wealth, 120; production more important than foreign trade, in Prussia, 123; and provincial barriers, *see* Tolls and internal customs barriers; Quesnay on, 134: note 33; and supply of bullion, 119; and taxation, 119; transit trade in Prussia, 126-7; and war, 119
tribunal, 113
Turgot, Anne Robert Jacques, 68, 129, 139, 164, 168; and French military strength, 78; and land surveys, 84; on peasants, 131; and poverty, 135; and productivity of land, 134; the Revolu-

tion and, 174; tax collection, 73, 74

Ulrike, Queen of Sweden, 65
Ursinus, 126, 176,c

Vauban, 35, 68-9
Varnhagen von Ense, 65
Varnhagen von Ense, Rachel, 65, 128
Vergennes, 55
Voltaire, 52, 55, 66, 82, 163, 177; and administration of justice, 90; and Beccaria, 159; and the Calas case, 96, 111; and the monarch's miraculous powers, 25; on moral actions, 156, 157; and reason, 157; and sale of offices, 95; and unrest in France, 28-9; and Wolff, 27, 152

war, constant preoccupation of governments with, 116, and consequences of this, 41, 68, 80; essentially warlike nature of absolutism, 41; military functions of absolute monarchs, 30; philosophers' hostility to, 37; seen as an art, 37; seen as a science, 116
wealth, and the Enlightenment, 159-60, 162; and power, 116-17; trade and, 117-28
William III, King of England, 35
Williams, Sir Hanbury, 62
Wolff, Christian, 26-7, 36, 50, 152, 156, 178-9, 180

Yorck von Wartenburg, 64, 204
Young, Arthur, 99, 129, 130, 132, 135, 137, 139

Zedlitz, von, 113, 114-15, 185